ANNA THOMASSON studied for an MPhil in Biography at
the University of Buckingham and her thesis was shortlisted for
the *Daily Mail* Biographers' Club Prize. She lives in London
and this is her first book.

❖

'Anna Thomasson has uncovered a remarkable story and brings these two
fascinating but forgotten figures and their brilliant world vividly to light.
An impressive debut'
                                                    JULIE KAVANAGH,
                                    author of *Rudolf Nureyev: The Life*
                                    and *Secret Muses: The Life of Frederick Ashton*

'*A Curious Friendship* tells the story of two wonderfully unlikely friends
and allies during the years between the wars. Moving, thoughtful, entertaining and magnificently researched, Thomasson's account of a bohemian
art student and sharp-witted – sometimes comically snobbish – spinster
is an outstandingly accomplished and original first biography from a writer
for whom we can predict a very bright future'   MIRANDA SEYMOUR,
                                    author of *In My Father's House* and *Noble Endeavours*

'Anna Thomasson is a wonderful writer, with a pitch-perfect ear and a
marvellous sense of style. I was also impressed by the thoroughness of
her research. I really felt she had come to know her characters intimately
with the result that one completely trusted her judgement every inch of
the way. She has, too, a brilliant visual sense so that one really sees Rex's
paintings and those magnificent houses'   SELINA HASTINGS,
                                    author of *The Red Earl* and *The Secret Lives of Somerset Maugham*

'It is a vibrant, admirably researched debut, tinkling with famous artistic
names. A non-fictional *Brideshead Revisited*, it's piquantly evocative of
that lost aesthetic echelon of 1920s and 1930s society which dissolved
amid the shadows of war; and the convention-defying friendship threaded
through it is enthralling'   CAROLINE SANDERSON,
                                    Associate Editor of the *Bookseller*

Anna Thomasson

❖

A Curious Friendship

The Story of a Bluestocking and
a Bright Young Thing

PAN BOOKS

First published 2015 by Macmillan

First published in paperback 2016 by Pan Books
an imprint of Pan Macmillan
20 New Wharf Road, London N1 9RR
Associated companies throughout the world
www.panmacmillan.com

ISBN 978-1-4472-4554-4

1 3 5 7 9 8 6 4 2

A CIP catalogue record for this book is available from the British Library.

Typeset by Ellipsis Digital Limited, Glasgow
Printed and bound by CPI Group (UK) Ltd, Croydon, CR0 4YY

Visit **www.panmacmillan.com** to read more about all our books
and to buy them. You will also find features, author interviews and
news of any author events, and you can sign up for e-newsletters
so that you're always first to hear about our new releases.

For my mother,
Annette Thomasson

'What do we any of us live for but our illusions and what can we ask of others but that they should allow us to keep them?'

Somerset Maugham, *The Sacred Flame*, Act III

Contents

❖

AFTER

List of Illustrations

❖

List of Illustrations

Introduction

❖

Several years ago I went to Plas Newydd on Anglesey, an elegant, neo-Gothic mansion on the banks of the Menai Strait and home to the Marquess of Anglesey. There I had seen the mural painted by Rex Whistler, begun in 1936 and now considered his masterpiece. The windows of the dining room look out beyond the sloping lawns and the stretch of grey water to the looming, cloud-capped peaks of Snowdonia. On the facing wall, the mural is a fantastical reflection of the view from the windows; the Welsh landscape is transformed into an enchanted, Arcadian panorama, with the crispness of Canaletto and the warm, dreamy light of Claude. Later I would learn that it was typical of Rex to turn his back on reality and reinvent it. I was intrigued by this man whose self-portrait stands discreetly at the corner of the mural, a solitary and rather forlorn figure dressed as a gardener with a broom in his hand and rose petals scattered at his feet.

Amongst the cabinets of letters, possessions and drawings in the permanent exhibition dedicated to Rex at Plas Newydd, one item in particular caught my eye: a love note written to a girlfriend in 1937 beseeching her to delay her departure to London. Around the note is a beautiful cartouche topped by a heart and crown. It is playful, fanciful, almost childish: a frivolous billet-doux. And it seemed to me like a relic of an earlier, more elegant age. In Rex there was none of the vigour, the confrontation and the agenda I had come to expect of 1930s art, of a 1930s artist; instead his billowing rococo clouds suggest a gentler outlook – one imbued with humour, whimsy and romance.

I began to research Rex's life. But in the process of trying to discover him someone else kept appearing in biographies, letters and footnotes. And in photographs too, there she was amongst the Bright Young People: Edith Olivier, a small, smart woman with shingled black hair, a large nose in a strong face, a cigarette in her hand and enormous gold earrings. She seemed dynamic, older than the others, but often at the centre of the group, laughing and holding court.

Rex first met Edith in 1925, when both were guests of their mutual friend, the mercurial young aristocrat Stephen Tennant, at a villa on the Italian Riviera. They were at such different stages of life, continuing along on very different trajectories, but the friendship that developed between them would be the most important of their lives. I see their meeting as a collision; it changed them irrevocably. Rex was then nineteen and a rising star at the Slade School of Art. Edith was fifty-two, an Oxford-educated spinster and the daughter of a Wiltshire rector to whom she had dedicated most of her adult life. It seemed to me such an unlikely friendship: a Victorian bluestocking and a bright young thing.

Edith was the most diligent of diarists and as I explored her archive, reading through the many journals she had kept, along with bundles of her private letters, the traces of her life, year by year, began to emerge from the pages. She was a passionate conversationalist, and at times, reading her diaries felt to me rather like we were having an intimate discussion, or that I was eavesdropping into her conversations with friends. They are idiosyncratic and tangential and filled with vehement underlining and wonderfully archaic spellings ('shew' for 'show'), and I have retained both her and Rex's original spelling and punctuation. Edith's diaries are written in a voice that is at once Victorian and modern, and at all times profoundly personal. As I desperately tried to decipher her impossible handwriting, I felt as though I got to know her.

Though she had dedicated much of her life to her father and to the local community, I discovered that there was nothing meek or humdrum about Edith. Fiercely intelligent, she had studied at Oxford, where she befriended Lewis Carroll. She had supernatu-

ral visions and a profound, preternatural sensitivity to place,
particularly the Wiltshire landscape, which she loved more than
any other and whose elemental energies she claimed to feel. In
the First World War she was instrumental in establishing the
Women's Land Army and was later given an MBE for her work. A
highly practical and rather eccentric spinster, Edith was terrifying
to the provincial world that knew her. After her father's death she
would move with her beloved sister to a house in a quiet corner of
the Wilton estate surrounded by woods that had inspired Sidney's
Arcadia. And so her life could have continued, amongst county
families, rural and relatively peaceful. But then her sister died,
along with the future that Edith had planned.

When she met Rex Whistler, a different life began. She
became a respected writer, publishing the first of a number of
novels in 1927, *The Love-Child*, which tells the story of a lonely
spinster who invents an imaginary child to be her companion. She
would become a celebrity, feted in *Vogue*, quoted in *The Times*,
the late-blooming centre of her circle of famous and talented
younger friends for whom her home, the Daye House, became
a retreat. And in Edith's archive they were there to discover too, a
host of friends from her earlier life and from her new one: society
women like Diana Cooper, Diana Mitford and Ottoline Morrell;
politicians such as Winston Churchill and Violet Bonham Carter;
the writers Evelyn Waugh and Vita Sackville-West; the poets
Henry Newbolt and Elinor Wylie; the writers and patrons Edith,
Osbert and Sacheverell Sitwell; the actors Laurence Olivier
(Edith's cousin) and his wife Vivien Leigh, and many more.

But of those friends, it was her close circle of younger men
that fascinated me most, and the way their lives gradually inter-
wove with Edith's own in the course of her diaries and letters. As
I opened the envelopes, read their letters, looked at their choices
of paper and ink, and their handwriting, those friends came alive
for me too: Stephen Tennant, amusing, self-obsessed, his florid
handwriting scrawled in kaleidoscopic inks on pastel-coloured
paper; Siegfried Sassoon, warm, concise, a neat hand on neat

paper; and Cecil Beaton, witty and name-dropping, his headed notepaper procured from grand houses and Hollywood hotels.

And then there were Rex's letters. For Edith and his other friends, these were prized possessions, still treasured by the families who inherited them. Not so much for what he wrote – which was invariably charming and self-deprecating – but for the delightful illustrations that wound like vines around the paper and out onto the envelope. Rex would later admit to Edith that he illustrated his letters as a delaying tactic while he tried to think of something to write, usually because it involved an awkward apology for forgetting a dinner party or declining an invitation for a weekend in the country. Better still was a rebus letter drawn for his friends' children and entirely composed of pictures that represented words.

Edith and the Daye House were a world away from Rex's own family and the small, suburban house where he had grown up. Edith lived an enchanted life, the river flowing past her cottage, and, beyond the woods, Wilton House with its graceful parkland, its old masters and aristocratic occupants. The magic of it all allowed Rex to escape from a childhood blighted by the death of his elder brother and by his unhappiness at boarding school, not to mention the expectations of his dearly loved and doting mother. On countless sightseeing expeditions Edith took Rex to all the places that she loved; she introduced him to society; she would guide him, inspire him and help to reinvent him, as in turn, Rex would help to reinvent her. At the very heart of their friendship was a profoundly romantic sensibility which they shared. It was what had drawn them together in the beginning with a sense of recognition and affinity, it was what they loved and nurtured in each other over the years that followed, and it was the source of Rex's art and Edith's writing.

And so I began to unravel Rex's seemingly charmed, but in fact rather troubled and ultimately tragic life. I came to understand why his art was so distinctively old-fashioned and why, at Plas Newydd, he had painted himself as a lowly gardener with a broom rather than a paintbrush in his hand. I also discovered why the love note that Rex had written to his girlfriend in 1937 was so symbolic, and so poignant.

The setting for this story shifts between London and Edith's beloved Wiltshire, a county humming with history and myth, rolling downland and chalk river valleys, graceful stately homes, combes, ancient forest and parkland. It is a tale both of this ancient landscape and of the time between the two world wars, an era that today seems fleeting, lost, charged with the knowledge of what happened before and what happened after. But in the 1920s, when this story begins, and to Rex's generation at least, it seemed that the world was changing for the better; a sense of optimism and liberation sprang from the ruins of the First World War. It was at this time that Edith and Rex met and their lives began to blossom, and, though so much of their friendship was a retreat from reality into the shared, romantic world of their imaginations, they were also very much a part of the artistic and aristocratic world, a world captured in the novels of Evelyn Waugh and Nancy Mitford.

Their story weaves through the 1920s, a time of extremes, the era of the Depression and the General Strike, but also of the Bright Young People with their endless whirl of parties, and the swarm of scandal and gossip that engulfed them. And in later years hedonism made way for sophistication, and seriousness, as another war began to loom. When the Second World War finally broke out at the end of the decade it marked another shift in the course of Edith and Rex's lives. For both of them it was a call to action, but it would divide them forever.

BEFORE

Edith

❖

In her talk, she danced over the world. Jane had hardly ever left home, but every book she read, every traveller's tale she heard, caught her imagination, and filled her with PLANS.

Edith Olivier, *As Far as Jane's Grandmother's*

She had always been good. A dutiful daughter and loving sister; staunchly conservative, devoutly religious and a committed townswoman; Edith was a pillar of society, just like her father. The Reverend Dacres Olivier was imbued with an unrealistic strength of character. Rather too formidable for real life, he was the kind of man that only appears in Victorian novels: swift of step, clear of judgement and resolutely composed. As rector of Wilton, the ancient capital of Wiltshire, and private chaplain to the Earl of Pembroke who lived at Wilton House, he had achieved a certain position in society, and of this he was proud. Dacres in turn had inherited his sense of duty from his father, Henry, who had lived further north at Potterne and been High Sheriff of Wiltshire in 1843. The Olivier family was of Huguenot descent and originally from Nay, near Lourdes, in the foothills of the Pyrenees. Edith's branch of the family anglicized the pronunciation of their surname so that it was pronounced 'Olivi-a' rather than 'Olivi-ay', like the family of her second cousin, the actor Laurence Olivier. To Edith's branch that was considered an unnecessary affectation, and not at all English.

Dacres's faith was not abstract and mystical; it provided him with the exacting code by which to live his life, and this pervaded all things: 'He was like a force of nature, moulding one's life, and yet never a part of it. He was too important to be that. The immense force and impetus of his personality came largely from the fact that for years he had disciplined himself to live by unalterable rules which extended to his every action from the least to the greatest.'[1] And so for his wife Emma, his children and the servants who looked after them, life at the Rectory was a regimented affair as he universally enforced restraint and self-discipline, instilling the house with an ecclesiastical atmosphere of duty and decorum. 'Nothing must be spoken of, of which he did not approve', Edith would later write.[2] But Dacres allowed himself one indulgence. He was devoted to the roses that grew beside the walls of the long Rectory garden. So sacred were these roses that his daughters were forbidden to arrange them in artful bunches or to pick them at any other time than early in the morning, before it got too hot. Instead they were under strict instruction to place only single stems in slender specimen vases that he provided, so that he could contemplate their individual beauty.

But beneath the rigid exterior was quite a different man. Over the years he had gradually eschewed the usual pleasures of youth – travel, hunting, music – to dedicate his life to the Church.

My father used to tell us that when he left Oxford, he decided that he disliked his handwriting, which was ugly, irregular, and illegible. He therefore changed it, making it firm, clear, and very balanced. So it remained. This too was himself.

There were in my father two people – the natural man, and the man formed by reason, judgment, and a religion based on the Church Catechism, and centred round the duty towards God, and the duty towards my neighbour. He did not ask from the faith which he so firmly kept, any mystical consolations: he demanded a definite line of conduct. Probably the fundamental traits in a character are never wholly obliterated, but by the time I knew my father, the Old Adam in him had become as completely sublimated as was his handwriting. He had adapted himself to the mould which he had made.[3]

With his foibles and eccentricities it would be easy to cast Dacres Olivier as a tyrannical paterfamilias: adamantine, a pinched and parsimonious Casaubon-like character, his face carved like 'a cameo'.[4] But Edith admitted that living with her father 'was great fun when he allowed it to be so'.[5] For the rest of her life, long after his had ended, she would record 'Papa's birthday' every year in her diary. Though she had found her father autocratic and intimidating at times, and though he had tried to dictate the course of her life, she adored him. She was very much her father's daughter.

Edith Maud Olivier was born in the evening of the last day of 1872, the eighth of Dacres and Emma's ten children and their second daughter. Mildred, known as Millie, was born three years later and became Edith's closest friend. As a child, Edith was rather mousy-looking, with dark eyes and a pensive expression concealing her startlingly bright mind. Industrious as well as clever, she revealed an early passion for reading, steadily working her way through the books in her father's library. However, while her brothers in turn – Boysey, Henry, Alfred, Frank, Sidney, Reginald and Harold – left home for public schools and later, careers in politics, finance, the army, the navy and the Colonial Service, Edith was not so fortunate. Dacres was a country parson with a large house and a large family but only a small living, and though personally of ascetic tastes, he considered it appropriate for a man in his position to live with his family on a grand scale. But economies had to be made and one of them was his daughters' education. It was left to their mother Emma to teach them and only later, when Edith was fourteen, did they acquire a governess.

Emma was the daughter of Bishop Robert Eden, of Moray, Ross and Caithness (Anthony Eden was Edith's second cousin). She was Dacres's second wife; his first had died after only a few years of marriage leaving a son, also called Dacres, who did not live at the Rectory and was an adult by the time Edith was born.

Edith would portray her mother as a shadowy, serene figure, forever wafting into her husband's study to soothe him out of his habitual ill temper.

The education of the girls aside, domestic economies had little tangible effect on life at the Rectory. It was a large, civilized, well-proportioned Georgian house, the kind of house that implies its inhabitants live civilized, well-proportioned lives. It easily contained the family of twelve as well as several servants. The house stood back from the road behind a brick wall, and carriages arrived at the front door through an arch built into the carriage house to the left of the main building. The Rectory facade was brick with yellow pilasters; a round white porch held up by pillars stood welcomingly before the front door. Inside, the light and high-ceilinged hallway spanned the depth of the house. At the far side of the hall, the garden door, which in Edith's memory was always open in summer, looked out onto the terrace, the walled garden and the seemingly infinite lawn that sloped away from the back of the house. The Rectory was linked to the church by a path of clipped and pointed yews to the right of the house. At the bottom of the lawn there was a pond with a waterfall and an island and beyond that the River Nadder where Edith and her siblings swam.

Though Dacres saw little of his children when they were very young, as they grew older he enjoyed having them about him. They were likened by a family friend to the 'Four and Twenty Blackbirds'; whenever Dacres wanted to open the pie, she said, they would always be there, poised to sing. Though her brothers in turn took flight, the girls, like Milton's daughters, remained at home and at Dacres's bidding. And he expected that there they would stay. 'Though he always sat alone in his study, he liked us within call', wrote Edith; 'he hated anyone going out to parties. The coming and going worried him. He was truly conservative. As the family party had been yesterday, so he wished it to be to-day, and to-morrow, and so on *ad-infinitum*.'[6] He wholeheartedly disapproved of careers for his daughters and in marriage only 'archbishops of good family' were considered acceptable suitors.[7]

Though their elder sister Mamie got married (to a young naval officer, Frank Carter, after a paternally imposed engagement of four years), Edith and Mildred stayed at home, within the confines of the Rectory and a social circle of local county families: 'The wheel of our lives then rotated slowly . . . its spokes were the successive events of the days, the weeks, the years. To these spokes we were bound. We rotated with them.'[8]

In 1895 when Edith was twenty-two she planned her escape. Some years earlier in 1889 she had attended a series of Oxford University extension lectures in Salisbury, on the Stuart period. At one of the lectures she had met Cosmo Lang, who would later become Archbishop of Canterbury. He suggested that she should sit for a scholarship to read History at Oxford. Her father's friend Bishop Wordsworth had established a scholarship in memory of his first wife at St Hugh's Hall, one of the women's colleges. Reluctantly Dacres let Edith take the exam on the assumption that she was unlikely to succeed.

Edith won the scholarship. And though she had been delighted by the prospect of the university, with its societies, debates and bicycles, she would find that for a woman a university career meant little beyond an improving diet of attending lectures and writing essays; 'women's colleges had then an untarnished school-girl complexion'.[9] Despite an ever-increasing female presence, Oxford was still an exclusive bastion of masculinity onto whose illustrious lawns, as Virginia Woolf would find, it was unwise for girls to trespass.

She did, however, enjoy an intriguing friendship. Charles Dodgson, better known as Lewis Carroll, was the author of *Alice's Adventures in Wonderland*, first published in 1865. He had been introduced to Edith by a college friend, Evelyn Hatch. Evelyn had been one of Dodgson's infant muses and had posed for him in the nude as a Gypsy child. By the time Edith went to Oxford Dodgson was no longer teaching but remained in residence at Christ Church. He enjoyed the company of a select group of female students whom he would invite to dine with him *'tete-a-tete'* in his rooms.[10] Edith occasionally found herself the guest at one of his intimate soirées. They always dined on mutton chops and meringues and discussed questions of logic. Occasionally they looked at his photographs. 'Mr Dodgson was very fond of little girls', Edith would later write.[11] It seems that he had been rather fond of Miss Olivier too, writing in his diary that he thought her a 'very nice girl' and regretted that they were on 'Miss terms' rather than 'kiss terms'.[12] Edith had grown into a handsome young woman with dark eyes, jet-black hair and her father's strong features. She had a dominant and slightly slanted nose, wonderfully high cheekbones and a heavy brow – with her naturally thick, straight eyebrows giving her a look of fierce determination that more than compensated for her height, being just over five foot.

Edith developed a great respect for the principal of the college, Charlotte Anne Moberly, known as Annie, a distant relation of her mother and a rigorously exacting but exciting influence on her students. Moberly was both deeply religious and an impassioned pioneer of women's education; she showed Edith the academic career path that she could take if she chose to. For an educated woman of Edith's background, a bluestockinged independence was one of the only options if she wanted to escape the family home. But Dacres would not have allowed it, and perhaps it was never even discussed. The other option would have been to find a husband, one which her father might approve of. Only once did she make a gesture in that direction. One weekend in term-time she brought home a young don to meet her family, but Dacres made him seem so inadequate that Edith put an end to the relationship. She never tried again. As it happened Edith developed asthma in Oxford and left after only four terms. By 1896 she was back at the Rectory and life continued much as it had done before.

Edith appeared to accept her lot. She lived, for the most part, a practical, useful sort of life – 'a home-keeping youth' – helping her father with his duties in the parish and becoming involved with countless local causes and committees, including teaching the choir at Netherhampton and running a branch of the National Poultry Organization Society.[13] With her natural confidence and inherited hauteur she proved adept, resourceful and persuasive. Wilton was the ancient heart of Wiltshire and proudly maintained political independence from the much larger city of Salisbury only a few miles to the east. It was a Middlemarch kind of town, and in Edith's youth it was steeped in tradition. She would remember with delight its fairs, pageants and unusually high number of processions. She had been named after Wilton's patron saint* and like her father she felt a responsibility, almost a noblesse oblige, to serve the town.

When their mother died in 1908 Mildred and Edith took over the running of the Rectory and the care of their increasingly irascible father. By then the sisters knew they would never marry. Mildred had had only one love affair, 'one radiant summer of perfect mental companionship and whimsical tenderness, and then it all went wrong'.[14] She remained dependent on her bolder sister, with whom she had made a pact that they would never leave each other, rather like Jane Austen and her sister Cassandra. In childhood, when Edith dreamt of adventures on the high seas, Mildred would weep for hours, fearing that she would be abandoned. Their friend Pamela Tennant recalled that Mildred 'would agonize if this beloved sister was out even walking down the village street,

---

* Saint Edith (or Editha) of Wilton was born in 961, the illegitimate daughter of King Edgar. She became a nun at Wilton Abbey, from where her mother had earlier been forcibly removed by the King and later returned as abbess. After her half-brother Edward was murdered she was offered the throne but chose to remain at Wilton. She was learned, pure and beautiful with a penchant for fine, golden clothes, a luxury for which she was rebuked. She responded by saying that this was irrelevant to God whose judgement could penetrate beyond clothes: 'For pride may exist under the garb of wretchedness; and a mind may be as pure under these vestments as under your tattered furs'. She died at the age of twenty-three. Her body remained sweet-smelling and uncorrupted in its grave, she was the source of several small miracles and a magnificent shrine was dedicated to her at Wilton Abbey. (Anna Jameson, *Legends of the Monastic Orders* (London: Longmans, Green & Co., 1867) p.96.)

beyond her sight'.[15] Another friend would later write that 'the two sisters were inseparable, and their little dark heads could be seen under the same evening cloak when there were wanderings after dinner in the Park'.[16] Edith and Mildred were bound to each other, and happily so.

In 1912 Dacres retired as Rector of Wilton and became a canon at Salisbury Cathedral, moving with his family to a house in the Cathedral Close, the inspiration for Trollope's Barsetshire novels, to live amongst 'scholarly canons and gentle old maids'.[17] In leaving Wilton Edith felt that she had lost her soul.

Two years later the threat of war hovered over the country but within the cloistered walls of the Close, the Balkans seemed too distant to contemplate. Soon after war was declared troops and army lorries began to pour into the city from Salisbury Plain, shattering its preciously maintained tranquillity and ushering the war into their lives. Within a month came news that Edith's youngest brother Harold had been killed fighting on the Aisne, leaving behind a wife and two small children. Edith later wrote with impassioned bitterness about the 'uprush of idealism and ignorance' with which the war began and how this faded away as the harsh realities slowly filtered back from the front.[18] Her friend, the poet Sir Henry Newbolt, wrote to her: 'This war is going to change the world for us all. Nothing will ever be the same again.'[19]

At first Edith's daily life continued as before; she remained busy with her duties in Wilton and enjoyed the novelty of making domestic economies. But a few years later, as the war rattled on far beyond its first Christmas and more and more men left to fight, Edith, as a member of the Wiltshire County Agricultural Committee, recognized that there would soon be a serious deficit in the number of farm workers. This, she thought, was an opportunity for women to show their capabilities. She met for tea with her cousin Sydney Olivier, the Fabian and, conveniently for Edith, President of the Board of Agriculture. He was commandeered to help implement her plans. Setting up the organization was the easy part. Convincing sceptical farmers, who loathed the idea of a

'Regiment of Women' working on their farms, would prove a harder task.[20] She became involved in recruiting volunteers and organizing their training on local estates and had soon built up a register of about 4,000 girls. Despite the farmers' reservations, her scheme proved successful and it soon became apparent that it would have to evolve into something bigger and more official. In 1916 Edith went to a meeting at the House of Commons to discuss the creation of a new national organization and she became a superintendent of its Wiltshire branch. And so the Women's Land Army was born. By late 1917 there were over 260,000 women working as farm labourers. Two years after the war ended Edith was awarded an MBE for her work.

Edith's role with the Land Army meant that she had to learn to drive. She acquired a little two-seater and was endlessly dashing about the Wiltshire countryside, from farm to farm, in her stiff khaki uniform. She loved to drive fast and had inherited a passion for sightseeing from her father. As a child she had gone for drives on Salisbury Plain with Lady Pembroke in her phaeton, and with her father she would set out on expeditions, her stiff straw boater flat on her head, as Victorian girls often wore them. Edith's attire would change over the years but her love of sightseeing remained a constant. And whereas Dacres's routes were always carefully planned, Edith liked to explore.

Secretly, as a child, she had devoured her brothers' adventure books and wished that she was a boy so that she could run away to sea. At night with Mildred she play-acted and told tales of worlds far beyond the Rectory walls. All her life Edith longed to be an actress but her father would not hear of one of his daughters going on the stage, a career he considered 'grotesque' for a woman.[21] 'My father thought a professional actress was as improper as a Restoration Play', she would write.[22] Dacres's mother Mary, so family legend told, had been friends with Mrs Siddons, the celebrated tragedienne. Siddons had tried to persuade Mary to go on the stage, so gifted an actress had she been. But Mary was 'the strictest of Puritans' and it was not to be countenanced.[23]

Edith's brother Alfred horrified Dacres by abandoning the Colonial Service to become an actor and she dared not follow suit. So Edith lived the theatrical life vicariously, through the reviews of Mr Walkley, *The Times* theatre critic, who came to represent all that Edith was denied by her father and the 'one link with the world of [her] dreams'.[24] Her acting was confined to charades at home and the town play, but the instinct never left her.

Beside the Rectory on West Street in Wilton stands the parish church of St Mary and St Nicholas. It was built in 1844 by Lord Herbert of Lea and his mother Catherine, known as 'the Russian Countess' of Pembroke. She was the daughter of Count Semyon Vorontsov, Russian Ambassador to the Court of St James's. Catherine had a fashionable fancy for Italian architecture and so the church was designed in the style of a Romanesque basilica, more suited to casting a lofty shadow over a Florentine piazza than over a leafy English graveyard. The interior is a shrine to caprice with black marble columns from the Temple of Venus at Porto Venere, windows made of glass looted by Napoleon's army and twisted, mosaic-studded columns from Horace Walpole's chapel at Strawberry Hill. The whole effect is fanciful and foreign. Even the orientation of the church is irregular; it lies on a south-west–north-east axis rather than the traditional east–west. Here Edith had been baptized by her father. Beside the church, as if countering the frivolity of its neighbour, stands the gracious, deep-red brick Georgian Rectory where Edith was born: square, solid and restrained. But between the two buildings there is an unexpected and strangely English harmony. And just as the flamboyantly romantic and the archly conservative sit side by side on West Street in happy contradiction, so they did in Edith Olivier.

As children, Edith, Mildred and the younger boys created their own realm within the labyrinth of cellars, attics and cupboards of the rambling Rectory. They enjoyed a clandestine independence, with their private jokes and family legends closely binding them like comrades. In the summer they played around the mulberry tree or in the disused duck-house on the island, and in the evenings they would run and dance along the flat roof of the Rectory watching passers-by on the street or their oblivious parents talking in the garden. Often they would slip beyond the lawn and across the river into the meadows and orchards of the Wilton estate so that they could play with Lord Pembroke's nieces and nephews, with whom they had been brought up and would remain close all their lives.

The aristocratically eccentric world of Wilton House fascinated Edith. Lady Pembroke, whimsical and wayward, planted ivy all over the park at Wilton, refusing to believe that something so delicate could harm the trees around which it coiled so prettily. Lord Pembroke had been one of Disraeli's allies and his sister Lady Maud had married Sir Hubert Parry, the composer of 'Jerusalem' amongst other things and 'a whirlwind of genius'; another sister, Lady Mary, married Baron Freddy von Hügel, the Christian philosopher; and his youngest sister was Lady Ripon, married to a famous shot and herself a 'dazzling . . . social queen' to whom her friend Oscar Wilde dedicated *A Woman of No Importance*.[25] As a child, at the Rectory, Edith was required to be silent and dutiful; a role she accepted willingly to avoid upsetting her parents. But at Wilton House she was encouraged to speak her mind and give free rein to her imagination. And though she looked like a mouse there was nothing timorous about Edith: she was spiky, energetic and bold. There is a photograph of her as a young woman in 1897, a grin on her face, her arms swinging in gleeful abandon as she skips along the gravel path behind the Rectory in a puff-sleeved blouse and long, tightly belted skirt of late-Victorian fashion. Edith would never suppress the 'natural' side of her personality as her father had learnt to do.

Her other education took place in the drawing rooms of Wilton House. As a young woman she would tramp across the estate to dinner at the big house with her sisters, galoshes over their satin shoes and the full skirts of their evening dresses pinned to their waists. Wilton House was 'the centre of our lives', she would write.[26] Socializing with the Pembrokes' circle of aristocratic and intellectual friends, listening to the conversations of dukes and duchesses, artists, historians, poets and politicians, had given her strong opinions and fanciful ideas. It gave her a sense of superiority, both socially and intellectually, that never left her. And she became a dedicated Tory in the aristocratic tradition. In the park at Wilton as a child she had seen Mrs Patrick Campbell perform in *As You Like It*. It had been played there before with Shakespeare amongst the company. The world within the walls of the estate was sheltered, grand and immutable. There, she would later write, her soul resided, and she came to realize that she never wanted to leave.

Edith enjoyed the elevated position in society that her link with Wilton House and her close friendship with Lord Pembroke's eldest son Reginald, or 'Regy' as she called him, provided. This connection meant that by the time she was an adult Edith had a large network of grand friends with grand houses set in beautiful estates. Amongst them, the Morrisons at Fonthill, the Radnors at Longford Castle, the Marchioness of Bath at Longleat, Lady Juliet Duff at Bulbridge, the Duchess of Devonshire, the Marchioness of Salisbury, Lady Desborough and Lady Violet Bonham Carter, the politically minded daughter of the Liberal Prime Minister. Reginald Herbert married Lady Beatrice Paget, sister of the Marquess of Anglesey. The Marquess's wife, Marjorie, a daughter of the Duke of Rutland and sister of the beautiful socialite Lady Diana Cooper, was Edith's friend.

Beyond the Wilton House circle, amongst Edith's closest friends were the American-born critic Alice Douglas Sedgwick and her sister Anne, who was a writer, a great friend of Henry James and married to the critic Basil de Selincourt. Another lifelong friend was the adventurous writer Yoi Maraini, who lived in Florence with her second husband, a sculptor. And nearby, across the meadows at Netherhampton House, lived Sir Henry Newbolt, the patriotic poet, and his wife Margaret. He shared with Edith a love of history and tradition.

But as the daughter of a country rector, and later as a very active woman in the community, Edith's social world was never confined to lofty patrician and artistic circles. She came into contact with everyone from church grandees to farmhands. She had resigned herself to an eternal spinsterhood, but Edith might have considered herself more of an Emma than a Miss Bates. She knew everyone and everyone knew her. Society people and townspeople marvelled at her endless energy and enjoyed her eccentricity.

Although she forged an independent life for herself, Edith was always rather contemptuous of the suffragettes, undoubtedly more for their conduct than for their cause. At St Hugh's, Annie Moberly had encouraged a progressive and quietly persistent attitude towards votes and degrees for women but without the drama or aggression of the later suffragettes, one of whom was enrolled at the college for a term in Edith's first year. Emily Davison, born in the same year as Edith, devoted her life to the cause of women's suffrage and later martyred herself beneath the King's horse at Epsom. Edith never mentions Davison in her memoirs. She deplored violence and found a way to assert her voice and freedom without upsetting anyone. One of Mildred's friends recalled Edith returning home from Oxford 'like a bright particular star a little out of its course and visiting a lesser firmament'.[27]

Edith remained good friends with Annie Moberly until her death in 1937. A respected and pioneering academic, Annie had another, more unusual side. In 1901 she had been walking in the gardens of the Petit Trianon at Versailles with Eleanor Jourdain, a fellow scholar, her close companion and, according to some, her lover. The two women suddenly found themselves in a scene from the eighteenth century and encountered various characters, who were, they were later convinced, Marie Antoinette and members of her court. They sought to 'rationalize' their experience and set about investigating it in the manner that was instinctive to them both as academics. After years of exhaustive research, they discovered that Marie Antoinette had been sitting in the gardens of the Trianon on 5 October 1789, when she was informed that a mob was marching from Paris. By way of an explanation for their vision, Annie and Eleanor formulated an elaborate theory that Marie Antoinette's memory of this terrifying moment had been so powerful that it lingered in the same place through time and that somehow they must have entered into it telepathically and witnessed the scene for themselves. They went on pseudonymously to publish their account in 1911; the bizarre story of the eccentric spinster-visionaries gripped the public imagination and quickly became a bestseller.

There are various theories as to what the two women actually saw, but the aspect that has most fascinated the critics of *An Adventure* over the years is the vehemence with which the two women defended their vision and the dedication with which they researched their claims. One explanation is that it was a case of contagious insanity, a shared delusion or *folie à deux*, or more specifically in this case, *folie imposée*, whereby the delusions of one person are imposed on another, revealing, it has been suggested, a repressed lesbian affinity.[28] Despite the authors' use of pseudonyms, their identity was known to acquaintances and some reviewers. Their academic status lent credibility to the story but the story did little for their academic reputation. Moberly and Jourdain were two of only a handful of women spearheading the burgeoning women's education movement at Oxford and Cambridge and the publication of *An Adventure* seemed to confirm the fears of their detractors. It cast an embarrassingly long shadow over the college and the careers of the two women.

Some of this folly clearly rubbed off on Edith, who never doubted the validity of the claims in *An Adventure*. She too had a curious combination of common sense, intelligence and a profound fascination with 'things past explaining'.[29] Edith was infatuated with history and the romance of place, believing that darker and more primitive energies existed deep within the Wiltshire landscape. Salisbury Plain with its 'great impersonal changelessness'[30] fascinated her: 'the hauntings of the Plain are not personal, they are universal. The word "Revenant" fits them better than "Ghost"', she later wrote. 'Abstract presences seem to come and go upon the Plain, and they pass like the cloud shadows which move eternally over its still, impassible face.'[31]

Late one afternoon in October 1916 Edith was wearily driving home through rain from a meeting of the Women's Land Army. Leaving the main road she came across a huge avenue of megaliths, beyond which a village fair was in progress. She realized that she was looking at the stone circle at Avebury. Though the stone circle still stood, it was some years later when she discovered that the avenue of stones had disappeared before 1800 and that the fair had been abolished in 1850; she decided that she must have stepped back in time to the eighteenth century.

But despite inexplicable things happening to Edith she didn't consider herself a psychic. She believed that her imagination was so finely tuned as to be receptive to the supernatural. Nowhere did she feel this more keenly than in Wiltshire, and Salisbury Plain in particular. 'It is not a question of "seeing ghosts" or of "having visions"', she would write, 'it is that sometimes, under the influence of that great spirit that seems ever brooding over the plain, one's own little outlook is lost and is incorporated into something older and bigger and wiser than oneself. One knows what the past was like.'[32]

Her sense of place derived from an elaborate patchwork of remembered anecdotes, local legends and folklore, history and literature. In the manner of Kipling in *Puck of Pook's Hill*, she had fiction and fact organically fused in her imagination. 'I know of no one who claims to have seen an apparition of one of the most beautiful and tragic funeral processions in the world's history', she would later write, 'when for two nights and the best part of two days, Sir Lancelot and his seven companions went on foot the long forty miles from "Almesbury unto Glastonbury", escorting the bier upon which lay, with face uncovered, the body of Guinevere the Queen . . . If strength and poignancy of feeling are the cause of hauntings', which she believed, 'one might expect still to meet those figures on that long way of sorrow, but the beautiful vision has never been seen'.[33] Undoubtedly Edith hoped that she would be the one to see these 'revenants of the Plain'.[34]

Edith's Christianity sat happily with her belief in visions, primitive energies and the predictive power of the horoscope. Every morning, throughout her life, she attended daily communion. She would go to evensong almost as often. With its ceremonies, rituals and symbols, Edith's Anglican faith was like a romantic ideology, one that was almost pantheistically tied up with nature. The perfect synchrony of the Christian year with the seasons delighted Edith, as did the aesthetic and sensory pleasures of the Anglican Church. And so it was that the lyrical world of Edith's imagination mingled seamlessly with her real world: that of laundry lists, of milk yields, parish matters and committee meetings. It illuminated her faith and the landscape around her and she responded to both with equal passion.

The farmers and parish councillors might have been bemused by her flights of fancy, but Edith had kindred spirits. One of them was her great friend Pamela Wyndham, the daughter of the Honourable Percy Wyndham and his wife Madeline. A statuesque society beauty, Pamela had the blood of French royalty and Irish nobility running through her veins. She was a year older than Edith, and as children they had played together on the lawns at Wilton. In 1895 she had married Edward Tennant (later Lord Glenconner), scion of the exceedingly rich industrial family whose fortune derived, rather more prosaically, from the invention of bleach by a Victorian farming ancestor. Eddie Tennant's sister Margot was married to Herbert Asquith, the Liberal Prime Minister. Of Pamela's five surviving children (a sixth, a girl called Hester, died a few hours after she was born in 1916) Stephen, born in 1906, was the youngest. At Clouds, her parents' home in Wiltshire, she had been brought up in a lofty but tolerant atmosphere amongst Pre-Raphaelite artists and socialist writers. William Morris had been a frequent guest. Pamela had keenly imbibed their values and carried them with her into her own family life, shunning society and the Tennants' London house in Queen

Anne's Gate as much as she could, in favour of a quiet country life. But Pamela's idea of country living was a Ruskinian ideal, one that belied the industrial source of the family's wealth.

Edward Tennant had built his wife a house, Wilsford, in the Avon Valley in Wiltshire, designed by Detmar Blow in the style favoured by the Arts and Crafts architects. There Pamela indulged her imagination, writing poetry and books on folklore, nature and her children. She loved her children, her 'jewels' as she liked to call them, more than anything. When her favourite son Bim was killed by a sniper's bullet on the Somme in 1916 (the son she had brought up to believe that fighting for one's country was the noblest cause) Pamela was distraught. Though she had profound faith Pamela was also a mystic. Like Edith she believed in second sight and it became her mission to contact Bim on the other side. With her friend and neighbour, the respected physicist and Christian spiritualist, Sir Oliver Lodge, who had also lost a son in the war, Pamela conducted seances at Wilsford and together they sought to conjure up the ghosts of their beloved dead. A few years later in 1921, Pamela published *The Earthen Vessel*, an account of her spirit-communication with Bim, and a curiously personal and painful relic of an age of mourning.

History has not been kind to Pamela. Later generations have vilified her as a vampire-mother whose own life overshadowed and warped the lives of her children. Rather than nurturing her 'jewels', her overwhelming love had drained the lifeblood from them. Edith privately disapproved of the way Pamela raised her children and of her incessant attempts to contact the dead. But despite these differences, the two women had a great mutual understanding. Edith admired Pamela's sensitivity and dedication to a life fuelled by the imagination. She also considered her to be a fine poet.

Dacres died two months after the Peace, in January 1919, at the age of eighty-seven. Edith and Mildred were in their late forties and finally at liberty to begin an independent life. They left the Close for temporary accommodation in a former laundry cottage on the Wilton estate, until they found a more permanent home of their own. Eventually they rented a house from Edith's friend Lord Bledisloe, who had helped her to set up the Women's Land Army. Fitz House was a fifteenth-century manor house with mullioned windows in Teffont Magna, perhaps the prettiest village in Wiltshire, and some miles from Wilton. A stream ran along the village street from the chalk down, and access to the house was provided by a bridge. Edith believed the water in the stream was the finest in Wiltshire after she was given an ancient recipe for an unguent that listed it as a magic ingredient. For the two years they lived there, the house was a happy place, often full of their many nephews and nieces and their friends' children. Reginald Pembroke's four children, Patricia, Sidney, David and Tony, as well as their cousin Michael Duff, often came to stay. Edith's childhood friends the Parry sisters, Dolly Ponsonby and Gwendolene Plunket Greene, by now had children of their own, and they too, along with Pamela Tennant's children, were frequent visitors. Edith's memories of Teffont Magna were that it was 'full of noise and laughter and children's games'.[35]

A photograph taken in about 1920 shows the sisters in the garden at Fitz House: Mildred, carrying a parasol to ward off the sun, and Edith, in profile, playfully gesturing to her sister. It is a picture of contentment and happiness. Mildred was Edith's beloved companion in all things. Like Edith, she loved conversation and the sisters talked to each other incessantly, about books, music, the piano – which Mildred played very well – their garden and their friends. They stimulated each other's minds and perhaps it felt to them as if their lives were complete. Dolly Ponsonby would later recall Mildred as a warm and sympathetic friend who was interested in everything and everyone around her.

> With Mildred we felt clever, amusing and attractive . . . Certainly she had the power of transmuting prosaic and everyday things into exciting and funny things. She could extract amusement from a door-scraper . . . she retained some of the absurd

caprices of youth, enthusiasms or dislikes for unaccountable things; there was the charm of the unexpected and the un-explained . . . Mildred never had a middle-aged point of view . . .'[36]

In 1921, Lady Pembroke offered the sisters the old dairy cottage, set in a corner of the Wilton estate. And joyfully they returned to the place that they loved. 'I found my lost soul in the park', Edith later wrote and Mildred described it as 'the most wonderful thing that ever happened to us'.[37] They hired a housekeeper and a maid, set about making alterations and planned a rose garden. They renamed it the Daye House, the old Wiltshire word for dairy. Soon, as at Teffont Magna, the house was teeming with children, camp beds filling up every available space. Edith and Mildred adored their young guests – indulging them by telling ghost stories and dressing up as witches or Indian squaws in a tent in the woods. And in turn the children adored them. At the Daye House there were no routines and nothing humdrum; all was fun and magic and adventure.

And so it could have continued. But then Mildred found a lump in her breast and was diagnosed with cancer. She had an operation on the dining table at the Daye House, while Edith sat nervously in the next room, the smell of ether seeping out from underneath the door. But it was to no avail. After months of debilitating radiation treatment, Mildred died on 19 November 1924. Edith was fifty-one, and she believed her life was over.

Rex

❖

It was heaven-clear to me, solitary and a dreamer; let me but gain the key, I would soon unlock that Eden garden-door.

Walter de la Mare, *Henry Brocken*

Just before the turn of the century, at around the time Edith Olivier returned home from Oxford, Helen Ward came out at a hunt ball in Basingstoke Town Hall. Like Edith, Helen was the daughter of a country rector; she had learnt French in Brussels, wrote poetry and played Chopin, and then appalled her family by making a mésalliance with a man in trade. In 1898 she married Harry Whistler at a church in Notting Hill and the couple honeymooned at Lulworth Cove. A builder, uneducated and un-sophisticated, was not at all what the Reverend Charles Ward had in mind for his daughter. But Harry was a gentle soul, quietly spoken and charming. His company, on the High Street in Eltham, south London, was modestly successful and carried out all kinds of jobs from building, decorating, sanitary work and electric lighting (the poster declared the company as the rather evangelical-sounding 'Agents for the Incandescent Light') to inventories, furniture sales, auctions and property lettings. It sup-plied everything from manhole covers stamped with the Whistler name, to architectural services, specializing in suburban houses in the popular half-timbered 'Tudorbethan' style.

Harry and Helen's third child, Rex, was born on Midsummer's Day, 24 June 1905, at the family home, a modest mid-Victorian detached house around the corner from the office. A photograph taken in 1911 shows the Whistler family formally arranged in their back garden, a portrait of pre-war, middle-class respectability: Harry, thickset and moustachioed, serious in a dark suit and boater; Helen, elegant in white and draped in a wicker chair; beside her, perched on the arm of the chair, their daughter Jess, then aged eleven; and their two sons, sitting in miniature chairs on either side of their mother, dressed in wide-collared sailor outfits and straw hats with upturned brims; on the right, Denis, and on the left Rex, with fat cheeks, grinning at the camera. Their last child, Laurence, was born the following year.

Harry had no social ambition and no desire to make gentlemen of his sons but Helen had other ideas and her boys were duly sent to local prep schools. Though she was a loyal wife and would never regret her rebellious marriage, it did not stop her hoping for better things where her children were concerned. Rex was christened Reginald John but Helen called him Rex from birth; it sounded noble and romantic.

Helen encouraged all her children to draw from a young age but as it became clear that Rex's talent was rather more precocious she began at once to nurture it. Pencils and paper were kept in constant supply and she would cherish his childhood drawings all her life. Between 1912 and 1923 he won a prize every year at the Royal Drawing Society exhibition.

These drawings were almost always dramatic, and usually suffused with Rex's own variety of gentle, absurd humour. As one looks at them now, they appear unrefined, inelegant and often gruesome, but they also resonate with the same sense of energy and delight in the grotesque as his adult work, hinting at the artist he would become. And they reflect, too, his inventive interpretation of history, literature and the Bible stories his mother read to him. The images burst from the page and invite a closer look. One picture, drawn when Rex was nine or ten, is of decapitated Moorish soldiers, their long ponytailed scalps bleeding beside them. There is a drawing of the crumpled carriages of a train crash; another of a drilling machine in a mine with pieces of rock spinning off it; and a cartoon of a wronged wife seeing her husband with another woman, about to smash his portrait and being carried off by the police. Invariably Rex coupled drama with farce, as he would always do.

For most of his life Rex preferred to draw from memory. His imagination served as a catalogue of learnt images, and his talent always lay in his ability to reproduce, elaborate and reinvent reality. Amongst his very earliest drawings is 'The Knoll Palace', in which he has romanticized and upgraded the Knoll, the family home at the time, to a palace. Another was entitled 'Prince Rex of Troy leaving for Grece [sic]'.

Rex was a popular little boy; sunny, open and affectionate. He worshipped his elder brother Denny and the two were inseparable. Where Denny led, the younger boy would follow and whatever they were doing, Rex was always striving to keep up with him. He would constantly seek to prove himself, always believing that he had failed.

One morning in February 1915 when he was eleven, Denny began to feel unwell at school. He left without permission and returned home. He had measles, then whooping cough and eventually developed pneumonia. An air of horror hung in the Whistler home as the boy lay in his bed upstairs. A month later he died. His mother, who had great faith in God but a constant, seemingly irrational fear of accident and illness, was inconsolable. She could not face the funeral and Harry went alone. For nine-year-old Rex, the sudden loss of his best friend was the beginning of an underlying sadness that would never leave him. He was also now the eldest son, and became the focus of his mother's hopes and expectations.

In 1919, when Rex was fourteen, he was sent to Haileybury, the public school in Hertfordshire founded to educate civil servants for India. A sporty, austere sort of school, it was an odd choice for a boy who wanted to do nothing but draw and paint. Rex was bright but not intellectual. He would later remember the relentless boredom he felt at Haileybury – a dreamy schoolboy, whiling away the hours in class doodling strip cartoons across the pages of his exercise books. In a letter to the school in the 1980s, Laurence Whistler would write that his brother 'owed nothing to the art school, which he didn't much frequent, and the art master thought nothing of his work'.[1] Yet Rex found that his talent won him friends, as it had at prep school: 'I did a drawing for a boy yesterday and after that I got no peace everyone asked me to do them one'.[2] So it would always be.

Rex left Haileybury in the spring of 1922, at the age of sixteen, and planned to go to art school. To his credit, Harry Whistler put no pressure on his elder son to take over the business that he had worked so hard to build. He was happy for Rex to become an artist and knew that Helen had greater things in mind for her son than the building trade. But she thought of Rex as a gentleman-artist, not a bohemian. She 'admired', Laurence Whistler wrote, 'the kind of artist who moved with grace in the world of affairs, such as Rubens . . . whose example she liked to fancy that Rex might follow'.[3] Rex was far more fortunate than many of his contemporaries. Both Evelyn Waugh and John Betjeman were considered a disappointment by their fathers because of their refusal to work in their respective family businesses. Cecil Beaton's father was a wealthy timber merchant and wanted his son to work in the City after coming down from Cambridge. For Waugh, Betjeman and Beaton, taking up the pen and the camera were acts of rebellion. On the contrary, Rex's parents actively encouraged his artistic ambitions. For his mother, becoming an artist was a sign of respectability and cultivation rather than insurrection.

And so Rex entered the Royal Academy Schools on a probationary basis. But as he was essentially self-taught, and limited by his inability to draw from life, in the end-of-term examination Rex failed and, to his horror, lost his place at the school. It was one of the worst moments of his life but he was determined not to give up. He decided to try his luck at the Slade School of Art where he was interviewed by Henry Tonks, 'the revered, redoubtable, dreaded and loved master', whose former pupils included Augustus John and Stanley Spencer.[4] When asked why he had failed at the RA, Rex replied: 'for incompetence'.[5] Tonks offered him a place, beguiled by his frankness and impressed by his talent.

At the Slade, girls with bobbed hair, sandals and Augustus John smocks hung about the entrance. Rex befriended Oliver Messel, later a fashionable designer of sets and costumes. At times, later, Rex and Oliver would find themselves competing for the same commissions. But that was in the future. 'Instead of always slaving away in the somewhat uninspiring atmosphere of life classes (always flabbily grotesque models) at the Slade', Messel would later recall, 'Rex Whistler and I were inclined to fritter away the time in each other's company, doodling and drawing fantasy palaces and imaginary people. During the weekends we started making masks of papier mache.'[6]

Several weeks into term the Honourable Stephen Tennant arrived at the Slade. With his whippet-slim frame, shiny golden hair and finely modelled face he had the elegant androgyny of a Beardsley or Erté illustration – and the attendant whiff of aristocratic decadence which that implied. In the many photographs taken of Stephen his expression is one of either patrician disdain or limpid-eyed ingenuity. He was much preoccupied by his own beauty and took the greatest delight in the beauty of things around him.

One lunch-break he noticed Rex sitting alone reading Edgar Allan Poe and introduced himself. Perhaps it was the choice of book that first attracted Stephen, or perhaps it was that in Rex, solitary, quieter than the other students, he saw a potential kindred spirit. Rex took a very businesslike approach to art school; instead of the bohemian garb favoured by his classmates he wore a proper suit and carried an attaché case. He wanted to be taken seriously, and although he had a charming and easy manner with the other students, he found it difficult to make friends. Stephen would later recall:

He was a deeply shy man, with a great tendency to making reservations in his judgement of others. While not censorious, he was critical and recessive in the extreme . . .

He had a quality of essential simplicity that continually opposed the curious sardonic melancholy of his maturity. He had an essential gravity which his fooling played and like summer lightning [sic]. Sometimes his face in repose was curiously sad and thoughtful. He was sometimes capricious and quixotic, uncertain of his own feelings and predilections.[7]

Rex's first impression of Stephen was of a 'slender figure and extraordinary beauty, like a more delicate Shelley'.[8] In contrast, Stephen saw Rex as 'a plump, thick set, very boyish man, with a manner both impulsive and diffident . . . His skin was pale, his eyes agate-grey, with a nuance of catkin hazel, almost topaz brown and grey depths . . . Something inhibited and repressed showed in his lips and the way he averted his head sometimes, when he was particularly thoughtful.' 'We both loved fairy tales, mythology, legends containing magic spells', Stephen recalled, 'and we found a strong reciprocal bond in the passionate vividness of our imaginations.'[9] They also shared a more contemporary fascination with Hollywood, the movies, fast cars: the glamour and gloss of America. Together they explored London; they went to parties, to the theatre, they set off arm in arm on moonlit walks and dipped their toes into the city's bohemia.

More than anything it was love of poetry that brought them together. Both young men were obsessed with Shelley, Keats, Chaucer, Tennyson and de la Mare. For Stephen it had been an integral part of his life but for Rex this overt worshipping of poetry was a new thing. Inspired by the poems, fantasies and fairy tales he was reading with Stephen, Rex had begun to compile and illustrate an anthology of his favourites. The violence and drama of his childhood drawings were giving way to romance and beauty. Now he adored the wildly dreamy illustrations of Arthur Rackham, Edmund Dulac and Kay Nielsen, as well as Rowlandson and Hogarth. Rex filled the pages of his book with lovers, Gothic ruins, gravestones, witches, stormy skies, windswept seas, silvery moonlight, sylvan landscapes and casement windows. There are poems by Shelley and Tennyson; Poe's 'Annabel Lee' (a favourite); Keats's 'To Autumn', 'To a Nightingale' and 'La Belle Dame Sans Merci'; some Herrick; Gray's 'Elegy'; selections from the *Rubaiyat*; and Edith Sitwell's 'Spring'. Rex was fascinated by the macabre, mystical world evoked by these poems; and he sought solace in their atmosphere of nostalgia and longing. There are more poems by Walter de la Mare than any other; to Rex, he 'was the supreme romantic of the modern age, creating a world of his own by transfiguring with strangeness what was familiar or at hand. Rex would often apply the epithet "de la Marish" to some scene in his mind'.[10]

At around the same time as he was compiling his anthology Rex drew an illustration of Henry Brocken, from the eponymous novel by Walter de la Mare, published in 1904. It was Rex's (and Stephen's) favourite novel and tells the story of the hero as he travels through a literary landscape, encountering legendary characters from fiction, such as Keats's palely loitering knight, Jane Eyre and Rochester, Bottom and Titania, Gulliver, Criseyde, La Belle Dame sans Merci and Lucy Gray. At the end of the book Brocken meets the forlorn heroine of Poe's 'Annabel Lee' on a desolate beach. In his illustration Rex casts himself as Brocken, wrapped in an overcoat against the wind, cowering beside the elfin girl, with the brooding sea, dark, looming rocks and billowing clouds, a whirl of grey behind them. Like the hero of the novel, Rex was longing to 'unlock that Eden garden-door' that would lead into a world of the imagination.[11] Very soon he would.

Rex and Stephen's friendship developed quickly, almost passionately, and soon Rex was invited to the Tennants' home in Wiltshire. 'I'm going down this weekend to stay at Lord Grey of Fallodon's house in Wiltshire!!!' he wrote excitedly to a school friend.[12] Stephen's father Lord Glenconner had died in 1918. Four years later his mother Pamela married Lord Grey, the former

Foreign Secretary and an old friend, long-time admirer and fellow bird-lover. Edward Grey, Pamela and the children continued to live in Wiltshire rather than at Fallodon, Grey's family home in Northumberland.

At Wilsford Pamela had created a luxurious paradise of mock rusticity and artful simplicity to the design of her own pastoral fantasy. It was a Petit Trianon kind of house, built of chequered stone and flint, with gables and mullioned windows, espaliered fruit trees and rough-hewn wooden bridges, an ilex-shaded lawn where peacocks stalked, and a garden ringing with birdsong, the air heavy with the scent of flowers. But, though the house looked as old as the Norman church beside it, and though everywhere hung an atmosphere of gentle decay, at Wilsford nothing was quite what it seemed. The weathered bricks concealed sophisticated, up-to-date heating and water systems, the rustic cottages in the grounds were a racquet court in disguise, and the mock village green was very much a private lawn onto which no villager was invited to tread.

The house was filled with simple furniture, Morris chintzes and beautiful plants as well as exotic animals, writers, artists, psychics and Pamela's ghosts. The bedrooms were named after flowers. But at the heart of Wilsford were Pamela's beloved children, her most cherished creations. She created a fairy-tale world for them to live in, filled with magic, poetry and beauty. She had built a round thatched house for the children to play in, with a ladder leading to an upper room. But, as V. S. Naipaul later observed, it was an idea conceived entirely by an adult, and left nothing to the child's imagination.[13]*

Pamela keenly cultivated her children's imaginations, and

---

* Naipaul lodged for a time on the estate. *The Enigma of Arrival,* published in 1987 by Viking, is a fictionalized autobiography that takes the narrator from his native Caribbean to a rented cottage on an estate in rural Wiltshire. Its themes are Proustian and pastoral; the narrative circles around perceptions and preconceptions about place. The narrator's mysterious, elusive, eccentric landlord was based on Stephen Tennant, Naipaul's own landlord at Wilsford.

published their infant mutterings in a book, *Sayings of the Children*. Stephen, her youngest child, after spending only a few days at school, where he had cried constantly, was allowed to return home. His mother dressed him as a girl until he was eight and encouraged him to believe he would have been more contented as a girl, perhaps in order to compensate for his wayward elder sister Clare, whom Pamela considered a disappointment. She 'bottle-fed' Stephen 'on a rarefied diet of beauty and culture' and nurtured his talent for drawing, organizing an exhibition of his Beardsley-esque drawings at a London gallery when he was fourteen.[14] He had his own reptilliary and a parrot house, and from an early age was encouraged to indulge every imaginative whim. Unsurprisingly he became profoundly narcissistic. He grew up with the belief that he was like the most rare and beautiful of his mother's hothouse orchids and claimed that he had heard the flowers on Salisbury Plain calling his name. When his father asked him what he planned to be when he grew up, Stephen answered, "'I want to be a great beauty, Sir'".[15]

In spite, or perhaps because, of 'Mummie's' suffocating love it was his 'belovèd Nannie', old, benign and uncomplicated, for whom Stephen felt the most affection. But though a current of tension and unhappiness ran deep at Wilsford, Rex found it to be a magical place. With reality kept out by the garden wall, Rex could escape into a fantasy world of poetry, indulgence, ease and a very gentle, English sensuality. It was a place where daydreaming wouldn't be tempered by the rap of a schoolmaster's ruler against his knuckles. Rex was dazzled by Stephen and the manner in which he made an art of his life. He was impulsive and effervescent; he could be generous and capricious, he made grand gestures and appreciated the smallest, most insignificant of things. His letters were a vision, his handwriting a loopy, rococo swirl of coloured inks eddying across equally colourful notepaper. Stephen was teaching Rex to see and appreciate things afresh: the delicate beauty of a shell or the song of a woodpigeon. And Rex was smitten.

Around this time, no doubt inspired by this new friendship, Rex began to draw vivid images of the high life, of exotic homes, fast cars and dinner dress. One design, entitled 'My Private Bathroom', is of a vast classical chamber with an elaborate carved and vaulted ceiling, pillars, braziers, elegant rococo seating, satyrs pouring hot and cold water and a cushioned, gilded gondola floating across the water. He designed a sophisticated and slim-fitting dressing gown for himself, modelled in the picture by a Chinese man who is in the process of spilling a cup of tea. It was typical of Rex to undercut fantasy with humour, and deflate drama with bathos. 'Sometimes I thought that he felt to be serious about anything was dangerous', a school friend would later recall.[16] His flights of fancy never entirely left the ground.

For Rex and Stephen their friendship was a 'Kingdom by the sea'. The envelopes of all their letters bore the line from Poe's 'Annabel Lee' on the back:

> *I was a child and she was a child*
> *In this Kingdom by the sea:*
> *But we loved with a love that was more than love—*
> *I and my Annabel Lee—*[17]

Rex declared that he and Stephen had 'got rather a "case"', school slang for a love affair between boys.[18] Stephen had been attracted to his own sex since his youth when his 'naughty behaviour' involved kissing and flashing at soldiers who were stationed on Salisbury Plain; he was even caught by a policeman 'doing something he shouldn't' with one of the soldiers.[19] Pamela chose to ignore his behaviour, perhaps realizing that what her son wanted most was not sex, but to be admired. She liked Rex and thought he would be a good influence. Rex had had homosexual experiences at school but his friendship with Stephen seems to have been fuelled by the power of their shared imagination rather than sexual attraction: 'by this age any homosexual leanings he had were not towards a male more feminine than himself' writes Laurence Whistler.[20] Theirs was a romantic friendship rather than a love affair. According to Stephen's biographer Philip Hoare, 'for either, the idea of putting their friendship on anything more than a "spiritual love" level would have been difficult to imagine . . . Stephen still apparently too ethereal to consider anything physical.'[21] Some years later, in a letter to Stephen, Rex would write of their relationship: 'Thank God it grew and lasted all this time owing nothing to unhappy and destructive SEX . . . physical love'.[22]

Stephen has long been suggested as an inspiration for the character of Sebastian Flyte in *Brideshead Revisited*, the beautiful young aristocrat who introduces Charles Ryder to a closed and intoxicating world. Like Stephen, Sebastian is egotistical and eccentric. He adores strange objects. And like Stephen, Sebastian is on a perpetual, almost infantile quest for novelty. He is both fey and feckless and entirely devoted to his teddy bear Aloysius, as Stephen was to his pet tortoise. Sebastian has a doting nanny whom he adores and a beautiful but controlling mother, whom he later describes as 'a *femme fatale* . . . She killed at a touch'.[23] It has also been said that Rex was an inspiration for Charles Ryder, who throws himself headlong into Sebastian Flyte's world, seduced by the 'entrancing . . . epicene beauty' at its heart.[24] A number of his contemporaries took it as given and the similarities between the real and fictional friends are often striking. Many of the characters in *Brideshead Revisited* are undoubtedly composites of people Waugh knew although he was notoriously dismissive of those who sought to identify the direct sources from amongst his friends and acquaintances. Waugh knew Rex; they occasionally attended the same parties and had a number of mutual friends. There is, however, no evidence, and perhaps, at most, Waugh had an idea of Rex and his friendship with Stephen in mind when writing *Brideshead*. But the novel is a captivating narrative of the time, both socially and culturally, and the parallels are a fascinating paradigm to the story of Rex's life.

Some years earlier Stephen had been diagnosed with tuberculosis. Living at Wilsford, in a damp river valley, was making matters worse. In 1924 his doctors prescribed an escape to foreign climes and cleaner air. And so in the autumn Pamela made plans for her son to spend the winter in Switzerland. He was to travel with a retinue: his Nannie, a manservant, and a doctor-tutor called Dr Macfie. Pamela told Stephen that his friend could come too. For nineteen-year-old Rex it would be his first trip abroad. Even though it meant missing all but the first two weeks of term, he received the invitation with the utmost delight: 'if I could have my own way, I'd pack my toothbrush (and Euthymol*) right away and follow you to the moon!' he wrote to Stephen.[25] His parents and Tonks agreed to the plan and soon letters were flying back and forth as the two young men planned their wardrobes in minute detail: 'jade green jerseys', 'rakeish' snow caps, and nothing white; 'I always thought white looked dirty . . . when seen against the virgin whiteness of the snow', wrote Rex.[26] Stephen had suede dressing cases made for them both with their initials gilded on the exterior and monogrammed glass bottles filling the interior. They were to go first to Paris, staying in a suite at the Hotel Meurice overlooking the Tuileries, and then take the night train to Montreux, and from there on to a chalet in Villars. They departed on 23 October, three days after their trip had been announced in the social column of the *Daily Mirror*.

---

* A brand of toothpaste.

Spring

❖

It seems a pause between two worlds.

Edith Olivier's Diary, 26 December 1924

It was the silence that bothered Edith. The house had always been full of noise: children on the lawn, Mildred at the piano, afternoons in the garden and evenings with friends in the Long Room. They had been happy, but when Mildred fell ill and died, Edith found herself alone for the first time in her life.

Although she had written in her diary every night for the past forty years, Edith allowed six days to pass following Mildred's death before she could bear to open the small leather-bound book. Sitting in bed that night in late November, a small, solitary figure against a bank of pillows, a pen in her hand and a writing desk on her knee, she wrote: 'I feel very weary . . . I cannot realize that I am going to be lonely <u>always</u>'.[1]

Edith was twelve when she had begun to write a diary. For an observant and opinionated but altogether dutiful girl like the young Miss Olivier, with a disapproving and autocratic father such as hers had been, it was a discreet act of rebellion. Writing became a necessary part of her life; it gave her a sense of selfhood and offered material validation to a seemingly inconsequential existence. Her daily entries are filled with anecdotes, confessions and indiscretions, as well as 'inevitable everyday-ness'.[2] At times contemptuous and at others affectionate, Edith had found a medium through which she could reveal her inner thoughts and impulses – and her writing became irrevocably interwoven with the fabric of her life. When, in 1887, she had been taken by her father to watch Queen Victoria's Golden Jubilee celebrations in London, the fourteen-year-old Edith was less interested in the spectacle itself than in its grand participants. In her diary she described that she had strained to glimpse the expressions on the faces of the royal party, the civic dignitaries and the exotically dressed maharajahs parading by. 'I must have been a funny little girl', she later wrote; 'the gorgeous pageantry of the day did not impress me. What I was looking for was the intimate expression on the faces of the people who drove by. I wanted to know what they were like. It was this which interested me'.[3]

For the young girl with an instinct for storytelling and an inclination to fantasy, who wanted nothing more than to become an actress, writing her diary gave her life a plot, made it a drama in which she played the central character. And so it continued for the next forty years, an unbroken private narrative, until Mildred died and the story seemed to have come to an end.

Though her many friends rallied round her, that Christmas Edith fled her house and its resounding silence for the sanctuary of an Anglican convent. And for a few days it brought her comfort: 'the atmosphere of this place gives a feeling of suspended life', she wrote in her diary; 'I feel unsubstantial – a thin shadow in limbo with the soft faint music of the psalms breathing through me. It seems a pause between two worlds.'[4] Edith had thought she might renounce the world and stay there indefinitely. But she was, the Mother Superior told her, 'too rebellious in mind' for a quiet life of prayer and contemplation.[5] With the New Year came an alternative, one that she willingly accepted: an invitation to a villa on the Italian Riviera. On board a Channel ferry Edith began the twenty-fifth volume of her diary. It was 21 March 1925, the last day of winter.

Part One

❖

THE LOVE-CHILD

1: San Remo

❖

It's sublime,
This perfect solitude of foreign lands!
To be, as if you had not been till then,
And were then, simply that you chose to be.

Elizabeth Barrett Browning, *Aurora Leigh*

Pamela had joined Stephen for Christmas in Switzerland and in
the New Year of 1925 she suggested that the party might journey
further south and take a villa somewhere in Italy. Stephen's tutor
was dispatched ahead of the group to find a suitably quiet location. Macfie travelled west along the Italian Riviera, and rented
the Villa Natalia on the Corso Cavallotti, just outside San Remo.
Stephen and his mother meanwhile compiled a list of guests who
might join them. Pamela proposed Edith Olivier, her old friend,
now in mourning for her beloved sister.

And so she came, travelling via Paris where she had spent a
few days with friends. Alighting at the station in San Remo, she
found Stephen waiting for her with a bouquet of violets in his
hand. She was weary from travelling and went straight to her room
to rest upon arriving at the villa, but in the afternoon she joined
the other guests on the stone terrace that overlooked the sea.
Pamela had since returned to England, leaving Stephen- and Rex
with Dr Macfie and Nannie. At dinner that first evening there
were 'terrific arguments' about 'the love of power', which Edith
and the young men defended.[1] Rex had been worried that this
scholarly country rector's daughter in her fifties would bring her

present grief with her and hinder their fun. Instead he found a sharp-witted, loquacious little woman with a cigarette in her hand who would absent-mindedly scratch her head or kick out her foot when she became particularly animated. Rex could see at once that Edith was no ordinary bluestocking.

Conversation was Edith's greatest pleasure and since Mildred's death she had been starved of it. It was lucky then, that 'Stephen talked like a rocket going off', as Cecil Beaton would later write.[2] She delighted in Stephen: 'he is the most sparkling talker . . . and perhaps the most amusing. He dances like a will-o'-the-wisp where other people stick in the mud . . . He can be by turns poetic, malicious, and nonsensical. His talk is very pictorial and he handles words as if they were paint on a brush.'[3] Rex's talk, on the other hand, was not intellectual or iridescent. He was enthusiastic and funny; he loved to exaggerate everything and he had a ringing laugh. But he enjoyed the duet of a conversation rather than a solo performance. He was a little quieter, gentler and certainly less confident than Stephen. But perhaps most appealing to Edith, he was interested in things. That first night in her diary she described him as 'a delightful keen boy who loves talking'.[4] Her first opinion of people as confided to her diary, though often revised later, could be brutal. But she liked Rex from the start.

The next day set the pattern for life at the Villa Natalia and Edith easily slipped into step with the young men. In the morning she walked with Stephen along the palm-lined boulevards into town and drank hot chocolate. And she bought a dress. Edith was delighted by San Remo: 'everything so gay and coloured . . . marvellously tropical'.[5] About twenty miles along the coast from Nice, the town had had its heyday in the late nineteenth century when European aristocrats had flocked to its grand hotels. But by the twenties, grandeur had given way to glamour, and Stephen loved glamour. The Villa Natalia, Stephen wrote to a friend, was 'a creamy villa in a grove of palm trees; our garden goes down to the sea and there is a heavenly terrace of stone actually in the sea where we sit and play mah-jongg or draw. Such a beautiful town, San Remo – white & red & glittering in the hot sunlight . . . the sea is roaring in my ears as I write . . .'[6]

At Cap d'Ail Stephen bought two red butterfly nets, later chasing his prey in the garden amongst the bougainvillea with an 'enchanting leaping movement'.[7] Another evening after dinner he was 'wildly excited' looking for frogs and newts in the waterbutt.[8] Edith wrote that 'all our misadventures enchant Stephen who is delightfully young and feels everything new is fraught with the romance of all the world'.[9]

For Rex too, 'all was new, the very streets he had been inventing years ago but placing farther East for his Arabian Nights'.[10] Edith was fascinated by his talent: 'R is unselfish and absorbed in the love of painting. The moment he comes in he sits down and begins drawing little imaginative pictures . . . Very <u>alive</u>. His facility and quickness are marvellous.'[11]

She was beguiled and revitalized by Stephen's joy in nature, by Rex's enthusiasm and by their delight in all things. She took it at face value, as a mark of their youth, and she found it contagious: 'we are writing a little book about our adventures. I write and the boys illustrate. Both full of invention and fun'.[12] The warmth and otherness of Italy and the company of these sweet, lively young men were like lotus-eating for Edith, a balm to her grief.

Afternoons were spent on the terrace, Stephen and Edith reading or writing and Rex drawing. At Pamela's request, Edith had brought a selection of books to provide the young men with a potted literary education. They were unusual but entirely characteristic: Gilbert Murray's *Euripides*, George Moore's *Ave* and Geoffrey Scott's *The Portrait of Zélide*, which had just been published. The young men were captivated by Edith Sitwell's haunting new poem 'The Sleeping Beauty' which she read aloud to them, and by the essays of Walter Pater. 'They did not know Pater', Edith wrote, 'and revel in every sentence'.[13]

Other days were spent shopping, visiting churches or walking in gardens filled with fountains and exotic flowers. There were trips inland, and along the coast to Monte Carlo. One afternoon they went to a thé dansant and watched with amusement the 'terrible' and 'very naked' German dancers with 'ballet skirts and bare dirty legs with garter marks at the knee [and] busts wobbling horribly in little sateen bodices'.[14] Later Rex and Stephen took turns to dance with Edith. One day they all donned fancy dress for tea, Stephen appearing in a tight-fitting black suit with matching skullcap and Rex, a red one. They dressed Edith in long gold trousers and a yellow velvet cloak and painted her face 'most wickedly and charmingly . . . Stephen wants to go to a Fancy Ball so this was a practice'.[15]

Rex and Stephen decided that Edith should be modernized. For a week they pleaded with her to have her hair cut and eventually she capitulated: 'A great day for me as after discussions all the week and the boys imploring me to do it I had my hair cut off – Bingled – this morning . . . I am afraid I am rather absurdly old to do it but it does suit me'.[16] In place of her old-fashioned bun and velvet ribbon, Edith's hair was cut into a bingle, an up-to-the-minute variation on the shingle with bobbed sides and a close shave at the nape of the neck. Perhaps it was then that she began to dye her greying hair to its original black. And that was only the beginning. On trips into Nice and Monaco she was persuaded to buy lipstick and shorter dresses. Edith was inclined to vanity and was thrilled by her transformation. Now she looked as contemporary as she felt. No longer would she look so conspicuously English and Edwardian amongst the suntanned Riviera habitués in their beach pyjamas and espadrilles.

On Easter Sunday, 'a radiant sunny day', Edith found the breakfast table laden with gifts.[17] From Stephen there were red carnations and a heap of gold chocolate coins and from Rex a watercolour that he had painted of the gardener telling the story in Edith Sitwell's 'The Sleeping Beauty'. Later they went to communion together. 'Happiness is there for me . . . it brings all near together and the past is not over'.[18] One day, towards the end of her stay, she saw swallows flying across the garden and wondered if they were on their way to England.

She too was about to return home, but much had changed. She had a new look and more significantly, a new friend in Rex. She left for England and Rex set off on a brief trip south to visit Florence, Pisa and Rome, rather apprehensively, because it was his first time travelling alone. Edith had given him letters of introduction to her friends in Florence. And they had made plans to meet again.

2: *The Daye House*

❖

Do you not see how all things conspire together to make this
country a heauenly dwelling? Do you not see the grasse how in
colour they excell the Emeralds, euerie one striuing to passe his
fellow, and yet they are all kept of an equall height? And see you
not the rest of these beautifull flowers, each of which would
require a mans wit to know, and his life to expresse? Doth not
the aire breath health, which the Birds (delightfull both to eare
and eye) do dayly solemnize with the sweete consent of their
voyces? Is not euery Eccho thereof a perfect Musicke?

Sir Philip Sidney's notebook

Edith returned to England in April. Before travelling home, she
stayed in London with American friends, the sculptor Francis
Howard, known as Tudie, and his wife Lura. There she received a
charmingly illustrated letter from Rex inviting her to join him for
tea at the Slade. 'My dear Edith', he wrote, 'I trust you won't think
it impertinent to address you thus!', and apologized for the 'very
common little notepaper'.[1] The following Monday they met at two
o'clock and spent the afternoon exploring the East End by bus.
'We mustn't be benighted in the slums', Rex had warned and
implored her to 'look very shabby' for the expedition.[2] Edith found
him as entertaining as before, perhaps even more so, as it was
their first opportunity to spend time alone together: 'He is a darling, so fresh and full of zest'.[3] That evening as they parted she
invited him to the Daye House for Whitsun.

It seemed that a different woman had returned to Wilton; she felt revitalized, transformed by her haircut and elegant new clothes. But though a lot had altered, some things remained unchanged. In the overgrown garden and in the house, empty but for the housekeeper and the young servant girl, Edith's thoughts turned to Mildred: 'It's exactly ten weeks today since I left here for Paris meaning to be a month away and here I am at last, so glad to be back. The little house welcomes me and holds all my heart and all my longing and memory. I cannot find Millee when I am staying about. Here she lives with me tho' without speech.'[4] She had decided to put together a book as a memorial to her sister. It was to be published privately with contributions from their friends including Stephen Tennant, Pamela Grey, and Francis and Lura Howard's son Brian. Henry Newbolt offered to write the biographical preface but then decided that he couldn't spare the time as he was working on a book of his own. Instead he suggested that Edith should write it. She wasn't at all convinced she was up to it, but Newbolt insisted, knowing that it would be a cathartic thing for his friend to do.

Waiting for Edith at the Daye House was another letter from Rex, illustrated with a drawing of them both looking down at a Wren church from an enormous, open-top bus. The letter announced that he was to arrive later that day as planned. There was little time then, for Edith to feel the solitude:

> Dearest Edith, I'm so looking forward to coming to you at the week-end. I am leaving Waterloo at 3 o'clock on Saturday, so I shall be at Salisbury station at 3.52 . . . What fun our little jaunt through the city of London was. I long one day to have plenty of time and ramble about and explore the lovely old city churches and odd corners. So looking forward to seeing you again.[5]

And so Rex arrived at Salisbury station. From there he was driven by a friend of Edith's the few miles to the house, which stood on the outskirts of Wilton, on the road to Netherhampton. Just before the town a narrow lane ran beside woods at the eastern edge of the Wilton estate. Passing the hamlet of Quidhampton, where Edith sometimes attended early communion, the ancient water meadows revealed themselves on the right side of the road, as if in a painting by Constable, with their distant views of the spire of Salisbury Cathedral. On the left ran a high brick wall, appearing at once to hold back the tall trees – the oaks, larch and pale, shimmering poplars – and to deter the curious from entering. A little way along, at a break in the wall, two high wooden gates opened to reveal, through a canopy of overhanging yews and willow, a drive, and beyond that in a clearing lay Edith's Gothic-looking, grey stone cottage, barely visible through a veil of honeysuckle, wisteria and roses.

The elegant Italianate house was, according to David Cecil, 'both sensible and fanciful. It might be a keeper's cottage if it were a little less elegant; and if it were not quite so sober and workaday, it could easily be one of those small pavilions of pleasure which were dotted about the park during the eighteenth century.'[6] Exaggerated gables jutted out from beneath the steeply pitched, slate-tiled roofs. Some windows had pointed arches; others were ordinary, rectangular farmhouse windows. A small turret with a weather vane on top nestled between two wings of the house. And a colonnade transplanted from a dismantled pavilion in the park led to the plain cottage door. Peaceful and secretive in the woods, veiled in 'green silence . . . within a "Charm of birds"', it seemed a fairy-tale house, 'de la Marish', and Rex must have felt so at once.[7]

Visitors to the Daye House always noticed the stillness, the silence broken only by birdsong or by the screech of bats on summer nights. It seemed as if there was an ancient magic in the woods. And perhaps there was. It was at Wilton, in 1578, that Sir Philip Sidney had written the *Arcadia*, a pastoral romance composed as an amusing diversion to entertain his sister Mary, the Countess of Pembroke. According to local legend, Sidney took inspiration from the park's shady woods and abundant harvests for his vision of a classical rural retreat from urban life, an earthly paradise where peace, innocence and true understanding could be nurtured. The seventeenth-century writer John Aubrey believed it to be true: 'these romancy plaines and boscages', he wrote, 'did no doubt conduce to the hightening of Sir Philip Sydney's phansie. He lived much in these parts, and his most masterly touches of his *Arcadia* he wrote here upon the spott, where they were conceived.'[8]

For centuries the Pembroke family had espoused Arcadian ideals with gusto, and not simply on an aesthetic level. For them, Arcadia meant conservative values, continuity, stability, unchallenged hierarchy, inclusion and exclusion, vast swathes of privately owned land: an ancient aristocratic ideal. Edith felt at home within Wilton's immutability.

By the twentieth century, but for the addition of the Daye House and its garden, little had changed of the landscape in Edith's corner of the park. To one side of the house was the rose garden that Mildred had planted but had not lived to see mature; it had become her memorial. To another was the Paved Garden, a little network of quaintly formal paths and beds filled with roses, violas and nasturtiums with a chubby lead cherub at its centre. The Deer Park stretched out beyond the hedge. The house seemed almost like an island, surrounded as it was by so much water: the water meadows opposite and beyond the edge of the garden, the River Nadder which flowed towards the sea. At the river's edge, beside a flight of steps leading down to the water, there was a bench where Edith used to sit to watch the swans gliding past or the kingfishers and egrets scouring for fish along the riverbank. From the little bridge beside the Daye House, beyond the Victorian boathouse with its barley-sugar columns, could be seen a distant glimpse of the eighteenth-century Palladian Bridge that spans the river. It linked the open parkland and pasture fields to the south with graceful, sweeping lawns, beyond which, shaded by ancient cedars of Lebanon, stood Wilton House.

Rex was to sleep in the Porthole Room at the Daye House; it had been Mildred's bedroom, and so named because of the *œil-de-bœuf* window that winked out from under the eaves and gave the room a jaunty, nautical atmosphere. Between this room and Edith's bedroom, which was above the colonnade and the front door, was a small chamber used as a chapel. There were three other bedrooms; downstairs, directly beneath Edith's room, was the Canary Room, with yellow walls and a black ceiling, named after a resident china canary on the mantelpiece. Upstairs, the Trellis Room overlooked the Paved Garden. The largest bedroom, above the kitchen, was shared by the two servants: Violet, the enthusiastic, seventeen-year-old daughter of Edith's recently retired housekeeper, and twenty-year-old Kathleen, newly employed as the cook and chauffeur. The space upstairs was more cramped than it might sound and, with only one bathroom and two lavatories in the house, it sometimes felt as if everybody – Edith, her guests and the servants – lived on top of one another.

Downstairs there was a small study known as the anteroom, really a passageway with a little walnut writing table and scarlet lacquered walls touched with gold. The kitchen was large and looked out onto the river and the vegetable garden. The dining room had pale green walls, magnolia-patterned chintz, a wall-hanging of baroque birdcatchers and haymakers and French windows that opened out onto the garden. The dining chairs had seats worked in tapestry-stitch by Edith with a wreath encircling images of the houses in which she had lived, each lovelier in turn, and each surrounded by high walls, set apart and sheltered from the world outside, where time stood still.

At the heart of Edith's house, and perhaps at the heart of her life, was the Long Room, a grand name for an old wooden army hut that the sisters had attached to the south-west corner of the house and converted into a drawing room and study. They had trained the honeysuckle and roses to ramble over its roof and year by year it was gradually disappearing beneath a verdant veil that encroached upon the windows. Edith's friend, the historian George Young, once compared the room to the British Empire, saying it had begun as a shanty and ended as a palace. Its panelled walls were primrose yellow, lit by shaded sconces, and lined from floor to ceiling with the precious books, silhouettes, paintings and *objets* that the sisters had accumulated through their lives. Edith was a passionate collector of things: not just books, but press cuttings, letters, drawings and photographs. The floor was pale wood with carpets scattered here and there; and cosy chairs, upholstered by Edith, stood beside the fireplace. On the far side of the room, next to the door, was a rosewood Regency sofa covered in blue jaspé fabric, which had been brought from the nursery at the Rectory, where it had doubled as a boat in the children's adventures. It was Edith's habit to lie on a daybed in the Long Room, with her head lower than her legs, nestling beneath a patchwork blanket, as she read aloud or talked with friends, in what Cecil Beaton would describe as her 'sibilant, jerky tones'.[9] It was in this pose that Edith would talk with Rex, he sitting at her feet or perched beside her on a chair. And in summer she would take out sun loungers, rugs, trays of lemonade and heaps of books and entertain her guests in the sheltered stone garden outside the Long Room.

Later that first afternoon Edith walked with her guest in the Deer Park. 'Rex is very happy talking in enthusiastic bursts', Edith wrote in her diary that night.[10] She loved his 'enchanting nonsense'. 'He excels at talking this', she added.[11] She found him endearingly curious: 'all pale before Rex's burning enthusiasm about everything he talks about, his subjects possess him.'[12] With her treasure-trove knowledge of history and literature, Edith was pleased, and eager, to teach him. It seemed natural to resume the role she had adopted in San Remo, and Rex's literary education continued.

Edith read on average three books a week and her taste was unsurprisingly eclectic. Her library was filled with classics – Shakespeare, of course, George Eliot, the Brontë sisters, Trollope and Thackeray, and plenty of poetry: Hardy, Herrick, Browning, Hopkins, Emily Dickinson and George Herbert, who had lived nearby at Bemerton. There was war poetry and Georgian poetry, including Ralph Hodgson and Walter de la Mare, a favourite for

Edith as he was for Rex. There were French novels, which she could read fluently thanks to her mother, and books on history, geology, art, needlecraft, gardening and cookery, including a trusty Mrs Beeton. Christian texts stood side by side with books on dreams, spiritualism and the occult, and others on contemporary psychical research, as well as an early edition of Miss Moberly and Miss Jourdain's *An Adventure*. Many of the books in her library had been inscribed to her by the authors, including a number by Pamela Grey and Henry Newbolt. Edith always kept up to date so there were contemporary works too – by Virginia Woolf, E. M. Forster, Aldous Huxley, Lytton Strachey, Robert Graves and Nancy Cunard, T. S. Eliot's poetry and a copy of Brian Howard's *The Eton Candle*. She particularly admired Edith Sitwell, whose poems she had read aloud to Rex and Stephen in Italy.

'Rex is too enchanting, such exhuberant burst of bizarre spirits and incongruous fun. He is very amusing indeed, also very serious', she wrote in her diary while he was staying with her.[13] In the eyes of Edith's family and friends this burgeoning friendship was an amusing aberration, perhaps even a little suspicious. She had always behaved so appropriately and dressed so demurely, and now she was back from Italy, suddenly soignée with boyishly cropped hair, shorter skirts and lipstick. Later, in June, family eyebrows were raised even higher when she invited Rex to dine and dance with her at the newly opened Gargoyle Club high above Soho on the corner of Dean and Meard Streets. The club belonged to David Tennant, Stephen's elder brother, and it would soon become the most fashionable and decadent haunt for London's haute bohemia, with glittering mirrored tiles and Matisse paintings on its walls, and Augustus John, Clive Bell, Noël Coward and Dylan Thomas, as well as Guinnesses, Sitwells and Rothschilds, at its tables. It is doubtful that Edith had been to a nightclub before, let alone invited a young man to join her. One of her nieces thought that she must be going mad and there is something of Nancy Mitford's mighty Lady Montdore about her makeover. But Edith didn't care; she was enjoying herself.

In the afternoon of Rex's first visit Edith took him to tea with Sir Henry and Lady Newbolt at their beautiful seventeenth-century manor house at Netherhampton, about a mile across the meadows from the Daye House. 'Rex was mad with delight over their house, which he thinks the loveliest he has ever seen', she wrote.[14] The following day she took him to meet her friend Lady Radnor at nearby Longford Castle. While they were there other guests, friends of Lady Radnor, arrived: 'Rex could not believe in such Philistines and it was most amusing to see his colour come and go as he tried not to contradict them', she wrote in her diary that night; 'they said all the stock things against Epstein's Memorial Panel to Hudson as if they <u>must</u> be caricaturing the bourgeois critics.'[15] *Rima*, Jacob Epstein's sculpture of a naked woman, had provoked a public outcry and the press had branded it 'The Hyde Park Atrocity'. But Edith was determined to impress her receptivity to contemporary ideas and culture upon her new young friend. She was keen to set herself apart from her own generation, in appearance, thought and action. Delighting in the shared conviction of their aesthetic superiority she wrote: 'Rex and I are prepared not to like it but felt we would defend it with our life's blood then! . . . As they drove away', Edith added, 'he fell on my neck letting off steam of his pent-up rage.'[16] They had become allies.

3: 'At the Shrine of Beauty'

❖

. . . the lovliness of Wilton was so soaked into me during my
stay with you, that I can quite clearly see in my mind all the
intoxicatingly beautiful spots that you showed me.

Rex to Edith, 4 June 1925

On the Sunday of Rex's first visit, Edith had returned from matins
to find him drawing the Palladian Bridge from memory. In the
1730s, the 9th Earl of Pembroke had swept away all trace of
Wilton's French-style, formal gardens. In place of a vast parterre
with its grotto, statues and elaborate fountains that threw rain-
bows into the air, the Earl created an idealized vision of nature, an
eighteenth-century Arcadia of meadows dotted with trees and
softly swelling downland.

Later, to add to the picturesque scene, a triumphant arch was
added at the summit of a distant wooded hill. A little to the
west of it, beneath the brow of the hill, a Doric temple stood in
pale relief against the bank of trees behind it, exactly as it was
intended, as if in a painting by Claude. Running through the landscape was a stream that had provided the medieval nuns of the
original Benedictine convent with their fish on Fridays. The Earl
had the stream widened into a broad stretch of river with stone
steps at intervals leading down to the water. He spanned it with
a colonnaded bridge of his own design, inspired by Palladio's
rejected scheme for the Rialto Bridge in Venice. Completed in
1737, it was a tour de force of Palladian architecture and the
centrepiece of the Earl's new garden. Edith later described it in

an article as 'the most famous English bridge' of the eighteenth century.[1] It would be copied at Stowe, Prior Park and elsewhere. Catherine the Great commissioned one for Tsarskoye Selo. For Rex it was to become the touchstone of all the qualities he tried to capture in his work.

The park, rich in treasures and natural delights, overwhelmed Rex on his walks with Edith. Two days into his first visit, Edith wrote that he was 'still busy drawing every garden house in the Park'.[2] He was enchanted. All about him lay centuries of ease and taste and wealth. Deep woods coursed with tributaries and streams from the two rivers that enclosed them. A medieval soufflé pond, which had once contained carp, now stood silent, ancient, under a low canopy of trees. Here and there statues from antiquity or long-outmoded architectural features, relegated to the depths of the park as fashions changed, lay half-hidden, waiting to be discovered. At the edge of the estate, a short walk from Edith's garden, stood a monumental baroque bridge, topped with bacchanalian statues, blackened with weathering and encrusted with lichen. Beneath the bridge a natural swimming pool had been created out of a dammed stretch of river and here, soon, Rex would be swimming with the Earl's children.

Writing to Edith to thank her after his return to London, Rex said: 'the lovliness of Wilton was so soaked into me during my stay with you, that I can quite clearly see in my mind all the intoxicatingly beautiful spots that you showed me'.[3] At the bottom of the page he drew a cartoon of a column with two figures prostrated at its foot, labelled 'you & me, worshiping at the shrine of beauty!'

In late September he returned to stay with Edith for a weekend. They walked along the path through the woods, then beside the river and over the Palladian Bridge to visit Wilton House for the first time. It had been one of the great estates of Renaissance England and the Pembrokes one of its most powerful families. Each century left its mark on Wilton; it is in part Tudor, Georgian and neo-Gothic, and some of the monastic fabric can still be glimpsed. Hans Holbein was possibly involved in the redevelopment of the original medieval abbey in the sixteenth century. The house was later substantially remodelled from 1647 by John Webb and Inigo Jones, the latter redesigning the south front and the staterooms in the Palladian style. He created the Double Cube Room, a heavily carved, richly painted and gilded cornucopia symbolizing fertility and wealth, in which hangs Van Dyck's enormous regal portrait of the Earl of Pembroke and his family. It was regarded by Edith as 'perhaps the most beautiful room in England'.[4] At the beginning of the nineteenth century, the later much-derided James Wyatt radically remodelled the house in the Gothic style.

In the late 1500s the house had been a centre of the arts and at its heart was Mary, Countess of Pembroke, the sister of Sir Philip Sidney and wife of the 2nd Earl. A poet and translator, Mary gathered around her a circle of painters, musicians, actors and writers including Edmund Spenser, Michael Drayton, John Donne and Ben Jonson. John Aubrey described her as 'the greatest patroness of witt and learning'.[5] The estate became a celebrated retreat from the travails and intrigues of life at court.

As centuries passed, Wilton became one of the greatest houses in England, its rooms a treasure trove with paintings by Tintoretto, Raphael, Caravaggio, Claude, Lely, Rembrandt, Brueghel, Reynolds and Rubens adorning the walls, and Roman, Greek and seventeenth-century sculptures lining the Gothic cloisters. For Rex, the house was a revelation.

In her diary Edith describes him 'sitting for hours studying the Wilton catalogue after seeing the pictures this morning, going over the paintwork of each picture'.[6] She was thrilled by his reaction: 'Walked in the Italian Gardens, to the Orangery, to Holbein Porch, and on the lawns with Rex – a divine companion – every bit of beauty delights him. His eye misses nothing.'[7] And she delighted in the frivolity of his imagination: 'He can't think why Lady P. doesn't add one more Temple d'Amour to the present beauties and was very extravagant and amusing planning one on the island at the Confluence. It is to be dwelt in by "12 of the most beautiful and blind virgins in Christendom" who will sing wondrous hymns and never be seen.'[8] With him she was appreciating things anew: 'Rex is a divine person to be with', she later wrote, 'as he sees further than I do and shows it to me.'[9] Thanking her for the stay in a letter, as he would always do, Rex addressed Edith on the envelope as 'Miss Edith Olivier (Queen and Saint) Dwelling in the Daye House'. 'Nine thousand thanks for the most delicious week with you', he wrote; 'I am quite unable to put into words how much I enjoyed it. Perhaps I can explain better by means of a small drawing', beneath which, at the bottom of the page, he had drawn a row of cartoon faces growing progressively happier; the last one beaming with a toothy grin.[10]

Rex never lost his fascination with fairy tales but it was beginning to wane, and soon contemporary realities would have no place in his imagination either. Now it was all historical fantasy, inspired particularly by Wilton, Rome and the pleasure gardens at Stowe, where his brother had gone to school in 1923. Rex was captivated by the romance of seventeenth- and eighteenth-century art and architecture; the whimsicality of rococo and the extravagance of baroque were perhaps the natural successors to his youthful obsession with Rackham and Dulac. Now he pored over paintings by Claude, Poussin, Canaletto and Boucher. It was 'a tremendous discovery', his brother recalled.[11] When he had visited Rome, briefly, in April after San Remo, Rex had had his first true taste of the baroque and found himself 'speechless with wonder at the amazing beauty and romance' all around him.[12]

First Stephen, and now Edith, had lit the touchpaper of his imagination by introducing him to their world of beauty, of indulgence and aesthetic sensitivity. Wilton was, as it had always been, an Arcadian fantasy on a grand scale, a retreat from the realities of life, and a crucible for invention and fantasy. And so it was becoming for Rex.

4: *The Darling*

❖

There could not be two more opposite people than Brian and Rex.

Edith Olivier's Diary, 7 November 1926

In May 1925 Rex returned to the Slade for the start of his final year, which he had delayed by two terms in order to travel with Stephen. At the time Professor Tonks had happily given his blessing to the trip. 'By all means take the opportunity', he had written to Rex. 'You are doing the grand tour not, alas, as it used to be done, behind the measured tread of horses, but at least in comfort. Make notes and really try and see the best things . . . It is certainly a great opportunity for you'.[1] He might not have been as generous to the other students. Naturally it had helped that Tonks was a friend of Stephen's mother but more importantly, Rex had become 'the apple of his eye'.[2]

Tall and angular, with the gaunt, ascetic aspect of a portrait by Van Eyck, Henry Tonks had a reputation as an exacting, sometimes terrifying, but inherently kind, teacher. 'He looked like an anchorite which indeed is what he was', his pupil Lady Cynthia Asquith later wrote; 'an anchorite of Art, who regarded painting as a solemn holy craft; himself as its humble dedicant.'[3] He was vehemently opposed to the modernist sensibilities championed by the artist and critic Roger Fry, a former Slade tutor. Tonks put the greatest emphasis on traditional teaching methods, drawing from life and studying classical art. Draughtsmanship was paramount. He took a rigorously puritanical approach to teaching, encouraging precision and careful observation above all, undoubtedly because he had trained as a surgeon and had taught anatomy. 'Human beings', he told Rex's fellow Slade student Nan West, 'though lovely, must still have backbones secreted under their clothes however voluminous; the artist enjoys all the frippery of life, but must hang upon the foundation of being.'[4]

Abstraction was alien to Rex. And though he might admit to Edith that he admired Impressionism, he felt that it was beyond him: 'Rex talked keenly of his aims and ideals in art and the different ways of putting on paints', she recorded in her diary. 'Says he can't paint the Impressionist way – like Velazquez or Whistler tho' he thinks it the greatest, but must always build up from form'.[5] He was entirely immune to the influence of Fry, Post-Impressionism or the avant-garde and was merely amused by Roland Penrose's Surrealist exhibition some years later. In 1927, with Edith, he went to look at Stanley Spencer's *Resurrection*, which was presented to the Tate that year. Edith thought it 'full of awkward beauty' but Rex, she recorded, thought it only 'badly composed'.[6] Rex's own style was polished and controlled, his perspective was accurate, and his palette restrained and elegant. His work remained purely, and unabashedly, figurative even though the themes were usually fantastical.

Rex found it almost impossible to draw from life and preferred – as he had when a child – to draw from memory and from his imagination. In life-drawing classes he would study the model intently, turn around and then begin to draw, often embellishing his nude with a panama hat or stockings. His sketches of the plaster casts of dismembered, antique busts have their missing limbs defiantly pencilled in. It is surprising, therefore, that he had very quickly become Tonks's favourite. But Tonks considered Rex to be a natural draughtsman, one of only a handful he had come across, along with his former pupil Augustus John. 'Never had I known Tonks so lyrical in anyone else's praise', their mutual friend Cynthia Asquith would later recall.[7] 'Whistler has extraordinary gifts', Tonks wrote in a letter to his friend Augustus Daniel, later director of the National Gallery:

> All except the power of observing anything in particular, and
> even this at times he has, when he <u>paints</u> from the model,
> but with a pencil in his hand he is incurably unobservant. He
> does things with ease I could not begin to do, he has all the
> qualifications of a great master, <u>except</u> what the bad god-
> mother arranged he should not have, the power of looking.[8]

Luckily Tonks chose to overlook Rex's unorthodox technique,
encouraging him to work to his strengths, to study the model and
then to draw it from memory, as Hogarth had done. Rex had been
awarded a scholarship at the end of his first year which was
renewed, along with other prizes in each subsequent year. Intui-
tively too, Tonks had decided to nudge him in the direction of
decoration and to develop his own decorative style. Before the
King and Queen's visit for tea at the Slade to mark its centenary,
Tonks had given him the task of improving the school's main staircase. The royal couple were to discover, beyond the palms,
hydrangeas and red curtains with gold tassels and fringes that Rex
had rigged up at the entrance, that the stairs appeared to be made
of solid gold. It was a characteristic solution to the task – both
fantastical and practical – and it had reportedly amused the King
and Queen greatly. For Rex it was a sign of things to come.

But Tonks had not entirely given Rex up to frivolity – far from
it. For some time he had been keen to encourage a renaissance in
mural decoration; he was interested in its social function and also
as a way for his students to make money without selling their
souls. In 1924, his friend the philanthropist Sir Joseph Duveen
had provided funds for two Slade students to paint a mural at a
club for East End boys in Shadwell. Tonks chose Rex and Mary
Adshead.* 'Whistler', Tonks wrote in a letter to a friend, 'would
set them dancing'.[9] And this Rex tried to do. In his mural, villagers
drink and make merry in the shade of an old, half-timbered inn,
as they are entertained by gambolling Gypsies dancing to the

---

* Mary Adshead, 1904–95, had a long and prolific career as a painter, mural-
ist, illustrator and designer.

music of a flute and a fiddle. Behind them two Gypsy caravans are moored at the edge of a village green, with a glassy duck pond reflecting the tall trees that surround it. A road dotted with elegant stone cottages winds off into open fields. It was a strange choice for the wall of a docklands boys' club, a well-meaning but perhaps misjudged philanthropic gesture. It offered a glimpse of a bucolic world that the boys would, in all likelihood, never get to see, a fantasy pastoral, an escape from the grimy reality of the riverside slums. It was this project, his first commission, on which Rex had worked during the summer of 1924, and perhaps Tonks thought that he had earned his trip abroad with Stephen. When Rex arrived at the Slade in the following summer for the start of his final year, it was 'as leading student . . . – "swept up into demigod circles" . . . and no doubt basking a little', wrote his brother.[10]

In January 1926 Rex spent a weekend with Edith at the Daye House. On the Sunday they sat in the Long Room, Rex working on drawings for *Mildred* while Edith read aloud 'two of Zélide's *Tales*, two stories out of de la Mare's *Broomsticks* and a bit of Henry James' *The Liar*'.[11] Rex was thinking of entering for the Prix de Rome, a scholarship that would give him three years' paid study in Italy. Though she would miss him, Edith thought it was a good idea – 'I feel rather in favour of three years paid for while he can really go on <u>studying</u> without having to make potboilers to support himself' – but Tonks opposed it, arguing that 'no Prix de Rome people have done anything <u>afterwards</u>'.[12]

In fact Tonks had other plans for Rex. Early in 1926 Sir Joseph Duveen pledged £500 to pay for a mural to decorate the walls of the refreshment room in the gloomy basement of the Tate Gallery on Millbank. A committee was formed that included Tonks and Charles Aitken, the director of the Tate. Evidently Tonks made a good case for his pupil, and Duveen must have remembered his Shadwell mural of the previous year, as Rex was eventually offered the commission. It was a great opportunity for any artist, but for a student who was not yet twenty-one it was an extraordinary honour. In a letter of December 1926 Aitken told Duveen that he thought Rex had 'unusual invention and capacity for so young an artist'.[13] And Tonks explained Rex thus to a friend: 'Such gaiety and ideas, so continuous, it is really a dream . . . I have never had anyone like him. He amuses me because he has a certain gift of humour, I can not describe it, very subtle, that touches some recesses in my mind, all hidden under a most respectful (and really respectful) manner', adding prophetically, 'if only we can save him from the Pit, because directly he is launched he will be an amazing success'.[14]

At the end of his final term at art school Rex was sad to leave: 'some of the happiest days I have ever spent have been at the darling Slade'.[15] He remained friends with Tonks, who retired from the Slade in 1930, often visiting him for tea at his house in the Vale in Chelsea, ever thankful for his teaching and for those first commissions. And until his death in 1937 Tonks keenly followed his protégé's career.

In March, Edith had visited Rex at the Slade where he showed her his first sketches for the Tate. 'It's a room 60 feet long', she wrote in her diary; 'he means to have a coach and four going on a journey all round the room, passing all over the world and collecting the things eaten in the Tea Room. It looks v. good. He is to have pupils under him to work at the unimportant parts – feels afraid they will be offended at having to carry out his designs entirely.'[16] Tonks had chosen Nan West to assist at the Tate. She soon came to realize that Rex turned up to work when he felt like it, sweetly apologetic and full of fanciful excuses. But despite his irregular hours Rex worked hard at the Tate, as he had to, often through the night, and he rarely managed a weekend away. In May on the first day of the General Strike that threatened to bring the country to a standstill, Rex stayed at home in Buckinghamshire. But on the following day he returned to the gallery and to his mural, oblivious to the commotion outside. He had a job, for which he was receiving £5 a week, and felt no compulsion to get involved.

At the Daye House Edith was busily thinking up money-making schemes of her own. Mildred's medical bills had used up all their savings and Edith had very little money left. She paid only a nominal rent to Lord Pembroke, but she had a car to run, servants to pay and regular guests to entertain. One resource that she could always call upon was her intellect. She had great confidence in her opinions and could conjure up an extempore talk on almost any subject that was thrown at her. She had begun to lecture for the Girls' Diocesan Association on topics such as 'Gambling' and 'Manners' and she also gave talks on literature, speaking persuasively, and with verve, on sweeping subjects like 'The Tide of Time' and 'Arthurian Legends' at girls' schools in Staffordshire, Buckinghamshire and Cornwall.

In the spring of 1926 she took two private pupils, foreign girls, who were to be taught English literature and history. Writing to Edith on 'Midsummer Night, 10pm', after a rare weekend at the Daye House, Rex, who was horrified by the invasion of their privacy, confessed:

> Edith my darling, I always thought you were rich . . . I had imagined that you only kept one car as you couldn't drive two at once, and that the reason that you don't keep a yacht at Southampton was that you were a bad sailor – etc. etc. . . . you say that you will pay for your new motor with the money you will get from these monstrosities [her pupils], – but my dear, will you ever be able to sell them? I can't think who on earth would buy them from you. Possibly petrified and white-washed they might be useful to a landscape gardener for use as statues, but not in my garden please!
>
> In love and pain, Rex.[17]

At the end of August Edith returned from a month in Ireland staying with an old friend. The day after she got back Brian Howard, son of her friends Lura and Tudie, arrived at the Daye House for the weekend. Also staying was Elinor Wylie, the feted forty-one-year-old American poet and novelist, whom Edith had recently met at Wilsford. Edith admired Elinor, but with reservation: 'exquisite . . . obviously expecting to be lionized. <u>Much intelligence and character</u>'.[18] Their friendship would later improve on closer acquaintance.

Brian also had poetic ambitions, and he too expected to be lionized. Edith had a difficult time indulging both egos, but kept them busy with sightseeing and poetry-reading sessions. Edith had known Brian all his life. As a child he had often stayed with Edith and Mildred, bullying the other children and provoking displeasure in everyone about him. He had been at Eton and went on to Christ Church, Oxford, which he had left under a cloud and without a degree earlier in the year. At twenty-one, he was determined to become a celebrated poet. 'Brian read his poems . . . he was touchingly anxious for approval and criticism', Edith wrote, on the second day of his stay.[19] With Brian she was patient and encouraging, a surprisingly open-minded sounding board for his often outlandish ideas.

At Eton, Brian had been 'the most fashionable boy in the school', and at Oxford, he, along with his friend and rival Harold Acton, had been at the heart of the 'aesthetes', the set that had so enchanted Evelyn Waugh.[20] He was flamboyant, openly homosexual and a great disappointment to his father, Tudie, who had wanted a hearty sportsman for a son, and to his mother, Lura, who sent him to a psychiatrist in an attempt to redirect his sexuality.

Brian Howard was considered by some to be a nouveau-riche charlatan, but this only added to his glamour. He embraced and embodied Modernism. His daring *vers libre* poetry had impressed Edith Sitwell; he adored the Ballets Russes, read Proust and Rimbaud, knew Cocteau and Diaghilev. He also had a reputation for seducing fellow undergraduates. Waugh based Anthony Blanche in *Brideshead* on both Brian and Harold Acton. Brian, like his fictional counterpart, was an 'aesthete par excellence, a byword of iniquity'.[21]

Brian was an unhappy, truculent young man, admired and

loathed in equal measure. His aggressive instinct and easy malice did little to help. In her diary, Edith was critical: 'A charming manner and disgraceful manners. Inconsiderate, unpunctual, insisting on people always doing what he wants.'[22] But she saw something beyond this: 'He is a born flâneur . . . He must be able to carry on and to carry out what he means to do.'[23] She admired his boldness and his ambition and was characteristically keen to defend Brian against what she considered to be narrow-minded and intolerant censure: 'Lady Pembroke is understanding of him tho' she knows and shares – in a degree – the prejudice'.[24] The day before this was written, Edith and Brian had discussed his un-popularity. 'He pathetically begs to know why', she wrote, adding: 'I can't tell him but I know. He is exotic, foppish, un-English, really too original for ordinary English Society. They think him immoral which he isn't!'[25] She might have been less supportive if she had known the full extent of his exploits.

One day during his stay, he composed a word portrait of Edith, a short vignette in prose, written in the avant-garde style of Gertrude Stein, the influential and experimental American writer and doyenne of modern art and literature, who lived in Paris for most of her life.

> In the brake, in the brier, in the chalk there was life in lines. A small black, a pointed back, a broomstick, a storm. Also quick carving, a quickness, a strict quickness and highly principled in abandon. A diffident dark flash but kind.[26]

Edith did not record her thoughts on this description although she kept the paper on which Brian had scrawled it in pencil. It is surprisingly perceptive; Edith's vitality pulses through its lines, intellectually agile but controlled, liberal and yet decorous. And though the witch comparison is not flattering to an ageing spinster with black hair and a large nose, Brian saw Edith in a way that she would later portray herself: as a woman inseparably bound to the Wiltshire landscape, receptive to its magical and elemental energy.

'There could not be two more opposite people than Brian and Rex', she wrote in her diary in November.[27] Brian had returned to stay until Christmas and Rex's arrival at the Daye House was a welcome relief. 'Brian being at his worst trying to make grand "art" conversation with Rex', she wrote, 'insincere and flashy and paradoxical. Rex honest and honestly bored.'[28] Edith of course sided with Rex, who in marked contrast to Brian's louche sophistication was boyish, clean-cut and gentle.

Brian's word portrait of Rex, composed at the Daye House, reveals something of the duality of his nature and also of his work: a charming, polished facade concealing something hardier, more visceral and melancholic. Perhaps it also hints at his change in fortune:

> Goats are slow but sure. Surely they are sure footed. A goat has a bland hand, a suave hand. Direction is rough, but this direction has smoothed its roughness. Laughter in the barroom, in the ballroom, in the bathroom, but the laughter is an urn. Goodness and gracious goodness, not an oath. Twisted power, strong as string so that it can be made powder. But power but goat.[29]

In historical terms, the difference between Brian and Rex is symbolic. In his study of decadence after the First World War, Martin Green makes the distinction between international aestheticism, represented by the bold modernism of Brian Howard, and English aestheticism, a more romantic, insular and nostalgic form, which Evelyn Waugh, John Betjeman and Rex would come to represent. It is a difference reflected in *Brideshead Revisited*. When Anthony Blanche dines with Charles Ryder, he warns him to avoid Sebastian and not to let his work be influenced by the charm of the Flytes. In England, the gentle nostalgic style would be found more palatable, especially amongst the upper classes. Unlike Rex's artistic career, Brian's success as a poet, in spite of his early promise, would never amount to much.

While Rex was grateful for Edith's guidance, intellectually and socially, Brian was less receptive; he already moved confidently in society. He welcomed Edith's criticism of his work, but he did not need it. Perhaps Edith was aware that Brian moved all too easily out of her own, somewhat provincial, social orbit. Rex, on the other hand, did not. It is interesting, though, that the inherently snobbish Edith, whose own social status appeared to have been raised by the grand company she kept, should accept Rex, a builder's son, so readily into her world. Like many people of her class, Edith distinguished between those who were firmly established in society and those who had 'arrived' in it. Even though Edith was not of the aristocracy, her high standing in local circles, her friendships with aristocrats, and her close connection with Wilton House, ensured that she was at least considered a subsidiary member; certainly she considered herself one. But this perhaps made her more sensitive to class difference. She relished her position in Wilton church in the second pew behind the Earl's family, and invariably gave visitors to the Daye House a tour of the estate. Her pride was almost proprietorial as she administered her 'Test for Guests', as she called it, which usually required them to declare spontaneous admiration as they came upon lovely views of the house and park.[30]

As for Rex, Edith saw herself, in part, as patron to a talented young artist. In that first year of their friendship, she set about gradually educating her young protégé in the esoteric ways of her world and introduced him to many of her rich, aristocratic and influential friends. There is a glamour about artistic talent; it has always been a passport into society and for Rex it was no exception. He was not a private artist who could only work in ivory-tower solitude and this worked in his favour. He enjoyed drawing, often spontaneously and seemingly without effort, for the entertainment of others. Edith often sat beside him as he drew, 'marvelling at his quick sureness'.[31] Many of his friends would remember Rex impulsively sketching ideas on hotel notepaper, on napkins or the backs of menus in restaurants or on whatever surface was at hand, clutching a pencil with his curious fist-like grip, as he whistled to himself or clicked his tongue, his toe tapping, wholly immersed in the drawing and perhaps at his most peaceful. He drew quickly, with a steady hand, conjuring up a world before the eyes of his audience, eager to entertain and delight.

At the Daye House, Rex had drawn a bookplate for himself, whilst Edith looked on. In her diary she described the pleasure of watching him at work: 'His speed is miraculous, such exquisite fine work, such free design, such spirit and enjouement'.[32] She had asked him to illustrate *Mildred* and he also began a tradition of drawing a frontispiece in every volume of the Daye House visitors' book, the first of which she found 'full of enchanting detail'.[33] In 1926, while working at the Tate, he was living at home in Farnham Common in Buckinghamshire, where the family had moved in 1924. He had, as Edith described it, an 'exhausting daily journey', a three-hour commute by train into central London every morning and returning in the evening.[34] There was no possibility of paying for a studio in London on his salary and Rex told Edith that he was in need of a benefactor, 'some artistic and philanthropic "Sir John or Sir James"' who would advance his rent for two years, at which point he would be able to repay the debt. 'He will certainly make money if he lives', Edith wrote; 'I only fear he will kill himself from over strain. He is a most lovely character and everything he says shews more and more the beauty of his nature'.[35]

Edith took Rex's hint, telling Mary Morrison, her old friend and wife of the immensely rich Conservative MP for Salisbury, about Rex's situation over lunch. 'She most wonderfully says she will give him £100* for his studio anonymously thro' me – I am to have the joy of helping him to this – It is too thrilling', Edith wrote in her diary that night.[36] Rex was overjoyed, promising to repay Lady Mary's generosity with pictures and writing immediately to thank Edith for her help:

---

* Over £5,000 in today's money.

Edith you <u>darling</u>!! For if this huge gift is not actually from you it was through your dear kind interest and trouble that it was procured . . . PS. I shall let you know, of course about the success of my studio searches. I'm <u>dying</u> with excitement. I shall keep it quite a secret with you until I'm established properly in it – then what fun!'[37]

On the face of it Edith's gesture sprang from a benevolent and disinterested philanthropy. But perhaps she was secretly hoping that it would help to extricate Rex from his home and his family. From the beginning of their friendship she had written fondly about Rex in her diary but by the end of 1925 her tone had become far more passionate. 'Rex makes my heart stand still', she had written in November, 'by telling me he saw an oculist yesterday who says his eyes are very bad . . . I see Rex is terrified – says he'd rather die or lose both his legs. Oh – the darling.'[38] Rex's eye inflammation was short-lived, but Edith's distress reveals the extent of the feelings she was developing for him. By the end of 1926, when Rex was still at work on his mural at the Tate, Edith wrote: 'I don't think him at all well. He looks strangely curiously ill at times. He will be such a very great man if he lives and I pray he may for the good of this poor earth.'[39] She had begun to worry that she might lose Rex, as she had lost Mildred, whose place he was taking in her affections.

5: A 'Dream Change'

❖

> . . . it just did express what Clarissa truly was to her – the
> creation of the love of all her being.
>
> Edith Olivier, *The Love-Child*

One sleepless night in the summer of 1926 Edith suddenly came up with the idea for a novel. *Mildred*, the book of essays in memory of her sister, had just been printed, with delicate illustrations by Rex and a drawing by Stephen on the cover. Edith had written the introduction and found that she had enjoyed the experience. Perhaps more importantly, her friends had enjoyed reading it and Henry Newbolt told her that she should have written the whole thing.

The Oliviers all tended to sleep fitfully, but unlike the rest of her family, Edith relished her sleeplessness. Alone and undistracted, she was able to put her rational, daytime self to bed, allowing her imagination to wake up. From childhood Edith's bedroom had been the crucible of her creative life, and it was a theme to which she would often return, writing in *Night Thoughts of a Country Landlady* in 1943:

> In bed at night most people suffer a 'dream change' of some sort
> . . . At nightfall, the most civilized and conventional people
> revert to the animal . . . Love and lust are both more potent at
> night, as the Hebrew poet knew when he wrote, 'I sleep but my
> heart waketh'. And the spirit too wakes into a new quickness, as
> the body grows drowsy.[1]

That night in her bedroom at the Daye House, 'a spiritualized animal took possession' of Edith and she began to write.[2] 'Till that night', she would later recall, 'I had never thought seriously of becoming a writer, and now I did not know whether what I was doing would ever be any good.'[3]

The Love-Child tells the story of Agatha Bodenham, a staid and neurotic thirty-two-year-old spinster, a woman without 'the power of getting into touch with her fellow-creatures' who finds herself alone for the first time in her life when her mother dies.[4] She had never been close to her mother, and yet, she is horrified by the sudden loneliness: 'Strange that she should feel so, for she had always been solitary – a solitary child, a solitary girl, and now, at thirty-two, a still more solitary woman.'[5] She remembers that when she was a child she had an imaginary playmate, an ethereal child called Clarissa, 'the one blossom of Agatha's imagination', whom she would conjure up in bed until 'the caustic drops' of her governess's 'common sense' destroyed the creature.[6] She was thus 'forgotten for many years, and now coming back to mind as a memory, not of a possession, but of a loss'.[7] She describes Clarissa as 'the only being who had ever awoken her own personality, and made it responsive'.[8]

And then one night Clarissa reappears. She stays with Agatha, who alone can see the child. But although initially she is ethereal and 'shadowy', Clarissa eventually becomes visible to everyone.[9] One day a policeman visits, requesting that Agatha fill in papers to register Clarissa. Her mysterious presence Agatha has explained by letting it be known that she is a distant relative whom she intends to adopt. Panicking at the intrusion of an outsider, Agatha refuses to fill in the form, and forced to explain her hesitation, she suddenly tells him: '"She is a love-child. She is my own"'.[10] Agatha does not care that she has lost 'her position, her name, her character' with this utterance, 'it just did express what Clarissa truly was to her – the creation of the love of all her being'.[11] Agatha's life is no longer empty; it revolves entirely and obsessively around the child: '"You can't really get away from me," [Agatha] said. "I've got you on a string"'.[12] And their days are filled with joyful games in which they play-act scenarios from real life:

> Agatha had enjoyed the acting games, in which she and Clarissa passed practically the whole of their lives, because, through all the stirring adventures that they imagined together, there ran the serene certainty that they were all the while in a world where the events were entirely under control . . . Clarissa, on the other hand, had found in them her nearest point of contact with the real world of adventure.[13]

Clarissa grows up and makes friends with Kitty and David, two fashionable young people who live nearby. She is fascinated by their excitingly modern lives, and wants to do everything they do. Now an adult, she is no longer contented with play-acting at life as Agatha wants to. Everything that Agatha despises and fears – driving, socializing, dancing – Clarissa is desperate to try. And Agatha allows her to, begrudgingly, but only if she accompanies Clarissa. Agatha is foolish and pathetically old-fashioned in these scenes. She begins to sense that Clarissa, her child, her own creation and her one companion, is slipping away from her, seduced by the glamour of modern life.

It gradually dawns on the girl that the adventures of the real world are far more interesting than those of 'the artificial world' that Agatha invents for them: '"if we really did the things we play at, they would be even more fun."'[14] '"I never thought it possible before, but now I see what a lot we have missed."'[15] Agatha starts to impose limits on Clarissa's world but to no avail. David falls in love with Clarissa and so begins a battle with Agatha for possession. In the climactic scene of the novel, David confesses his love to Clarissa and they kiss in Agatha's moonlit garden. Agatha watches as, instantly, the girl disappears. Agatha 'had seen her go out, like the flame of a candle . . . She knew that it was possible for a star to escape its orbit, and to break the secret link which held it to its sun.'[16]

Clarissa's survival depended entirely on Agatha and when the exclusivity of their bond is broken by her love for David, she dies. Agatha is distraught and hysterical. David is convinced that she is mad, 'an old maniac'[17] and 'a vampire',[18] who has kidnapped or killed Clarissa. But in a frenzy, she tells him that he has murdered her child and must leave at once. There is a strange calm at the end of the book, as Helen, the parlourmaid, watches Agatha happily talking to herself with 'a mindless face' and playing ball with someone who is not there.[19]

The Love-Child is an intriguing book. It is slight, odd and whimsical but the whimsy is countered by its inherent darkness. Edith's prose is elegant and spare, almost prim. The authorial voice is far more cautious and restrained than that of her diaries. The novel is both a fairy tale and a study in madness; it defies definition. When the book was republished by Virago in 1981, Hermione Lee in her introduction questions whether Edith had chosen Clarissa's name as a tribute to Virginia Woolf's *Mrs Dalloway*, published the year before Edith began writing *The Love-Child*. She suggests that Edith 'might well have had in mind the split in that novel between madness and the social self'.[20] Edith read and admired Virginia Woolf's novels even though she did not much care for their author. But she makes no mention in her diary of reading *Mrs Dalloway* although she would later write that she enjoyed *Orlando*, which was published in 1928. Certainly, her novel met with nothing like the critical success of *Mrs Dalloway*. But though *The Love-Child* is written in the traditional format of the third person and is far less experimental and sophisticated than Woolf's stream-of-consciousness narrative, Edith's book, with its inward focus, its engagement with private fantasy, estrangement from the world, repression, sexuality and motherhood, is stridently modern.

Fantasy novels were popular at the time. Pamela Grey had written several, and perhaps it was her prolific literary output that first inspired Edith to have a go at writing herself. *Lady into Fox* by David Garnett had been published in 1922; Edith had a copy in her library. It is an enigmatic novel about a woman who, as the title suggests, inexplicably turns into a fox.* Her husband's initial reaction is to pretend that nothing has changed. He sends the servants away, dresses his wife in clothes and plays cards with her, but she soon gives in to her feral instincts and he has to release her into the wild. Like Edith's novel, *Lady into Fox* ends on a tragic note as the fox is savaged and killed by the local hunt. Rex introduced Edith to Garnett's writing and perhaps she had in mind the haunting atmosphere of *Lady into Fox* and the strange, intimate and secretive relationship at its heart.

A more obvious influence, and one that was later pointed out in reviews, is *Lolly Willowes* by Sylvia Townsend Warner, which was published in early 1926. After her father's death, twenty-eight-year-old Laura Willowes is sent to live with her brother and his family in London. After years of a dull and dutiful existence she finds herself 'groping after something that eluded her experience'.[21] She decides to escape to the country and moves to a village in the Chilterns. And there she sells her soul to the devil and becomes a witch. '"We have more need of you,"' she tells the devil. '"Women have such vivid imaginations, and lead such dull lives. Their pleasure in life is so soon over; they are so dependent upon others, and their dependence so soon becomes a nuisance."'[22] Warner's novel is a delightfully wicked and satirical answer to the question of what to do with the spinster in Society. Lolly takes matters into her own hands. '"One doesn't become a witch to run round being harmful, or to run round being helpful either, a district visitor on a broomstick. It's to escape all that – to have a life of one's own"'.[23] Lolly, like Agatha, escapes the confines of her prescribed way of life with magic. Or does she? With both characters it is never made clear whether they have supernatural powers or are, after all, delusional. Either way, both Lolly and

---

* The novel won the James Tait Black Memorial Prize in 1922 and the Hawthornden Prize in 1923.

Agatha choose to harness and embrace the madness and the darkness in their hearts.*

At the end of *The Love-Child* Agatha's fantasy appears to shatter as reality reimposes itself. But she is seen playing with an imaginary person, and the reader is left to decide whether Clarissa has returned, whether Agatha has gone mad, or whether she was mad from the very beginning. There are echoes of Freud's 1919 essay on the uncanny in the ambivalent shifting between reality and fantasy, hysteria and the supernatural, intimacy and detachment, repression and release. But any Freudian resonance was almost certainly unintentional since Edith disapproved of psychoanalysis. However, it is quite probable that she would have read Hoffmann's tales, on which Freud's essay focuses, and also the writing of Edgar Allan Poe, who was influenced by Hoffmann, and that she would have absorbed their Gothic, uncanny atmosphere.

The pages of Edith's diary are filled with gossip and caricatures, as well as observations and analysis of the behaviour of those around her. She was intrigued by the caprices of the human brain and fascinated, too, by states of insanity, schizophrenia and split personalities, themes to which she would return almost compulsively in her writing. She had witnessed at first hand, if not insanity, then her father's suppression, by sheer strength of will, of the less rational side of himself, flickers of which she glimpsed from time to time. Edith herself, of course, had inherited this divided self, but she lived happily with the two sides rubbing along together, forging her character and making her the singular woman she was. Perhaps it was awareness of this that led her to explore ideas of duality again and again in her writing.

---

* In a letter to Cecil Beaton in 1927 Edith wrote: 'I am staying my hand as to Sylvia T. W. till we have talked. At the moment I feel antagonistic to her but I may change!' It is tempting to speculate that the source of this antagonism might have been a literary rivalry. Perhaps the English publishing world was too small for two books about spinsters dabbling in the dark arts. (EO to CB, 5 July 1927, BA)

With Agatha, she explored the effects of grief and loneliness and the dangers of excessive introversion and introspection. In her adult solitude Agatha retreats entirely into her imagination. Pygmalion-like, her childhood fantasies take root and grow, forming Clarissa: 'She justified it to her common sense by considering that, as other women found their recreation in Society, or in novel reading, or in gossip, so she, who had never been amused by these things, found hers in the creation of her own imagination.'[24]

One day Agatha and Clarissa read *Sturm's Reflections** and learn of 'the attractive powers of bodies,'[25] a theory they take as the 'scientific truth which lay behind the appearance of Clarissa'.[26] Edith, influenced by Annie Moberly and Eleanor Jourdain's similarly 'scientific' explanation for their vision at Versailles, and by the numerous books about psychic phenomena in her library, rationalizes Clarissa into being. Through Agatha, she draws a direct link between psychic ability, an open mind and the strength of the imagination:

> Here at last was the great scientific truth which lay behind the appearance of Clarissa. It was the body of Agatha Bodenham herself which had attracted those minute particles of matter from which had been compounded Clarissa's exquisite little form, and then, from those particles, by a perfectly normal law of nature, a rational being had come into existence.[27]

Although Clarissa's existence stems from the maternal longing of a childless woman, it is often described in strangely erotic terms. Agatha guiltily indulges her fantasy, 'the Clarissa Game',[28] as if it is an illicit addiction and finds herself 'looking forward toward bedtime as if something wonderful was going to happen'.[29] Her 'love-child', formed not by passion but by loneliness, becomes bitterly ironic. Their relationship is strange, slippery and undefined.

---

* *Sturm's Reflections on the Works of God and His Providence Throughout All Nature*, Christoph Christian Sturm (1740–86).

With Clarissa, Agatha acts out scenarios from life, like a child playing at being an adult. Clarissa, an 'elfin, impish little girl', can be seen to represent Agatha's wilder self, her madwoman in the attic. Clarissa is the free-spirited child that Agatha, and perhaps Edith, was never allowed to be.[30] She stains her pristine white dress with raspberry juice, 'makes a terrible mess of the carefully arranged cottons and silks' in Agatha's workbasket and throws her carefully gathered hair 'combings' out of the window.[31]

Ultimately, though, at the close of the novel, Agatha's imagination is triumphant. It allows her to find a happiness and fulfilment that she had never known before. Edith places the importance of nurturing the imagination at the very heart of the story. She casts Agatha's total immersion into the world of her mind less as a retreat and more as a liberation – a journey into a life that to the outside world is mere madness but which she finds entirely rewarding.

Though Edith was obsessed with history she chose to write a book about the present. It would have been easy enough for her to whip up a historical romance if all she wanted to do was to make money, but she was scathing of the form: 'the "historical novel"', she would later write, 'is, as a rule, but a hybrid artistic form, and is commonly neither historical nor a novel'.[32] *The Love-Child* is a contemporary story about a woman's confrontation with modernity, a novel of ideas for which Edith could not have guaranteed a publisher. Modernity notwithstanding, Agatha Bodenham was almost certainly named after another cloistered spinster, Cecilia Bodenham, the last abbess of Wilton Abbey before the dissolution of the monasteries, and in a number of ways she is the antithesis of Edith. She is reserved, socially stunted, a victim of her situation who struggles to keep up with Clarissa and her young companions. By contrast, Edith was fascinated by the modern world and drawn to it; she delighted in the amusing escapades of her young friends. In Agatha, she created a self-consciously parodic portrait of the woman she could have become as a result of her upbringing: the provincial spinster that she was on paper. In her memoirs, she would later acknowledge drawing on her own life for inspiration. Edith, like Agatha, had known a life dominated by a despotic parent who sought to suppress her creative instincts. Agatha, like Edith, enters into her imagination as solace from reality – and that imagination is powerful enough to entertain ideas of the supernatural. Agatha's intimate, imaginary relationship with Clarissa recalls the make-believe of Edith and Mildred's private world. And as Agatha's alter ego, the wayward Clarissa indulges in everything that Dacres would have forbidden his own children to do. After Mildred's death Edith had lost her closest companion and, like Agatha, faced an 'utter and irremediable loneliness – a loneliness that could not be broken'.[33] Her life was similarly 'emptied of companionship'.[34] Like Edith, Agatha's imaginative impulses take place at night: 'in the night, as she lay in that half-sleeping state when the spirit wakes because the mind is weary, when impossibilities seem possible, and when dreams come true – then, all of a sudden, she found that she was playing with Clarissa, quite simply and naturally.'[35]

And what of Rex? Had he become Edith's love-child? Certainly to the outside world their friendship would have looked odd, perhaps as foolish and illusory as Agatha's relationship with Clarissa. Edith's friendship with Rex sprang from the isolation she felt after her sister's death; from the same feverish desire for companionship that drives Agatha to invent Clarissa. Rex had come to fill the void. He had brought affection, youth and vibrant modernity into Edith's life, and her imagination, which had been lying dormant for so long beneath layers of practicality and duty, had begun to blossom.

In confessing that she has a love-child Agatha shatters her own respectability, breaking out of the conventional mould of a genteel spinster, as Edith was appearing to break out of hers. Like Agatha, Edith was possessive of Rex and anxious about losing him. Clarissa's seduction by modernity could perhaps reflect Edith's fear that Rex, who was becoming increasingly well-known for his work at the Tate, would be drawn out of her sphere into the sophisticated milieu that Brian Howard inhabited.

But were her feelings towards Rex maternal or romantic? Rex's brother Laurence insisted that they were simply friends – 'anything more amorous would have been grotesque'.[36] In her diary, at this time, Edith presents Rex as childlike and clearly she was convinced that there was no impropriety about their friendship. She had introduced Rex to an aristocratic world in which he was essentially an orphan, her surrogate son. She was educating him. But, as in *The Love-Child*, their relationship relied on a certain amount of role play and invention. As long as realities such as their age difference, Rex's family, the lure of the sophisticated, urban world and the inevitable siren call of sex were kept at bay, they could maintain a suspension of disbelief. The dynamic of their relationship could continue to hover, indistinctly, somewhere between mother and son and virgin lovers. Together, rather like Agatha and Clarissa, Rex and Edith could retreat into the private world of their shared imagination. Though to outsiders it seemed a strange relationship, it suited them, and it was transforming them both.

Part Two

❖

TABLEAUX VIVANTS

6: Bright Young People

❖

One can be serious about the frivolous, frivolous about the serious.

Susan Sontag, 'Notes on Camp'

In February 1927 Edith and Rex stayed with Stephen, his mother and Lord Grey at a villa in St-Jean-Cap-Ferrat on the Côte d'Azur. La Primavera was 'a low long rambling house . . . in an enchanting garden hanging over the sea'[1] with an orchard of orange trees, formal parterres and masses of scented flowers in the garden; 'a tangle of colours'.[2]

Also staying at the villa was Stephen's friend Zita Jungman, with her sister Teresa, known as Baby, new stars of the London social scene. The gamine and vivacious daughters of the artist Nico Jungman, their mother's second marriage, to a Guinness, had propelled the sisters into the highest echelons of society.* Another guest was Dolly Wilde, the lesbian niece of the playwright, and a witty conversationalist. Loelia Ponsonby, later the Duchess of Westminster, along with Tanis and Meraud Guinness, visited from their villa at Cannes.

Nights at the villa were mistral-battered and days were 'radiant' and 'deep-coloured' in the winter sun.[3] There was play-acting in the garden, everyone 'painted up to the eyes'; swimming in the sea; singing at the piano; sunbathing on the terrace and lunches

---

* Cecil Beaton described them as 'a pair of decadent eighteenth-century angels made in wax'. (Cecil Beaton, *The Book of Beauty* (London: Duckworth, 1930), p.33)

with a glamorous, continental crowd and English aristocrats in the South of France for the season: 'Princes and Dukes and Princesses with lovely romantic names and exquisite hand-kissing manners. Talk mostly French but very agreeable and easy. I can talk French easily at parties', Edith wrote in her diary.[4]

She was sharing a suite of rooms with Rex; it seems that the strength of their friendship had by then been universally acknowledged and accepted. But still Edith felt the need to justify it in her diary: 'my bath is really in his bedroom but we are so easy with each other that this seems all right. He looks on me most simply as a Mother'.[5] Sitting in her room late one night, Rex amused Edith by recounting the story of his uncomfortable journey, made worse by some undesirable fellow traveller. '"May hell devour her"! He . . . exclaimed', wrote Edith, adding that 'this was so surprising from his good earnest honest respectable lips that I laughed till I went to sleep.'[6]

Rex was escaping from his work at the Tate and Edith, meanwhile, was 'mad with joy', having just heard that *The Love-Child* was to be published by Secker.[7] As soon as she heard she had dashed off to Netherhampton to tell Henry Newbolt the good news. He had been the first to encourage her and was thrilled, promising to act as her agent and oversee the contract. But until the last minute she had been despairing about the book. 'At last wrote and typed the whole thing. Rosemary and I in agony over it – as we both think it bad – patchworky – not quite right', she had written the previous month.[8] Rosemary was the daughter of Edith's favourite brother Sidney. She was immensely fond of her niece, who had lived with her and Mildred for a while at Fitz House and had since become a kind of unofficial amanuensis. In the coming years she would type most of Edith's manuscripts and help creatively with several of her books. Edith had particularly struggled with the climactic love scene between David and Clarissa in *The Love-Child*: 'I am trying to make it very trance-like and my fear is that it will be pretty and cloying'.[9] Three days later she was still agonizing over it: 'It wants great delicacy. The least wrong thing spoils it and it feels to me all wrong now. Felt very depressed and hopeless.'[10] Romance was something of which she had little experience.

She had been greatly encouraged by the enthusiasm of Alice Sedgwick, who had been staying at the Daye House when Edith wrote the first chapters. She had then sent the manuscript to Alice's sister Anne, who in turn sent it to Secker on Edith's behalf. When it was published in August, Sir Henry Newbolt wrote that he thought it 'flawless – the best "first book" I have ever read . . . perfect'.[11] Other reviews, both in London and America, where it was published by the Viking Press, were equally complimentary: The *Telegraph* declared it 'delightful' while the *Daily News* called it 'a thing of rare tenderness and beauty'.[12] The *Saturday Review* said:

> Here is a book that many will like and more will not. But those who like it will be loud in its praise, will vaunt its limpid simplicity of style, its steady march of incidents each slight in itself, the delicate precision with which it holds its balance true, the restraint of its leashed emotion. A delicate, shimmering thing, it has the immateriality yet the radiance of a bubble, and like a bubble when it bursts all its elements are dissolved into air. Miss Olivier is a newcomer in the field of fiction, but she should go far.[13]

For the first time Edith thought that she might be able to earn a living from writing, that it might be possible to make a career of it. Success emboldened her and made her even more at ease with the young people holidaying at Cap Ferrat: 'We all had very amusing conversation about my Love Child', Edith wrote in her diary at the end of one day, 'Rex saying he would have one too "one way or another" and everyone saying that it was the thing to do. Suddenly', she added, 'I saw Mrs Lion [a fellow guest] who had come in in the middle of the conversation, looking very grim and shocked and . . . I realized that she didn't know it was the name of a book'.[14] In Nice Stephen bought make-up and that evening, after dinner, Edith submitted to his paints; he 'admires artificiality, saying he infinitely prefers make-up to human skin'. There followed a discussion about it, Edith and Pamela agreeing that subtle, nature-improving techniques were best. '[Stephen] couldn't believe in my innocence in these matters', she wrote; 'the result was rather horrible – <u>much too rouged</u>.'[15]

At Cap Ferrat old and new worlds were colliding and Edith spanned the gulf between the two. When Queen Victoria's daughter Princess Louise, Duchess of Argyll, arrived early for lunch at the villa, it was Edith who recognized her and rushed forward into a sweeping curtsey to greet the guest. And she was unimpressed by Betty Balfour, the celebrated silent film star. Stephen and Cecil had spotted her at the hairdresser's and were 'wild' with excitement. 'She is secondrate and ugly', Edith declared in her diary, asking herself: '<u>what makes a Film Star?</u> Stephen and Co. are to lunch with her on Monday. I would more gladly lunch with a charwoman.'[16]

'Cecil Beaton has arrived', Edith noted towards the end of the month. 'A marble face and voice – hard polished surface, but not unattractive. He has a great reputation as a photographer and has only got the little camera which was given to him when he was 12 – and for studio his sisters' bedroom!'[17] It was Stephen who had invited Beaton, keen to befriend the twenty-two-year-old whose 'sunburst' had 'electrified London'.[18] And Cecil was desperate to develop his acquaintance with the golden androgyne he had first met at a dance in December. Cecil's first impression of Edith was of 'a rather swarthy middle-aged woman wearing a tall purple pixie hat . . . she seemed to eye me with definite disapproval', but after a few days they had begun to warm to each other.[19] She had been introduced to Cecil by Pamela as 'a figure in the archaeological and ecclesiastical life of Wiltshire'.[20] 'Later I discovered this was true', Cecil would write in his memoirs, 'but the description was far from resembling the dashing, dazzling person who so soon was to become a lifelong friend. After we had confessed our mutual shyness and struck a chord of mutual sympathy, I began to rely upon Edith Olivier for advice on every conceivable variety of subjects . . . she wielded over me a wise and efficacious influence.'[21]

It was noted, at the Villa La Primavera, that the boys looked smarter than the girls. A photograph taken at Nice of Stephen, Cecil and Rex alongside Edith and Zita, would suggest that this is true. Stephen and Cecil stand side by side with languid poise, all considered nonchalance and wasp-waisted in their Oxford bags, their fair hair perfectly parted. Rex in a pale jacket with plus fours and long socks does not fare so well, but he looks relaxed and happy beside Edith, chic and sportive in a short and jaunty white dress with pearls and white stockings. In the following month the *Sketch* dedicated a page to the party at La Primavera with pictures of the young men perched elegantly with sketchbooks on their knees and one of Pamela, the beneficent hostess, on a stone bench.

Cecil soon set to work 'taking photographs of faces among flowers and foam'.[22] Rex and Stephen he photographed as camp idols on the rocks above the sea, with leopard skin bound around their bodies. Stephen, perched like a delicate Nereid, and Rex, his muscular physique spreadeagled like a shipwrecked sailor, as the waves crash around him. And out came Beaton's camera again, some days later, for what appears to have been an exclusive session with Edith: 'Cecil photographed me in the morning in all the most amazing poses, generally upside-down, on the floor, in a flowerbed and what not'.[23] She thought his photographs were 'amazing . . . incredible that they are photographs at all.'[24]

Cecil was beginning to make his name as a society and fashion photographer. In 1925 he had left Cambridge without a degree and was doing all he could to avoid working in his father's timber business or any other prosaic office job, by busily taking photographs, going to any and every society gathering and designing elaborate costumes for the endless rounds of fancy-dress parties. By the spring of 1927 his photographs had begun to appear in the *Tatler* and elsewhere, his sisters willing mannequins and his nanny helping to develop the negatives in the bathtub. In early summer he signed his first contract with *Vogue* to supply photographs and illustrations for the magazine, which later that year declared that his work sounded 'the death-knell of the foggy school of impressionist photography'.[25] Cecil's greatest skill was to make people look good with clever lighting techniques, retouching and cropping, but it was his artful innovation that was attracting notice. His photographs were theatrically stylized and painterly in composition; like Rex he was frequently inspired by Watteau, Fragonard and Gainsborough, but it was a very modern, modish timelessness he sought. And his style was refreshingly makeshift and consciously artificial with shiny fabrics, shimmering sequins and jewels, elaborate make-up and fanciful costumes. He used surrealist touches: liberal quantities of draped or twisted cellophane, banks of balloons, faces reflected in mirrors or the shiny lid of a piano, debutantes presented as 'Soapsuds' and society hostesses' and actresses' heads appearing under glass domes like exhibits in a cabinet of curiosities.

Beaton had an extraordinary talent for publicity but his success was largely owing to the Sitwells. 'I wouldn't bother too much about *being* anything in particular, just become a friend of the Sitwells, and wait and see what happens', a friend had advised him at the start of his career.[26] At the vanguard of avant-garde culture, the trio of aristocratic siblings were the pioneering taste-makers of the twenties, prolific writers and united as a cultural phenomenon. Dressed in austere monastic robes or rich brocade gowns with heavy glowing beads, Edith, a poet, was 'a tall, graceful scarecrow with the white hands of a medieval saint', who claimed that as a child she had fallen in love with a peacock.[27] Her painterly, experimental poems were rich in image, atmosphere and elusive symbolism, and coursing with melodic rhythms. In *Façade – An Entertainment*, first performed publicly in 1923, Edith recited her poems through a megaphone in time to a musical accompaniment, the score written by the young composer William Walton, a Sitwell protégé. It was a *succès de scandale*.

Edith's brothers Osbert and Sacheverell were aesthetes and writers. All three were fascinated by the baroque and the rococo, by all things bizarre, obscure and theatrical; everything that countered the ever-increasing homogeneity and soulless functionality of modern life. With their aristocratic pedigree and their incredible facility for publicity, the siblings were ensured plenty of coverage in the press and 'their taste became news'.[28] But they were generous with their fame. 'We were on the lookout for geniuses', Sacheverell remarked in an interview many years later.[29] In Cecil Beaton they had found a natural ally. He defined and presented the image of the Sitwells, as carefully cultivated and curated as their idiosyncratic tastes.

Back in England, Stephen commissioned Cecil to take his portrait for a twenty-first birthday present to himself and was thrilled by the results: 'I am <u>nearly crazy</u> at their beauty', he wrote to Beaton on receiving them.[30] In one photograph Stephen is standing in front of a silver-foil backdrop wearing a perfectly tailored pinstriped suit, over which he has slung (or so it seems) a shiny black mackintosh. Everything in the picture gleams, from his golden marcelled hair and his limpid eyes to his glossy pursed lips. Stephen knew his own beauty, the high cheekboned arrogance of his face, the sinewy slenderness of his body; he celebrated and worshipped it. Cecil's photographs captured it for posterity. As with the Sitwells, Cecil tapped into Stephen's personal fantasies of himself, perfecting them and then presenting them back to him as prints. It is little wonder that his work was becoming so popular or that Stephen, who was now also contributing to *Vogue*, was being hailed as 'the brightest of the bright young things'.

The Bright Young People, as the press styled them, were a loosely connected set of sybarites, almost invariably rich and predominantly aristocratic, whose antics filled the gossip columns and both fascinated and appalled 1920s society. They were of the 'lost' generation after the First World War, determined to enjoy themselves and to defy their parents, especially the fathers who had sent their sons into the mindless carnage of the trenches. They were seen as another symptom of what was considered to be the moral dissolution of the post-war era, a time of increasingly open promiscuity, of both the homosexual and the heterosexual variety, and of a rising divorce rate.

In their subversive defiance of authority the Bright Young People rejected the seriousness and obligations of adulthood. They adopted a pose of decadent infantilism embracing everything that was childish and hedonistic. They took superficiality seriously, with Stephen exhorting his *Vogue* readers to maintain an expression of 'vacuous boredom'. Misrule was the order of the day, which would soon be captured by Evelyn Waugh in the farcical anarchy of his novels *Decline and Fall* and *Vile Bodies*, published in 1928 and 1930. In place of the pre-war language of elegant restraint came an inflated, explosive, idiomatic vocabulary, both in speech and in writing. Conversation leapt to a superlative, exclamatory pitch, anything and everything was 'too divine', 'ghastly' or 'shame-making'. When not affecting boredom, they howled, screamed and shrieked with laughter. Gone were the buxom femininity of the Edwardian lady and the bluff machismo of the Edwardian gent. The new woman lopped off her hair, first bobbing it, then shingling it (much as Edith had done in San Remo) and then cutting it all off into an Eton crop, the shortest of all. She wore cloche hats and sporty, androgynous-looking jumpers, her breasts bound beneath them. She wore scarlet lipstick, she smoked and drank. And as the girls looked like boys, so the boys looked more like girls. They shaved their beards so that their faces were as smooth as their lacquered hair. Some wore make-up. This look of infantile androgyny both denied maturity and knowingly undermined the conventional distinctions of sexual difference.

The Bright Young Things listened to jazz, drank cocktails, sniffed cocaine and went to the theatre to watch themselves parodied in Noël Coward's highly successful and scandalously modish plays. They favoured nightclubs over private dances, and they played elaborate versions of children's games: sardines, hoaxes, treasure hunts, fancy dress and charades. It was a strange mix of sophistication and childishness; when Susan Sontag later declared in her 1964 essay on the meaning of camp that 'one can be serious about the frivolous, frivolous about the serious', she could have been writing a manifesto for the Bright Young People.[31]

The tabloid press – the *Sketch*, the *Tatler*, the *Daily Mail* and the *Daily Express* – eagerly lapped up their exploits, regaling its readership with tales of glamour and scandal. Gossip columnists were soon seen at every party; Patrick Balfour, the *Sketch*'s 'Mr Gossip'; the aristocratic Lord Castlerosse and the well-connected, left-wing provocateur Tom Driberg, more than most. The outrageous antics of the group proved far more entertaining than the polite society announcements of old. The news that the French Ambassador was in town or that Lady So-and-So was spending the summer at Monte Carlo suddenly paled in comparison. And for the Bright Young People the publicity was part of the appeal; for one in particular it was a pleasure. After a party in 1927 the *Daily Express* reported: 'The Honourable Stephen Tennant arrived in an electric brougham wearing a football jersey and earrings'.[32]

Vogue became the self-professed champion and chronicler of Britain's youth and the exploits of this *jeunesse dorée* sprang from its pages. The agenda of the magazine was closely aligned with the iconoclastic sensibilities of the group and its emphasis on youthfulness, originality and subverting conventions: 'Youth', according to Christopher Reed, 'in the journalistic nomenclature of the "Bright Young People" or "Intelligent Young Persons", was an identity defined not by biological age but by an attitude of delighted transgression against convention.'[33] For the *Vogue* of the twenties, clothes, interests and ideas were of equal relevance – all fashionable, all subject to the same transience, all relevant for as long as they were 'amusing'. What was required, the magazine suggested, was a youthful mental elasticity. Identity and, it implied, sexuality, were equally transient and unfixed. Androgyny became the ideal and with it, dress, gender and ultimately life became a perform-ance, played out in the gossip columns. Exaggeration, artificiality, affectation, superficiality, humour, idiosyncrasy, frivolity, mas-querade, theatricality, all associated with the sensibility that was later defined as camp, were the order of the day. And their style was not just confined to dress but applied to literature, ideas, art and design. It was a way of life: the artificiality of Cecil Beaton's photographs, the decadent, gender-bending juxtaposition of Stephen Tennant's pinstriped suit and his lipglossed mouth, the Sitwells' taste for novelty and baroque excess, all these exemplify 'the Amusing', as the style came to be known.

Inevitably, the sensational behaviour provoked a backlash from the more conservative members of society for whom Stephen's, as well as Cecil's, appearance and manner were provocatively dandi-fied, hinting at dissipation and, more dangerously, at homosexuality, a crime that was punishable by imprisonment. Sex between men was nothing new but society operated on a tacit code of conceal-ment; it was tolerated as long as it wasn't made obvious. In a codified world where sexuality, as well as class, was manifested by appearance and behaviour, Stephen and his friends were not obeying the rules. Edith was concerned that they were jeopardiz-ing their reputations. She noted that at a party 'Stephen, Rex and others seem to have created a scandal by appearing in very outré dresses as beggars, with very painted face . . . they . . . shewed too much thro' their rags'.[34] She rushed to their defence: '[Stephen] is misunderstood and people hate him and say such beastly things about him. As I say it's vieux jeux on their part, as now-a-days so many boys are girlish, without being effeminate. It's the sort of boy which has grown up since the war'.[35]

In September 1927 the hostility escalated. At a ball at Wilton House to celebrate Sidney Herbert's coming-of-age, Edith danced with Rex, Cecil and Stephen in the Double Cube and walked with them along the river in the misty moonlight. She thought it was a heavenly night, but unbeknown to Edith, at some point in the evening Cecil, who was heavily made up with rouge and mascara, had been unceremoniously dumped in the River Nadder by a group of hearties. 'Do you think the bugger's drowned?' he heard one of them shout.[36] It was a symbolic gesture, as the water was only knee deep. Lady Pembroke (who was fond of Cecil) was appalled and ejected the troublemakers from the house, but Cecil was mortified, saying nothing to Edith, with whom he was staying for the weekend. When she did find out Edith made her allegiance clear: 'What an amazing thing is this hatred of the unusual – from Shelley onwards. Dear loyal Rex, tho' saying he sees no objection to Stephen's painting his face if he does it so well that it doesn't shew, [but now] is concerned because . . . he "puts on as much as a girl". This is silly, but not enough to throw people into rivers for!'[37] A few days later she added: 'there's violent anti-Stephen feeling about. People think that Cecil is immoral and S is tarred with the same brush . . . All this makes me miserable and helpless and I went to bed really depressed. <u>Are</u> these boys depraved?' she asked herself. 'I will not believe it. Rex is goodness itself, Stephen innocent and ignorant, Cecil perhaps has been in a bad set but I believe him to be absolutely alright now'.[38]

What Edith saw of her close young friends convinced her that they were nothing more than amusing children. She accepted their juvenile behaviour at face value; she was charmed by their invention and mannered flamboyance, which she thought creative and entertaining. Stephen rapturously chasing butterflies amongst the bougainvillea at San Remo or Cecil spouting persiflage, cocktail in hand, on the terrace of the Villa La Primavera: to Edith this was innocent rather than scandalous. She happily perpetuated their personas as they were perpetuating hers, having transformed her from a faded country spinster into an elegant woman of fashion. But she failed to acknowledge the full implications of their appearance and behaviour as she had refused to accept, on hearing of her scandalous affair with Vita Sackville-West, that her friend Violet Trefusis was a lesbian. To Edith, who had lived all her life without it, sex was not significant.

Though Cecil and particularly Stephen were at the heart of

the beau monde Rex always remained on its fringes – and in Edith's eyes he was anyway above suspicion. Unlike Stephen, who lived on a seemingly infinite inheritance, he had to work for his money. Of course Cecil had to work hard too, although he liked to give the impression that he didn't. In the way that he dressed, fancy-dress parties and leopard-skin togas aside, Rex was markedly, and increasingly, conservative in comparison to his dandyish friends. Stephen might sprinkle his hair with gold dust, rouge his cheeks, smear Vaseline on his eyelids, paint his lips, don earrings and mist himself with scents from Worth and Molyneux, but for the most part (despite his brief flirtation with plus fours) Rex dressed 'unostentatiously' in corduroy trousers or well-cut suits.[39] He was conscious of the significance of how he looked. According to his brother, 'He liked rich and unusual colour-effects in shirts and ties and pullovers; and soft dark hats worn with a rakish brim.'[40] However, he always sought to present a more conventionally masculine demeanour. It was not just for Edith's benefit, although undoubtedly her good opinion mattered to him. Stephen was rich and aristocratic. Rex was neither, and though his friend was happy to court controversy Rex did not want to be tarnished, or have his career thwarted, by accusations of immorality.

With the money that Edith had secured for him he had been looking for a studio to rent. He had found 'either luxurious flats at £5 per week or dark little almost-no-windowed "bed sitting-rooms", whatever they may be!' he wrote to Edith. '(It somehow suggests a person spending all their time just sitting on the bed!)', he added, with the inevitable illustration of a wide-eyed young man perched awkwardly and redundantly on the edge of his bed in a tiny room. He told Edith that he was focusing his search on the warren of streets around Fitzroy Square and Charlotte Street, not far from the British Museum. Several Slade students had studios in the large and relatively cheap Adam houses and the area, later known as Fitzrovia, had long been colonized by artists. It had a worn charm and had, Rex told Edith, 'gone down in the world'.[41] The Fitzroy Tavern on Charlotte Street was a favoured meeting place for Augustus John, George Orwell, Dylan Thomas and hordes of intellectuals and artists. The Eiffel Tower restaurant in Percy Street had been for decades a favoured haunt of bohemians who were welcomed by Rudolf Stulik, the genial Austrian proprietor. The Vorticists gathered there, Wyndham Lewis had illustrated the menu and it was soon to become Rex's favourite restaurant.

Eventually he found a studio on the first floor of 20 Fitzroy Street and at the end of May 1927 Edith went to visit his 'two charming Georgian rooms'.[42] His studio was at the front and double doors opened onto a bedroom at the back. Not for Rex Stephen's 'Silver Bedroom' at Mulberry House, the family's new London home on Smith Square, with its silver curtains, bed draped in brocade and foil-lined walls. And neither did he want the iridescent lamé adorning the dining room of the Sitwells' Chelsea house. In contrast Rex's studio appeared unstudied, genteel and spartan. It was dominated by two vast sash windows through which light poured in; at one end of the room two bookcases with busts on top stood either side of a simple daybed and at the other end a homely fireplace was laden with frames, books and invitations. Eschewing the radical chic of his friends, Rex had styled his rooms in imitation of an eighteenth-century artist's studio, a room in which Gainsborough or Romney would feel at ease. One friend, a frequent visitor in the early thirties, later recalled that 'there were a few chairs which were piled as high as possible with books and papers and things and I'm sure that the lady who came to clean for him sometimes didn't dare touch anything in case she was going to spoil or interfere with something. So if you did move something off a chair with great effort in order to sit down you were sat in clouds of dust. I don't think he noticed anything like that.'[43]

With his conservative clothes and traditional studio he was cultivating an image for himself that was quite distinct from his modish friends. For Rex, this had a greater purpose than as a signifier of his aesthetic sensibility. It masked his comparatively humble origins and enabled him to reshape and then to control his own identity. It allowed him to reinvent himself. Commenting on his new friend in his diary in August of the following year, Cecil wrote:

> Rex, so romantic with his luminous face, Roman nose, and large crown to his head, exudes warm-heartedness and sympathy, but he is a strangely remote person. I doubt if many people even impinge on his inner feelings. He seems to accept me as a new bosomer, but I wonder if, apart from his deeply reciprocated devotion to Edith, he has really loved anyone.[44]

At first Cecil had been sceptical about Rex, whose air of remoteness he thought exaggerated, although he had quickly 'come forth from his shell' to charm him and they had become good friends.[45] But Rex's elusiveness would remain one of his most frequently noted characteristics. His letters were witty, warm and ebullient, and they could be intimate, but were often taken up with divertingly decorative illustrations. For a few days only, in 1926 and 1927 – and never again – Rex kept a diary, declaring with great intention on its front page: 'This is the Diary of Rex Whistler – The good and noble minded'.[46] He never bought an engagement book, but preferred to write dates on narrow strips of paper decorated with drawings. And even though he worked very hard, he seemed almost cavalier about his work.

Rex was one of a growing breed in the twenties: people who didn't belong to the aristocracy but for whom creativity was an entrée into high society: novelists, artists, actresses, photographers and composers, middle-class meritocrats such as William Walton, Sybil Colefax, Cecil Beaton, Beverley Nichols, Noël Coward and Evelyn Waugh. And with celebrity came the burden of a public image to cultivate and protect, or not. Some met with a better reception than others. It was often said, as repeated by Laurence Whistler, that the only sound during the two minutes' silence on Remembrance Day was that of Lady Sybil Colefax climbing.[47]

Cecil Beaton was from an urbane and relatively wealthy London family and yet he was considered an upstart *arriviste*. With the help of the Sitwells, Beaton's social climb, which he called 'the uprise' in his diaries, was energetic and flagrant; he revelled in his new-found fame. Beneath a photograph of Cecil in the *Graphic* he was succinctly described as: 'Mr. Cecil Beaton, an elegant first-nighter, who designs pretty frocks for his friends, takes exquisite photographs, and is generally artistic, as well as being very popular at tea parties in town.'[48] In the process he made a lot of enemies. He would soon become a victim of the biting satire of Evelyn Waugh (with whom he had been at school), appearing in *Decline and Fall* (and several later novels) as David Lennox, the enterprising society photographer. Lennox arrives at a house party with the effete and decadent Miles Malpractice, perhaps based on Stephen (which delighted him): 'They emerged with little shrieks from an Edwardian electric brougham and made straight for the nearest looking glass.'[49] Cecil was bitchy and outspoken, provoking the wrath of society ladies with his gently satirical caricatures in *Vogue*. When he had been dunked in the River Nadder during the Wilton Ball, Stephen had also been a guest, more painted and perfumed than Cecil. But Stephen was protected by his status, by his consumptive fragility and by his impenetrable self-confidence. Though Beaton enjoyed perpetuating the myth that he was a direct descendant of Mary, Queen of Scots's lady-in-waiting Lady Mary Beaton (a story born from his having cannily dressed his sister Baba as Lady Mary for a well-publicized fancy-dress party), he was not in the least aristocratic, neither was he as self-assured as he liked to appear.

When he published his diaries many years later, Cecil entitled the chapter covering this period 'The First Rung'.[50] Although his relationship with the Sitwells was far less intimate than that of Rex and Edith, the dynamic is in some ways comparable. Both men benefited from their friendships with older, well-connected people. But whereas Cecil's rise was noisy, Rex's was seamless and apparently effortless. Undoubtedly, a large part of this was to do with how the two men dressed and behaved. With his easy charm and artistic *sprezzatura*, Rex tended to make more friends than enemies. And there was a lingering aesthetic snobbery that rated painting as a greater talent than photography. The other important factor was his friendship with Edith. The Sitwell family's patronage of Cecil Beaton was like a heralding fanfare at the gates of the citadel of high society. Edith's support of Rex allowed him to slip through the back door. Most of her friends were not at the cutting edge of the artistic world but she knew, and had introduced Rex to, the aristocratic circle that was to become his milieu. She was educating him in the esoteric lore of that world. She nurtured his old-fashioned gentleman-artist persona. Unlike Cecil, Rex was kept beneath the radar of social contempt. Though Cecil was a flamboyant diarist he was also a perceptive observer of character:

> Rex's poetical appearance – the profile like ivory cameo, and pale unseeing eyes – was, I soon discovered, in contrast to his rugged health and independence of character. In spite of his vagueness and inability to cope with worldly affairs, he could be extremely caustic and was by no means removed from the down-to-earth reality of high life . . . Rex was always a refreshing companion: each time one met, his frankness and honesty of purpose seemed to grow in effect. Everyone reacted with delighted surprise whenever he entered a room.[51]

Beaton seems keen to emphasize that despite Rex's air of retirement he was, like himself, courting the beau monde. And he also hints at a conflict in his friend's personality. Rex was a part of the flamboyant, predominantly homosexual circle that centred on Stephen, Cecil and Oliver Messel, but he was also set apart from it, perhaps he even held himself back from it. Had he been born an aristocrat, or if the Sitwells and not a fifty-three-year-old provincial spinster were championing his cause in society, things might have been different.

7: *Town and Country*

❖

The double strain, of the orthodox and the bizarre.

The Times, 21 November 1927

From Cap Ferrat Edith travelled south to Florence to stay with the writer Yoi Maraini, who lived with her husband Nello, a sculptor, and their fourteen-year-old son Fosco, at Torre di Sopra, an ancient frescoed farmhouse with a watchtower, surrounded by olive groves and overlooking the city.

While there Edith received a parcel from Cecil Beaton, containing a letter and the results of their portrait session at the villa. 'Thank you so much for sending them to me and for your letter', she replied, 'the only scrap of news I have had from La Primavera since I left. So but for you I should feel utterly out of it and homesick, and like the old woman in *Those Barren Leaves* who hated going to bed because she thought something amusing would be said or done when she wasn't there.'[1]*

The woman in Cecil's photographs, in one reclining on a rug and looking seductively at the camera, bears almost no resemblance to the modest Edwardian spinster of a few years before. She is dressed in a gold-striped, sleeveless and drop-waisted dress with painted eyes, lips and nails, the bright Mediterranean sun

---

* *Those Barren Leaves* by Aldous Huxley was published in 1925. A satirical novel, it centres on a group gathered at an Italian villa to relive the splendour of the Renaissance. Each character in turn is revealed to be superficial and vacuous in spite of their sophisticated posturings.

catching her earrings, necklace and bracelets and glistening on the foliage around her. Later, when her family saw the photographs she wrote that they 'disapproved fantastically'.[2] But Edith was thrilled:

> <u>Could</u> there be two more different people in the world than that grave Fakir or Dervish, holding a grim black cloak rigidly about an unmobile form who has sat for years in contemplation without becoming religious – and that abandoned woman (more to be pitied than censured) who sprawls voluptuously on the ground in dazzling stripes of gold? I think both photographs have much character and I long to see the others when you have reprinted and re-touched items. I have so seldom been photographed that it is most interesting to me to see these outside impressions of myself and I stare at them for hours. Yoi Maraini thinks the prostrate one <u>very good indeed</u>.[3]

Edith had begun to resemble a glamorous Gypsy, with dangling earrings of semi-precious stones, theatrical rings, and dyeing her hair a dark blackish-plum colour with henna. She was giving a lot more attention to her appearance than before and taking her clothes to Foyle's, the dressmakers in Wilton, to be altered and shortened. Her sister-in-law Esther, who had a dress shop on Grafton Street in London, was now advising her on corsetry to look slim.

Her literary career was burgeoning and her world was opening up. In late July a portrait of Edith, taken by Cecil, appeared in *Vogue* alongside other contemporary writers, Elinor Wylie, Sylvia Townsend Warner, the Sitwells and Rosamond Lehmann, above the heading 'Some of the Younger Generation of Writers'. Edith's inclusion stretched the definition somewhat; at fifty-four she was the eldest of the group by thirteen years (Elinor Wylie was then forty-one). But for *Vogue* youth was not defined by age but by a certain mentality, which they evidently considered Edith to have, one that aligned her with the Sitwells and her bright young friends. Like Edith, the magazine was a combination of the traditional and the modern; amongst the usual advertisements that year for trousseaux, Worth perfumes and Poiret dresses, were others for sanitary towels, cars and sportswear. More importantly perhaps for Edith, her presence in *Vogue* signified her metamorphosis into a writer of note, a literary ingénue: 'Miss Edith Olivier's charming first novel, "The Love Child", is an example of the modern tendency to the fantastical in fiction'.[4] 'I was very proud to see myself on that page of distinguished authors', she told Cecil in a letter from the Daye House. And she updated him on *The Love-Child*'s progress. Her publisher Martin Secker had told her: 'The book sells steadily but <u>slowly</u>. This surprises and disappoints me as it seems as if so many people have read it. And I am told that a Sunday paper announced it as a Best seller a fortnight ago'.[5]

But despite the slow sales Edith was now thinking of her future as a writer, and a fashionable one at that. 'I <u>long</u> to write for Vogue – and to plan with you on what subjects', she told Cecil. I want to Pot-boil if I can find a pot to boil – a fire to boil on – and anyone to partake of the feast – Stephen told me that you are now the King of Vogue.'[6] And on this she was persistent. After attending one of his parties in London (where she usually stayed with her sister Mamie, Lady Carter, at her house in Chelsea), Edith wrote to thank Cecil:

> What perfect parties you give! That one was so overflowing with interesting guests that I hated being one of the first to overflow into the drear and dusty streets after I had only sipped at your honey . . . I was very sad at having to go before the Editor of Vogue arrived. Will you say that I am ready to review <u>anything</u> . . . I should <u>like</u> to do the Book of the Month from Paris but if they don't like that I'm not particular . . .[7]

Whether Cecil actually intervened for Edith at *Vogue* is unclear – perhaps he was too busy cultivating his own career – but it would be many years before she wrote for the magazine. Her relationship with Cecil was fast developing in the summer of 1927. But it was not all one-sided. Cecil had decided to make a book of his drawings and photographs of society women and in August wrote to Edith for advice on its title. 'Have you yet thought of a thread on which to hang the jewels of your tableaux I wonder?' she asked in reply. 'One wants to be obvious but not banal. Anything good sounds precious and affected . . . the idea of "Scenes from the Great Book of the World" of course gives you unlimited scope. If it would attract enough . . . but one wants something more like <u>Pictures of Beauty and Fate</u> or <u>Fatal Beauty</u> – we want the sure journalistic touch.'[8]

Edith had become an honorary bright, if not young, thing. Like Rex, her young friends found her inspiring, an open-minded confidante with daringly cropped hair who read Walter Pater, listened to jazz, danced the Charleston with Rex in the Long Room, smoked cigarettes and drank cocktails; all without compromising her strong sense of morality. They were drawn to her wisdom and her tolerance. And they gravitated to her out of a natural affinity; though she was of their parents' generation she was a 'good' example of an adult, having resisted the shackles of marriage and the burdens of parenthood. She was free, as they were. Being so much older than them she seemed sexually unthreatening; she didn't make impossible romantic demands of these mostly homosexual or sexually confused young men. And in turn this made them unthreatening to her; their presence in her house and in her life posed no risk to her reputation. Edith appeared to be rebelling against the life that her father had dictated for her, just as much as her young friends were themselves. 'Suddenly the country robin emerged as a bird of paradise', Cecil later wrote.[9]

But Edith straddled two worlds. It was characteristic that in the same month that she appeared in *Vogue*, she was compiling a selection of country recipes and cures for a Women's Institute book called *Secrets of Some Wiltshire Housewives*. Amongst other rustic offerings it recommended that rainwater collected on

Ascension Day improved the eyesight and that baked apples made excellent poultices for earache. The Dowager Countess of Pembroke, perhaps troubled by her own digestive system, submitted a laxative recipe, another 'to allay constant sickness' and suggested raw egg yolk and castor oil for diarrhoea.[10] Edith wrote the foreword and provided ten, rather more sophisticated recipes, including raisin wine and raspberry brandy. In the foreword she wrote that she thought 'Lily Brandy', a remedy for cuts, sounded like a drink from 'Fairyland' and that she was pleased with the addition of a sore-throat remedy used by Adam and Eve: 'its great antiquity must increase its efficacy'. She confessed that she feared she would be burned as a witch for publishing the 'Cure for Falling Sickness' which began with the words 'Take a man's skull that has not been above a year buried', although she couldn't resist including an equally arcane recipe of her own for an ointment made from adder's tongue, to be gathered in the New Forest. 'This is not so poisonous as it sounds', she reassured her readers.[11]

One day she might be entertaining Elinor Wylie, dining with the Sitwells or drinking champagne with the Ballets Russes in London, the next she would find herself back in her old world. More pressing than a commission from *Vogue* was the need for a new set of false teeth and that she had to prepare a series of embroidery lessons for the Wilton WI. At 'an appalling genteel tea party', with her niece Rosemary, Edith found 'eight sickening women sitting round making up sentences to say to each other . . . one awful woman . . . dressed and looked like diarrhoea. This was my conversation. "Cathedral Cities generally have many antique shops." "Yes. There are some at Exeter." "Many at Salisbury" . . . we fled'.[12] It was a party of provincial upper-middle-class ladies, a group to which by rights she belonged, but no longer felt that she did. She described herself as a 'half-caste', hovering between the older and the younger generations.[13] At the end of 1927 she was recruited to play an old woman in an amateur production of *The Monkey's Paw* in Salisbury. It was a role she abhorred: 'I can't play the old woman and they know it . . . It is misery to work at it – a part quite alien to me . . . it depresses me beyond words', and so she decided to 'play it like a Greek dancer'.[14] She was forced to buy flat shoes for the part, which also depressed her. 'I have too much spring for an old woman', she lamented after one of the rehearsals, which took place in the local branch of Lloyd's bank.[15] One morning, later in the year, just before Christmas, she visited the old ladies of Wilton to give them their traditional festive gift of a half-crown. 'Mrs Stephen Musselwhite (now 94) was very funny', she wrote, 'asked why I hadn't been to see her lately. "Been looking for a husband, I expect" – I said I had had no luck. She answered "They'll never leave you out, with that good looking face." I glowed till I remembered that she had been too blind to recognise me when I came in'.[16] She could laugh about this because, despite having a large group of friends of her own age, she identified herself with her young friends rather than those her own age: 'We old ones talked of the modern girl', she would write in her diary a couple of years later, 'and somehow when I find myself doing this with my own generation I always feel a fraud – eavesdropping – as if I really belonged to the young!!'[17]

Things could have been very different. Edith's next novel offered an alternative narrative for the life she had lived and was living now. Eager to keep her name alive in the literary world, she had begun to write again and for the first time she was using a typewriter, the results of which were almost as difficult to read as her frantically scrawled and often indecipherable handwriting. The title of the book was not new; *As Far as Jane's Grandmother's* had been a family saying in her childhood and later, as adults, Mildred and Edith had thought it a wonderful title for a novel. Edith had even written down some ideas for the first chapter but had put it aside, until now. It tells the story of Jane, a girl whose life is so dominated by her overbearing grandmother that she can never escape her influence. An influence marked quite literally by the measure of distance and the implied limitation in the title. Mrs Basildon prevents her orphaned granddaughter Jane from marrying and eventually from taking the veil. Impotent against the force of her grandmother's will Jane remains entirely at her mercy. She takes to wearing a hair shirt and when her grandmother dies, Jane, at thirty-five, has become a replica of her grandmother.

As a young woman, behind a veneer of obedience and tightly calibrated emotions, she lives within the limitless world of her dreams, happier in fantasy than in reality. In *The Love-Child*, Agatha, through the power of her imagination, manages to transgress the boundaries that her upbringing and society have drawn for her in the real world. But though Jane longs to become a *salonnière*, with a group of brilliant friends, her imagination slowly ebbs away from her and with it she retreats out of the social world, sequestered in the austere mausoleum of her grandmother's Queen Anne mansion. Like an antelope in the jaws of a lion, she finds peace in surrender. 'The real questions were whether by now the mask had not grown so close to the face that it would never come off; and if it did, whether the face beneath would have taken forever that vapid mould.'[18]

In this dark, unrelenting novel, which Edith dedicated to her niece Rosemary, she returned more bitterly than in *The Love-Child*, and in a surprisingly outspoken way, to the subject of her own circumscribed life, her thwarted romance and ambitions, and to the tyranny of autocratic adults. 'I liked this subject', she would later write; 'it is a character which charms me, mostly because I could never be at all like it myself . . . The story of Jane with her few ineffectual struggles is really a symbolic picture of life in my own father's house'.[19] Mrs Basildon is a grotesque, malign version of Dacres. Why does Jane yield to her grandmother's clutches? Why did Edith never rebel against her father? These are the questions she explores in the novel, and perhaps she was trying to justify her own submission to her father's will. Characters such as Dacres and Mrs Basildon, 'are rare to-day', Edith wrote:

They suggest a life lived in a secure and unshakeable setting. The tides of varying opinions may sweep to and fro outside it, but all the time it remains completely watertight . . . a personality such as this sounds harsh and forbidding, and it may be so at heart, but in the case of my father, I had seen it veiled in an outer garment of courteous old-fashioned manners, which simply made him impossible to argue with. If one ever attempted such a thing, he could always finally and definitely place one in the wrong. The longer one knew him, the more one came to see that his system *worked* . . . the first reaction of youth was naturally to rebel against this overmastering authority; but in order to rebel successfully, the rebel must have his own conception of life, equally complete and equally believed in. Not many people possess this.[20]

Edith claimed that she toed the line that her father had drawn for her because his will was stronger than hers and because she was convinced that he was right. Only when he died was she free. But in the character of Jane, Edith highlighted everything that she was not herself. Jane's search for a useful existence, for salvation and her feeling of redundancy, reflect the inherent impotence of the spinster in the society of old. For Jane, the only escape from bondage is into another form of bondage, either by marriage or by joining the Church. Edith had avoided both, and she had made herself useful. And though she lived, and had always lived, within high walls, Edith was not immured or cloistered from the outside world and neither did she wish to be. The Daye House was a retreat, not a prison; she moved freely in and out of society as she chose, and she could live an imaginative life without having to hide it, as Agatha Bodenham must do, or deny it entirely, like Jane.

While Jane becomes increasingly prudish and disapproving of the young people she meets, Edith loved and admired Stephen, Rex and Cecil; she envied their youth and was amused by their exploits. For Edith the end of the First World War, coinciding as it did with her father's death, was a watershed in her life as it was for society at large. In conversation with friends of her own age

Edith defended the behaviour of the post-war generation. And she delighted in the freedom of the modern woman. The disapproving voices of those friends echo loudly through the sentiments of Jane and her grandmother:

> The War was over at last. In the eyes of Mrs. Basildon and Jane it had killed the old England, and the society which now began to rise from the ruins was a vulgar travesty of that which they had known in the past. This England was a thing kicked together by the feet of grotesque dancers, in place of a noble edifice carefully constructed by honest builders according to a considered plan.
>
> Jane and her grandmother deplored the certainty that the many unsexed women and girls whom they descried around them would never consent to return to their 'pre-War' life of dignified leisure. They were spoilt for it by these years of driving lorries and of making munitions side by side with men; of messing with men, smoking with men, and even swearing with men.[21]

A scene in the novel in which Julian, an aesthetically minded young man with theatrical friends, is locked in the pound, was inspired by Cecil's dunking in the Nadder. It was a declaration of support for her young friends. She had recently been horrified to discover that one of the instigators was Roger Chetwode, the son of her Wiltshire friend Star, Lady Chetwode (and John Betjeman's future brother-in-law). But when Edith read the manuscript to Rex one weekend in October she disagreed with him on the extent to which this should be obvious: 'he wants me to sharpen the point still more of the ragging scene so as to shew up the Cecil affair – but I won't turn it into propaganda. As it stands it is the way to shew Jane's character reacting to various milieux. Everything else is by the way – tho' the by-products <u>May</u> be effective.'[22] She wanted to defend Cecil, but not to go beyond the bounds of propriety herself. She still had some limits.

A few days later Rex sent a letter to thank her for the weekend:

> My darling Edith,
>
> . . . Never has the country looked more lovely and never have you been more delightful. I'm terribly excited about <u>Jane's Grandmother</u> which I think is going to be <u>enchanting</u> and I feel <u>sure</u> a huge success – except with the 'Rowdies' and 'hearties' of the Wilton ball of course! (May hell devour them all!) Don't forget to write and tell me every word that passes between you and that Chetwode 'rough' when you meet at Oxford. You really can't go on liking him <u>and</u> keep your self respect, I'm sure.
>
> . . . My paintings are to be opened on 30 November it is now arranged – whether finished or not.
>
> Much love Rex[23]

With the Tate deadline looming Rex was beginning to despair that he would ever finish 'the detestable room', as he described it to Edith, confessing that he was tempted to 'whitewash the walls and columns as they stand and the room would look considerably cleaner and brighter; I should then burn my brushes, palette and boats, and leave for China or the Azores'.[24] He told Cecil: 'I literally live – day and night – at the Tate now-a-days'.[25] In September Edith had gone to see him at work in the steamy subterranean gloom of the refreshment room amongst 'curious and tripperish tea drinkers'. She thought he looked ill, 'very strained and <u>done</u> by the atmosphere', and was worried when he ordered only milk and biscuits for supper, which she supplemented with two peaches from her handbag.[26]

The room he was painting was about sixty feet long and thirty feet wide, with a door at each end and three windows running along one wall. He had created an energetically continuous scheme, with clever use of trompe l'œil to accommodate doors and windows. At first glance resembling a hunting party on a tapestry, it follows a journey through a picturesque oriental-inspired landscape, painted in sylvan shades of emerald, teal, jade, sepia and umber. But if the landscape is reminiscent of Claude with its tall, feathery trees, shadowy mountainous depths and softly diffused light, the playful narrative of the mural is in the spirit of Watteau or Fragonard. An expedition, in pursuit of rare game, departs from a baroque palace. Dressed in a mix of modern, Victorian, Edwardian and eighteenth-century dress, a party of characters, including a girl with an Eton crop and a moustachioed man with a bowler hat and an eyeglass, sets off on foot, on horseback, on a bicycle and in a vibrant red chariot that appears to dart, incongruously, through the moody landscape inhabited by shepherds and shepherdesses. This whimsical, uncanny fusion of styles, the unexpectedly modern details within a romantic landscape of pagodas, Georgian mansions and classical bridges and pavilions, helps to lift the work out of the realms of pastiche and infuses it with a mischievous wit, a poetic *jeu d'esprit*, which playfully undercuts the initial sense of formality. In November *The Times* arts critic would interpret the mood of the mural as 'The Sitwell Family, emulating the Swiss Family Robinson, after a course of the novels of Thomas Love Peacock'. He noted the 'unconscious symbolism of the double strain, of the orthodox and the bizarre . . .' 'Up above', he added:

> Where the attention of the visitor may be supposed to be alert, the two strains are more or less consciously pursued; down here, where more basic needs are in evidence, they are properly mingled in the unconscious. We are in the basement of the building and the mind alike . . . In both spirit and execution the scheme is a great success . . . on nothing is he to be congratulated more than on keeping up the dream condition, in which things seen, imagined, and read about are all interfused throughout.[27]

It was to the realm of the 'dream condition', with its inevitable Freudian resonance, that Rex would return again and again in his work. Like Wilsford's rustic grandeur or Wilton's eighteenth-century Arcadia, it is a world of aristocratic capriccio, where all is not what it seems, a world of magic realism that shuffles reality and artifice, ancient and modern, suffusing it with a surreal, dreamlike quality. This was Rex's personal vision of pastoral, a retreat from the real world into the Arcadia of his imagination. It was not an unchanging landscape though there were some constants, his beloved Palladian Bridge in particular. Each manifestation over the years that followed would reflect where Rex had been and what architecture was inspiring him at the time. But each work is immediately recognizable as his. And so the tea-drinking Tate visitors were not faced with modern art, there was no glimpse of a brave new world or reflexive engagement with their politically troubled present. Instead in the refreshment room beneath Millbank, as cars and buses endlessly rattled past on the road above, Rex's mural offered an escape out of the gallery basement and out of the modern urban world altogether. Not to the rustic idyll of a, albeit idealized, village scene, as for the boys of Shadwell, but to a soothing, innocent and entirely imagined world. And to make that passage a more convincing one, the fixtures and fittings of the room were designed to echo the mural, with gilded canvas on the dado and gratings and red lacquered wicker furniture to complement the vaguely oriental theme. The style of the mural was much less vigorous and theatrical than at Shadwell. It marked a shift in Rex's work to a far more restrained, elegant and consciously decorative mood; the Tate mural is flat and formal, like Chinese wallpaper.

Edith and Rex decided that the mural needed a narrative. Over several weekends at the Daye House in the winter of 1927, they devised a story to elaborate on the scenes that Rex had painted: *A Guide to the Duchy of Epicurania with Some Account of the Famous Expedition in Pursuit of Rare Meats*. Rex described his mural and Edith turned it into a story. The painted characters were given names, mostly anagrammatic. Rex had filled the mural with autobiographical details – the Palladian Bridge, the Corinthian arch and the Boycott Pavilion at Stowe – but the story that he invented with Edith is perhaps an allegorical record of his own entry into a bountiful aristocratic Arcadia. Rex was cast as Król Dudziarz (Polish for Whistler), an impoverished bicycle-riding nobleman, who joins the expeditionary party in pursuit of rare meats with which to improve the limited diet of Epicurania. Tonks, a key factor in Rex's present success, appears as a bust on the stone belvedere at the palace. Król joins the Princess Claudia, her maid Gilabia Telemonte and the Colonel-in-Chief, in a red chariot; the Colonel's aide-de-camp Captain Paradier on a white horse and Tillet Murd, a pantry boy, who runs unwillingly at the back. The group is led by Prince Etienne (French for Stephen), 'a youth of rare beauty and promise, an aristocrat from the top of his high brow, to the tips of his long and pointed finger-nails' out of the Palace of Epicurania.[28]

Always fearful of pirates, ghosts and food poisoning, they travel through exotic lands, past ruined castles and vaporous mountains, encountering mermaids, deer, gazelles, leopards and snakes. They notice a shipwreck and meet a sailor who joins them. In a jungle Król spots a unicorn, but fails to catch it as he is armed only with a bicycle pump; instead they seize a black boy whose mother darts up into a tree to hide. Reaching a ruined Palladian Bridge they believe that they have arrived at Wilton House but soon realize that it is the Palace of Joisigonne (Inigo Jones, who had advised on the building of Wilton House). Król and Etienne long to stay the night amongst the romantic ruins and the next day, as they depart, they steal an urn to carry any caviar that they might find on the journey. Inside the Grotto of the Gluttons, which is guarded by two monsters with lustful faces, so real that they cannot tell whether they are facing painted statues or real creatures, they find the walls lined with foie gras. Passing the Great Wall of Cathay, pagodas and Chinese bridges, they gather lobsters and eggs, and in Woste (Stowe), a park on the edge of Epicurania, they find truffles with the help of truffle hounds. Eventually they return to Epicurania, passing a gardener who thinks his son Saidon (Adonis) has gone mad for having fallen in

love with a statue of Venus. They arrive at the palace triumph-
antly laden with food, to be greeted by a municipal party and
much cheer. The Prince lays out a magnificent leopard skin, the
Dowager Duchess dies of overindulgence, the Captain marries
the maid and Epicurania becomes a world centre of gastronomy.

In one land the party fails to notice that a boy playing with a
hoop has fallen into the river, his arms outstretched; he cries in
vain for help as he drowns. Later, on a cliff, they pass a dilapidated wooden cross, placed in memory of an earlier, fallen
traveller. They replace the cross with the urn that they have found
and inscribe on it the initials 'D. A. W'. This was Rex's tribute to
his brother Denny and a memento mori, a reminder for the viewer
that death exists, even in Arcadia.

It was typical that he should depict himself travelling through
Epicurania on something so prosaic as a bicycle. Rex had been
catapulted into society. As a bright new star of the art world, he
was inundated with social invitations and commissions from the
beau monde: 'he has so many he knows not how to fit them in
without making people wait too long'.[29] But it had all been so
sudden, and whenever he could, Rex escaped London for the
balm of Edith's indulgent company and the cherished 'cosiness' of
the Daye House. Though he enjoyed the glitter and the parties,
the madcap saturnalia that was life in London did not altogether
suit him. He felt out of his depth financially and perhaps he was
still a little socially unsure.

In October, Edith wrote that Rex was 'so happy to be here,
throwing himself about on chairs saying how he adores it' and
'wants to laugh all the time'.[30] Later, in December, he was 'in
anguish' over the prospect of the Fonthill ball which they were
both due to attend that evening: 'He says he dreads going out so
much that he is wretched all the day before. If he is going to a
party – says that he only likes coming to me here – or going out
with me in London – of course I <u>adore</u> this. All day he exclaims
against "these monsters" who are coming tonight to disturb our
peace'.[31] No doubt this was said, in part, to please Edith but Rex

knew that with her he did not have to play the bon viveur. '<u>No visits I love more than these to you</u>', he told Edith in a letter, and underlining it, for emphasis.[32]

Wilton seemed entirely removed from Rex's life in London. There he could retreat into a gentle, almost childish world of imagination, slipping into the 'dream condition' with Edith, his loving comrade, beside him. One afternoon in September they walked to the temple on the estate: 'Rex's passion, he wants to decorate the room when they restore it – and in that ashen atmosphere he moved like a flame, lighting it with his vision'.[33] Another night they walked about on the downs watching the moon 'glinting thro the trees. We were suddenly standing in the Fairy Ring', she wrote, 'weirdly shaped toadstools, like mad bits of the moon and all about were twisted crooked gnarled little hawthorns which we thought were witches. Owls . . . all round, but at first no nightingales. At 10.30 they began. A miracle in the dark silence.'[34]

There were days when Rex and Edith would climb into her car and motor off together through the Daye House gates and beyond the sheltering walls of the park, into the depths of the Wiltshire countryside. Edith was taking Rex on expeditions to all the places that she loved to visit in the county she adored. Humming with the primitive and mythical energies that Edith claimed to sense, Wiltshire is an ancient, rolling landscape of hidden combes; green ridges and high chalkland; laced with trout streams, bubbling springs and clear-running rivers lined with willows. Vast swathes of smooth, empty land lie beneath a huge empty sky; a sacred, immemorial solitude where time passes like shadows over the downs. Layer upon layer of history are as tangible and integral to the landscape as the seams of chalk within it: ancient, pagan, Christian. It is the land of Salisbury Plain, of standing stones, burial grounds, abbeys and towering cathedrals. The land of Old Sarum and Camelot and the royal hunting ground of Cranborne Chase. It is the land of 'moonraking', of eccentric William Beckford's Gothic fantasies at Fonthill; the lakes, temples and grottoes of the man-made Arcadia at Stourhead; of the picture-perfect village of Lacock and of majestic Longleat, the seat of Edith's friend, the Marquess of Bath. On summer nights Edith would drive up to Grovely Wood, high on a chalk ridge above Wilton, a royal hunting ground haunted by four sisters murdered as witches, to listen for the sound of nightingales. They motored down roads that Edith knew to be old cattle droves, Tudor highways, market roads or dry, flinty footpaths that followed the long curves of the downs. Sometimes they left the road entirely. On sightseeing trips with her father they always had to follow a planned route, but Edith preferred to explore. Many years later she would write in her memoirs:

> Rex Whistler is the perfect travelling companion. He follows no prearranged plan: he is ready to respond to any unexpected invitation. When one drives out in the morning with a certain destination in mind, Rex soon wearies of the important road which leads to it and is attracted by some side road which appears to meander nowhere in particular . . . So much of the day is spent in these unpremeditated détours, that night is sometimes falling by the time we reach our ultimate destination; and this adds immensely to the first view of a very beautiful scene.[35]

Sightseeing was suddenly fashionable in the 1920s as Britons sought to outrun the ever-expanding urban sprawl and 'rediscover' the countryside in their shiny new cars: modernity heralding nostalgia. It gave rise to a boom in the sale of tourist maps, guidebooks and topographical writing. In *Vogue* in October 1928 a page entitled 'The lure of the open road and English wayside – sport, speed, motors and motorists' featured photographs of chic people beside their elegant cars.[36] But the fashion for sightseeing didn't inspire Edith; she had always done it, although it could well have motivated Rex's expedition around the walls of the Tate refreshment room. Edith believed that the landscape would only yield up its secrets to the initiated few and believed herself one of them. Edith as guide, vividly conjuring up the spirit of a place as they motored along in her Baby Austin, had a perfect companion in Rex, whose imagination was brimming with fresh ideas and images as he sat snugly on the seat beside her. In November, Edith wrote in her diary: 'We are entirely in sympathy and adore each other'.[37]

8: Revels

❖

Strange creatures – with just a few feathers where brains should be.

Lytton Strachey to Roger Senhouse, 27 October 1927

A passer-by walking beside the River Avon near Wilsford, one morning in October 1927, would have been forgiven for thinking that they had stepped back in time. Perhaps they had stumbled into a time slip, one worthy of the Misses Moberly and Jourdain, or more prosaically, that they had chanced upon one of the countless costume pageants that seemed to keep high society occupied in these parts. That is, of course, unless they happened to subscribe to the *Tatler*, or if they knew who it was that owned the chequered stone manor house at the top of the lawn on the opposite bank. Perhaps then they would know of Mr Tennant's exploits and the scene would have come as no surprise.

Ranged along a rustic wooden bridge that spanned the river, a group of seven young people dressed in the garb of eighteenth-century gallants playing at shepherds were adopting poses with varying degrees of self-consciousness. The water was motionless beneath them, reflecting the louring autumn sky, and the riverbanks were a barren tangle of rushes and weeds. The scene was one of rococo splendour, transposed to the damp south Wiltshire countryside, and as alien to that landscape as the emerald-coloured lizards that were now and then spotted in the surrounding fields, having escaped from Stephen's reptilliary.

It was not immediately obvious whether these giddy Meissen figurines were men or women; all had painted faces and cropped, side-parted hair; all wore billowing blouses. Some were perched on the bridge's handrail, others leant against it. Below the bridge a footman was taking photographs. Now and then one of the performers appeared to be orchestrating the group, dashing down to look through the camera's viewfinder before returning to his perch on the bridge. They held their poses. The shutter snapped.

Days like this were rare for Stephen. Now he was often confined to his bed, albeit perfectly coiffed and wearing smart pyjamas, with his paints and poetry scattered all about him. Though he'd been declared the brightest of his bright young friends, in reality he was spending more time in enforced exile in the country than glittering around Mayfair. But rather than missing out on society, he now invited it to come to him, at Wilsford.

That weekend in mid-October, Stephen gathered friends for a house party dedicated to fancy dress. The guests included Rex, Cecil, Osbert Sitwell, his brother Sacheverell with his Canadian wife Georgia, Zita and Baby Jungman, Christabel McLaren (later Lady Aberconway) and William Walton. Also invited was Siegfried Sassoon, the celebrated war poet and pacifist. The first evening, at dinner, Stephen sat beside Sassoon. Later some of the group dressed as nuns and later still they danced in pyjamas to a gramophone. 'The weekend at Wilsford will be deliriously amusing', Osbert had promised Sassoon, who wrote in his diary that night: 'It was very amusing and they were all painted up to the eyes, but I didn't quite like it'.[1]

Stephen and Cecil had planned an elaborate group photography session, involving various tableaux in which they were to imitate the *fêtes galantes* in the paintings of Lancret, Watteau and Fragonard. The next morning Stephen, Cecil, Rex, Walton, Sacheverell and Georgia Sitwell and the Jungman sisters dressed in the costumes that had been acquired especially for the occasion – buff canvas breeches, long white stockings, plain or floral calico jerkins and frilly, high-collared silk blouses and silk cravats. They powdered their faces, lined their eyes with kohl and carefully painted their lips. Out in the garden Stephen arranged the group, Cecil positioned the camera and William the footman pressed the shutter. Adopting their ancien-régime attitudes they posed for pictures on the bridge, beside a haystack, and upon the leaf-strewn lawn, with baskets of artificial flowers arranged about them. There were individual portraits too: Cecil and Stephen duelling daintily with foils and Rex, a lovesick troubadour, playing a guitar while reclining in the long grass of a wooded bank.

Inspired by the commedia dell'arte, the *fêtes galantes* paintings of the eighteenth century were frivolous and irreverent. They represented artistic freedom, expressing a culture of pleasure and self-indulgence, a shift from warfare to love, a celebration of the libertine spirit of the age. It is unsurprising that the style was appropriated by the Bright Young People, and that Harlequin and Pierrot, both stock characters of the commedia, made frequent appearances at their fancy-dress parties. In the original paintings rosy-cheeked maidens and their swains hold courtly conversations in Elysian Fields and make gentle love in the sylvan shade. But the photographs that they took that day in 1927 were a different matter. There is no courtship, no sensuality and certainly no sex. In fact there is no sense of a conversation at all between the androgynous gallants on the bridge; instead all is performance, aloofness and self-expression, rococo made modern.

'The Lancret Affair' as Sacheverell dubbed the day's proceedings, was Rex's 'dream condition' brought to life, a witty and achingly contemporary refashioning of history. Dressing as eighteenth-century courtiers who were themselves disguised as rustic shepherds, they were sophisticates playing innocents, in the Arcadian tradition. And it was only appropriate that this should all play out at Wilsford, a theatrical house of mock-rusticity and false antiquity, with its racquet court masquerading as cottages and its lawn disguised as a village green. Pamela had inherited her parents' romantic socialism and reinterpreted it as an Arts and Crafts fantasy; now, Stephen too was playing at pastoral with his friends on the lawn.

These photographs are perhaps the most iconic images of the 1920s *jeunesse dorée*. Taken only a year after the General Strike and two years before the start of a global depression, they represent a detachment from reality, a lack of political consciousness and an extravagance as blinkered and dangerously decadent as the artificial rusticity of Marie Antoinette's own Arcadian idylls. But that was the point.

Present that day but pointedly absent from the photographs was Siegfried Sassoon. Fazed by their childish frivolity, he lurked in the background, 'the tired and middle-aged author'.[2] But later that afternoon, after the bucolic gambolling was over, he drove some of the group to visit his friend Lytton Strachey at Ham Spray, his house near Hungerford, in the north-west of the county. Strachey was delightedly appalled by Stephen and his friends, describing them in a letter as 'strange creatures – with just a few feathers where brains should be', adding, 'though no doubt Siegfried is rather different'.[3]

Strachey might well have dismissed the dressing-up but Edith, who dined at Wilsford that evening, was indulgent as usual, recording in her diary that they had all donned elaborate outfits for 'a hectic lovely dinner party': 'Rex and Cecil clothing me in coat and trowsers striped gold and coloured tissue with long fringed sleeves and a little cap covering the head made of gold beads. Hours passed and the guests grew hungrier and hungrier while Stephen still dressed'. Georgia Sitwell was dressed as a young lover of Catherine the Great, Baby Jungman wore silver trousers and a tunic, Zita refused to dress up 'tho' terrified at not having' and Cecil 'looked a pretty creature in gold and rose coloured gauzy tissue with a rose coloured cloak and lots of rouge'. Eventually the Sitwell brothers, Sassoon and Walton led the flagging guests into the hall and offered them champagne. At a quarter to ten a message came from Stephen telling his guests to begin dinner. Stephen at last made his grand entrance dressed in a white Russian suit, a bandeau around his head and a silver train flowing behind him. 'He moves like Mercurius', Edith wrote, 'with winged feet'. Walton, dressed at his own request as an Indian and pretending not to know English, played waiter for the evening. Later they played hide-and-seek in the dark: 'everyone was too frightened to move, so there was no hiding or seeking, only the faint sound of slow footsteps, breathing, and whispering'.[4]

Somewhere in the darkness that night, Stephen was attempting to seduce Sassoon who, at forty-one, was nearly twenty years older. And though he was, as Lytton Strachey had assumed, 'rather different' from the bright young butterflies, though he had disapproved of all the frolicking on the lawn that day, Sassoon in turn was finding himself attracted to Stephen. In the early hours of the next morning the two men drove to Stonehenge and didn't return until dawn. Stephen was 'simply intoxicating my senses', Sassoon later wrote.[5]

Sassoon was born in 1886, the middle of three sons of Alfred and Theresa Sassoon. The Sassoons were Sephardic Jews, originally from Baghdad, merchant bankers known as 'the Rothschilds of the East'. Alfred deserted the family home when Sassoon was a small boy. Soon afterwards he died, leaving Theresa, a smothering mother, to bring up the three boys at their charmless Gothic mansion in the Weald of Kent. Sassoon was educated at Marlborough and Cambridge, which he left without taking a degree. He then set out to pursue a simple life, hunting, playing cricket and writing passable pastoral poetry, a life that was interrupted by the outbreak of the First World War. He joined up on the first day, became a distinguished officer and was awarded the Military Cross for bravery. He lost his younger brother at Gallipoli and witnessed the horrific first day of the Somme. As the war dragged on his patriotic eagerness changed to bitterness. He turned against the bloodbath of the war and began to write the powerful, compassionate, anti-war poems that would make him famous. Encouraged by Lady Ottoline Morrell, Bertrand Russell and the pacifists at Garsington Manor, he renounced his commission and protested against the war in a letter to *The Times* that was read out in Parliament. Rather than being court-martialled he was diagnosed with shell shock and was sent to Craiglockhart, a hospital for neurasthenic officers near Edinburgh. There he received psychoanalytic treatment from Dr William Rivers and befriended the awestruck young poet Wilfred Owen. 'My wound is healed,' he exclaimed, 'but my soul is scarified for ever.'[6] In 1918 he voluntarily returned to the front.

After the war he became for a short time literary editor of the socialist newspaper the *Daily Herald*. But Sassoon was a man of many contradictions. At heart profoundly conservative and a snob, he was both a war hero and a pacifist, and though he appeared to conform to a hearty, masculine stereotype, he was both homosexual and a poet. While he hankered after the leisured life of an English gentleman, he was half-Jewish, and he revelled in society and the company of urbane aesthetes like Osbert Sitwell. All these contradictory impulses jostled for supremacy, a struggle that would remain unresolved for most of his life.

At the time he met Stephen, Sassoon had a mixed reputation, revered in some quarters as a vocal pacifist and a visionary poet, feted by literary society, and acknowledged as a brave soldier, and yet vilified in others as an anti-Establishment troublemaker. In the spring of 1927 his aunt died, leaving him a quarter of her fortune. He was free to dedicate his days to poetry and foxhunting and his life oscillated between the country and London, where he pursued relationships with a string of lovers. His friends the Sitwells meanwhile were particularly keen that he should meet Stephen Tennant and engineered several opportunities. Sassoon took the bait and Stephen immediately expressed a desire to see him again. So he came to Wilsford. And soon they were lovers.

Edith Sitwell dubbed them 'the old earl and little lord Fauntleroy' and they were, on the face of it, an unlikely pair, one a painted narcissus and the other a courageous soldier, whose poetry had railed against the horror and injustice of the war.[7] Sexual attraction, however, is not as simple as ideological compatibility. Rugged, misanthropic, melancholic, with a suggestion of latent wildness lurking behind his neat, ascetic demeanour,

Sassoon was everything that Stephen was not. But he was also handsome, heroic and experienced, and had lived another life; he would become a father figure for fatherless, mollycoddled Stephen. Perhaps most importantly he was a famous and respected poet, who moved in the loftiest literary circles. Above all else Stephen admired a life dedicated to creativity and beauty.

Stephen 'symbolises all that I should ordinarily regard as idle and pleasure-loving and self-indulgent', Sassoon wrote in his diary, 'yet he does it all with such grace, and I have realised more and more that he is essentially childish, in spite of his veneer of sophistication'.[8] Sassoon felt a strong sexual attraction to Stephen. And he was youthful, he seemed untainted and fresh; his child-like, intense enjoyment of things was infectious to the war-wearied poet. The snob in Sassoon also delighted in his aristocratic status. But there was something more. Stephen was intelligent and witty and in spite of almost no formal schooling he was perceptive about literature. And perhaps Stephen's tuberculosis, that most decadent and romantic of diseases, redolent of imminent tragedy, inspired protective feelings in Sassoon. It was a role that allayed some of the misgivings he felt about his homosexuality.

Sassoon's comment about that first night at Wilsford, that he 'didn't quite like it' although he could see that it was 'very amusing', was, as one of his biographers writes, 'an ambivalence that would characterize his whole relationship with Stephen'.[9] But for now that didn't matter to Sassoon. He had been at work on a book that he had begun towards the end of the previous year, which would become *Memoirs of a Fox-Hunting Man*, a semi-autobiographical novel, a rangy, Proustian recollection of his passage from childhood to manhood. But his writing had ground to a halt. For now his growing obsession with Stephen, his 'Stephenitis', as he called it, eclipsed everything else in his life.[10]

9: 'Adored Sons'

❖

It is unbelievable that these two barn door fowls can have hatched this wild swan.

Edith Olivier's Diary, 3 May 1929

'Cocktails will be served' assured the invitation to the exclusive private view of Cecil's first one-man show on 23 November. Edith joined the celebrities, society luminaries, gossip columnists and art critics swarming up the stairs and into the throng at the Cooling Galleries on New Bond Street. 'The occasion was certainly one of *the* events of the week,' declared the *Sketch*, 'for Society flocked to admire presentations of itself and its friends. Indeed the gallery was so full of distinguished people that it was difficult to see the wood for the trees'.[1]

The *Lady* spotted Stephen in the company of Oswald Mosley and Oliver Messel, and indeed his presence and his portraits were much noted by reporters. He had lent a recently completed bust by Jacob Epstein to sit alongside his photographs in order to offer a three-dimensional perspective on his beauty. The Sitwell brothers were there too. Osbert had written the foreword to the catalogue, but their sister Edith, whose portraits were perhaps the most discussed, was enigmatically absent. 'The chosen few', noted the *Sunday Times*, 'were privileged to wander round the rooms, waving a cocktail glass in one hand and one of those Tunbridge Wells wafers, than which there is no more fashionable food stuff today, in the other'.[2]

The show featured Cecil's photographs and drawings of the

most talked-about actresses and society ladies. Tilly Losch, the Viennese dancer, was photographed in a tree trunk. Cecil's sisters Baba and Nancy (whom he was always keen to promote) featured prominently. The scandalous American film star Tallulah Bankhead posed as Sarah Bernhardt and there was a photograph of Freda Dudley Ward, the mistress and confidante of the Prince of Wales. Others of Pamela Grey, Ottoline Morrell, the Duchess of Marlborough and more titled ladies of varying ranks lined the walls. '[Cecil] is not a great artist and is of the moment, ephemeral, but very gifted. His photographs brilliant. All the world was there', Edith wrote in her diary.³ 'We were greeted with many repetitions of the familiar "Too marvellous" and "Divine"', commented the man from the *Tatler,* and 'not to have seen his exhibition is to own yourself a nobody', the *Sunday Herald* declared.⁴

The following day Edith wrote to Cecil congratulating him on his success and wishing upon him correspondingly lavish financial rewards. Money was never far from her mind these days. 'I must send one word to tell you how <u>really</u> impressed I am by your exhibition', she wrote to Cecil. 'Your sure hand – your brilliant wit – your individual and amusing point of view as well as the decorative beauty of your pictures. I knew your photographs, the drawings were a revelation.'⁵

Edith was not alone in her praise. For the most part the tabloids and the broadsheets alike hailed Cecil's show as a sensation and praised the work for its freshness and innovation. Naturally there were a few voices of dissent and his show ignited a debate about the value of photographs as art. 'I cannot see how a young society man has contributed anything of importance to modern photography by including in his exhibition portraits of people seen upside down, or showing both profiles at once', wrote an evidently unimpressed 'O.R.' in a letter to the *Daily Express.*⁶ But the art critic of the *Sunday Herald* wrote that he 'found the work of this clever and unconventional artist . . . very refreshing after a view the day before of some chocolate-box family portraits by Laszlo, for so long the pet portrait-painter to Society with a big, big S.'⁷

The unveiling of Rex's (unfinished) murals at the Tate on 30 November was a worthier affair than the cocktail-soaked whirligig that was Cecil's private view. Edith was there, along with Christabel McLaren, Lady Lavery and Edith and Osbert Sitwell (whose presence it seemed was a necessary endorsement at any cultural gathering) but instead of a sparkling assortment of socialites there were the altogether more sober figures of Ramsay MacDonald and George Bernard Shaw. With Lord D'Abernon, Henry Tonks and other grandees from the art world, and alongside scores of journalists, business managers of hotels, theatres, banks and railway companies, they strolled along the red carpet that led into the basement of the gallery and into the refreshment room, to listen to speeches promoting the renaissance of public art.

Rex was led onto a platform 'like a lamb to the slaughter, pale and very calm and still', observed Edith, there to sit sheepishly beside Lord D'Abernon, chairman of the trustees of the gallery, who was to unveil the murals, and Bernard Shaw, who had won the Nobel Prize for Literature two years earlier and whose presence at the Tate, it was hoped, would give a lofty, impassioned edge to the plea for British Art.[8] In unveiling the paintings D'Abernon described the murals, quoting Milton, as 'buxom, blithe and debonair' and said that it was necessary to educate the rich to give work to young artists.[9] And in a second *cri de guerre* to potential patrons, Shaw was, according to Edith:

> very funny and having at the rich, saying Rex was quite unlike the other Whistler, who was a <u>Gentleman Artist</u>, while Rex could be treated like the plumber, would touch his hat and call them 'Sir' and never be mistaken for the dukes and duchesses who came to luncheon, tho' he and his bag of tools might be sometimes in the way! Said the other Whistler <u>could not</u> have done Rex's paintings. (This R afterwards said, was 'very ambiguous').

Shaw told the audience that he personally could not afford to be a gentleman and that had been the key to his own success. It was a lesson that Rex did not heed, but it would have been well to do so.

> Tonks followed, speaking very affectionately of R and saying how he 'a dreamy creature' wandered into Gower Street one day with some drawings in his pocket and 'found' Tonks who did not therefore find him tho' he knew at once what a 'find' he was. R found all this much more shy-making than Shaw's gibes . . . A marvellous triumph for Rex though he afterwards said he felt it was 'a tragedy – not knowing how to live through the ordeal' . . . never was anyone so entirely simple and unaffected and real all through. It's a marvellous thing to be so truly a great genius and yet, at the same time, this gay spontaneous affectionate boy . . .

'Mrs Whistler', Edith noted, 'was rather hurt with Shaw I think for implying that her precious pet was not a gentleman . . . Saw Rex's father for the first time – a short dark secondrate man'.[10] It was not the first time that Edith had met Rex's mother, whom she had described dismissively earlier in the year as 'a woman in a background' and 'a pretty woman of the schoolteacher kind'.[11] It was a strange situation. Edith was only two years younger than Helen Whistler and had become Rex's best friend. It must have seemed that he had acquired for himself a substitute mother.

Though Edith's diaries are teeming with every detail of Rex's present life and his plans for the future, in those first years of their friendship there is little mention of his past, his family or his home. She invariably relayed conversations in detail in her diary, but if they talked about his family and his history during those evenings in the Long Room, it is telling that Edith chose not to record it. It was as if he had come to her as an orphan, a changeling with no past, a palimpsest onto which Edith would help to write a new life. Of course it may be that Rex chose not to discuss these things with her. Perhaps it suited him too.

Until Edith met Helen for the first time in June 1927, her diary makes no reference to either of his parents. And it is interesting that over two years had passed before Rex introduced Edith to his mother. Of whom was he ashamed – Edith or Helen – or was it merely circumstance that kept them apart?

For Edith, Helen was, and would remain, the focus of a simmering rivalry. In return, according to Laurence Whistler, Helen was jealous of the time that Rex spent with Edith, feeling that she had usurped her place in his heart. As for Harry Whistler, the snob in Edith found it hard to accept that her darling Rex had such a brusque, uncultured and common father. Her opinion of his parents did not improve on closer acquaintance. 'A man really of the lower classes. A shopman kind of man. He talks a lot and I think they are rather frightened of him . . . Rex <u>cannot</u> be his son', she wrote of Harry after an overnight stay with the Whistlers in 1929.[12] Two days after that she came to the conclusion that 'his home is cramping to his mind', adding that 'he adores his mother but she is <u>really</u> a kind pretty governess and his father is <u>terrible</u>, an awful little clerk with black hair and moustache, laying down the law about trivialities. Rex perfect to them both and has space to work there as there are several little sitting rooms . . . It is unbelievable that these two barn door fowls can have hatched this wild swan.'[13]

Rex, she felt, was a product of her influence, more her son than theirs. No doubt she kept these thoughts from him, confining them to the pages of her diary, which no one, not even Mildred, had ever been allowed to see. And it wasn't just Rex. When Edith met Cecil's sister Nancy, she was unimpressed by her 'affecting society airs', adding: 'Cecil is indeed a marvel to spring out of his very commonplace family'.[14] It was one thing for these young men to blaze a glorious trajectory out of the middle classes and into society but it seems that their families were not welcome to join them.

Laurence Whistler later wrote that Rex did not guess the vehemence of Edith's thoughts about his parents but that 'it merely annoyed him . . . to hear her putting on for our father's benefit the special joviality she kept for bluff farmers'.[15] For their part, Helen and Harry 'found Edith surprising, decidedly eccentric, and quite comic . . . Under easy talk they were of course uneasy with this intellectual friend from the grand world; were trying hard to raise their customary level of intercourse, and treat each other's notions seriously'.[16]

Laurence himself fared a little better. In August 1927 Rex had arrived at the Daye House for a weekend bringing with him his brother, then fifteen years old and on holiday from Stowe for the summer. He was 'rather a dear little boy', Edith decided, 'with white face, dark eyes and a nose'.[17] Laurence joined in with all the things that Edith and Rex usually did alone. They went to Netherhampton to paint pictures of the Newbolts' house, 'funny little Laurie crouched about like a goblin'; they spent an afternoon 'drowsily pretending to read' in the Daye House garden and in the evening after dinner Edith read de la Mare aloud. They drove out to Netheravon Down, 'careering over turf like tanks ourselves' to watch 'an enormous display of tanks, armoured cars and other mechanical weapons' which had been put on for the benefit of 'Winston' [Churchill], then Chancellor of the Exchequer in Baldwin's government.[18] And on the final day of their visit Edith wrote:

> After luncheon we made our last Beauty Pilgrimage – to the Park School – and then I drove them to Salisbury station and returned very sad. I suppose Rex has faults, but I can't find them and when I drive with him I have the feeling I had with Mildred – nervous of accident, with such precious freight. When I drive alone I don't care what happens. He has everything I want – genius, brilliance, intense interest in things of the mind, lovely looks, funniness, the power of creating new beauty and <u>shewing</u> it, tenderness, affection, and real goodness, sincerity and truth![19]

Laurence on the other hand was always made to feel like a pale reflection of his older brother when he visited the Daye House. Dining alone with him in 1930 at the Randolph in Oxford, where he was then a student, Edith wrote: 'He is far duller without Rex who gives him all his character'.[20] Laurence at the Daye House, with his older and greater claim on Rex's affections, disrupted the delicate illusion of her relationship with Rex. He represented Rex's other life and his real family. Writing Rex's biography years later, Laurence sought to redress the balance. Of that first visit, he remembered 'the light . . . truly spanking in the patrician trees', the Palladian Bridge 'loftily absorbed in some cool, exclusive day-dream'; and on the Sunday, en route to church, the facade of which he found 'more arrogant than elevating', the bells 'pealed out with all the mindless hilarity of a smart wedding'.[21] To Laurence, Wilton seemed theatrical and intimidating. And then there was Edith and the Daye House, and her talk of the beau monde which baffled the boy:

> That little house no bigger than our own; the servants pleasant country girls like our own; our hostess a country clergyman's daughter like our mother – it was surely the best possible introduction to social life for a childish boy who had never stayed away except with relations. All the same to a child brought up among the reticences of a more middle-class mode of life there was something to alarm in the casual freedom of the aristocratic one, long since adopted by Edith, who anyway was rather alarming in her own right. It was then that I first heard the impressive name Lebohmord, some-times shortened to 'Bohmord', though never, I think, by Edith; but I was doubtful of the spelling, for it was said in such a quick, dismissive and superior tone.
>
> Why did Mr Hicks call Edith Edith, when Edith never called him anything but Mr Hicks?
>
> 'Well, I suppose he likes to think he's in Lebohmord.'
>
> So it was some kind of club or society, but surely one would know if one belonged to it? Apparently not. A little later it seemed to me that the name was not often mentioned by those who undoubtedly did belong, which made me wonder whether Edith was not in some sense a country or associate member.[22]

Over the years, Laurence would be welcomed at the Daye House, and though he grew closer to Edith, he was never allowed to enter the intimate, imaginative world of Rex and Edith's friendship. He never became one of Edith's 'adored sons', as she called them; he would make his own way in the world and he remained on the periphery of that colourful circus in Wiltshire.[23] With fascination, disdain and perhaps a little envy, he would remain an outsider, looking in.

10: Bird Songs

❖

'Surely you can see all those towers and spires?'

Edith Olivier, *Without Knowing Mr Walkley*

'I have liked 1927', Edith wrote in her diary on the last night of the year, her fifty-fifth birthday. 'I saw Florence for the first time and crossed the Alps, published my first book and have really had a success – tho' <u>not</u> financially. Made friends with Cecil and have got to know several interesting new people and Rex has become famous by finishing this big work. He and I have deepened our friendship.' But she added a cautionary note: 'unless I can earn more I shall be really bankrupt this coming year. I rather dread 1928'.[1]

A few days later the Thames broke its banks, flooding the basements of riverside buildings in London. Several people were killed. Of immediate concern to Edith, however, was the news that the Tate's basement had been engulfed with water and that Rex's mural had not escaped: 'Talked to Rex on the telephone. He says he went there yesterday. The scene of desolation in Tate Gallery indescribable'.[2] Luckily, there was little damage as the mix of oil colours and turpentine he had used rendered it waterproof.* But it was an inauspicious start to the year.

Later that month saw the first night in Salisbury of *The*

---

* According to his brother, Rex was still planning to complete his scheme at the Tate but by the time structural repairs had been done he had moved on to other work. 'By then the impetus had decayed', Laurence writes (L & U p.113). It remains incomplete to this day.

Monkey's Paw, in which Edith was playing an old woman, a role she hated. She complained that there was hardly anyone in the audience but a few local friends who had come to watch, including 'the "Upper ten" Herberts', as she called them. Aside from the play the next few weeks perhaps allayed Edith's prophetic New Year's Eve diary entry. She went to Wilsford to watch the 'silly' films they had made at the house party in October: 'Stephen always looks beautiful . . . Cecil knows exactly how to make his effect – and looks very lit. Osbert and Sachie v. good at character parts and so – to my surprise is Willy Walton – who is really a comic lead.'[3] And towards the end of the month Rex came to stay. They went sightseeing in Bath and Rex, who thought it rivalled Florence, was overjoyed by the Pulteney Bridge and Prior Park.

Less than a week after the unveiling of his Tate murals Rex had received an invitation to the British School in Rome, not as a conventional prize-winner but as a guest of the Chairman Lord Esher, with free passage, studio and accommodation. He was invited to stay as long as he wished. In December he had written:

> My Darling Edith
>   . . . think of seeing Tivoli for the first time!! I don't know <u>what</u> I shall do, when I find myself standing (or sitting!) and looking at (and I hope, sketching) the immortal waterfalls and grottoes and treading the ground hallowed by Claude and Poussin, Piranesi and I don't know <u>how</u> many other Immortals. This letter sounds just like a débutante's, written the day before 'coming out'!
> Much love Rex.[4]

He planned to leave in April.

February was one of those months that epitomized Edith's life. She was busy trying to finish *As Far As Jane's Grandmother's* and preparing lectures for girls' schools. Then she was asked by the Bishop of Salisbury to be secretary of his Women's Diocesan Council, a post he likened to being a lay female archdeacon; and she was elected to the National Council of Women which campaigned on social welfare and philanthropic issues and the promotion of rights, education and economic independence for women. Its members were encouraged to become active citizens and to involve themselves in local politics but it sought to avoid being labelled as a feminist organization. This meant that it could engage with often divisive issues such as divorce and birth control without being seen as radical. It was akin to the Women's Institute, of which Edith was a devoted member. Edith's branch of the Institute met weekly at Quidhampton to discuss community issues and to campaign for improvements to housing and utilities. It also encouraged its members to stand in local elections. The WI too actively avoided allegiance with feminism and in doing so made itself more appealing to the average (usually conservative and middle-class) woman who didn't want to be seen as a radical but who wanted to become engaged in the world beyond the domestic realm. It also helped to legitimize these associations in the eyes of society, drawing women in from the radicalized margins of politics. This was particularly pertinent after 2 July 1928, when the Representation of the People (Equal Franchise) Act was passed in Parliament, finally giving women electoral equality with men.

That same year the writer Vera Brittain lamented that feminists were considered to be 'spectacled, embittered women, disappointed, childless, dowdy and generally unloved'.[5] It would have been easy for Edith to fit into this mould, but she continually fought against the stereotype. She had never identified herself as a feminist and was critical of the drastic measures taken by the suffragettes, but she had always had strong political convictions, and had always been and would become increasingly engaged with local issues and politics. For many years she had been a member of the Conservative Association, attending their conferences in London, and had even held a Conservative summer school at Wilton House in 1923.

Towards the end of February Edith travelled to Cornwall to give her series of lectures. On Ash Wednesday, 'one of those blazing Cornish days which turn February into June', she drove out of town in her Austin.[6] Standing on the cliff at Land's End she looked out across the Atlantic. Miles out at sea she saw a town, 'a jumble of towers, domes, spires and battlements' – it was clearly an important place. At first she thought it must be the Scilly Isles and enquired of a coastguard.

'"There is no town there," he told her. "Only the sea."

"Surely you can see all those towers and spires?" she replied.'[7]

He could not. And though Edith realized that the bright winter sun must have conjured up a mirage on the horizon, she nurtured the hope that she had seen a vision of the Arthurian city of Lyonesse, shrouded in myth and mist, sunk beneath the waves off the Cornish coast, 'the phantom circle of a moaning sea', as Tennyson put it.[8]

A few days after Edith had returned from Penzance, Rex telephoned to tell her that Heinemann had rejected their 'Guide to the Duchy of Epicurania' with 'most crushing criticism'.* Perhaps the success of *The Love-Child* had made her a little too self-confident. Edith and Rex had hoped it would be seen as they saw it, as a *jeu d'esprit*, a children's book for adults. But Heinemann thought it a rather smug in-joke, 'involved, stupid, bad and likely to damage Rex's lovely drawings'.[9] Playful whimsicality had succeeded on the walls of the refreshment room but didn't translate into a book. 'I feel quite humiliated and so depressed', Edith wrote.[10] Rex sent a consolatory letter, with an angel weeping large tears down the back of the envelope: 'Darling Edith, I'd been feeling so confident of its acceptance hadn't you? Had we not been so <u>encouraged</u> I don't think it would have been so <u>devastating</u>.'[11] To add to Edith's misery her brother Frank was dying of cancer. She went up to London to see him at their sister Mamie's house and he died peacefully a few days later with Edith beside him.

Still in London later in the month Edith went with Rex to a 'marvellous' Dürer exhibition at the Colnaghi Gallery in Mayfair

---

* It was eventually published by the Tate Gallery in 1954.

and afterwards they drank hot chocolate and talked of Rome. Three days later he was gone. 'I shall miss him dreadfully', Edith wrote in her diary that night.[12]

But she was not alone for long. That afternoon she went to the cinema with Cecil. They dined at Boulestin in Covent Garden, which Cecil thought 'the prettiest restaurant in London'.[13] After supper they went to the theatre with Sassoon and Stephen to watch Noël Coward in S. N. Behrman's *The Second Man*. Cecil had brought a suitcase to the theatre containing a fancy-dress costume that he planned to slip into later in the evening. After the play Edith had to dissuade him from changing in a cab shelter and instead took him back to her sister's house. Once transformed they both set out for a 'bottle party' that Stephen was throwing with some friends, Cecil looking 'enchanting' in a dark blue military uniform from the 1840s and Edith in a 'very becoming' combination of evening dress and hussar's hat. The party was held in a maisonette belonging to Olivia Wyndham, one of the Bright Young Things and a good friend of Brian Howard. Edith recorded it all in her diary:

> Two tiny rooms and 200 guests at least – an extraordinary scene. Dazed drunken faces slowly rotating in a room tightly packed and where dancing was really impossible. A mixture of fancy and ordinary dress. Upstairs people lay talking in heaps on the floor, as there were no seats. Here and there a vivid face shone out. Stephen in huge gold earrings, as a sailor, wearing a succession of different coloured blouses. Oliver Messel, marvellous, painted as a Chinese mask . . . I knew lots of the abandoned guests and was very much amused tho' very frightened that I <u>must</u> end by being drunk as I knew not how potent the drinks might be. But I was brought back, quite sober, by Cecil at 3am.[14]

'What a night we had! I adored watching that party', she wrote to Cecil a few days later; 'the slow revolving of abandoned faces in that crowded little dance room. The heaps of promiscuous people on the floor upstairs. Oh dear that sounds very wicked and as if you and I ought not to have been here. But I hear it was even more "orgiastic" after we went so discreetly early'.[15]

In the months that followed, Edith spent more time alone with Cecil than she had before, getting to know him well. For the most part, she liked him. 'Your talk is as good as your photographs', she told him, 'and this is saying a great deal. It is such fun to hear you discussing people with equal ease from the points of view of Angel, Dog or Man. You <u>do</u> see all round them.'[16] She admired his sensitivity and his humour, and although she didn't think his talent compared to Rex's, Edith was impressed by his ability to get on in life. 'I always quote you to my slack and stupid friends', she had written to him in February, 'as one who <u>always brings things off</u>.'[17]

On 5 May Edith returned home and Cecil arrived later that afternoon. They sat in the garden until it grew dark and gossiped about their friends. After breakfast the following day Edith and Cecil went to the Rectory orchard to pick branches of cider apple blossom for Cecil to take back to London to use in photographs; all the time Cecil taking pictures of Edith amongst the branches. 'Your portrait of me picking apple blossom is a really successful one', she would write to Cecil a few days later when she received the prints, adding mischievously: 'but nevertheless I hope you will make something of the one with legs bare enough to make Captain [surname illegible] turn away his eyes.'[18] That night, after Cecil had left, she summed him up in her diary. 'One meets him on the surface, a surface of sharp incisive facets, sending off sparks and new lights on to what he touches . . . he has no affection I think, except for his sisters, but enjoys congenial society and indeed <u>any</u> society for he loves being able to criticise.'[19]

Later in the month a drawing of Edith appeared in *Vogue*, a product of Cecil's afternoon in the garden at the Daye House and his increasing fascination with her world. He now had a regular column, 'How One Lives from Day to Day', in which he regaled readers with anecdotes from his life amongst the beau monde. It was characterized by much dropping of names, most of them titled, as well as names of the nightclubs and restaurants that were fashionable that month. The text was accompanied by cleverly observed sketches of the society ladies who had recently crossed his path. There at the bottom of the page in the late May 1928 edition, along with Lady Evelyn Guinness and two debutantes (one of them Nancy Beaton 'in a fairylike frock'), sat Edith, a picture of contentedness and bucolic elegance, reclining in an enormous deckchair, her head held aloft as she peers down past a sharp and haughty nose at the embroidery in her lap. Beside her on a table stands a tea urn with a cup and saucer. She 'sits in the sun in Wilton Park' reads the description, 'doing her embroidery and wondering how the public will like the new novel which she is just finishing'.[20] 'Of course I glow with pride at being honoured by your drawing in Vogue', she wrote to Cecil the following day; 'the Pembrokes tell me it is very like me but I of course do not know that view of myself. I see you have taken an inch or two off my leg and put it on my nose – thus satisfying with the stroke of the pencil les Covenances and the spirit of caricature.'[21]

As with all his subjects, Cecil flattered Edith with his drawing, and with his attention. Their letters to each other were witty; with Cecil Edith could gossip about people they knew and people they didn't. Cecil's observations and comments were always amusingly on-point and needle sharp. Her friendship with Cecil was different from her relationship with Rex, shallower, less loving, but affectionate nonetheless. Although Cecil was a star of the London social scene he was determined to make an entrée into the grander circles of the country-house world that Edith inhabited. He knew that Edith could help him.

Edith encouraged and indulged Cecil, and later in the year when he began work on a book she helped him to write it. It was to be a collection of his pencil sketches along with critiques of the women he had photographed (or tried to photograph) over the previous two years. Discussing the book in a letter Edith offered lots of amusing ideas and suggested that he could find old poems dedicated to women with the same name as his subject. 'Chaste Dian' beside a picture of the celebrated beauty, Diana Cooper, she thought 'would be terribly funny'. 'I have got a very amusing idea for my next book – if I can bring it off – and wrote the first page yesterday', she added.[22]

Cecil would never rival Rex, who, a few months later, wrote to her lovingly from Rome:

> Most darling Edith
>
> How I <u>adore</u> Rome! and I do rather dread having to leave quite soon – until I think of all the Heavenly people and places I shall be seeing when I get back to England – 'that land so witchery-sweet'. And when I read your news that the <u>Temple has been perfectly restored</u> I really felt like packing <u>at once</u> and rushing off straight back to Wilton.
>
> . . . I owe you more than I could ever repay – as the stock phrase goes. Though I do mean to try and repay <u>something</u> of what I owe!!
>
> . . . I should so <u>adore</u> to be at the 'Temple-warming party' unless there are likely to be a lot of <u>tiresome</u> people at it. If so, we will have our own 'warming', very <u>secret</u> and <u>rustic</u> and deliciously pagan, with much red wine 'with beaded bubbles winking at the brim', and (<u>you</u> at any rate) 'with purple stained mouth'! . . .
>
> Much love Rex.[23]

Despite the critical success of *The Love-Child,* Edith continued to be disappointed that literary success did not automatically bring with it great financial rewards. In November 1927 she had received a cheque for the royalties due by the end of June that year. They had amounted to £17.5s.7d (about £920 in today's money). She was even more surprised that royalties from the American sale of 3,000 copies of the book yielded only £40 (about £2,126 today). It was not enough for her to live on, to pay the servants and to keep the car and the household running. And so the economies and the lectures continued.

On 8 May, the day after Cecil had left, Elinor Wylie arrived at the Daye House. She had brought with her a book for Edith to review, sent from New York by her husband, William Rose Benét. Benét, whom Edith had met at the Daye House in 1926, was a poet and the deputy editor of the *Saturday Review*, the American magazine which had enthusiastically reviewed *The Love-Child* and championed Edith as a novelist to watch. The book she was to review was *A Mirror for Witches* by Esther Forbes, a novel about Salem. 'I am deep in a book about witchcraft which is sent to me to review (oh how grand!)', she wrote to Cecil, 'and I am learning many malicious tricks'.[24] Now that she had established a literary reputation, she hoped reviewing would provide a means to supplement her income.

Edith had gradually warmed to Elinor Wylie since they had first met at Wilsford two years before. Since then Elinor had visited Edith in Wilton and she had stayed with Elinor at her rented house on Cheltenham Terrace in Chelsea. In July 1927 Elinor had given a 'delightful and interesting' dinner party for Edith but it was still with some trepidation that she was received at the Daye House in May 1928.[25]

In New York, Elinor was a literary celebrity; her poetry and historically inspired novels were extravagantly praised. She was friendly with Dorothy Parker and Aldous Huxley; W. B. Yeats admired her work, as did F. Scott Fitzgerald and Ernest Hemingway. Elinor was ethereally beautiful and tall, with copper-coloured hair and pale skin; she favoured dresses of clean-cut black or silver silk from Parisian couturiers and she was extremely vain. The first time Edith had seen Elinor she was shimmering down a staircase at Wilsford in 'a dress made of stiff shiny silk' that 'looked like frozen green water'.[26] She liked to create an effect whether in a room or a garden. Having walked with Elinor in the park at Wilton, Edith observed that 'Miss. W moves serenely through it sure that she contains within herself more perfect loveliness'.[27] Later, recalling her first glimpse of Elinor, and tempering somewhat the pertness of her original observation, Edith wrote:

It was beautiful, that appearance of hers, and consciously so. She loved beauty; sought it; created it; – in her person and her surroundings, as well as in her writing. It was, in a sense, the passion of her life. Hers was, throughout, the deliberate pursuit of a loveliness which she valued most, perhaps, when to others it might appear far-fetched and precious.[28]

Elinor was a highly romantic and changeable woman; she was obsessed with Shelley and claimed to have had a vision of him. Her delicate, sparkling poems were often compared with miniatures and likened to jewels. Her novels were fantastic and fanciful. *Mortal Image* was a fictional sequel to Shelley's drowning in the Mediterranean and *The Venetian Glass Nephew* tells the story of a cardinal who seeks a nephew to be his heir.* He stumbles upon the workshop of a glass blower who crafts a beautiful nephew out of glass. A beautiful woman falls in love with the glass nephew and when she realizes that he cannot return her love she decides that she must be turned into glass to be with him.

Elinor was as fragile as her poetry, and her life as melodramatic as her novels. In her diary, Edith called her 'a stormy petrel, looking lovely, clear cut and clean carved and in a black dress,' and continued: 'The talk <u>only</u> of herself and her writings'.[29] Elinor's vanity irritated Edith's friends and made her vulnerable to teasing. On Midsummer's Eve in 1927, Elinor had been a guest at a Wilsford house party. Late that night it was suggested that the party should drive up to Stonehenge. When they arrived Elinor, dressed in a silver lamé evening dress, was lifted up onto one of the stones to be worshipped as a moon goddess and began to recite her poetry to the worshippers at her feet. After a while she realized that she was the butt of a collective joke and was driven back to the house in tears. 'No one can tell what is going to send her into a frenzy of emotional offendedness!' Edith told Cecil.[30] But Edith liked Elinor. She admired her writing and Elinor's novels were

---

* *Mortal Image* was published in 1927 and *The Venetian Glass Nephew* in 1925.

almost certainly an inspiration for Edith's later novels. She enjoyed the breathless whirlwind of Elinor's conversation, she was always happy to talk about poetry and history, which Elinor adored, they often went sightseeing together and Edith would have been more sympathetic than most to a woman who believed that she had seen a vision of Shelley.

In 1910 Elinor had left her first husband and infant son and fled to England to live with a married man, Horace Wylie, who later became her second husband. Later, back in New York, she left Wylie for Benét, and they married in 1923. But that marriage was as unsuccessful as her previous two. Early in 1928 Elinor had returned to England alone. She was thrilled to be back in her little house in Chelsea. In London she fell in love again, with another married man, Henry de Clifford Woodhouse. After she arrived at the Daye House that day in May Elinor told Edith of the love affair. 'She is possessed by it,' Edith wrote in her diary.[31]

Later in the month Elinor was at Woodhouse's home when she fainted and fell down the stairs, having had a small stroke. She was already suffering from Bright's disease and the fall exacerbated its symptoms. She was also convinced that she was pregnant with Woodhouse's child. Arriving at the Daye House to stay with Edith in June, she was 'almost demented'. But gradually, looking out of the round window in the Porthole Room, 'her room in the trees' as she thought of it, she could see only green leaves and the fretfulness began to subside.[32]

That weekend Elinor sat in the Long Room and read her new love sonnets to Edith. They were full of silvery beech trees and drooping willows and evidently inspired by the Wiltshire landscape that she was coming to love. In pain, depressed, troubled by chronic headaches, dizziness and numbness, she often talked of suicide and when she wasn't writing about love she was writing on scraps of paper about Christianity, death and the afterlife, in mystical, metaphysical poems heavily influenced by Donne and Shakespeare.

Elinor had also written a series of poems that she called 'Bird

Songs', and she dedicated them to Edith to whom she had given handwritten copies. They were inspired by the pastoral charms of the Daye House. One of the poems she first entitled 'Holiday' and then changed to 'Little Prayer':

> My best content were death:
> Yet let me have
> A lightly taken breath
> Above my grave.
>
> Content I cannot win
> Save by that sleep,
> Yet count it folly and sin
> Living, to weep.
>
> Permit me, while I live
> Still to be gay,
> Till Thou consent to give
> True holiday.[33]

With 'beloved Edith', Elinor found some respite from the turmoil and sorrow that now almost entirely engulfed her life.[34] She had always considered England a haven and had first been drawn to Wiltshire because William Beckford had lived there – she had a penchant for eccentrics – but for her the Daye House and the countryside beyond it had become a sylvan retreat with, at its heart, a wise, sympathetic friend of profound faith. She decided to look for a suitable property nearby and soon found an Elizabethan cottage with mullioned windows at Chilmark, a village a few miles west of Wilton.

She planned to dedicate a book to Edith but in mid-October Elinor had a second stroke that left her partially paralysed. On 29 November she gave Edith lunch at Chilmark, her last day there before travelling first to London and then sailing on the *Aquitania* to New York, to spend a quiet Christmas with her husband. She planned to return to England permanently in the spring and Edith promised to come to Southampton to meet her off the boat. From

New York Elinor sent Edith several letters complaining that she felt unwell. The last of these was written on 16 December, a few hours before she died, suddenly and quietly of a stroke, at home. That day she had been preparing the manuscript of *Angels and Earthly Creatures*, a new book containing her latest poems including the love sonnets inspired by her last affair. She picked up a volume of Donne's poems and asked her husband for a glass of water. As he returned with it, she stepped towards him, said: 'Is that all it is?' and then fell dead on the floor in front of him.

Two days later when Kathleen brought up her breakfast tray, Edith glanced down to see that her newspaper had been folded at the second page. There she read with horror of Elinor's death. A few days later Edith wrote to Benét in New York. 'I have felt impelled to write something about Elinor. I give it to you to use as you like . . . I have written of her as I knew her, trying to convey something of the rarity of her nature.'[35] Edith's tribute would not appear in print until 1942 when Benét published a volume of Elinor's last poems. 'I hope it may remind [Edith] of the genuine and deep affection the poet had for her. To Elinor, Edith Olivier represented those noble and gallant qualities that adorn the England whose cause today is so utterly our own.'[36]

11: Król Dudziarz

❖

'I fancy there will be a boom in Whistler.'

Henry Tonks at the unveiling of Rex's murals at
the Tate in November 1927

The *Daily Mail* had hailed the Tate refreshment room as 'a dream of a tea room' on the day after Rex's murals were unveiled, declaring that 'the floodgates of fancy are opened and the waters leap into the air'.[1] Other reviews were equally enthusiastic. Edith gleefully recorded that the artist and critic William Rothenstein had commended Rex's work as 'witty and scholarly', which she thought 'perfect praise'.[2]

Lord D'Abernon's call to the rich in his speech at the Tate seemed to have worked. Soon Rex received his first private mural commission, a panel for the industrialist Sir Courtauld Thomson in the hall of his Buckinghamshire home, Dorneywood, a Queen Anne-style house, built in 1920.* He set to work in a style already evident in the Tate mural, a dynamic combination of flatness and depth, delicacy and solidity. Within an architectural trompe l'œil frame, which functions like the proscenium arch in a theatre, a red velvet curtain is tucked behind a bust of the mural's patron (a nod to classical tradition) to reveal a playful stage-set scene worthy of a comic opera. Beyond a black-and-white tiled and balustraded loggia where a dog sleeps peacefully in the shade and a

---

* Later, in 1943, Sir Courtauld Thomson presented the house to the nation for use as a country house for a Minister of the Crown.

squawking parrot swings in a gilded cage, a world, once removed from reality, reveals itself. A formal lawn, lined with statues, runs down to a hazy horizon strewn with Rex's customary style of feathery, Claude-inspired trees. Windsor Castle rises in the distance and the Wilton Column stands at the centre of the lawn in front of a loggia. To one side, an Edwardian couple is playing croquet. In the foreground a blonde, Botticelli-esque Flora clutches the hand of an attendant Cupid; having swept down from their perch atop the column, they beckon the viewer to enter the dreamscape.

The synthesis of historical periods and the intermingling of fantasy and reality recall the 'double strain, of the orthodox and the bizarre' that *The Times* critic had admired at the Tate. These caprices were becoming a key element of Rex's signature style, along with the use of statuary, heraldic motifs and diverting naturalistic details dotted here and there to keep the viewer intrigued and entertained.

Rex's style, with its spirited treatment of classical motifs, its innocence and its whimsicality, links directly to the mindset of the Bright Young People. His mural at the Tate had been hailed by Henry Tonks as 'the most amusing room in Europe'[3] and, in an *Architectural Review* article endorsing the 'Amusing' style, Osbert Sitwell had praised Rex's 'deft and light-hearted frescos' as embodying 'the criterion of our changed taste'.[4] His style was not modern in the conventional sense; there were no cool, sleek Art Deco lines. The knowing and gently mocking nostalgia of his work suited the cosmopolitan mood of his wealthy and aristocratic clientele. The purpose of a mural is to transform a room, to offer a false window onto an alternative reality; and to a generation that seemed to know that it was living on borrowed time, his fantasies charmed because they offered a glimpse of a kinder, more elegant world.

A large part of Rex's developing appeal, both artistically and socially, was that he and his art appeared to be one. The Rex Whistler who was being welcomed at luncheons, dinner parties and country weekends was beguilingly self-deprecatory, entertaining and rather shy. His beautifully illustrated and vehemently under-lined letters and his exuberant, exaggerated way of talking enchanted their recipients. He seemed to have sprung from the Arcadia that he depicted, he was Król Dudziarz on his bicycle. But the Rex Whistler who appeared to the world was, like his murals, part reality and part invention: a performance on a stage within a classical frame. And illusions are by their nature deceptive, even dangerous.

At Dorneywood, Rex added a self-portrait, a profile on a trompe l'œil medallion. It was an elaborate signature; just as many artists had done before him, Rex was claiming the work as his own, presenting himself not as an anonymous artisan but as an artist. In doing so he was defying George Bernard Shaw's sugges-tion that he was a jobbing painter. But in spite of his sudden success, Rex had begun to question the legitimacy of his work. There had been no struggle, no dingy garret but, thanks to Edith's intervention, an elegant studio in a Georgian house in Fitzroy Street. At the Slade Henry Tonks had encouraged him to focus on decoration and had put him forward for the Tate commission. But it is interesting to consider, had Rex not won the Tate commission or had he been tutored by someone less indulgent than Tonks, how his style might have developed. Perhaps he would have been a freer, more experimental artist. If he had never met Stephen or Edith, never seen the Palladian Bridge at Wilton, and if they had never introduced him to the aristocratic world that was becoming his milieu, for whom would he have worked and what might his influences have been?

Before the First World War British art had been influenced by continental movements such as Cubism and Futurism but the development of modernism had been stunted and reshaped by the war. Rex's work, with its nostalgic link to England's past and to the landscape, was as much a product of the increasingly insular, post-war artistic community as that of pastoral artists like Christopher Wood, Ben Nicholson, Paul Nash and Eric Ravilious. But that similarity was not enough to save Rex's reputation as a fine artist. 'Cecil admires beauty but has not got Rex's sensitiveness to it', Edith wrote in her diary in March 1928; 'he thinks R. not modern enough – too 18th century and that people like [Augustus] John would think him negligible because of this'.[5] But Rex continued to be wholly unconcerned by contemporary art. 'Had he not simply disregarded what had happened to art since *Les Demoiselles D'Avignon*? Well, yes, but he had found a manner and a public at once', his brother later wrote.[6]

Conservative and romantic, Edith encouraged those aspects of Rex's nature and his work. A few years later, after visiting an exhibition of paintings with Rex, Edith wrote that she had seen 'lots of <u>very bad</u> ones by Vanessa Bell and her friends'. She thought them 'meaningless and lacking in design which', she added, 'is what they aim at'.[7] There are, of course, many possible answers to questions about what his style might have been. Yet it is easy to imagine a different Rex, one who had been exposed to more contemporary influences, and was welcomed into the world inhabited by people like Christopher Wood, which centred on the Brasserie at the Café Royal – the heart of artistic bohemia – instead of the aristocratic one in which he found himself. But as his brother later wrote: 'I doubt if he ever entered the Fitzroy Tavern'.[8]

But in that other world, Rex was seen as an interior decorator. According to the design historian Anne Massey: 'Interior decoration never enjoyed the status of architecture or even interior design, being regarded as a branch of fashion.'[9] 'May they be called mural <u>paintings</u> instead of decorations?' Rex had asked Edith as he went over the manuscript for their *Guide to Epicurania*.[10]

There was a long tradition of artists who were muralists, from Giotto and Michelangelo to Diego Rivera and Stanley Spencer. But in England, with a few exceptions, usually religious ones, murals tended to be painted for commercial or wealthy private clients. They were ornamental and ephemeral. Rex's work offered a delightful reverie for the rich and aristocratic patrons who had come flocking as soon as the Tate murals began to make his name. A steady stream of visitors had come to watch Rex at work in the refreshment room. One dowager declared that his murals were 'Too, too divine!' and begged him to paint her on her bathroom wall.[11] Even Augustus John did not escape criticism when it appeared that he was concentrating his efforts too exclusively on lucrative society portraits. 'Rex was funny and farcical and also serious. He wants to do a lot of wall painting in his life. But <u>now</u> to have a rest from work done to order', Edith had noted in her diary before the unveiling of the Tate murals. 'Rex wishes to paint a lot at his whim and for the sake of studying what he wants to do'.[12] But it was wishful thinking on Rex's part. His course had been set.

Rex was 'very ashamed', as he confessed to Edith, 'of his delight in his studio and his joy in making it lovely'.[13] 'The serious artist', he told Edith, 'only wants <u>a room to paint in</u>, and wants to do nothing in it but paint'.[14] And despite or perhaps because of his success at the Tate, Rex wanted to be taken seriously. His choice of studio – in Fitzroy Street at the traditional heart of the artistic community – suggests that he wanted to identify himself with the art establishment. And he was now trying to develop his style, spending his time reading about architecture and filling his sketchbooks with notes on Andrea Palladio and studies of classical details. At Edith's suggestion he was also reading Vasari, Ruskin and Cellini. If classicism was to be his style, then he wanted to be a fluent classicist. But he was rarely satisfied. Stephen later recalled that Rex 'showed an almost exaggerated modesty about his own work. I think his extreme facility made him skeptical towards a talent which he wished to discipline'. The 'artist is a child of sorrow', he concluded.[15] And Rex continued to be unnerved by his rapid success and confided in Edith, she wrote in her diary:

> In the evening he told me of three miserable days . . . when he seemed to have begun with some sort of visions of the frightful miseries of people in the Slums. He broke down and

found himself crying and he could not forget it. It still haunts him and once again I know he feels he ought to give up all his art and go to work and live there. It's quite magnificent and I know not how to advise him, as though it is heroic but his art is heroic too and it is a sublime gift. But yet, why does he have these visions sent him? I so fear advising him against his real conscience but could one advise the sacrifice of that genius?'[16]

After the philanthropic Shadwell mural and the Tate refreshment room Rex's commissions were almost entirely from private patrons. There was nothing radicalized or politically engaged about his work and there was no railing against social injustice. Misgivings about the direction of his career nagged Rex for much of his life.

Glimpses of the melancholy aspect of his nature began to appear in Edith's diaries, an aspect which would assert itself more and more over the years; a longing for something indistinct and out of reach, a sense of diffidence, of dissatisfaction, of *et in Arcadia ego*. One January afternoon at the Daye House Rex had lain in bed drawing his own memorial urn. It was a stock classical motif and pleasing to draw, but for Rex, writes Laurence, 'the urn was more than an amusement'; that 'hollow-sounding symbol of mortality' for Rex 'could strike a chord of gravity and gaiety at once' and was 'heard often in his talk and sometimes in his work, a very English ambiguity of mood – equivocal as the look of English weather'.[17] And from Rome in May 1928 he wrote to Edith to say that he was dreading his birthday the following month. He thought twenty-three was 'a <u>horrible</u> age – no longer really young'. He was going to Capri, he told her, 'to drown all regrets in the Blue Grotto'.[18] At the top of the letter he had drawn a cartouche with Rome written within it, pierced by a rapier dripping with blood; beside it a rose sheds mournful petals. He was exaggerating, of course, tragicomic about his age and about his regrets. But as always with Rex, he was only half-joking.

Unsurprisingly perhaps, Rex and Edith frequently discussed

religion. For Edith it was a buffer against the miseries of life but faith offered Rex little comfort. For him, art was a religion, a tangible solace rather than an abstract concept. And Edith was saddened that he only half-believed in life after death. Perhaps Denny's death had put paid to any real faith Rex might have inherited as a young boy, whereas Mildred's death had, if anything, strengthened Edith's belief in the afterlife. Edith was convinced that Rex had been held back by his upbringing, by the idea of religion that he had inherited from his mother, although she doesn't say so explicitly:

> He persists in identifying Religion with the Church of England and thinks its only connexion with art is the banners and altar vases which he despises. Thinks Art is a Religion to the real artist . . . He is not metaphysical. In the back of his mind I see he <u>fears</u> religion, thinking that if he listened too closely to it, he would be told by his conscience that he ought to give up painting for good works and this he knows he couldn't do but to deny his conscience would make him forever uneasy. He must have imbibed a Puritan religion which is still his fundamental sense of God. He hasn't been able to accept a broader truer one and this from the feeling that if he did, it would really be making it easier for himself and pretending that painting was pleasing God while knowing it was pleasing himself.[19]

Edith continued to be adoring and wholly uncritical and her diary is littered with digressive encomia in praise of Rex and his talent. 'I love him very much', she had written in August, 'funny, earnest, brilliant, conscientious, loving, unexpected – oh so unexpected'.[20] And then later that month: 'Rex such an angel. I love him more and more. He seems to me quite without flaw and not only that but overflowing with charm, brilliancy, tenderness, sympathy and funniness. Added to this he is a real creative genius.'[21] In September 1928, she was driving with Rex and Laurence and crashed her car into the park wall. Although they would later laugh about it, at the time Edith was horrified:

> Then came a frightful thing. Tho <u>blessedly</u> also a salvation – we were driving to Wilton for matins in the rain when the car skidded violently, banged into the park wall and was broken literally into fragments. We were none of us hurt – unbelievable as we saw the wreckage. Laurie was frightened and faint and was knocked out for most of the day . . . Rex too angelic and thank GOD not injured – his valuable hand and arm not broken and he was so calm and serene and unselfish. They were both very concerned for <u>me</u>. Especially R of course . . . God has indeed <u>saved</u> us from great and sudden danger and I can't cease to thank Him for sparing Rex to the world and saving me from harming him.'[22]

Laurence recalled that Edith's first thought was for her beloved: '"Rex darling!" she shouted', although because she 'slightly slurred her "r"s, it became "Ryex darling, your <u>hands</u>? Are your <u>hands</u> all right?"' 'It did not matter what had happened to my members', Laurence added wryly.[23]

Edith's frequent references to their mutual affection in her diaries suggest a need for reassurance. At times she even sounds like Agatha in *The Love-Child*. Her ever-increasing protectiveness and adoration were at once romantic and maternal. But then Edith had had neither lover nor child and in Rex, in a way, she had found both. It was therefore the first time that she was able to write with such intimacy in the pages of her diary. She enjoyed the physical closeness of their relationship, and often recorded his actions and gestures, describing in detail what he was doing and her joy in watching him do it. She loved his boyish laughter in the cinema and loved seeing him draw, 'his absorbed face – his sure hand – his quiet suggestive strokes'.[24] And when they went together to look at the Tintoretto at Wilton House, she recalled that she loved 'to watch his absorbed face before such a picture – his worship of its loveliness – his <u>careful examination</u> of the painting'.[25]

Rex confided in Edith more and more. One bitterly cold night in December 1927 he had told her how terribly unhappy he had been at Haileybury School, speaking of 'the ugly, dirty sordidness of it, demoralising and debasing' and saying that he would not send his own son away to school.[26] He returned to the subject in the following month, telling Edith of 'the full extent of his miseries at Private Schools and the way the masters treated him. Such fools men must be – so without all understanding of a child', she declared. 'He was so unhappy at his Private School that his parents (he now knows) thought him very ill and were always writing to the school about it. He knows it was his misery and fear of the master'. As a final, triumphant note, she added: 'But of course he was afraid to tell his parents thinking it would only make a fuss and he would have to go back more in disgrace than ever. He has never told them. How helpless a child is!'[27]

Walking with her in Wilton Park, however, Rex could give himself up to the beauty of his surroundings. 'Rex's love and joy knows no bounds', Edith recorded. 'He swims in beauty, floats in it. We were a long time on the Palladian Bridge watching liquid moonlight rippling beneath it and the lights and shadows on the columns . . . never was a guest more deliciously, openly happy'.[28]

But Rex's worries were always present. The invitation to the British School in Rome was an honour, but it only exacerbated his self-doubt. He wanted to be taken seriously as an artist, but, as he again confessed to Edith, he still doubted his ability:

> After dinner a great talk about R's work. He is dissatisfied with himself, thinks he does not work hard enough, is too facile, avoids difficulties. Doesn't grapple with them but paints gracefully round them. Thinks other young artists go in more seriously for mastering technique . . . I don't want to harm him by saying he is perfect as he is . . . I think the Roman stay will be his chance of intellectualising his technique . . . he has a lovely nature, so inspired and so humble and so profoundly <u>honest</u> – that is his fundamental

character on art, in Religion, in Life. He can't be other than crystal true'.[29]

Tonks had told him that the British School would be the turning point of his life. Rex hoped it would be. But from Rome he wrote to Tonks: 'I am distressed to find that I simply can't paint straight from nature at all . . . I of course knew it would be hard, but it is infinitely harder than I had imagined, and seems to be far beyond my powers and I don't feel I shall ever be equal to it'.[30] In another letter, to Edith in June, Rex asked her to kiss the Palladian Bridge for him: 'I shall love it more than ever when I return now that I know and love its relation here!'[31] He explained that he had started an 'honesty campaign':

> Darling Edith,
>   . . . I am trying very hard to paint exactly what is before me, painting trees where they really are and not where I would have them, or 'bending' them to please myself . . . hardest of all, perhaps, to paint colours as they really are – to my eye. This last is the hardest of all because it needs the most discipline. Grass, for instance, is such a hideous colour I often think, and it is very hard not to 'improve' upon it! The results of this 'honesty' campaign, however, would make you quite sick! And they make me somewhat depressed . . . I'm sure Tonks is right in saying that I must paint from nature in order to learn and that if I continue to paint out of my head always I can never hope to improve . . .
>   Much love Rex.[32]

He was overwhelmed by the beauty of the baroque buildings that seemed to appear at every turn, by the clusters of parasol pines and the warm light that anointed each scene with an apricot veil. The Borghese Gardens, he told Edith, 'are full of such lovely things, innumerable exquisite statues, vases and sham ruins and such beautiful, absurd Rococo gateways, delicious little lakes and fountains and legions of busts on pedestals. And all these enchanting things are half in and half out of the indigo shadows of vast ageless ilex trees. Never', he wrote, 'have I <u>seen</u> or even <u>imagined</u> such trees. The incredible beauty of these ilexes leaves me with a sort of aching longing to do something <u>with</u> them, to paint them to draw them, to do anything rather than <u>waste</u> them!'[33] And so he was filling a sketchbook with drawings of classical architecture and landscapes, inspired by public buildings, gardens and sleepy side streets that he stumbled upon as he wandered through the city. This book he labelled as his 'Baroque notebook', quite distinct from his ordinary sketchbook. He was trying to intellectualize his work, to broaden his understanding of architecture, even reading a book about Le Corbusier which he recommended to Edith, thinking it '<u>wonderful</u> . . . like an <u>icy-cold</u> shower bath, which is quickly penetrating to the skin in spite of all my Classical and Baroque "mufflers" and "wraps"!!'[34] At heart though, Rex felt that he was immobilized by his inability to get things done. In a letter to Edith he told her that he had become 'indolent in the heat' and reminded her that she had said she thought concentration and sheer hard work were fundamental to the artist's progress:

Well if you're right, I am certainly doomed to never rise above small achievements, for I have now come to realize and perhaps for the first time I face it as a <u>fact</u>, that I am incurably and hopelessly lazy and lacking in the power to concentrate. I <u>know</u> it and have always known it really, only I used to tell myself: 'you can exert yourself if you <u>want</u> to'. I've been wasting my time here <u>abominably</u> . . .

Though this is only a trivial matter, of course, the little scribbles which I do on the envelopes and at the tops of my letters are the greatest proof of all, perhaps, of my feeble will and dilatoriness.

For though naturally I hope they may amuse you a little and make my letters more attractive, I'm afraid I must admit that that is not really why the sketches are there! When I tend to write a letter I first of all get an envelope and address it and then waste a little while scribbling on the back my monogram etc. I then get my sheet of notepaper and prepare to start, but I <u>simply can't</u>. I have to start scratching some futile little thing at the top – anything rather than begin the letter! One of my great difficulties is to prevent myself from 'decorating' my business letters! It is this same <u>inability to concentrate</u> which has prevented me from doing all the work and sightseeing which I had planned, before coming here.[35]

Guilt pecked at him, and not just about his work. 'My darling Edith . . . You are an angel to write so often to me and I should die if you stopped though that is all my laziness in answering deserves . . .'[36] It was a common theme, and many of his letters to Edith would begin thus. There was devotion, in return for hers, but also a suggestion of an increasing and uncomfortable sense that she was not the epicentre of his life, as he had become for her.

There were diversions to stem the brooding, however. He was swept into Rome's grandest circles and it was probably the Sitwells who gave Rex an introduction to Gerald, Lord Berners, who lived for part of the year in Rome at a grand antique-filled house overlooking the Forum. Rich, homosexual, an eccentric aesthete and a wily practical joker, Berners was an amateur artist, writer and composer, an admirer of Surrealism and a friend of Cocteau. He would be immortalized by Nancy Mitford as the bizarre if benign Lord Merlin, who encircles the necks of his whippets with diamond necklaces and who dyes his doves pastel colours. Berners had been keen to meet the young darling of artistic London and soon Rex was joining him at three o'clock every afternoon to sketch on the Palatine Hill, and being chauffeured in his vast Rolls-Royce around the city and on expeditions out into the Campagna. 'You'll be relieved to hear that I'm <u>wasting my time terribly</u> for I've hardly done any drawing or painting at all', Rex told Cecil, which was more amusing than truthful. He had been to Tivoli, he told him, a journey that had taken ages. 'But once there!' Rex wrote, and then had drawn a little sketch of stars and fireworks exploding,

> fountains <u>thousands</u> of feet high, oozy dripping grottoes on <u>every</u> side, vast ancient ilex groves, in whose shadows strange old goddesses recline with jets of water leaping from their green and slimy breasts and staircases of streaming water from terrace to terrace so <u>ravish</u> one that one is left completely exhausted.[37]

Berners was a pleasant and encouraging companion, but his own painting was such an impressive example of dedicated perseverance that Rex was shamed into working harder. 'I have been getting on a <u>tiny</u> bit better lately though I find it still incredibly hard', he told Edith, adding 'and, I do <u>horrible</u> paintings! Alas if only I could paint sunlight like Sickert! But I don't make any attempt to do so as I know that I have not the sort of mind and eye to be able to put on paint in that purely impressionist way.'[38]

Rex returned to England in the second week of August and telephoned Edith to ask her up to London. This was followed by a letter telling her how lovely it had been to hear her voice and how much he was looking forward to seeing her again. At the top of the letter he drew a wonderful sketch of Fitzroy Street, with little figures scurrying up and down the road as they go about their business, Edith arriving in her car to be greeted by a red carpet rolled down the steps of number 20 and Rex waving to her out of his first-floor window. When they were at last reunited, Rex regaled Edith with stories from his time at the British School. He had hated the atmosphere within its lofty, Lutyens-designed walls, he told her. He was appalled that the devotedly modernist students all seemed to hate Rome and to sneer at his taste for baroque architecture, shutting themselves in their studies rather than exploring the city as he had done. But in spite of what Edith had written in her diary, Rex had adored Rome; he had made friends amongst the architects and archaeologists, spent nights drinking and dressing up with them and had travelled alongside them on an expedition to Capri. Whether or not he had exaggerated his despair for Edith's sympathy or amusement, the trip to Rome had been less of a success than he had hoped or that Tonks had predicted for him. Just as he had turned his back to the model in life class, Rex needed distance from the baroque world that he adored in order to reproduce it. But he had *seen* all that he needed to see. Perhaps it needed to come to him indirectly, through the filter of his imagination. 'It seems so futile for me to try to put this lovliness on paper', he had confessed to Edith, 'and if my picture is to be only approximate I may as well wait till I'm home again.'[39]

Earlier in the month Edith had received a letter from Osbert Sitwell inviting her to stay at Renishaw, his family home near Chesterfield in Derbyshire, and insisting that she bring Rex too. The Sitwells greatly admired Rex's ability to conjure up the baroque world that they so admired and it was almost inevitable that they should want to cultivate their friendship with him. And, of course, they were to thank, in part, for Rex's success. Osbert was in the vanguard of Rex's early admirers. Soon after the Tate refreshment room had opened, he had commissioned a bookplate from Rex for which he received an elaborate rococo cartouche. It was the first of a number of commissions from the family, including later, in 1929, the dust wrapper for Edith's *Alexander Pope* and in 1932 the illustrations for *Bath*. In 1929 Rex would paint a small portrait of Edith wearing a brocade dress and glistening amber beads, sitting in a vast Venetian rococo chair (one of a pair at Renishaw), her long, elegant fingers clasped around a book.

On 25 August Edith set off from the Daye House on the journey north to Renishaw with Rex beside her in the car. 'He and I adore trips together', she wrote to Cecil a few days later, 'turning our little car into the gate of every lovely house and church we passed on the way and having such fun'.[40] As they were driving through Nottinghamshire, Rex realized they were passing Newstead Abbey, once home to Lord Byron. 'It's lovely', thought Edith, 'but haunted by that spirit of despair . . . Rex didn't see why but I know it.'[41]

The Gothic mood prevailed in Derbyshire. Renishaw was a vast and brooding house, predominantly eighteenth-century, with crenellations and pinnacles running along its parapets; beyond it lay the unseen coalfields that were the source of the family's fortune. Rex and Edith arrived in the early evening; Gerald Berners and William Walton, their fellow guests, had already arrived. Edith was immediately struck by the 'air of mystery and madness', worthy of *Northanger Abbey*, that hung about the house with its warren of rooms lined with heavy tapestries and menacing family portraits.[42] Sir George, the 'shadowy' patriarch, she thought 'exquisite and cruel and sinister and blade-like' while Lady Ida, his wife, seemed to have had a stroke. 'The three young ones are haunted by them', she wrote in her diary that night. Earlier in the evening, Berners and Walton had played 'mad duets' on the piano after dinner in defiance of the gloom and to send Sir George to bed. But she thought Rex appeared rather muted in this boisterous atmosphere: 'Rex is very quiet in this sort of party. No one would know how he rattles his nonsense when alone with a kindred spirit, but they all love him'.[43]

Edith Olivier loved Renishaw. 'What a marvellous place this is – literally <u>haunted by loveliness</u>', she told Cecil. They went to Hardwick Hall and on other expeditions into the countryside, 'we revel in sightseeing', she wrote.[44] Edith Olivier was still rather intimidated by Osbert, who seemed to her both amusing and cruelly two-faced about his friends, Virginia Woolf and Stephen Tennant included. But she thought him a master of the art of conversation with 'the dignified air of 18th century social life – very malicious and yet friendly!'[45] With his mordant wit, and ever poised with an epigram, he was like 'a character from the circle of Horace Walpole'.[46] His sister she liked without reservation.

Edith Sitwell shared Edith Olivier's obsession with history, one rich in kaleidoscopic detail and veiled in nostalgia. In her poetry as in her prose, she sought to evoke and resurrect the lost worlds of the past, as seen through a fancifully baroque and distinctly personal lens. Edith Olivier's romantic sensibilities were always tempered by the solid and practical core of her personality, where Edith Sitwell's floated freely. But even so, Edith enjoyed the company of her Sitwell namesake, who was fourteen years her junior. Behind the austere, acidic and eccentric image that Sitwell liked to present to the world, was a warm, loyal, sincere and surprisingly girlish woman. 'I had a wonderful morning with Edith who read me her new poem ["Gold Coast Customs"], finished today', Edith Olivier wrote, 'about Ashanti Civilisation – really a passionate, modest, macabre poignant, agonising picture of our civilisation, terribly powerful and intensely felt.'[47] Sitwell burst into tears as she read the poem to Olivier who began to cry with her. She had long admired and collected Sitwell's poetry, but there was another possible reason for the affinity between the two women, one that Edith Olivier did not mention in her diary and one that perhaps remained unspoken. In the previous year, at the age of forty, Edith Sitwell had fallen in love with a young painter, Pavel Tchelitchew, a homosexual Russian émigré, to whom she had been introduced by Gertrude Stein in Paris. She had quickly become his patron and a tireless champion of his work. He adored her, but from a distance, as a muse. He enjoyed painting her portrait and designing costumes for her to wear. According to her biographer, Victoria Glendinning, Tchelitchew found in Edith:

> A beautiful sheltered eroticism, the purely passive female sensibility that lives forever, a glass flower under glass, behind the opaque façade so remarkable in itself. He did not, as real lovers do, try to grasp the creature behind the façade; he helped her to elaborate and perfect her façade, since the one thing he feared was that it would crack, and he would be left face-to-face with a living, bleeding, demanding woman.[48]

This relationship tormented the lonely, virginal and vulnerable Edith with a little pleasure and a great deal of pain. Both she and Edith Olivier had remained unmarried from a combination of circumstance and parental oppression. Both were surrounded by and inspired a circle of predominantly homosexual young men. By comparison to Sitwell and Tchelitchew, Edith's friendship with Rex seemed, at this time, much simpler, more innocent and un-sullied by any sense of sexual attraction or repulsion. But both relationships were built on a similar dynamic, that of an elaborately constructed collaboration. Glendinning links her subject's dormant sexuality to her 1924 poem 'The Sleeping Beauty'. It 'must be', she writes, 'the only version of that well-known story in which the Prince never breaks into the palace to kiss his bride awake'.[49] Perhaps it was significant that this was the poem that Edith Olivier had read to Rex and Stephen at San Remo. She had delighted in their enthusiastic response to it. Rex had painted a watercolour inspired by the poem which he had given to Edith on her birthday. It had been his first gift to her.

12: 'The Trail of the Serpent'

❖

... they are all very sensitive to difference in meaning and
mean so many different things!

Edith Olivier's Diary, 24 April 1929

Later in September 1928 Brian Howard's friend and fellow dandy-
aesthete, Harold Acton, came to stay with Edith at the Daye
House. They had tea together in the Colonnade, walked in the
park and gossiped. But she disliked him: 'the trail of the Serpent
is on him – a habit of seeing evil everywhere'. During his stay, he
made what Edith described as 'an evil suggestion as to the friendship between Siegfried and Stephen', presumably telling her that
they were lovers.[1] Edith was either being naive, or some lasting
vestige of Victorian delicacy refused to acknowledge the possibility that their relationship was anything other than platonic. To her,
Stephen was a child, and of course she would always defend him
against parochial disapproval. In January she had talked 'of the
Stephen-Rex set' with Hester, the rector's daughter, who 'said
she couldn't like them as they were <u>Half-Wits</u>!!' to which Edith
replied, 'they may be only <u>Half-Males</u> but as for <u>Wits</u>!'[2]

Three years later in 1931, fifty-nine-year-old William Lygon,
the Earl of Beauchamp, married but homosexual, was outed to
King George V by his brother-in-law, the Duke of Westminster.
'I thought men like that shot themselves,' the King reputedly
responded. Beauchamp fled the country, planning to commit suicide on the continent but then changed his mind. Instead, he
lived in exile for the rest of his life. His friendship with the King

did not save him and no one, it seemed, not even a lord of the realm, was safe from scandal. Diana Mitford, a friend of Beauchamp's children and ever defiant in the face of public opinion, later claimed that her entire generation was on Beauchamp's side.

But in the summer of 1928 the mood amongst older members of society had become even more hostile than the year before. Like Romans at their most decadent height in their dying days, the parties of the Bright Young People in what would be their final season grew ever more wild and inventive, and with it a conservative backlash began to gather momentum. The young were becoming too liberal, louche and licentious; it was felt that something must be done. In July the 'Great Mayfair War' erupted. On the 10th, Stephen and David Plunket Greene (son of Edith's childhood friend Gwendolene) had taken two uninvited guests, Nancy Beaton and Elizabeth Lowndes, to a ball at Bridgewater House on Park Lane. Noticing their presence the indignant hostess, Violet, the Countess of Ellesmere, asked them to leave. It was the excuse that society had been looking for. The *Daily Mail* reported the scandal and it caused a furore. Angry letters and reluctant apologies flew back and forth. For many weeks the papers, and particularly the *Daily Express,* to whom Lady Ellesmere had relayed the story, gleefully fanned the flames. 'The ball at Bridgewater House', the *Express* declared, 'promises to be as famous as the one before Waterloo and to lead to nearly as much fighting'.[3] Interviews were published, the exchange of letters was printed – Stephen's apology, Cecil's defence of his sister, Nancy's plea of innocence, Lady Ellesmere's rebuttal – and large photographs of the gatecrashers and their consorts, even graphic illustrations of the expulsion, were splashed across the pages of the tabloids. In their wake came a tide of letters and articles declaiming the decline of standards and the rise of immorality in contemporary society. Cecil, who collected and catalogued every newspaper cutting in which he was ever mentioned, filled the pages of his scrapbooks with the evidence. The story reached newspapers in Czechoslovakia, India, Australia, Canada, China,

New Zealand and Egypt. The American press revelled in the sensation of what it called a 'civil war' in London society. It was, as the *Daily Express* noted, 'a piquant climax to the season'.[4]

At tea with a friend Edith discussed the debacle. 'Much talk of course about Stephen', Edith wrote that night:

> She thinks the hostesses had agreed to make an example of 'Gate-crashers' and that it's <u>very</u> bad luck that he is the scapegoat – as he is <u>not</u> one. My point is far more Violet's <u>unpardonable</u> action in putting it all into the vulgar papers. There she <u>has</u> let the upper classes down in the eyes of the mob. It's a much bigger thing – and a much worse thing than gate crashing. Helena thinks if they hadn't made it public they couldn't have stopped it which is an amazing point of view and means that if a hostess objects to a guest coming down late for dinner she will write to the *Daily Mail* and ask it to pillory that guest, hoping he or she may be shamed into punctuality.[5]

Edith saw the amusing side of the incident, but Stephen's mother Pamela was horrified and sent an 'SOS', summoning her to Wilsford. Pamela said that she had been warned that it was 'the beginning of a "Round-up" of Stephen and his foppish friends' and that he would soon 'be suspected of real immorality'.[6] She begged Edith to dash to London to stop Stephen from appearing at the fancy-dress party he was planning to attend the following night. Edith eventually managed to persuade Pamela that letters might be just as effective and they were summarily dispatched to both Stephen and Sassoon. Pamela was wary of her son's friendship with Sassoon but she was wise enough to acknowledge its existence and perhaps hoped that he would be a grounding influence. Edith had reassured Lord Grey that Sassoon was a good man and that Stephen was in safe hands. He was besotted. At Sassoon's suggestion, at the end of August Stephen was dispatched with Nannie Trusler to Haus Hirth, a pension run by Walther and Johanna Hirth in the Bavarian mountains at Untergrainau, near

Garmisch, where he had already stayed at the beginning of the year to receive treatment for his tuberculosis. Sassoon had paid for William Walton to join Stephen on that earlier trip, presumably in order to keep an eye on him. In September, Sassoon travelled out to join Stephen in Germany and then drove him down into Northern Italy to stay with the Sitwells at their castle, Montegufoni, outside Florence.

Bright Young Things and their misdemeanours were not Edith's only preoccupations that summer. At the end of July, Martin Secker had agreed to publish *As Far As Jane's Grandmother's*, although, like Heinemann, they had rejected the *Guide to the Duchy of Epicurania*. However, Rex was to do the illustrations for the novel and in late September Edith received a letter from Martin Secker telling her how pleased he was with both book and illustrations, but still Edith feared that it would not be well received. 'I feel', she wrote when it was published that November, 'it is in a very quiet subdued key for a season which has produced *Orlando* and *Elizabeth and Essex* as well as Siegfried's exquisite book'.[7]* *The Times* thought it 'well-written and accomplished' but found Jane's failure to escape her grandmother's clutches 'exasperating'.[8]

But first came her annual stay with Muriel Clanwilliam at her house Montalto, in County Down. It was to be more of a working holiday than anything else and Edith was dreading it. She was to teach Muriel's daughter and give a series of lectures on such subjects as 'The Late Nineteenth Century in Ireland', 'Gothic Cathedrals', 'The Novel' and 'English Houses'. Writing to Cecil, with whom she had spent an entertaining evening in London before she left, Edith told him: 'Though I won't go so far as to call you the Lord of Hosts yet there's no doubt you are the <u>Crown Prince of</u> Hosts and I always realise this anew when we've had an evening out together'. She begged him to write to her: 'I feel

---

* Virginia Woolf, *Orlando: A Biography*; Lytton Strachey, *Elizabeth and Essex: A Tragic History* and Siegfried Sassoon, *Memoirs of a Fox-Hunting Man*.

banished here . . . I have been busy since I arrived trying to learn the names of the 99 dogs who live in this (as in every Irish house) and trying too, to escape from their lickings, scratchings and rubbings . . . Today I give my first lecture to the aristocracy of Ulster, who all loathe literature and the Arts', adding again, as a final note: 'do write'.[9]

The hearty, out-of-doors life at Montalto appalled Edith. Her days were spent with Muriel, surrounded by a pack of wet, stinking dogs, except when she could escape to her room to work on her new book, *The Triumphant Footman*. In the evening after dinner she sat with Muriel listening to the wireless: 'a wild orgy, an opera from Hamburg, Cabaret from somewhere, lecture from London illustrated by piano, a Swedish speaker and a concert from Paris – all at the same time. Too frightful for words.'[10] Lecturing on Gothic cathedrals she struggled to keep up with the lantern slides she was using to illustrate the talk and kept losing her way. On 31 October a Halloween party failed to improve her mood: 'We tried to be Hallowe'en in spirit but the nuts we put on the bars of the fire did not crack and this was typical of the whole party, no snap about it.' She longed to be back in England and surrounded by her friends, who were so different from the rowdy young people at Montalto. 'I have never been bored by the young till now', she wrote despairingly in her diary, 'but I hardly know how to bear these screeching chattering idiots! . . . it's an amazing thing their lack of interest in anything except baby games . . . So unlike the present day when the young are generally overflowing with ideas.'[11]

Edith was preparing to return from Ireland on 20 November when she read in the paper that Pamela Tennant had died of a stroke. Pamela had been alone at Wilsford when she collapsed in the garden. She had been carried unconscious to her room and died in her bed some hours later. She was fifty-seven. 'The sudden loss of this most rich, varied and inspiring friendship is heartbreaking', Edith wrote in her diary that night. 'She was so infinitely worthwhile, her lovely mind so stored, her spirit so lofty and for those who knew her well, she had the deep humility of a little girl. I couldn't get my mind away all day from the sad house, with those men without her and her body left in her room, the soul flown.'[12] Her immediate concern, of course, was for Stephen, 'lost in central Europe with that Foxhunting man', as Rex had put it, in a letter to Edith.[13] Stephen and Sassoon were at their hotel in Versailles when a telegram arrived with the news. Aghast, Stephen made plans to return to London the following day, propped up by the last two pillars in his life, Sassoon and his ever-loyal Nannie.

Edith hurried back to England and travelled straight to London by train. Pulling the blind down in her carriage she changed into a black evening dress, made modest by the moleskin coat she put over it, and arrived just in time to attend the memorial service at St Margaret's Westminster for Pamela, who had been buried that day at Wilsford. The following day she wrote to Cecil in New York, where he had sailed on the *Aquitania* on 3 November. She was overjoyed to escape from Ireland, she told him, 'the people of Ulster all dour Protestants and <u>quite without minds</u>'. She had made £25.17s.6d from her lectures and doubted that it was worth the boredom of being there. Of Pamela, she added, 'it's quite impossible to believe that anyone so full of colour . . . is gone. One who <u>gave</u> so much with both hands and seemed to pour ideas into one's mind like wine into an empty glass'.[14]

Edith returned to Wilton the following day to find a letter from Stephen begging her to go to him at Wilsford; she dashed to the telephone but was told that he had already set out for the Daye House. Reassured by the spiritualism that he had imbibed from his mother, he was convinced that her spirit would not leave him and Edith thought he was being very brave. 'It is a marvellous tribute to her – to her spiritual influence. He feels her presence all the time – has none of those doubts which sometimes come when people lose one whom they love with all their heart . . . He was so touching and childlike and <u>alone</u>, begging me to be with him and to help him', wrote Edith, pleased, as ever, to be needed.[15] Mulberry House in London was left to Stephen's eldest brother

Christopher. He and his wife were to have Stephen's bedroom: 'they will paint its walls a quiet cream colour, & that silver dream will burst like a kettle', she wrote.[16] Stephen had inherited Lake House, and Wilsford would go to David, his elder brother. But it was one thing for Stephen to lose his Silver Room in London, quite another that he should be prised from Wilsford to which he seemed symbiotically bound. It helped that during the one night David's wife Hermione slept at the house she had been woken up, she was convinced, by the troubled ghost of Pamela pacing around the bed. David anyway thought Wilsford antiquated and Edwardian and he agreed that his brother could rent the house. And so Wilsford became Stephen's, in all but name, for the rest of his life.

Pamela never left Wilsford either. She was buried beside the house, a few steps from the mock village green, in a moss-lined grave in the small graveyard of the Norman church that she had restored years before. Rex, who had always sensed the steel beneath Pamela's softness and who had always felt that Wilsford was a place of sadness for all its loveliness, was asked to design her gravestone. It still stands beside the gate, its dainty shells and flowers all but lost beneath weathering and moss, and so, like everything at Wilsford, looks older than it is. Whether Pamela's restless spirit haunted the house as people said or whether she lay quiet in the ground, it was left to Stephen to keep her spirit alive. He would spend the rest of his life doing so.

At the beginning of December Edith went up to London to stay with Stephen and Lord Grey at Mulberry House in order to help with arrangements. She found Rex with Stephen who was given up to elegant mourning in his Silver Room: 'in bed in a black jumper with great piles of silver pillows heaped beside him . . . very few lights, and lovely gleams and shadows alternating and moving on the silver walls, very magic . . . Stephen so pale in bed. Heaps of Lilies and Orchids and Carnations. All very exotic and mysterious.'[17] That night she stayed with Stephen and they dined together in his room, he in bed and Edith sitting beside him on a chair. The following morning he called her out to look at some-thing in the square. It was a gift from Stephen, 'a lovely darling little new 1929 Austin Seven'. 'I can't say what I felt. Quite mad with joy', she wrote that night; 'it was a lovely enchanting thought of his and a tremendously expensive and vast present . . . He is an angel and he was such a darling about it so excited at giving it and yet making nothing of it as if motor cars were rained down on heads as presents every day.'[18]

After Pamela's death, many of Stephen's friends rushed to comfort him but none more so than the lover who was now almost constantly by his side. The paternal role was one that Sassoon preferred to adopt in his romantic relationships, but it was al-together more exaggerated with the newly orphaned and eternally boyish Stephen.*

Edith saw nothing but good in Stephen's friendship with Sas-soon. And it was perhaps around this time that she also began to come to terms with the nature of their relationship. Undoubtedly it was made more palatable by the esteem in which she held Sassoon and the evident attention and affection he lavished on Stephen. 'We were both alone for a moment and he at once spoke with great love and <u>comprehension</u> of Stephen', she wrote in London, 'he is a God-sent friend at this time'.[19] Increasingly though, Stephen was not their only common interest. That night, at Mulberry House, Sassoon gave Edith a special edition of his 'Ariel Poem'. 'He likes me finding a motto from his own poems for him', she wrote; 'I have sat silent – angry at what they uttered'.[20] Two days later Sassoon gave Edith a copy of his 1926 *Satirical Poems* and inscribed it to her with his new 'motto', a quote from his famous sonnet 'Grandeur of Ghosts'. He also sent her a 'charming and <u>praising</u> letter' about *As Far As Jane's Grandmother's*,

---

* A photograph of the two men taken abroad some time at the end of 1929 seems to encapsulate the dynamic of their relationship. They sit beside each other on the floor, Stephen, upright and child-like beside his caged parrot, look-ing at the camera. Sassoon, reclining, leans into Stephen and gazes at him like an indulgent and captivated parent.

which 'pleases me more than anything which has been said about it'.[21]

Women adored Sassoon. They half-fell in love with him, with his intelligence, his poetry, his quiet, contained strength, his robust yet unthreatening masculinity and his dry, droll humour. Generous and loving, he seemed to lack all artifice. Edith was intrigued by the ascetic way of life he favoured when he was working, 'a curious lonely existence' in which he wrote all night, breakfasted at midday, walked alone in the afternoon and perhaps played the piano, afterwards dining nearby in a restaurant or at his club. At forty-two he was closer to fifty-six-year-old Edith in age than to Rex, Stephen and the others; older and undoubtedly wiser. Certainly she saw in him an intellectual equal. And he was a link to an earlier literary world, being a friend of writers she so admired like Gosse, de la Mare and that master of the pastoral, Thomas Hardy. She had been very impressed with *Memoirs of a Fox-Hunting Man* which had been published in September, and even more impressed by its success, which was beyond her wildest dreams for her own books. Nearly 8,000 copies had sold in the first two months, reviews were gratifyingly good and he had won both the Hawthornden Prize and the James Tait Black Memorial Prize. 'Siegfried is the Prince of Best Sellers', she would write to Cecil in January 1929, 'and gets enchanting letters from Masters, Huntsmen, whips and hounds . . . who all tell him no one before has understood them'.[22] Later, she wrote: 'Siegfried is by turns violently intolerant, sympathetically appreciative, and savagely satirical. Sometimes silent in company but when with intimates he wakes up and his conversation is very racy and amusing . . . Siegfried is the best of friends.'[23]

Sassoon increasingly liked and respected Edith too. Apart from Rex he had little time for Stephen's friends, whom he thought immature and foolish. Cecil in particular he considered a malign influence. With her capacity for understanding, her sensitivity, intelligence and her infinite ability to listen, Edith was fast becoming his confidante, especially in regard to Stephen. One afternoon at Wilsford in the New Year he told her about his experiences on the Somme, and Edith, who was impressed by the modesty with which he dismissed his wartime heroics, enjoyed watching him talk, 'his quick, sudden urgent phrases as if he saw Truth before his eyes and hastened to pounce on it. And then so amusing with the unexpected laugh breaking in'.[24] Though he was attracted to Stephen's youthful vitality, Sassoon confided that he was 'happiest, really, with elderly people because they can talk about the past.'[25] Edith wasn't exactly elderly but she could and was always very happy to talk of the past, a past that was instantly recognizable to them both and whose loss they both lamented. She shared his fascination for Englishness and nostalgia for the rural paradise they had known before the First World War. It loomed large in her imagination and would dominate her later non-fiction writing just as Sassoon's *Fox-Hunting Man* was a celebration of, and an elegy to, the countryside of his childhood.

Later, in 1930, Edith and Sassoon discussed his relationship with his mother. Theresa Sassoon had learnt to tolerate her son's close friendships with men but she still hoped that he would marry. 'She is Victorianly intolerant', Edith wrote in her diary, 'and if she really knew what he is like she would be shocked', adding: 'I think Nature meant parents to know no more of their children when they are grown up, as animals don't, but spiritual nature won't accept this and so we get friction'.[26] No doubt, this was said with Rex in mind too. One night at the Daye House in February 1929, Edith, Sassoon and Rex stayed up late, talking about books and listening to jazz on the gramophone. 'Rex <u>would not</u> go to bed', Edith wrote. 'I told him I should ring up his mother at midnight, saying "Bad news about Rex. He won't go to bed". He said she would fall unconscious'.[27] Beyond the jokiness of this little exchange is an echo of the sentiment she had earlier expressed in her diary. Though in some ways Edith thought of her place in Rex's affections as a maternal one, she clearly felt that the dynamic of their relationship was different, freer than the claustrophobic one he had with his real mother. Edith dearly wanted her younger friends to see her as liberal, open-minded and set apart from their parents' (and her own) generation. That she could accept Stephen and Sassoon's relationship, despite her strident Christian values, illustrates the extent of her affection and indulgence towards them.

In January 1929 Stephen's doctor concluded that his tuberculosis had recurred. He was sent again to Haus Hirth with his valet and Nannie Trusler. It soon became clear, however, that it was his seventy-year-old Nannie who was dangerously ill; she had a longstanding heart condition and was becoming increasingly confused and incoherent. 'If she were to die I believe it would kill Stephen. I long to be with him', Edith wrote to Cecil some weeks later.[28]

In Stephen's absence, she invited Sassoon and Rex for a weekend at the Daye House in February. She sensed that Rex felt that Sassoon was becoming too possessive about Stephen and the invitation was her attempt to reconcile the two men. On the Saturday evening they drove down from London in Sassoon's car, a slow crawl through dense fog. Towards the end of the journey, perhaps more as a result of Sassoon's notoriously erratic driving than because of the fog, the car ended up in a pond outside the inn at Winterslow, a few miles from Wilton. Much to their (later) amusement, the owner came out, not to help them but merely to erect a sign that said 'THIS POND IS PRIVATE'. 'Hours passed, fog became very thick and I got terribly anxious. At 8.15, the telephone rang. Rex's voice came shattered and agitated', Edith wrote in her diary that night. 'They had run into a frozen pond at Winterslow Hut and couldn't get out . . . Rex looked quite dead. Siegfried fairly well and evidently determined not to moan and groan. He was too enchanting and like himself . . . they brought caviare and chocolate and huge photographs of themselves'.[29] Together they had a cosy weekend, they wandered around the rooms at Wilton House, Rex drew in Edith's visitors' book and in the manuscript book for Sassoon's latest work. They stayed up late listening to music on the gramophone and talking. 'Siegfried loves stories about people', she wrote, 'as well as talking about books.'[30]

Edith worried that Rex was jealous of Sassoon but she was wrong. He was jealous of Stephen. And Sassoon was convinced that Rex was falling in love with him. 'Am feeling rather worried about R., who is showing signs of falling under my spell', he confessed. 'I fear he is on the verge of a precipice . . . It would be easy enough to succumb, but would be no joke, once it began . . . R. is desirable, but I can't divide my heart into partitions, and if I were to try the experiment, I should find myself betraying [Stephen] . . . I don't want to be unkind to R. So far he has said nothing, but his behaviour has given the whole show away'.[31] When he first met Rex at Wilsford in 1927, Sassoon had 'scarcely registered his existence' but later that year, visiting Rex at the Tate a few days after the unveiling of his murals, he wrote in his diary that Rex 'interested him in more ways than one'.[32] The attraction, it appears, was mutual and they had begun to spend time together. But sitting for a pencil portrait in Rex's studio that winter, Sassoon talked only of the absent Stephen, whose Beaton photograph faced him on the opposite wall. It was amusement, companionship, nothing more, and Rex had to content himself with that.

It is easy to understand how Rex could have fallen under Sassoon's spell. Discussing the possibility of his brother's earlier sexual attraction to Stephen, Laurence wrote in *The Laughter and the Urn*: 'any homosexual leanings he had were not towards a male more feminine than himself'[33] and that, though 'he wanted to be forceful . . . [he] had an inclination to be yielding'.[34] Rex could see how the handsome, avuncular war hero cared for and protected Stephen. Laurence later questioned the extent of his brother's attraction to Sassoon, writing that only a month later, Rex was telling Edith how he had fallen in love with a girl he had met. Rex had been invited to stay with Lord and Lady Longford in Ireland by Laurence's history tutor at Stowe, Martin MacLaughlin, a 'brilliant teacher and starved homosexual', who had sought Laurence out at school for an introduction to his brother and about whom Edith wrote, without explanation, that he 'sounds to be an evil man'.[35] When he returned from Ireland at the end of March, Rex discussed the trip with Edith. 'R then fell in love with a very pretty girl', Edith wrote in her diary, 'and now feels a fool and ashamed of his response to her sex appeal. He kissed her and has never had an affair of the kind before. <u>How</u> I love his exquisite sensitiveness and candour. Talking of the love affair, he said, "I felt so far from <u>you</u> in Ireland and as if I should never see you again, and so . . .".'[36] The sentence was unfinished.

The girl, Gwen Farrell, later told Laurence that she had not realized that his brother was particularly attracted to her and that the kiss had not even been on the lips. 'I had not heard of her,' Laurence recalled, 'when, sitting pensive with elbows on the table, he wistfully shook his head and murmured "Gwen! – Oh, Gwen!", not too lugubriously. It struck me', he added, 'that he meant to make display of a grieved heart more than to invite inquiries'.[37] Rex had an almost Ruskinian attitude to women, once confessing to his brother that he thought defecating ought to be something that only men should do. Girls still dwelt primarily in his imagination. In his fantasies, as he confessed to his brother, Rex wanted to be the submissive one, wanted to be saved. Laurence writes that 'the interplay of force and submission held an interest; and even cruelty observed had a fascination'.[38] He also describes Rex's occasional erotic drawings. In one, 'the girl is seated naked on the edge of the bed consoling her lover who kneels between her knees, in tears. It is the tune of the desolated child', he wrote, 'transposed into the key of adult sex, the need for confession, absolution, reassurance in the arms of a mother who is also desirable and young and childlike herself.'[39]

And then there was Edith, with whom he could flirt, gently and flatteringly, telling her in a letter: 'since seeing you against that pink pillow in bed the other day, I feel I must, in honesty, raise your marks for seduction from 5 to at least 8!'[40] In her diary, there is no hint that Edith had noticed Rex's attraction to Sassoon. Rex, as she kept repeating emphatically, was wholly 'good'. He would not have told her. Ultimately, although she turned a blind eye to Stephen and Sassoon, sexuality for Edith was inextricably linked with morality. She would not even entertain the possibility that her Rex was attracted to a man.

Sassoon didn't succumb to Rex; his devotion to Stephen cast everyone and everything else in the shade. But it did not stop him cultivating a friendship, even trifling, with Rex. Whatever under-lying friction there was, it seems to have waned by the spring; Rex must have realized the futility of his longing and it remained unfulfilled. At the end of March, Sassoon travelled to Bavaria to be with Stephen and Nannie Trusler at Haus Hirth and in a char-acteristically generous gesture, paid for Edith, William Walton and later Rex to join them. He had also given Herr and Frau Hirth £500 to build an extension to the house and to replace the snow-damaged roof, telling them that he believed that they had saved Stephen's life. Haus Hirth was a typical Bavarian chalet with a select clientele; it was popular with English tourists with its Alpine promise of fresh air and fresh milk, standing amongst gentian-carpeted meadows, beneath wooded slopes and snow-capped mountains. Walther Hirth had inherited a Munich newspaper but had lost his money in the German inflation; to Stephen and soon to the rest of the party he became 'Onkel Walther' and his wife, 'Tante Johanna'. When he was not with Stephen, Sassoon was working on the sequel to his *Fox-Hunting Man*, which would become *Memoirs of an Infantry Officer*. Walton was at work on his Viola Concerto, later considered his first masterpiece. He spent much of his time at the piano or toying with the affections of a fellow guest, an American girl called Alice-Leone Moats, whom Edith described as having a face 'of the Henry James type'. In her diary, if not in person, Edith made her opinion of Alice immediately clear: 'she is self-satisfied and self-conscious. Quite certain, as Americans are, that she knows everything and can do everything. Her appearance very good.'[41] Beneath a radiantly blue sky in the hot spring sunshine, Edith sat, reading, working on her book or talking with her friends and shoring up observations to relay to her diary at night.

Stephen had given Nannie Trusler a new red velvet Bavarian

1. Edith as a child, with her hoop.

2. Edith in 1897, at the age of twenty-four, dancing along the path at the back of Wilton Rectory. The shadowy figure dancing with her is probably one of her brothers.

3. Edith and Mildred at Fitz House, Teffont Magna, about 1920.

4. Denny, Laurence, Jessy and Rex Whistler, 1913.

5. The Daye House.

6. The south front of Wilton House with the Palladian Bridge in the foreground.

7. Stephen Tennant, 'the brightest of the bright young things',
photographed by Cecil Beaton, 1927.

8. Rex, Edith, Zita Jungman, Stephen and Cecil at Cap Ferrat, 1927.

9. 'The Lancret Affair' on the lawn at Wilsford, as captured by Cecil Beaton, October 1927: Stephen, William Walton, Georgia Sitwell, Zita Jungman, Rex and Cecil.

10. Rex photographed by Cecil Beaton on the rocks at Cap Ferrat, 1927.

11. The hunting party in pursuit of 'rare meats': a detail from Rex's mural in the Refreshment Room at the Tate Gallery. Rex, as Król Dudziarz, gestures to a passing unicorn as he hurtles through the bountiful Arcadia on his bicycle.

12. Edith photographed by Cecil Beaton at Cap Ferrat, 1927.
'I have so seldom been photographed that it is most interesting to me to see these outside impressions of myself and I stare at them for hours', she wrote to Cecil.

13. *Conversation Piece at the Daye House*, 1937. Rex's painting of Edith holding court in the Long Room with Lord David Cecil, Lady Ottoline Morrell and himself, a brooding figure by the fireplace. Rex loved this painting and wrote to Edith, 'if I die first, please bring it with you when you come.'

14. Rex painted this panel in the Long Room when Edith had gone upstairs to dress for her 'one and only party' in September 1933.

dress and Edith wrote that she thought 'his exquisite affection for Nanny is really beautiful. They are so <u>protecting</u> of each other'.[42] Talking with Nannie one day in her room at Haus Hirth, they discussed Pamela's lack of discipline with her children, which Nannie deplored, and how it had affected each child in turn. Edith decided that Stephen was 'amazingly unspoilt by it. Its lack', she decided, 'has given his genius – spiritual and artistic – full play'.[43]

Edith thought Sassoon 'a delight' and 'most vivifying and so lovable', adding: 'everyone here adores him, host and hostess and servants, and he adores them all'.[44] They talked often of Stephen, both agreeing that he had a unique and extraordinary personality. One day Edith and Sassoon went into town together and stumbled upon an old shop selling traditional Bavarian trinkets. Sassoon bought a heap of hand-woven silk handkerchiefs, two of which he gave to Edith along with a pair of peasant-style earrings, 'great gold rings set with little emeralds'. 'He is as happy as a boy in his generosity', she observed. '<u>Loves</u> giving things. No one would recognise the rather grim alarming aloof poet of London in this gay creature . . .'[45]

There was happiness too that Stephen's health seemed to be improving. He had had a third operation to collapse the lung in order to rest it and his German doctor wrote to report on his good progress. 'Tante Johanna . . . says the specialist from Heidelberg writes full of hope over Stephen's physical recovery, tho' wondering how anyone so heavenly, so "<u>unerdlich</u>", so spiritual, can face this rude world – Thinks him like a Fra Angelico or a Botticelli. Is dazzled by his personality'. Edith thought this 'marvellous from a great German scientist'.[46] Sassoon, suspicious and ever possessive of Stephen, had a different interpretation.

To improve her German, Edith was reading a book on the *Art of Riding*, a series of love letters superficially about horse management but in fact a treatise on life and love. It gave her the idea that she might write a similar book of her own, 'Letters to my Niece on the Art of Embroidery'. And so for the next couple of days she wrote several letters to her niece Gillian. At first she had been excited by the idea but she changed her mind: 'I fear it may be too preciously moralising and old-maid-ishly epigrammatic'. Later that day she lay in the garden talking with Sassoon about her writing. '[He] would teach me to be a good writer if I lived with him', she wrote. 'He seizes one's half-born ideas and shews one what to do with them and <u>wants</u> one to do it well.'[47] It was a talent she shared.

Rex was due to arrive before the end of the month and Edith decided to go and surprise him on the platform at Munich station. He planned to break his journey to Haus Hirth with a night or two in the city to revel in its German rococo splendours. And so he and Edith set out to explore, albeit lamenting the loss of his Rome sketchbooks which he had left on the train and which, in spite of their toing and froing from the station to the lost-property bureau, he would never retrieve. That night they went to see *Così fan tutte* at the Residenz and before heading on to the pension they went to visit Johanna Hirth's brother, the artist Willy Preetorius, whose portraits in particular Rex admired. On the train they played a game together, Edith drawing a scribble and Rex making a picture out of it. 'He was brilliant at this'.[48] Soon Rex had relaxed into the somnolent mood of the place and sat drawing a pencil portrait of Walton as he played at the piano, as well as an enchantingly illustrated advertisement for Haus Hirth to be placed in English magazines, with a drawing of the house and enthusiastic endorsements from Hon. Stephen Tennant, Miss Edith Olivier, Capt. Siegfried Sassoon, Mr Rex Whistler and others.

It was a happy, peaceful interlude; Edith's pleasure in the companionship of her most beloved friends is evident in her diary entries, which overflow with love for them. Easter Sunday, 31 March, was Stephen's twenty-third birthday and a table was piled high with cake, presents and flowers. In the afternoon he descended from his sickbed upstairs to receive his gifts and birthday wishes, 'looking heavenly' in an orchid-mauve velvet dressing gown and matching silk pyjamas. 'No one else on earth could so deliciously have enjoyed and thanked for and welcomed his presents', Edith wrote, 'such an embarrassing thing for most people – unpacking – with the whole party sitting round.'[49]

Edith left for England several days later. Rex and Walton travelled with her as far as Garmisch from where she continued on alone along the Rhine, 'ending with a huge mis-shapen moon on the canals and flats of Holland – very like the hand of the Marsh King's daughter.'[50] Stephen and Sassoon, and Nannie, were left alone to their Bavarian idyll and happiness, for now.

13: 'Bells at Midnight'

❖

My anxieties make me non-creative! They tug at me with fretful fears.

Edith Olivier's Diary, 1 January 1930

Back in England Edith threw herself into the local Conservative campaign for the forthcoming general election, working alongside Tory friends like the Pembrokes and Lord Salisbury. Her old friend Hugh Morrison of Fonthill, who had been MP for Salisbury almost continuously since 1918, was standing again and Edith was prevailed upon to speak at rallies. She loved the thrill of campaigning, the heckling, roaring, singing and tub-thumping, and the hurtling about in cars with her comrades from meeting to meeting in coffee houses, pubs and the Market House.

There was an added relevance that year. On 2 July 1928, the Representation of the People (Equal Franchise) Act was passed in Parliament, finally giving women electoral equality with men. Edith wondered if the influx of women voters would affect the outcome; she thought not, as some women had told her that they planned to abstain, saying that they didn't understand enough. On Polling Day she voted and spent between 8.50 a.m. and 9.15 p.m. driving other voters to the Poll with an hour off at lunch and at teatime when, as she wrote that night, 'I sat in the Colonnade and drenched my soul in Sachie's most lovely *Visit of the Gypsies*'.[1] For Edith, the day after the election, 31 May, was 'a disastrous day throughout the country, Conservatives going down, Labour going up and Liberals queering the pitch'. Hugh Morrison had won Salisbury, but Labour had won nationally, although not with a clear majority and Edith assumed there would be another election soon. 'Labour's hands are tied, and they cannot nationalise or do any real harm', she concluded with relief.[2]

Rex had also returned to England in April and soon Edith received a letter from Johanna Hirth mourning the loss of her guests and Rex in particular, 'this darling whom we all miss most terribly'.[3] There was talk that spring that Rex might travel with the architect Sir Edwin Lutyens to India to decorate his Viceroy's House at Delhi. It was an exciting plan but one that never transpired. And for all his new-found success, Rex was still struggling with money. '<u>Do</u> forgive me for not having written before, but I have been working so hard – driven to it by the approach of dreaded Rent day and an empty feeling at the Bank', he had written to Cecil from Fitzroy Street in the previous September.[4] It was becoming a common theme.

Earlier in 1929 Sassoon had taken Rex to dinner with his friend the poet Edmund Blunden. In turn Blunden had introduced Rex to the publisher Richard Cobden-Sanderson, whose firm was planning to publish a book that would imitate the quaint, nostalgic charm of Victorian annuals. Rex was asked to illustrate the book, *The New Forget-Me-Not* as it was to be called, and it was the first of several successful commissions for Cobden-Sanderson. But it was one thing for Rex to illustrate books as a favour for friends like Edith and the Sitwells, quite another to do them to order, and what was worse, to a deadline. In February the Cresset Press had made the inspired choice of asking Rex to illustrate 'an Edition de luxe' of *Gulliver's Travels*.[5] There were to be a hundred and ninety-five copies printed on handmade paper and ten on vellum, all hand coloured to Rex's specification. Rex was commissioned to produce twelve illustrations, four head and four tail pieces; later several maps and a title page were requested too. 'He is rather depressed and <u>rattled</u> by all the illustrating work he has accepted,' Edith wrote in her diary in May, having been with Rex that day to see the work of William Nicholson, who was illustrating a new edition of Sassoon's *Fox-Hunting Man*. '[Rex] shall undertake no more of it – distracting – underpaid and not what he wants to do. Says his only really good kind of work is Tate Gallery.'[6]

But at the end of June he was escaping once again, this time to Rome as Gerald Berners's guest at his house in the Forum for five weeks. Though Rex complained that he was underpaid and overworked, this was his second free foreign holiday of the year. There were trips into the Roman countryside and to Tivoli, which he painted from the road, bathed in a soft amber light in the manner of Claude. They stayed in a hotel near the gardens and Rex described to Edith how his window overhung the waterfalls so that he could hear them endlessly overspilling at night. He sat at the roadside contentedly painting with Berners and at night, as he packed up his paints, he told Edith that 'it seemed as if the whole place had been <u>stricken</u> with its own beauty – heavy scented silence.'[7] During his time in Rome he painted a portrait of his balding, moustachioed and rosy-cheeked host painting at an easel at his house in the Forum. It was 'only too like him!' he told his mother. 'And so it cannot give much pleasure. He is so charming and kind.'[8] It was a leisurely and luxurious few weeks; 'this is how I spent my [twenty-fourth] birthday last Monday', he wrote to Stephen:

> I got up about 8.30 and had breakfast with B in the loggia overlooking the Forum – a breakfast of little hot rolls and butter and coffee followed by peaches and figs. At ten we drove to that spot nr. the Arch of Constantine and I began the picture which I have mentioned before. After lunch I rested in my dark and shuttered bedroom till 4 when we drove out of Rome to Frascati. A very beautiful place and high up above the Campagna. We painted all afternoon in the gardens of the Villa Aldobrandini, full of old fountains and ilex trees, and a view across the plain which takes the breath away. In the faint haze of the afternoon sun it looks more like a vast expanse of <u>sea</u>, stretching away and away

toward the horizon and the dim peak of Mount Soracte –
and in the other direction the long silver gleam which is
the real sea. We have been several afternoons painting. B had
a written leave from the family. On Friday while I was painting I looked up and saw a sallow face peering down very
hard at me from a terrace above. It was 'Il Duque Aldobrandini', just returned. Fortunately B was sitting not far
away and Aldobrandini waved to him and came down and
talked to us.[9]

There was none of the anxiety about productivity that there had
been in the previous year and his Gulliver drawings lay untouched
in his room. But even in Italy Rex was hounded by financial
worries. He had borrowed money from Cecil, and Edith, who
could ill afford to, sent him a cheque which he promptly returned,
with a reassuring letter: 'If I wrote to you as much as I loved you
and valued your friendship – you would hear <u>every</u> day![10] He
travelled back to England with Berners in his chauffeur-driven
car, a meandering, sightseeing journey up through northern Italy
and France that took two weeks. According to Berners's biographer, Mark Amory: 'It is hard to believe that Berners too had
not enjoyed himself, taking pleasure in his ability to bestow so
much beauty and luxury – the ducal gardens, the evening hush,
the figs, the Rolls-Royce – on a congenial young companion. They
parted and remained friendly acquaintances rather than friends,
let alone lovers.'[11] Perhaps there had been a subtext to Berners's
benevolence, but Rex had chosen to ignore it, as he would again.

After the election Edith was free to return to her own work.
She was still writing The Triumphant Footman as well as lecturing
for the WI, preparing a series of lectures about Stonehenge to
raise money for the Stonehenge Fund and organizing a weekend
for newly married couples at the Bishop's Palace in Salisbury. On
top of this she was making frequent trips up to London and elsewhere to visit friends and family and, most pleasurably for Edith,
inviting friends to stay with her at the Daye House. In June she

spent a weekend at Greenlands, near Henley, with Lord Pembroke's daughter Patricia and her husband William Smith, now
3rd Viscount Hambleden and chairman of W. H. Smith since his
father's death in the previous year. They had married the year
before at Wilton and Edith had been overjoyed by the wedding
luncheon in the Double Cube, the 'lovely Bride' in medieval dress,
sitting at the centre of a long table, looking 'like a banquet in
some Palace of the D'Estes and she like one of the Princesses'.[12]
Edith thought them a perfect match and she had been thrilled to
receive the invitation to Greenlands, a vast white stucco palace
sitting on the banks of the Thames. There she met Lord David
Cecil, then aged twenty-seven, youngest son of the Marquess of
Salisbury, a historian, literary biographer and fellow at Wadham
College, Oxford. He was an engaging conversationalist and Edith
thought him 'quite heavenly'; they would remain good friends for
the rest of her life. 'I adore him', she wrote after this first meeting,
'how he talks, vivid, pale – quick, brilliant.'[13]

Later that month a guest arrived at the Daye House who
would never receive Edith's unequivocal praise: William Walton.
He had brought with him Alice-Leone Moats, the American girl
from Haus Hirth, and a woman whom Edith had never met
before, Imma von Doernberg, the Princess of Erbach-Schonberg,
a young widow and the first cousin of Princess Alice, Countess of
Athlone (Queen Victoria's granddaughter). Walton spent his time
flirting with both women and told them all the story of his life 'so
that', as Edith noted archly, 'we should realise that he rose from
the ranks and so far has made no money, so isn't marriageable'.[14]
She thought him 'a piteable little cad – a diseased one too, rather
like a maggot – but I believe he has more character than appears.'[15]
The opinion that she had formed in Bavaria, that Alice was a fool,
did not change that weekend and she filled the next few days of
her diary with snide comments about the girl. Imma, on the other
hand, she admired at once for her charm and intelligence, and
also undoubtedly because she was a princess and not an American. They drove into Wilton together to buy postcards and Imma

told Edith that Walton was glad to be the only man at the Daye House: 'if Rex had come', Edith repeated, 'he would have been quite in the shade as Alice likes R so much better and he would have had all her attention'.[16] Alice Moats would later tell Laurence Whistler that she had been in love with his brother, but that he had shown no interest in her and she thought that he was homosexual. Walton, Imma and Alice returned for a midsummer al-fresco supper at the Daye House some days later, the roses in full bloom and the trees bowed with blossom, a backdrop to Edith's walnut table which was set with her green glasses and a large green bowl filled with strawberries. She hoped the picturesqueness of the scene would distract from the fact that there was only soup and cold tongue for supper. Later that evening, from her daybed in the garden, she was amused to observe the dynamic of this unlikely trio, Alice talking incessantly and believing herself to be at the centre of things while Imma and Walton, who were swiftly falling in love, threw longing glances at each other. That night they drove off into the Wiltshire darkness with Alice skirtless at the wheel, 'partly because she didn't want to spoil it and partly because she thought this was rather audacious a thing to do'.[17]

In April Cecil had returned from America in triumph, 'looking very hard and manly and with a much deeper voice!' according to Rex, who also told Edith, 'he is to be seen in every restaurant and at every cocktail party and first night. I think so but I'm not there myself to see!'[18] Cecil had been disappointed by the absence of reporters waiting for him on the dock when he sailed into New York on the *Aquitania*, but had quickly got into his stride. On his second day he had been summoned by Edna Woolman Chase, editor-in-chief at *Vogue*; she admired his work and immediately commissioned several articles and drawings of society ladies. Soon he was offered an exclusive photography contract with Condé Nast Publications. He was thrilled by the vibrancy of the bustling, burgeoning city, which was everything that he had long dreamt about. It was 'eggs-ill-ahh-rating', he later recalled.[19] Armed with advice and letters of introduction from the Sitwells and other friends in England, he quickly built up an impressive list of contacts, being feted by New York society ladies, attending their luncheons and parties in the city and weekending at their estates on Long Island. He was getting his name, and his work, into the papers and made sure that news of his success filtered home to England. It worked: 'Your life giving off sparkling mondanité like electric sparks. I feel I shall not recognize you so smartly equipped by New York savoir faire', wrote an envious Stephen, for whom the idea of New York, with its jazz, skyscrapers and movie stars, held the promise of an almost mythic glamour.[20] In January 1929 an exhibition of Cecil's old and new portraits was held at the Elsie de Wolfe gallery on Fifth Avenue and soon all the most famous film stars were lining up for him to take their picture. Now he had Condé Nast's drawing room as a backdrop, a *Vogue* expense account at his disposal and an income of $300 for every set of twelve prints. 'How rich you will be when I see you again if ever you can tear yourself away from that land of Dollars', wrote Edith to Cecil that month; 'are you thinking of marrying an American Heiress?'[21]

Money, or a lack of it, had been on her mind from early that year and though she had been swept off to Bavaria by Sassoon's generosity, it was only a brief respite from a rising sense of panic about how she was going to keep afloat. Before travelling to Germany, she had written to Cecil to beg for his help promoting *As Far As Jane's Grandmother's*, which was being published in America by the Viking Press later in March. 'If you have the chance', she asked, 'give me a little preliminary publicity or even draw an entirely imaginary and very beautiful little picture of me for any paper. Don't forget your impoverished friend', she pleaded.[22] She was expecting to receive some money from Secker at the beginning of April but she despaired at his decision not to advertise her novel more than once or twice in spite of the enthusiastic reviews it had received.

On 12 July she went up to London to attend the presentation

of the Hawthornden Prize. Though she envied Sassoon's success it gave her great pleasure to be associated with him. The prize was being given to Sassoon in absentia, with Edmund Blunden standing in for him, as he had insisted on staying with Stephen in Bavaria. 'He is not returning for it, but angelically staying with me', Stephen had told Cecil.[23] Three days later Edith went to a rehearsal of new Stravinsky ballet music and heard the young Russian composer, sixteen-year-old Igor Markevitch, who had recently been discovered by the impresario Diaghilev and brought to London. Afterwards there was a cocktail party in the foyer where she joined Edith Sitwell, who was looking 'exquisite dressed in moon light colour, a very <u>swathed</u> turban round her head'.[24] Later she lunched with Cecil at Boulestin and they had fun watching, and no doubt commenting on, their fellow diners.

Edith's weekdays were spent lecturing and writing her book and most weekends she had guests at the Daye House or went to stay with friends and family. But more and more her social life outweighed the money she was earning from writing and lecturing. Entertaining at home or going up to London, even though she always travelled in third class, was taking its toll on her financial situation. One way of saving money, a trick favoured by spinsters in the novels of Jane Austen and countless real impecunious spinsters over the centuries, was to stay for extended periods of time with friends. In late July Edith shut up the Daye House for three weeks and travelled to north Wales to stay on the Vaynol estate as a guest of Michael Duff, its young landlord. The Georgian manor house stood in the midst of Snowdonia, on the banks of the Menai Strait opposite Plas Newydd, the home of the Marquess of Anglesey, and the two families saw a lot of each other, crossing back and forth across the water by motorboat. From Vaynol she went straight to Northamptonshire to stay with Sacheverell and Georgia Sitwell at Weston Hall. Edith Sitwell and William Walton were also staying, Walton pining for Imma who had returned to Germany and Edith Sitwell complaining that Sassoon had abandoned their friendship for Stephen. They sat up late, Edith regaling them with stories of her visions at Avebury and Land's End and those of Miss Moberly, whom she had been to visit earlier that day at her home in Oxford. Miss Moberly had persuaded Edith to go to Paris that year; she believed that the time lapses she had witnessed happened every seven years and it had been twenty-eight years since her visit with Eleanor Jourdain in 1901. Edith longed to go with Rex and they made tentative plans for the end of the year.

Returning from Rome in July, Rex had plunged straight back into a whirl of illustration commissions and as if to compound his irritation at doing them he had been asked to redo the *Forget-Me-Not* drawings as the originals were too fine to print. Occasionally he went out of town for weekend parties. In the past he and Edith had usually been invited as a pair but that happened less frequently now. In August he escaped for a weekend at the Daye House. 'He looks ill', Edith thought, 'not as if he has been in Italy'.[25] It had been many weeks since she had seen him, and perhaps she sensed that he was slipping out of her orbit, which might explain the critical comment, a first for Rex. Soon, though, they were out in the car, motoring to Fonthill: 'Rex after Chartres now loves all Gothick equally with Classic', she wrote in her diary. It was Chartres, but also his enthusiasm for Kenneth Clark's *The Gothic Revival,* which had been published the previous year, that had opened Rex's eyes to a visual language beyond the Classical. And as if to counter that, they drove off to see the gardens at Stourhead, a Rex landscape brought to life, where he was 'quite off his head with desire!' she wrote. 'It is absolutely his place, this "Demi-Paradise" as it was described in a poetical epitaph to its maker which we found in the church.'[26]

In mid-June Nannie Trusler's health had deteriorated further and she was sent back to England. At the end of the month Stephen and Sassoon received word that she had been admitted to hospital in Chelsea and that they should return before it was too late. Stephen was determined that he should see her and this he managed to do, making several tearful visits to the hospital before she died peacefully on 14 August. That day Edith went with Rex to visit Stephen, who she thought 'looked exquisitely beautiful and bronzed . . . his face beside Rex's looked marvellous. R looked fat and white and <u>un-modelled</u> by him. He really has such beauty.'[27] Again, an uncharacteristic criticism of Rex although, watching his gentle affectionate manner with Stephen, she also observed that 'Rex is deeply <u>sensitive</u> of his feelings. He has such great love for his friends.'[28] The next day Rex went to draw Nannie on her deathbed, a tender pencil sketch of her head upon a pillow. It was, according to Laurence, Rex's first glimpse of death. Rex too had loved Nannie, and loved the way in which she had devoted her life to Stephen. She had perhaps been more important to Stephen than his mother, certainly a more steady and easy presence in his life. It had been less than a year since Pamela's death and now Stephen was entirely alone but for Edith and his friends. From now on, he would become entirely dependent on Sassoon, and Sassoon in turn devoted himself to Stephen's well-being.

A few days after Nannie's death Stephen returned to Wilsford, and another few days later Sassoon followed, effectively moving in. Stephen began planning to renovate and redecorate Wilsford and he had moments of great excitement thinking about it, entertaining Cecil with elaborate descriptions in his letters of how he was going to revamp it. But in spite of his plans and Sassoon's unwavering presence he felt alone and depressed. 'You can't imagine how lonely it is without my mother & Nannie', Stephen told Cecil; 'I am in some ways so completely desolate . . . In a way, luckily, I don't feel able to have fun like I used to – or to tire myself out – & think it is more than worth it – which I used to'.[29]

On 23 October Edith spent a day seeing all her favourite friends in London. She bought a new hat at Harvey Nichols en route to tea with Sassoon at his 'eyrie' overlooking Campden Hill Square. They talked of the Sitwells, of Stephen and the travails of writing books. He showed her William Nicholson's illustrations for his novel and she thought that the drawing of Sassoon for the

frontispiece was 'appalling . . . making him an Israelitish groom!'
After tea she dashed back to her sister Mamie's house in Chelsea
to change, gathering a picnic of pigeon, foie gras, Russian salad
and strawberry creams to take to Rex's studio on Fitzroy Street.
They had a 'very gay' hour or two, eating the food with a knife and
spoon as Rex had no forks. Later they went together to the first
night of *Three Sisters* at the Fortune Theatre in Covent Garden,
starring Sassoon's friend and one-time lover Glen Byam Shaw.
Edith found that she enjoyed it less than other Chekhov plays she
had seen but loved the 'mad Russian scene in the midst of the
weight of tragedy when they all wildly danced together'. And then
the night ended at the Savoy where she joined Cecil for dinner
with his sister Nancy, whom she damningly described as a 'boring
. . . round pink and white beautifully dressed piece of bread and
butter'.[30]

And then all her friends were off in different directions. On
9 November Cecil sailed again for New York, this time with
Hollywood in his sights. Towards the middle of the month Edith
went to see Stephen and Sassoon at Wilsford before they left to
winter in Italy for Stephen's health. She found Stephen in bed
and 'in great spirits' bestowing upon her cyclamens, orchids, new
pyjamas and scent.[31] The two men departed a few days later with
countless suitcases, Stephen's valet and Poll, his pet parrot, in
tow, travelling first to Rapallo to visit Max Beerbohm and then on
to Sicily.

Earlier that year Brian Howard had invited Edith to a modern
art exhibition in London, 'a Private View of Pictures by an
unknown artist from Lübeck – Bruno Hat,' Edith recorded in her
diary. 'Brian Howard took me to one side and confided that this is
a hoax. <u>He</u> painted them.'[32] To Brian and the others involved,
including Evelyn Waugh and Tom Mitford, brother of the famous
sisters, this was a hilarious in-joke. It was the kind of amusing
game that the Bright Young People excelled at. Two years previously Edith might have found it entertaining; now she thought it
foolish. Rex and the others were no longer bright young things,

they were growing up. The parties were petering out, girls like Zita Jungman and Diana Mitford were getting married, careers were blossoming and horizons were broadening.

Rex was too poor and too busy with his *Gulliver* illustrations, on which he was making lamentably slow progress, to go to Paris with Edith that winter and the plan was forgotten. In December though, she and Rex caught the eleven o'clock train from Waterloo back to Wiltshire. The night before, a storm had flooded fields and brought down trees, and the rain continued relentlessly that day. But Rex longed to spend a day exploring: 'R thirsted for little, lost, forgotten out-of-the-way villages'.[33] And so that afternoon they set out in the car on an expedition. That night they had 'delicious talk all the evening', Edith dressed in the pink brocade pyjamas that Stephen had given her and a coat of chiffon velvet and white fur.[34] And then the following day they set out again for a last drive together before Rex returned to London. The weather was as bad as it had been the day before but Edith wrote that they had seen 'a pair of magpies and drove thro' a flock of sheep which lucky omens got us over the most alarming, slipping, skidding, bog-sinking journey. We often could not think how we could possibly get over the next few yards. Rex was driving and so well'.[35] That weekend had been like any other they had spent together, and would again, but Rex seemed remote. In September, Edith had thought him 'ill and depressed', as if he were 'going through something and hasn't told me'; she was also disconcerted by his new interest in Freud.[36]

On 14 October Edith had sent the manuscript of *The Triumphant Footman*, which she had dedicated to Sassoon, along with Rex's cover design to Secker. At first she had been pleased with this latest book, a farcical historical satire, a celebration of self-reinvention and an affectionate portrayal of a successful social climber. It was an ebullient departure from her previous novels, but as she sent it to the publisher she began to doubt herself. To her surprise though, Secker had replied three days later with the news that it had been sent to print.

The Triumphant Footman, published by Secker in 1930, tells the tale of Alphonse, an adventurer who, fleeing his master's house, having stolen the family patent of nobility, masquerades as an aristocrat and various personae in the courts of Europe.

> My father owned a collection of family papers which had at one time been carried off by a footman. Among them this man had discovered an ancient patent of nobility given to a member of the Olivier family. The adventurous footman adopted the title and travelled all over Europe as a marquis. This amusing idea was at the bottom of *The Triumphant Footman*.[37]

Edith used her fascination with role playing and personality in a far more light-hearted, frolicsome fashion than in her earlier novels. Perhaps she was inspired by Thackeray's *Barry Lyndon* but also, more simply, by the extraordinary social mobility and self-reinvention of some of her young friends. Though the story of the footman is fanciful, beneath the narrative lie the universal truths that we are none of us one person and that we are a different person to everyone we encounter:

> So while his mother always clung to the soft Parisian syllable of his full name, Alphonse was known to his father and to all his London friends simply as 'Alf'; and the Superintendent of the Sunday-school wrote him down in the register, without question, as 'Alfred Biskin'. In Spain, his master had called him 'Alfonso', and Alphonse accepted this variant of his name as readily as the others. Each new appellation, too, seemed to call out a slightly different aspect of his character.[38]

Alphonse leaps from persona to persona, narrowly escaping discovery and even execution. And in the end she allows him to triumph, as the title suggests. The novel was hailed by *Harper's Magazine*, when it was published in America in the same year, as 'a piquant, chuckle-tempting story – perfect summer reading'.[39]

By the beginning of December she had written the first few

pages of what she hoped would become her next novel, for which she had the title, *Dwarf's Blood*. But by the middle of the month, only weeks after Wall Street had crashed and devastated America's stock market, heralding the start of a global depression, Edith was having a financial drama of her own. And it was hampering the progress of *Dwarf's Blood*: 'my anxieties make me non-creative! They tug at me with fretful fears.'[40] She had now begun to doubt that it was possible to make enough money to live on by writing books. 'I can't', she wrote in bed one night, 'tho' I know my books are perhaps precious and limited in their appeal . . . I am going thro' a bad money crisis. <u>No</u> dividends and therefore on as before – Huge debts pile up like gigantic waves and my little ship is down in the trough. I have been awake the last two nights trying to see a way out, and began to feel I must leave this house and live <u>nowhere</u>.'[41] That night she had been dining in bed when Violet, her maid, came in to see her. She told Edith that she knew she had been worrying about domestic expenses and that she had a plan. She would be Edith's only servant and Mrs Lea, the current cook, could be let go. Violet would keep house on 24 shillings a week saving Edith about £180 a year and she would do all the washing. And they agreed that there must be no more guests at the Daye House. 'Whether we do it or not', Edith concluded before she went to sleep that night, 'she has cheered me marvellously by her pluck and loyalty and affection'.[42]

Late on the last night of the year, and the decade, Edith mulled over the plans in her diary. 'I feel that when once the new regime has begun, it won't be bad. I don't care how little I have to eat if I can live here, but it's the change-over that I hate, and people knowing about it', she lamented. 'An unhappy end to the year. I mean to tell none of the family till they find out! And must go on at present for a month – till Mrs Lea's notice is up.' Her resolution made, Edith sat in bed waiting for 1930 to begin. 'Listened to the bells at midnight.'[43]

Part Three

❖

REVERSIBLE FACES

14: Moonraking

❖

'Oh, no other county can compare to Wiltshire!'

Edith Olivier, quoted in Cecil Beaton, *Self-Portrait with Friends*

'No guests', Edith had written emphatically in her diary in December 1929. She had come to the depressing conclusion that if she was going to save money she would have to abide by her new regime and curb her love of entertaining. But in the New Year an alternative opportunity presented itself. Her old friends Sir Richard and Lady Glyn were to go on a cruise that would last some months and they offered Edith their house, a Georgian mansion in Wimborne over the border in Dorset. She could shut up the Daye House and stay for free at Gaunts House with their servants to look after her, dedicate her days to writing rather than anxious economizing, have guests to join her and afford to travel up to London to see her friends.

And so Edith settled into a temporary life of luxurious solitude and committed herself to finishing her novel. She invited Rex to come down to join her for her first weekend but he wrote to tell her that he was still working on his *Gulliver* illustrations and couldn't escape. 'My dearest Edith, if I came to stay with you', he wrote, 'I know perfectly well that, with all unknown Dorset lying round to explore with you, I should not remain drawing 10 minutes! Do let us have some fun and driving about when this fearful cold is over and there is some prospect of summer. Preferably', he added, 'you will be able to take me in your Rolls Royce by then which will be more fun still – that is if only Secker will pay up punctually!'[1] And so instead, the following month, Edith went up to London. She lunched with Rex at the Eiffel Tower on Percy Street and then spent a 'delicious afternoon' around the corner in his studio poring over sketches, drawings and studies.[2] As well as the *Gulliver* illustrations he had been commissioned to decorate Edith Sitwell's book on Pope, and for his hero Walter de la Mare's *Desert Islands and Robinson Crusoe* he was hard at work on galleons, dolphins, windswept seas and swaying palm trees.

Edith's resolve lasted only as long as she stayed away from home. And her visitors' book is testament to this. When she returned to the Daye House at the beginning of April, she immediately invited Rex and Cecil to stay with her that coming weekend, 5 to 7 April. She was happier with guests, happiest when the guest was Rex. And though she had always liked to fill the house with friends, family and children, now the Daye House was evolving into something else – it was becoming a kind of provincial salon. More and more, it was not just Rex but many of her other friends who were making of Edith's cottage a refuge from the feverish world of London society, and from their increasingly eventful and complicated lives. In the coming years as she drew more of her young friends to Wiltshire, the Daye House became the centre of their little world. In the future there would be new guests, like Osbert Sitwell, whom she feared would alight on her inadequacies as a hostess; the art historian Tancred Borenius, who would come to Wiltshire as director of the excavations at Clarendon Palace; the artist Henry Lamb; and Lord David Cecil, who would move to a house in the nearby village of Rockbourne about ten miles from Wilton, with his wife Rachel, daughter of the literary critic Desmond MacCarthy. In November 1930 Rex's Slade contemporary Oliver Messel visited Edith. She took him on her usual tour of the park and he pleased her by being suitably impressed by its wonders. 'It's delicious to wander there', she wrote to Cecil, 'and to know the newcomer will <u>see</u> each loveliness as it comes into sight.'[3]

At Christmas 1931 William Walton gave Edith a piano. She

put it in a corner of the Long Room, beside the door. It had been sent in preparation for the New Year, when she had invited him to stay so that he might begin work on his first symphony. By then Edith would have grown to like him, never as unreservedly as the others, but she admired his 'genius' for music and was pleased that she could offer him a haven in which he could work.[4] Walton made much of his humble roots, played the working-class hero and the inverted snob when it suited him, and was frequently given financial assistance from the Sitwells, Sassoon and others. His social rise was practised in a far more subtle, insinuating fashion than Cecil's energetic ascent. Of Walton's friendship with Edith, his biographer Stephen Lloyd writes that she was 'one of several society ladies whose hospitality Walton cultivated with care, and doubtless, even cunning. They after all', he adds, 'could effect the right contacts and offer him tastes of the artistic and society life so typical of the period, with long weekends at large country homes, mixing with both up-and-coming and well-established artists and other personalities'.[5] Edith had grand associates and a circle of artistic friends but unlike most of Walton's society ladies she was not a rich patron.

But neither lack of money or space, or having to share a bathroom, would deter Edith from inviting her friends to stay with her, often, like the now increasingly desultory Brian Howard, for extended periods of time. Her early life had been spent in a house filled with siblings and then she had lived with her intelligent, fun-loving sister Mildred as her daily companion. And so her friends had become the stimulating, sustaining centre of her life. She felt lonely and old without them. 'These boys are delicious to an old hag like me – making me feel <u>they</u> feel me their contemporary', she wrote in her diary in December 1930.[6]

In turn, in the peaceful, cosseting atmosphere of the Daye House, cut off from the world by rivers and high brick walls, Edith could offer her friends a pastoral retreat. She loved the fact that, over 300 years after Wilton had inspired Sir Philip Sidney, a new generation of artists considered her house a sanctuary and the park an inspiration. It was just the kind of romantic connection that she delighted in. Edith 'continued without effort on her part', Cecil Beaton recalled some years later, 'to discover young people of promise and bring them to her house. So many of the young writers, painters and poets came to her with problems about their work and life, and they knew that after she had listened intently to their outpourings, her advice would be unprejudiced, wise and Christian'.[7]

The Daye House wasn't an intellectual and political hothouse in the Garsington mould, however, and it had none of the biting wit of Bloomsbury. And outside her indulged and indulging circle of friends, there were those less captivated by Edith's charms. In January 1929, Julia Strachey had stayed for a night at the Daye House. Strachey was distinctly unimpressed by what she perceived as her hostess's lack of sophistication in both dress and thought. Bloomsbury venom, it appeared, could seep as far as Wiltshire: 'Edith wore a suburban georgette dance-frock for dinner, her hair like a negress's on one side and flat the other. The second night, an argument about religion, Tommy [Stephen Tomlin] telling her his atheistical views and that "the time has really come for people to throw away the crutch of religion". She, being deeply, passionately religious, couldn't take in what it all implied.'[8] Similarly Virginia Woolf had dismissed Rex in her diary as 'steamy, grubby, inarticulate Rex Whistler' when she had met him (in his painting clothes) at Duncan Grant's studio.[9] Bloomsbury this was not.

Edith was no lofty muse. She wasn't simply a catalyst or a conduit for inspiration; she had a career of her own. And in her friendships she found inspiration and stimulation for her own writing. At the beginning of the year Dick de la Mare, son of the poet and an editor at Faber, had written to Edith with an offer to publish *Dwarf's Blood*, which he had heard she was writing.

De la Mare was Sassoon's editor and his fiancée, Katta, was the daughter of the Bishop of Salisbury, so Edith had two sources of recommendation. His offer, an advance of £100 and 15 per cent royalty on the first 5,000 copies, seemed very attractive and she immediately accepted it, abandoning Secker. That year she was also co-editing a book called *Moonrakings: A Little Book of Wiltshire Stories* to raise funds for the Women's Institute. There had been a competition to gather old tales from the ladies of the county and it was Edith's job to make the selection. As her own contribution she submitted the script of the Quidhampton Mummers' Play, which had never been written down but was passed down verbally through the generations. It had last been performed in 1913; 'then the War killed it', Edith wrote in the Preface. She visited the last surviving Mummers and wrote as they dictated their individual parts from usually very rusty memories, eventually piecing it together as a whole. The idea of collecting and saving from oblivion these stories – history, personal memories, games and customs, superstitions and ghost stories, rhymes and folk songs – was very dear to Edith's heart. She felt passionately the need to preserve these vestiges, moonrakings, not only of Wiltshire's past, but of her own. 'The natives of Wiltshire are famed for the fruits of their rakings', Edith explained, 'there is no telling what a Wiltshireman may pull out of a pond'. Legend told that the men of Bishops Cannings, a village in the Vale of Pewsey, informed passing excise-men that they were raking the pond for a cheese that had fallen into the water.* The excise-men took them for fools and went on their way, for it was plain to see that the men were thrusting with their rakes at the moon's reflection on the surface of the water. Once the excise-men were out of sight the local men returned to their task, which was to extract the kegs of smuggled whisky that had been deposited in the pond for safekeeping. And so the inhabitants of Wiltshire were given a colloquial name: 'Moonrakers'. 'Cheese, moon-shadows, or spirits', wrote Edith, 'you cannot guess what may be found in a dewpond – that quiet miracle which lies on the downs, a mere ring of water

---

* The exact location of the pond is a matter of fiercely fought local conjecture. Edith believed that it was Bishops Cannings.

reflecting nothing but the sky, and holding a secret in its shallow depths, – the secret of its making, which has been handed down from father to son in the dry upland country.'[10]

Edith's literary success had only enhanced her inherent intellectual self-confidence and with it, no doubt, her faith in the supremacy of her own opinions. She had always been a voracious reader but now that she was writing reviews for publication, she was honing her critical faculties. One day in March 1931 Edith would pay a visit to a friend, a local farmer and milk retailer in his late thirties called Arthur Street. 'She called on me without any warning, and swooped into the room as only Edith Olivier could swoop, waving in her hand a cutting from the *Salisbury Times*', Street later recalled in a wonderfully evocative account of this encounter.

> 'This is charming, Arthur, charming. You must write a book. I insist.'
>
> Edith Olivier, I knew, would, and could, and did insist on anything at any time from anybody, so I gave her a cigarette in order to gain time. Write a book, indeed. Easier said than done . . . so I asked with what subject was this book of mine to deal.
>
> Edith waved her cigarette airily – even when she was sitting down her hands talked expressively in the language of Edithian swoops. 'With the one thing which you know something about, of course. With farming . . .'
>
> 'But, Miss Olivier . . .' I protested.
>
> 'But me no buts. Promise me that you'll try to write a book about this farm. Promise me to make a start, and to let me know how it goes.' So, of course, I promised, because in that particular mood Edith Olivier was an irresistible force against which I dared not attempt to play the role of immoveable object.[11]

And so, at Edith's behest, Street began to write, often late at night in bed after haymaking in the wet summer of 1931. *Farmer's Glory* was published in the following year by Dick de la Mare at Faber, almost certainly at Edith's suggestion. With its warm, simple scenes evoking farming and life in rural Wiltshire and western Canada, where Street had spent several years as a farm labourer, it met with much acclaim and launched his career in writing and broadcasting. He would go on to write another twenty-nine books – essays, novels, country calendars and farming commentaries – and become a regular and well-loved voice on the wireless for many years. *Farmer's Glory*, his first, and most famous, book was dedicated to Edith.

In the Long Room, over the years, Edith gathered such relics of her friendships. More and more of the books that filled her shelves were affectionately inscribed to her by their authors: Siegfried Sassoon, Elinor Wylie, Sacheverell and Osbert Sitwell, Walter de la Mare and countless others. Space on her walls disappeared behind paintings that had been given to her, many of them by Rex. In her scrapbooks she wrote out her friends' poems in her own hand, some by Sassoon and others that Elinor Wylie had composed at the Daye House in 1928; she added prayers, quotations from essays and charms against poison. She pasted in postcards from friends, from Cecil in Hollywood or the South of France, from Stephen and Sassoon in Sicily. There were Rex's drawings on scraps of paper, newspaper cuttings and photographs that Cecil and others had taken. On a rather formal, bookish portrait photograph of Edith, probably taken for book publicity, one of her friends had jokingly drawn on her nose a pair of pince-nez, perhaps to enhance her look of a lady of letters.

The Long Room was still, and would always be, at the heart of Edith's world. It was where she gathered her guests and where she sat to talk with friends or to write her books; the most autobiographical room in the house. To the right of the fireplace stood Edith's desk, a robust bureau with a fold-down lid. At the back of it were secret compartments and pigeonholes stuffed with papers and trinkets. On top of the desk stood a little pot stuffed with pens and quills, a heap of papers, a large, elegant glass egg timer and an ink blotter. Illuminating all this was a shaded lamp made out of a figurine of Nelson. Ranged along the shelf at the back of the desk was a row of large photographs. As she sat there writing, the faces of Rex, Sassoon, Walton and her father looked back at her, presiding over the desk like household gods. Beside these photographs was a drawing that Stephen had made from memory of Mildred to illustrate her memorial book; her head is in profile, emerging from a vast collar – a pretty, youthful face framed by dainty curls.

It was to Edith and the Long Room that Cecil was increasingly drawn for inspiration. Writing to Cecil's biographer Hugo Vickers in 1980, Stephen recalled that 'Edith Olivier was C's Egeria, Erda, she was all the muses to him' and that she had 'stimulated Cecil as no one else has done. I adored her too. C loved her most appalling vitality, her writing a diary at 3.30 in the night . . . She was utterly adorable'.[12] 'She galvanized a man already galvanized by his own rare gifts', he wrote; 'her talk was a blitz of fireworks. Her interests were legion . . .'[13] Galvanize was then a very modish word, which Stephen and Cecil used liberally. But it does describe the kind of influence Edith had on her friends. She counselled them into action, encouraged them, and helped them to focus on bringing their ideas to fruition, to make them coherent rather than untethered flights of fancy. She offered them real, practical and usually highly opinionated advice, whether they chose to take it or not. And she wished the same kind of success upon her friends that she was enjoying.

'The remarkable Edith has left after a visit of three days when I have had the opportunity of seeing her at her astounding best', Cecil would write in his diary in June 1931:

> So often I see her when I am surrounded by many people and this is not satisfactory. It is an abuse of her for her great qualities are not enjoyed in a crowd. She is 63, maybe more [she was 58], and one treats her as a contemporary. From the vicarage in Wilton it is inconceivable that this penniless

spinster should have blossomed into the extraordinary livewire that she has become – she has unlimited energy and vitality – she talks and listens intently all day – she relates long stories with heroic gusto. She is witty, full of jokes and at night she retires to bed to read three books and write a detailed journal after which she reappears next morning as fresh as ever . . . she has infinite sympathy and is one of the kindest people in the world. Everyone goes to her with troubles knowing they can trust implicitly in her and that her advice will be wise and easy. There are details of her complete unselfconscious behaviour that sometimes irritate one but I really adore her and love her more than almost any friend I have. If she were to die I would know that no-one would ever be able to fill the breach.[14]

The previous August Cecil had sent Edith a selection of pieces he was writing. '<u>Very</u> good Cecil', she replied, adding, 'I should go over them again. <u>Polishing</u>, improving and shortening a sentence here and there. You will find the places if you read the stories out loud . . . I don't believe writing can be an art unless it has more <u>form</u> than this.' Warming to her theme, she contrasted Cecil's prose with his photography:

I saw this week . . . your photograph of Christabel [McLaren] on her staircase. <u>There</u> you succeed perfectly, every detail of hall and staircase falls into place. And yet the eye is impelled to concentrate on the figure. I think that is what art should do. Use the details to build up something which is in the artist's mind – and <u>not</u> in the details . . . You are so amazingly observant which is the foundation of satiric writing – though <u>don't</u> give up your satiric <u>pencil</u> for a satiric pen. The pencil is far <u>rarer</u> as an instrument. <u>Anyone</u> can write. Hardly anyone can draw.[15]

In the autumn of 1930, Cecil asked Edith to proofread *The Book of Beauty,* his anthology of well-known beauties which was to be illustrated with his own photographs and drawings and published by Duckworth. Having read the manuscript Edith urged him to restrain his instinct for prose of a very purple hue. 'You twice speak of "Raving Beauties"', she pointed out to him; 'I suppose you can <u>say</u> this but on paper it looks as if the Beauties raved like madwomen.'[16] She also suggested that he should reduce the sections on his sisters Nancy and Baba, advice that he ignored: 'you know how spiteful people are – quite ready to say that the whole book is a Boost for them'. 'I have not helped you much to find new adjectives to replace "lovely" and "glamorous" etc.', she added, 'which is what I think is what you wanted me to do. But I advise your leaving out the adjective altogether, whenever you can . . .'[17]

Cecil later recalled how he had sprawled on the floor of the Long Room with Edith, scissors and paste in their hands as they reorganized the order of his book. It was published in November 1930 and received good reviews. In Edith's copy Cecil wrote: 'To my <u>Darling</u> Poppet Edith who has written this book for me the angel! Love from her very affectionate Cecil'.[18] She wrote to him when it arrived in the post:

> What a <u>perfect lovely beautiful priceless</u> present . . . The whole book leaves an impression of amazing technique, great imagination and originality, the most sure sense of Beauty. Artistically it is a real achievement and a <u>lift</u> for Photography, proud and haughty as that art has already become. The inscription makes me very proud and I love it but it's quite untrue . . . The whole book is a marvel – I feel it <u>must</u> be the ultra-fashionable Christmas present of the year.[19]

Most of the entries were laden with compliments about their subjects. The Jungman sisters he described as 'a pair of 18th-century angels made of wax, exhibited at Madame Tussaud's before the fire'.[20] One can only imagine what he had written before Edith's editorial input curbed his excesses. It is perhaps unsurprising, therefore, that Virginia Woolf took exception to her inclusion amongst the beauties. She had earlier refused to let Cecil take her portrait, dismissing him to Vita Sackville-West as 'a mere Catamite' and she was now appalled to find herself featured in his book.[21] In a letter to *The Nation and the Athenaeum* she protested that Cecil had never asked her permission and that she felt herself a victim. 'Mrs Virginia Woolf is one of the most gravely distinguished women I have ever seen', Cecil had written.

> In her we do not find the conventional pink cheeks and liquid eyes and childish lips. Although she would look like a terrified ghost in an assembly of the accepted raving beauties, she would make each one separately appear vulgar and tawdry in comparison with her . . . Her fine skin is parchment-coloured, she has timid startled eyes, set deep, a sharp bird-like nose and firm pursed lips . . . her old-fashioned dowdinesses are but a conscious and literary game of pretence, for she is alertly contemporary, even a little ahead of her time. Many of her confrères see her as a Juno, awe-inspiring and gaunt, but she herself is frightened, a bundle of tentative gestures, and quick nervous glances, as frail and crisp as a dead leaf; and like a sea-anemone she curls up at contact with the outer world.[22]

Cecil was more pleased than perturbed by the publicity that Woolf's letter aroused. Edith, who barely knew and cared little for Virginia and undoubtedly delighted in Cecil's caricature of the literary grande dame, wrote to him: 'Don't dear Cecil let the growl of people like Virginia Woolf get on your nerves. These carpings and yappings will pass and your book and your pictures will remain. Everyone who counts realises that she is only being Bloomsbury so let her bloomingly bloom.'[23]

Edith was influential and generous to her friends not just in regard to their work but in every aspect of their lives. Back in April Rex and Cecil had both accepted Edith's invitation to stay at the Daye House for the weekend. Though Rex was in despair at the slow progress of his *Gulliver* drawings (he still had six more to do and felt 'deadly weary of them') it was a jolly, uproarious weekend. Edith thought that Rex looked tired but wrote that 'both boys' were 'in wild spirits'.[24] On the Saturday David Herbert came over from Wilton House, bringing with him his teenage cousins, Caroline and Elizabeth Paget, Lord Anglesey's daughters, both beautiful with bobbed black curls and pale skin. Lord Pembroke's twenty-one-year-old second son seemed to be following in Stephen and Cecil's flamboyant wake. He had been living in Berlin, where he had befriended Harold Nicolson and Cyril Connolly and found work singing in a cabaret, performing as a German sailor, and had been briefly engaged to a German girl – to the surprise of his friends who knew him to be homosexual. Soon he would make a career for himself decorating the New York houses of rich Americans and established a home for at least a part of each year at the Park School on the estate, in what was essentially a baroque bungalow, and Edith began to see much more of him.

At lunch they ate trout caught from the river at the edge of the lawn with strawberries from her garden and they drank white wine out of Edith's tall green goblets. The young people playfully 'bullied and chaffed' Edith, and after lunch Cecil and Rex decided to transform her into a woman in a painting by Matisse. She submitted with delight as they dressed her in Cecil's imitation leopard-skin dressing gown, a jet-black cape and a sable collar with a magenta rose pinned to it. They added countless beaded necklaces, a huge black hat and three coloured chiffon veils and then, to complete the transformation, they painted her cheeks vermilion, with scarlet lips and eyes heavily rimmed with black. 'No one ever looked more extraordinary', she thought.[25]

Thus attired, Edith began energetically extolling the virtues of Wiltshire. For Cecil, it was a conversation that would prove of the utmost significance. Until recently his world had been entirely urban but for some months he had been thinking about taking a house in the country. He had already discussed the idea with Edith. 'And so you are going into retreat?' she had written to him the previous September. 'Why don't you find this cottage somewhere near here, so that you can now and again break out of your

Hermit's Cell and come and converse with the cloistered nun walled up at Wilton?'[26] Now, amidst the landscape that so possessed her imagination, tall trees all about and the river flowing past beyond the dining-room window, drinking from a green goblet and dressed as a Matisse, Edith conjured up the *genius loci*, the spirit of Wiltshire, for her guests. Her infectious passion for the landscape already held Rex in its thrall and now worked like an incantation on Cecil. She invoked Wiltshire's mystical energies, both sacred and profane, telling seductive tales of endless skies, of immemorial hills and ancient streams that carved the landscape, the county's earliest architects.

Suddenly Edith had a plan. Stephen Tomlin had recently told her of 'a Grand Meaulnes sort of place' that he had found while walking on the downs above his cottage.[27] It was a crumbling Georgian manor house obscured by ilexes and nestling in the hollow of a remote chalk valley high on Cranborne Chase. And, to Cecil's delight, she said that it had a grotto in the garden, which aroused his most baroque, Sitwellian instincts. With her face still painted and her body still bound in Cecil's leopard-skin dressing gown, Edith hurriedly ushered her guests into the car and they motored off to Tomlin's stone cottage at Swallowcliffe. When they arrived Tomlin said he would show them, and they climbed back into their cars and set off, 'an astounding party', Edith wrote, 'Cecil and the girls well-dressed moderns, Rex a gentle youth, Tommy [Tomlin] a corduroyed workman, and I this figure of fun'.[28] They drove off along the road towards Shaftesbury and then veering off the main road turned up a steep chalk track that led onto the downland. Eventually they got out of the car to walk the last mile down to the house.

Standing before them was a small portion of a much larger mansion built in the 1740s and then partially demolished in the 1870s. What remained was the east wing of the original house with the L-shaped former stables opposite. The house was elegant enough for Cecil to admire but dilapidated enough for him to imagine reawakening its beauty himself. 'It was as if I had been touched on the head by some magic wand', Cecil later wrote. 'It was love at first sight, and from the moment that I stood under the archway, I knew that this place was destined to be mine'.[29] It was to be Cecil's own Arcadia, a place where he could play at the pastoral life in a fantasy world of his own design. He had visions of weekends in the country, picnics on the lawn, fancy-dress parties to which he would lure his friends down from London. For Cecil the discovery of this old, melancholy house asleep behind a heavy veil of ilexes was Edith's moonraking brought to life.

But as they stood gazing upon the house a gamekeeper appeared and asked them to leave for fear that the owner would sack him if they were discovered on the estate. Rex and Cecil stood aside as Edith, in her extraordinary attire, stepped forward to enquire whether the house was occupied and whether they could take a closer look. But the gamekeeper held his ground and soon sent them on their way. It was late afternoon as they set off back to Wilton, Rex driving 'perfectly' along grass tracks as the car teetered above steep drops. They arrived home for a late tea and Cecil implored Edith to telephone the Glyns who knew the 'cantankerous' owner, Borley.

A 'wild evening' with Rex and Cecil followed their afternoon of romantic discovery. That night Edith wrote:

> They wanted me to be a <u>tough baby</u> (Cecil's American word) and insisted on drinking <u>all</u> the little bottles of sample liqueurs. I can't think why we were not drunk. We sat after dinner in darkness and did table turning and then Rex made lovely drawings and burnt them all. They had terrible fights over the hot water bottles when they went to bed – tearing the sheets off each other and making a terrific noise. Both <u>so</u> funny all day trying to be ribald, and lewd, and obscene and yet being such darlings . . . to these boys it's just absurd – a joke which they laugh at from outside.[30]

Rex and Cecil returned to London the next day and Cecil immediately sat down to write to Mr Borley, the owner of Ashcombe.

'No matter what the difficulties', Cecil wrote, 'I would overcome them all; considerations of money, suitability, or availability, were all superficial. This house must belong to me'.[31] Cecil would eventually succeed in claiming Ashcombe as his own, if only for a time. But for now it remained, for both him and Edith, only a lovely prospect. 'I adored our weekend. <u>How</u> funny you both were, imagining all that mischief', Edith wrote to him a few days later; 'you made me feel like a Courtezan (far more like me than trollop or strumpet which apply to you and Rex) so that since you left, while I have been reading a book about one I thought all the time that it was about <u>me</u>. And <u>I still think so</u>.' Her thoughts then turned to Ashcombe: 'I would so love you to be there', she told him; 'I feel it the place to inspire real creative work, either writing or painting and might make a new epoch in your life and shew you the way to some great achievement. Also <u>what fun for us all</u>!'[32]

15: Ashcombe

Is it what you can, at this moment in your life, make the chief thing in your life?

Edith to Cecil, 30 June 1930

Owning a house was something that Rex only ever daydreamed about, usually with Edith on one of their expeditions into the Wiltshire countryside. Coming across a particularly beautiful valley, a sleepy village or a Queen Anne rectory, they would conjure up elaborate images of the life that he might lead there and his visions of the future were as fanciful and extravagantly impossible as his pictures of the past. 'Looking upon a supreme view', she wrote after one such trip, 'Rex said he would like a kingdom and planned his Summer Palace just where we were sitting and a Versailles down in the Vale . . . The large still golden light on the downs was ineffable and how Rex loves it and feels it and absorbs it'.[1]

But domestic fantasies troubled Rex. He was happy to evoke Arcadia in his paintings and to improve other people's houses with his murals and designs for architectural features but a home of his own in the country was quite another thing. And he had the Daye House, which had become a second home for him but with none of the conventional familial ties. For Rex, unlike Cecil, buying a house was inextricably associated with a wife and children and the kind of grown-up life that he didn't have, and wasn't even sure that he wanted. Of course, he was still only twenty-four and no doubt it seemed that there would be time enough for that. Only recently he had been planning to share rooms and a studio with

Edith's young editor Dick de la Mare but those plans were thwarted when de la Mare got engaged early in the year. 'He feels that he has "lost a friend" and is "miserable about it"', Edith wrote in her diary in February.[2] Rex had, however, bought himself a car, a second-hand Vauxhall saloon, an ex-showroom model with elaborate interiors which he called his 'drawing-room'.[3]

By this time Rex was arguably as successful, or at least as well known, as Cecil. Photography though, was immediate and lucrative and Cecil, at only twenty-six, could soon afford a chauffeur as well as a country house. Rex had to toil away at commissions for months, and he was earning far less money than his friend. This was exacerbated by the fact that Rex, out of some exaggerated sense of propriety, tried to avoid the subject of payment with his clients. Perhaps he felt it inappropriate for a gentleman to dwell on something as banal as a fee. And it was usual for these clients to rely on Rex to propose an amount, which he invariably kept low out of modesty. He was in an odd position. He was increasingly welcomed in the country houses and drawing rooms of the aristocratic world, but it was not the world he had been born into, and though he was a guest he was often also an employee – his rich and cultivated clients were now usually his friends. It meant that the work he produced for them could be entirely personal and intimate but also, dangerously, that he was continually mixing business and pleasure.

Overwhelmed and depressed by his workload and whipped up into a wealthier world that was not his own, he was increasingly living beyond his means. He was also incredibly generous. Rex hated doing book illustrations but the work kept him afloat. He had begun to support his ageing parents, even to the point of paying his brother's fees for Balliol, which Laurence entered in the autumn of 1930. In the early summer of 1930 he was still at work on his *Gulliver* drawings. Rex had been paid a fee of £195 (about £10,780 today), which equated to about £7.10s per drawing (£415). At first glance this seems generous but the effort and the time the drawings were taking meant that his fee had to stretch over more than a year, and it was his principal commission. When Dennis Cohen of the Cresset Press offered to buy the originals for a total of £150 (about £8,300 today), Rex gladly accepted. Cohen immediately resold them for over double the amount he had paid for them. According to Laurence, 'Rex was innocent, and he was needy.'[4]

'He feels very stale over Gulliver tho' I think his drawings still <u>full</u> of invention', Edith wrote in her diary at the end of May, and again, only a few days later: 'Can't finish Gulliver. Each picture takes him 3 times as long as the early ones and he is inundated with orders for lovely rooms and ceilings, none of which he can ever begin'.[5] Two days later he arrived at the Daye House for the weekend. 'Rex came at 7 having meant to come earlier in the day. He is driven and distracted by his contracts. Still a drawing and two maps to be done for Gulliver'. He had just signed what Edith described as 'a really <u>fraudulent</u> contract' with Elizabeth Godley to illustrate her book *Green Outside* for Chatto & Windus. Rex told Edith that he had been forced to sign it in a hurry and then realized that the terms were most unfavourable; 'he gets practically nothing but must deliver 10 drawings by the end of June. He thinks they will sue him if he is late and said <u>I feel inclined to let them. I would gladly let them have all the money I've got in the Bank but could they seize my easels?</u>'[6]

Perhaps Rex's lamentations were exaggerated for Edith's benefit, and no doubt overstated further by the ever-doting Edith in her diary, but it seems that Rex really did feel these things deeply. 'When he gave me a print of the first Gulliver drawing', Stephen later recalled, 'he wrote sadly of its inadequacy, from his own point of view – particularly as he had taken great trouble over this series. The deep sadness in his voice when he spoke of this revealed a realisation of the essential tragedy of each endeavour.'[7] But the illustrations that gave Rex so much pain are now considered his finest. They are crisp, confident and finely wrought, playfully and elegantly recreating the Swiftian world. Scenes from the narrative play out within a proscenium arch formed by wide rococo frames, themselves made up of an ornate and intricate filigree of images drawn from and elaborating on the scenes they contain.

If illustration work was as much of a trauma as Rex claimed, then it was his very facility and remarkable versatility that were his undoing. Though he longed to be respected and admired as a fine artist, each lovely mural that he painted, each book that he illustrated so deftly, took him further and further from his wish. Since 1929 he had been employed by the theatre impresario Charles Cochran to design costumes, curtains and stage sets for his popular revues. It was a coup for Rex who went on to work with Cochran on several productions; more importantly, it would open up a new world of opportunities for him in the theatre.

As companies began to recognize the value of art for commercial purposes, Rex was increasingly called upon to create adverts, posters, Christmas cards, greetings telegrams, stamps for the Post Office and illustrations for the *Tatler* and *Vogue*; he was also commissioned by Guinness, Wedgwood Pottery, the London Underground, Fortnum and Mason, Imperial Airways and others. With its energy, ingenuity and light-hearted wit, Rex's work charmed and entertained, but it was also striking enough to arrest the attention of someone flicking through the pages of a magazine, walking down the street or waiting on a London Underground platform.

In 1932 Jack Beddington, the innovative and artistically enlightened publicity director of Shell, who would also employ Paul Nash, Graham Sutherland, John Piper and others, commissioned Rex to produce a poster for Shell Motor Spirit. Cars increasingly represented freedom and leisure, the ability to escape into the countryside, to explore the British Isles and to discover its heritage. But the advertising campaigns that Beddington commissioned are filled not with images of cars or petrol pumps, but with the promise of liberty and leisure; he wanted Shell Motor Spirit to become synonymous with the spirit of the age. For Shell Rex painted a view of the Vale of Aylesbury, not far from the house to which his parents would move at the end of 1931. The foreground is cast in the deep shade of a tree, below which the silhouetted figure of his brother sits in peaceful contemplation; beyond, the gently sloping wooded valley unfolds into the distance, bathed in late summer sunlight. The Chilterns rise on the horizon beneath scudding clouds in a duck-egg blue sky. It is the essence of English nostalgia, an Englishness that was becoming increasingly commercial and that slipped effortlessly from Rex's paintbrush.

Edith and Cecil had been in almost daily contact since their momentous discovery of Ashcombe in April. And all the time that Rex was labouring over *Gulliver*, letters flew back and forth between Cecil and Borley, the owner. 'Say you are a very quiet invalidish gentleman with no dogs or guns and you won't interfere with the game', Edith had urged him.[8] Cecil was determined to buy the place but Borley informed him that the loss of the house would devalue the estate and that his gamekeeper already lived in a part of the house. He also told Cecil that he had heard he was a friend of Miss Olivier 'who is considered hot stuff in this part of the world'.[9] Edith thought this was very entertaining: 'I am writing to my lawyer and bringing an action against Mr Borley for saying (1) that I am a friend of yours when I consider you far too tough to be on my visiting list. (2) that I am hot stuff. When every reviewer calls me <u>cool and restrained</u>. I shall be in London on Friday night and alone', she told Cecil, adding, 'I suggested to Rex that we should go to see Cochrane [sic] (he had asked me to go with him some time). He is stubbornly silent – as is his wont. So I shall probably be left in the lurch. What are you doing that evening?'[10]

The silence was evidently broken, as that Friday night Edith had a raucous supper with both Rex and Cecil at the Eiffel Tower restaurant on Percy Street. 'We walked through the streets, the boys in wild spirits and pretending I was drunk', she wrote; 'I can't think why the police didn't arrest us as they led me along with my fur coat wound round me (often over my face) and kept pushing me so that I reeled and then they caught me and supported me.

Lifted me at last into a Taxi . . . both real schoolboys and enjoying themselves vastly. Very funny and absurd'.[11]

After a telephone call from Edith, Borley was finally persuaded to let Cecil have a proper look at Ashcombe. At the end of May, when Edith returned from her annual visit to Ireland, she drove Cecil to Shaftesbury to collect Borley and the trio set off up the treacherous pathways that led to the house. At this second visit Cecil was 'in a haze of ecstasy' and in spite of the absence of electricity, water or plumbing, he was more determined than ever that Ashcombe should be his.[12] Eventually Borley agreed that Cecil could take a seven-year lease on the house. The nominal rent of £50 a year reflected the amount of work that was needed. Edith spent the next week planning what architect Cecil should employ to make the improvements. 'Cecil dear how I hug myself and you (the latter alas! only spiritually) when I remember Ashcombe', she wrote to him in London a few days later; 'can you believe that in a few months you may be established there in a vast noble studio which as yet does not exist in that noble <u>shell</u>.'[13] She was overjoyed that he would be living nearby but felt the need to offer the deliriously excited Cecil some cautionary advice:

> I think it is really unique, and uniquely romantic. You won't find such another place and the rent, I should say, not high for what it is . . . I myself should love it and make it my home but I'm not sure if you could – could you? Are you too urbane and civilised to enjoy a bucolic existence when you begin to <u>live</u> it? And would the kind of work you do be at all possible there? . . . I come back to it again, <u>in itself</u>, Ashcombe is perfect. But is it what you can, at this moment in your life, make the chief thing <u>in</u> your life?[14]

Undaunted, Cecil recruited an architect to oversee the alterations and employed a builder from Wilton, at Edith's suggestion. Rex was recruited to prettify the facade of the house and soon set to work designing a chimney piece for the sitting room and a new surround for the front door, in early eighteenth-century vernacular style and topped by a stone pineapple within a broken pediment, to be carved in Bath stone. He also suggested the addition of ornamental urns along the parapet.

A month after Cecil had signed the lease on Ashcombe, Rex and Edith lay in the Long Room discussing their favourite characters in fiction. They concluded that the best were not the 'ideal noble creatures' but those with flaws and foibles.[15] Often when she saw Rex now, Edith commented in her diary about how ill he seemed or how tired he looked and her well-intentioned anxiety can have done little to raise him from his malaise. He seems to have written far fewer letters to her that year, in their place only hurried little cards with none of the usual illustrations winding around the text. And, increasingly, those cards were sent to refuse her invitations to weekends at the Daye House. But Edith was not the only friend to be shunned; many letters and telephone calls remained unanswered. 'He finds it difficult to refuse invitations and yet he hates parties and interruptions to his work', she wrote in her diary that October; 'his only chance is not to see anyone or answer a telephone call so that he <u>gets</u> no invitations'.[16]

By August, Rex was working on a new commission, a twenty-foot mural in the hall of 19 Hill Street, Mayfair, for Captain Euan Wallace MP and his wife Barbara, the eldest daughter of the architect Sir Edwin Lutyens. He was happy to be painting again but still, to Edith, it seemed that he was suffering: 'Joined Rex at the Euan Wallace's in Hill Street at work on a mural picture which will be lovely. He looked dead tired and is feeling life a great strain', she wrote, adding that he 'has no money and is overworked and filled up with engagements he can't keep. Works there till 4 everyday and eats nothing'.[17] At the end of the month he travelled up to Wilton for a rare weekend at the Daye House and was as charming with Edith as he had ever been. The next day, though, they heard the news that the troubled twenty-nine-year-old artist Christopher Wood had killed himself three days earlier. 'We are both obsessed by the suicide of Christopher Wood at Salisbury station', Edith wrote in her diary that night. 'He left his mother and sister outside and went in and threw himself under the train.'[18] A precociously talented and much-admired painter, Wood had become addicted to opium and with it had become increasingly paranoid. Wood's parents lived not far from Wilton at Reddish House in Broad Chalke. He had travelled up to Salisbury to meet his mother and sister for lunch and to show them his latest work. After lunch he left them outside the station and jumped under a train. At the request of his mother the papers reported his death as an accident but somehow Edith discovered the truth. 'Rex is haunted by the thought of the misery this implies,' she wrote in her diary and perhaps she was haunted by the idea that another, dearly loved, young man might feel the same.[19]

Edith finished writing *Dwarf's Blood* on 10 October 1930 and as usual she was disappointed by the final result. But when she sent the manuscript to Dick de la Mare he wrote to congratulate her, saying that Faber would publish it in the spring of the following year. The novel, a Gothic romance, centres on an old English family called Roxerby. After a disappointment in love, the younger son leaves for Australia. Years later his son, Nicholas, succeeds to the Roxerby baronetcy and returns to England to claim it, along with a crumbling estate. With wealth acquired in Australia he sets about restoring the family's fortunes and returns the house to its former glory. He falls in love with and marries a beautiful local girl and when a son is born to them it seems that their happiness is complete. But it soon becomes clear that the child is a dwarf and Nicholas begins to behave irrationally and shun the baby. Eventually it is revealed that his own mother had been a dwarf, which he had kept secret. The dwarf son Hans is a charming, poetry-loving, precociously gifted artist. Though his mother loves him his father finds that he cannot, a feeling exacerbated by his shame at his mother's dwarfism. And so the family breaks apart and a fanciful, fairy-tale plot ensues that takes the reader from England to the mountains of Bavaria.

Underpinning the story is a theory that Edith seems to have

invented for the purposes of her novel, that the blood of a dwarf affects the mind as well as the body. Though Nicholas is of normal size it is his soul that is dwarfed and wizened by the dwarf's blood in his veins, whereas in the body of a dwarf the blood bestows extraordinary mental gifts. And so Nicholas's mother makes for herself a fortune and Hans is an artistic genius. 'I have always noticed', Edith later wrote, 'that there are certain mental and moral characteristics which seem to spring from dwarfishness'.[20] This of course begs the question, how many dwarves had Edith come across in her life? No doubt she was also influenced by Walter de la Mare's *Memoirs of a Midget* and the dwarf in Aldous Huxley's *Crome Yellow*. What Edith was undoubtedly fascinated by was the idea of suppression and its dangerous emotional consequences. It is hard to believe that Edith didn't read Freud, as his influence seems to hover over so much of her writing, but she had never been convinced of the merits of psychoanalysis. Even so, the sins of the father was certainly a common theme in her books, lives stunted and thwarted by parental figures, drawn from her own experience of an all-powerful, patriarchal influence. Other Freudian themes, those of childhood, madness, repression, release and hysteria, recur again and again in her writing, along with the idea of truth irrepressibly working its way to the surface.

Amusingly, this novel, in which Edith dealt with the subject of heredity, she dedicated to Rex, whose own background she found so persistently irksome and whose drawing of the bound and tormented Prometheus adorned the tail piece. Perhaps she channelled some of Rex's present wretchedness into the troubled Nicholas. When the dwarf child grows up he becomes an artist; his first exhibition in London is a great success and it is Hans who provides his father's salvation. Ultimately the novel is about the transformative and redemptive power of art.

In late October Edith drove over to spend the day with Cecil, who was busy transforming Ashcombe. 'Two things outstand', she wrote in her diary that night, '(1) That Cecil is spending far more than he knows or intends – so much that he won't be able to enjoy it (2) that the road is really <u>impassible</u> – all cars have to be pushed up the first bit – it is so slippery – wheels whir round roaringly! It is going to be quite beautiful – but is now a mason's yard.'[21] Though the courtyard was still a heap of bricks, and some of the rooms remained half-built and unpainted, some without windows and others without doors, Cecil was determined to start life at Ashcombe and invited Rex, Oliver Messel and a new friend, Peter Watson, for an inaugural weekend in November:

> The wild winter's evening arrived eventually when Rex, Oliver, Peter and I ventured down the steep chalky hill of the valley to spend the first weekend at Ashcombe. We savoured the chill smells of paint and freshly carpentered wood, combined with the warm smell of calico, new rugs, and crackling log fires. The small habitation, for so long abandoned to its loneliness, suddenly became alive and took on its own personality. It was unlike any other abode, admittedly fantastic and strange with its bright colours and silver trumpery but to me, at any rate, infinitely charming.[22]

Cecil had met Watson in the summer. He was a friend of Oliver Messel, possessed a fortune and charisma and, according to Cecil, 'the face of a charming cod-fish'.[23] He was to become the love of Cecil's life but Edith thought him rather sinister. The following year she wrote that he was being friendly towards her 'having heard (I presume) that I think him ill-mannered. He now calls me "Edith" and "darling" which I think equally out of place.'[24] Cecil would be obsessed with him for the next four years but Watson gave him only great torment and unhappiness in return.

Edith, along with the socialite and interior decorator Sibyl Colefax, had been invited for lunch that first weekend. 'Drove to Ashcombe soon after 12', she wrote in her diary that night:

> Missing somehow on the way Rex and Oliver Messel who came here to fetch me . . . it's quite magic. The drawing

room full of amusing Rococo chairs, tables and couches. A riot of carved gilt with bunches of wax flowers like wedding cakes. A roaring fire in the lovely grate we bought in Salisbury which is exactly right for the fireplace. The bedrooms have as yet <u>nothing but</u> beds in them, except Rex's – a little Virgin room with bed hangings of white satin. The food was Lucullan. Lady Colefax said Belshazzar's Feast which I felt was mal-apropos. Every sort of cocktail of every sort of colour – tomato, Cocoa-Kola. Luncheon began with Foie Gras and Caviare, then chickens with every vegetable on earth, a delicious whipped cream sweet from the Women's Institute Cookery Book and a great dish of pineapple, grapes and other luscious fruits. It was a Renaissance banquet, not a 20th Century luncheon . . .

The boys made me stay for dinner. Peter Watson rather a wet blanket. Sits apart, seems sulky, and is <u>very</u> grand, and at last retired to his bed, saying he felt ill. He is gauche, saying when I arrived having missed Rex and Oliver, 'Rex didn't <u>at all</u> want to go and fetch you.' I repeated this, when they were all there, and Cecil looked agonised. Rex and I sat together and talked . . . Later we all (except the sick Watson) lay on Cecil's bed and he read extracts from his old diaries, leaving out, in spite of our imploring, all the most shy-making bits.[25]

The next weekend Edith drove up to Oxford. When she had delivered the manuscript of *Dwarf's Blood* to Dick de la Mare he asked her if she would write the preface for a new edition of *An Adventure*. Edith was overjoyed; she believed entirely in Jourdain and Moberly's account and had always defended it; now she had a chance to do so publicly and definitively. Eleanor Jourdain, who had succeeded Moberly as principal of St Hugh's, died of heart failure in 1924 in the midst of a row over the sacking of a tutor. Later that year the third edition had been printed using the authors' real identities for the first time. Edith feared though that a visit to Miss Moberly would be in vain; she was convinced that her old principal would be against the idea of exhuming the scandal. After lunch with David Cecil, now a don at New College, she went to see Miss Moberly at her house in Norham Road and to Edith's delight found that she was very enthusiastic about the plans. It was a chance to rehabilitate her reputation. At eighty-four she struggled with the present but her memory of the past was still as acute as ever.

In her preface Edith sought to prove their account scientifically. Four pull-out maps were added to this edition and Edith focused on the academic meticulousness of their research, which had been deposited in the Bodleian, describing her old friends as 'true and conscientious scholars':[26]

> The book does not contain a ghost story, and now-a-days, no well-educated person would think that it could be explained by calling it one. It is the record of an unexplained extension of the limits of human experience: and it describes an experience of a type with which science is more and more concerning itself.[27]

She was not alone in her defence of the story. Several scientific writers were also sympathetic and she asked one, J. W. Dunne, the author of *An Experiment with Time*, to contribute a note at the close of the preface. He suggested that *An Adventure* confirmed Einstein's theory of relativity. But when the book was published in 1931, in spite of Edith's impassioned preface and Dunne's scientific explanations, for the most part the episode was considered an intriguing tale more than anything else.

On Sunday 7 December after early communion and matins at Wilton Edith drove to Ashcombe to stay overnight for the first time. Cecil's tenure had begun in earnest. Each weekend he piled his Ford with heaps of flowers from Covent Garden and motored down to Wiltshire. In the years to come he would lure an extraordinary array of friends to his country retreat: aristocrats and society luminaries, eccentrics like the Marchesa Casati, Salvador Dali, Ottoline Morrell and Gerald Berners, French neo-romantics like Jean Cocteau and Christian Bérard, as well as friends from

New York and glamorous film stars from Hollywood, all to be photographed on the lawn or in the house as if in a painting by Gainsborough or Fragonard.

That weekend, Edith inspected the progress of the studio and approved of the new decor in the sitting room, 'with its pink walls and the dull old gilt ornaments and furniture softly winking in candlelight'. The sculptor Frank Dobson, his wife and baby, were also staying and Edith was most amused to see Cecil pushing the baby along in its perambulator when she arrived: 'Cecil loathes [the baby] but he hides this very well and is so kind to it'. Another guest was the fashion designer Charles James whom Edith described as 'a little dressmaker who argues incessantly, enunciating like American talkie actors with no consonants. Cecil is giving me a Xmas present of a dress made by him which excites me very much.'[28] In the evening they played games, writing composite novels and drawing composite images, and that night Edith slept in a bedroom that was clad entirely in white satin with a pair of Cupids hovering over the bed. The following week she wrote to thank Cecil: 'What a magician you are for no one else could possibly have made it already a fairy palace.'[29]

Late on Christmas Eve William Walton and Imma arrived at the Daye House to spend the festive season with Edith. It was no longer safe for Imma to be in Germany as the Nazi party's hostility to the aristocracy was becoming more vociferous. The couple were still very much in love and Edith vicariously enjoyed the glow of happiness they brought with them. On the 28th all three lunched at Ashcombe where they found 'an enormously noisy and quite incongruous party . . . Cecil flitted about, producing the most marvellous viandes. Caviare, Smoked Salmon, Foie Gras, Mushrooms, about eight sorts of vegetables, Green Beer (which apparently is the very latest fashion and quite disgusting) and huge dishes of fruit'.[30]

Imma and Walton planned to leave the following day. Edith sat with Imma in her room as she packed 'with German efficiency and South German gaiety' while Walton dashed in 'at intervals to fasten down boxes very <u>maritalement</u>'. She noted with amusement:

> He is far more restful than musicians generally are and I think to live with the Sitwells must be a marvellous training. The guests left at noon – driving off blissfully together. He is <u>sure</u> they will marry. She – not so, but resolved <u>not</u> to marry him if it is going to harm his career. She is however quite as much in love as he is and I never saw two people whose frustrated love made them more radiant.[31]

In the New Year Imma returned alone to stay with Edith. Walton was working on a composition for a BBC concert in Leeds, which would evolve into his dramatic choral cantata about the Jews in exile, *Belshazzar's Feast*. Osbert Sitwell had constructed the text using selections from the Bible and the piece was dedicated to Gerald Berners. Walton joined them at the Daye House on 17 January. Edith met him at the station. 'I think he is really getting on with *Belshazzar's Feast*, though he won't allow himself to think so. He and Imma gazed at each other with that peculiar, quiet, burning look of theirs!'[32]

In April Cecil returned from a trip to America armed with a new contract from *Vogue* 'to give them 4 things in each number and the rate is £60 each so far as I could gather. This would mean £480 a month', she wrote in her diary. 'Can it be so?'[33] But it was not long before Edith, who was still trying to live on a budget of about £5 a week, realized the benefits of America for herself. *Dwarf's Blood* was published in the spring by Faber in Great Britain and by Viking Press in the United States. In May *Literary Guild*, an American magazine, wrote to tell her that they were dedicating their entire July issue to her and the launch of *Dwarf's Blood*. They requested her biography, an article and, to her horror, a portrait. They also invited her to go out to New York in the summer but she declined; her brother Reginald was coming to stay with her to recuperate after an operation. In August she received a cheque for £1,811 for American royalties and learnt that 5,000 copies had sold there in the first week of the novel's publication.

The following weekend Cecil arrived at the Daye House in his two-seater car with Rex, Oliver Messel and piles of luggage and furniture. Edith 'climbed in on to anyone's knees' and they 'hurtled along thro' blinding rain and cruel wind, skidding round corners which Rex could hardly bear'. She had an evening of fun at Ashcombe, the young men 'like schoolboys, rushing after each other, and fighting and shouting till all hours of the night. I suppose', she wrote, 'the enemy would say they were all drunk but as a matter of fact after one cocktail they all drank water.'[34] Writing to thank Cecil a few days later, Edith said: 'Every hour you add to the beauties of your beautiful house. I have never been so aware of the Act of Creation and feel that I have assisted in the first chapter of Genesis. One of the great things that is so marvellous is the flood of colour which you have poured into the place . . . you have made it alive . . .'[35]

Cecil adored publicity. He loved to invite hordes of fabulous, famous friends to enjoy life in his country retreat and to capture it all with his camera. He began a tradition of asking his guests to draw around their hands and then to sign the drawing on his bathroom wall, a particularly demonstrative alternative to a visitors' book. But that Ashcombe was so hidden, so inaccessible, delighted him too. It meant that he was entirely in control of his image-making machine. It also meant that he and his friends could enjoy a more liberated way of life away from prying eyes and twitching curtains. There were times when Edith was not invited, when the fun was less innocent, when the writing and drawing games played by firelight in the studio took a mischievous turn. They drew 'Heads, Bodies and Legs; or Titles and Pictures', Cecil recalled in his memoirs, adding that 'Rex, of course, excelled at this.'[36] In the Beaton archive at St John's College, Cambridge, amongst letters from Rex to Cecil, some of the drawings from these games still exist. They are drawn with the salacious humour of the schoolboy, plenty of giant penises, schoolgirl lesbians, the

Swiss Family Robinson naked and peacefully occupied on a beach and, beneath the title 'The Campbells are Coming', a drawing of bodies huddled in an embrace, naked but for their tartan bobble hats.

It is easy to imagine Rex giggling with the other young men in the studio firelight, their heads bent over paper and pencils as they vied to outdo each other's naughtiness. It is harder to imagine him enjoying the fights, tears and recriminations that marked Cecil's relationship with Peter Watson, and other such romantic and sexual dramas that played out in the highly charged atmosphere at Ashcombe. Nonetheless, like Edith, Rex, who was often invited for the weekend, admired the world that Cecil had created. It was just the kind of pastoral idyll that Rex adored – Georgian, hidden amongst trees in a lonely valley. Later, in 1936, he would paint the house, the ilexes beside it, the neighbouring studio with the imported white doves fluttering on the lawn. By then, the annual 'Ashcombe Sketching Competition' had been established, with Cecil and Rex the competitors and Edith judging in the shade of a green-lined parasol. He enjoyed the solitary days when they sketched together on the lawn but grew increasingly tired of the endless round of parties and pageantry and began to dread receiving Cecil's invitations. 'He liked to be with Cecil Beaton, if not too often', Laurence later said.[37]

When Cecil began busily transforming his bedroom into a circus-themed extravaganza he asked Rex to design a canopied four-poster bed; it had barley-sugar brass posts, and a bearded Neptune, attended by Cupids and a unicorn, frolicked in waves on the bedhead. One weekend Cecil invited Rex, Gerald Berners and others down to Ashcombe to help him adorn the walls with paintings of circus characters. Edith was also invited. 'When I arrived they had all just begun to paint Cecil's bedroom and this went on till dark', she wrote. 'It was an amazing metamorphosis. His room is at last the Circus Room of his dreams.'[38] But the weekend was followed by just the kind of petty, tedious incident that Rex despised, and which seemed to happen all too frequently at Ashcombe. He recounted the events in a letter to Edith:

I am rather distressed at the moment, (though I am making a mountain out of rather a molehill!) about the terrible offence I have incidentally given to the little Bismarcks – you remember them at Ashcombe? On the Monday after they had gone, Cecil and I went on painting in different parts of the room and I repainted a good deal of the not very good 'strong man' with the fig leaf that Bismarck had done – do you remember it? I had not the faintest idea that it would give offence. Oliver had particularly besought me to go on with <u>his</u> figure and I feel certain that Cecil told B that we should do a little more to <u>his</u> figure too. However Cecil tells me that they, (the Bs) came over from Biddesden last weekend and though <u>he</u> didn't mind <u>so</u> much Jacky B flew into a passion that I should have touched his work and could not say nasty and mean things enough about me Cecil says. I suppose it <u>was</u> wrong of me but it was quite unwittingly done. <u>I</u> treated all the paintings we did that day as mere <u>jokes</u>; we all helped each other surely and I thought that any of them would be altered or washed out even, if we had another idea for the walls later on. I am sad about it because I so hate to appear bumptious and greedy and also because I did so take to Jacky Bismarck and thought her enchanting and it is shocking to hear that she has been beastly about me when I had been thinking about her affectionately and believing we were friends. But what do you honestly think? I suppose it <u>was</u> in very bad taste my touching his painting though I <u>truly</u> believe that I should not be offended and bitter if, say, the Bs had stayed longer at Ashcombe and altered or made additions to that fat woman I painted. In my conceit I might probably think they had not <u>improved</u> it, but that is all, I think.[39]

Instead it was at the Daye House that Rex sought peace and ease. He adored the 'coziness' of time spent with Edith. There he was free to do his work and he wasn't required to be sociable, to perform. 'He often told me that he was happier there than anywhere else and that he feared so much the day when Edith might die, for he could not bear to have to face such a loss', Cecil wrote years later in *Ashcombe*.[40] But with commissions piling up and an endless round of social engagements to occupy his time, Rex's visits were becoming even less frequent.

Since he could not come to her, Edith resolved to go up to London to see Rex. At the beginning of December they had met for lunch at Gunter's Tea Shop in Berkeley Square. Rex told Edith that he had had dinner with Virginia Woolf and that she had railed relentlessly about Cecil's impudence at having put her in his *Book of Beauty*. 'R loathed this dinner where he alone was Cecil's friend'. Writing in her diary that night Edith delighted in the 'very delicious intimate talk' she had enjoyed with Rex that day.[41]

But a couple of months later, after supper at the Eiffel Tower Edith returned to his studio and Rex drew her portrait. She was appalled by the result: 'he drew me, making me look a very sad old woman.'[42] The previous year Edith had been diagnosed with high blood pressure after months of feeling irrationally irritable and tired. Her doctor had advised her to improve her diet with more vegetables and fish and she was determined to do as he advised. It seemed to her friends that she had as much vim and energy as she had ever had. And she continued to take a great deal of care with her appearance, dyeing her hair and, when she could afford it, commissioning outfits from her dressmaker, including a pair of 'amusing' pyjamas for evenings lounging in the Long Room.[43] She had been delighted by Cecil's Christmas gift of a dress and matching bolero from the couturier Charles James. The skirt was blue and white and the bodice was orange; Edith was fascinated by how cleverly it had been cut and draped to slim and enhance her figure. She had spent a delightful afternoon just before Christmas being measured and pinned and fussed over in James's atelier in London. In photographs Edith always appears self-assured and feminine, almost sexy. Although she was an ageing spinster, she did not feel the need to hide beneath long skirts or matronly shawls. But she disliked the reality of ageing. 'I hate my appearance so much that I don't like looking in the glass', she wrote a few years later.[44] She knew that she wasn't beautiful but she hoped that she achieved a certain modish elegance. Living amongst the young made her feel younger than she was and she was used to Cecil's flattering lens and to the compliments of her young friends. And so for Rex, the most dear of those boys, to adhere too keenly to the truth, although no doubt honestly striving to capture a true likeness, came as something of a shock to Edith: 'I am horrified that he <u>thought this like me</u>. It is a terrible eye-opener'.[45]

16: 'Peintre de Luxe'

❖

'We can't live in the past.'
'I can and I do.'

Edith Olivier, *The Seraphim Room*

'It's painted in rather my old boring way', Rex told a friend, of his mural for Captain Wallace at Hill Street in Mayfair.[1] He had painted it to what had become a successful formula: a window onto a picturesque landscape with wittily reworked classical details. In the foreground stands a terrace, flanked by ivy-clad columns against which Cupid leans, his quiver and bows set aside as he nonchalantly eats an apple stolen from a fruit bowl on the table. He looks out onto the real world, as at Dorneywood, inviting the viewer into Arcadia. And within, reality and fantasy, past and present, combine in an impossible landscape. A silvery river coils through the Claudian countryside of rocky promontories and grassy mounds into the vanishing distance. Mountains and a fortified town of baroque domes and Gothic spires rise on a horizon rendered in hazy shades of emerald. The Boycott pavilion at Stowe crumbles under foliage, sacks of flour from the watermill next door lean irreverently against its lofty facade. At the centre of the painting crisp, Botticelli-esque leaves and flowers carpet the earth and creep onto the terrace, a fountain spurts crystalline water, equestrian figures and hunting dogs prance along as if on a tapestry. As ever there are personal details: the family picnicking in the grass and the naked figures of the Wallace children perching on the rocks about to leap into the river. For those boys Rex painted a spider which one day appeared to have scurried a few inches further down the column on which it hovered.

The spider was a typical symbolic gesture. It was pleasing and amusing, and Rex loved to entertain. For his private patrons, it was the act of painting and not just the finished product that they were buying from Rex. He became their artist in residence. 'I have fun looking down from my scaffold on the guests as they arrive', Rex wrote while he was working at Hill Street. 'Sometimes I'm dragged to lunch too, but I try to get food sent up on a tray.'[2] After completing the commission he was even invited to join the Wallace family on their skiing trip to Switzerland.

In the foreground of Rex's mural at Hill Street, beside a swept pile of swiftly scattering autumn leaves, a black, liveried footman casually rests against an urn. It is a touch perhaps inspired by the grand aristocratic portraits of Zoffany and Reynolds in which black servants attend to their masters or entertain their master's children. But this is the 1930s, not the eighteenth century. Rex's footman has put down beside him the tray of drinks he has been carrying and has instead plucked a rose from a nearby bush which he dangles between his fingers. Within this topsy-turvy world, misrule is the order of the day; without, in the real world, things were no less shifting. At the centre of the terrace, an artist has just disappeared, abandoning his easel and his palette with the glistening oil paints he has been using. It entirely reflects the liminal position in which Rex found himself in this and in other houses where he worked. Has he slipped into the painting or is he lunching with the family? Is he lost in his own imagination or too busy socializing to engage with art? His own fears about the validity of his artistic output, as well as echoes of Henry Tonks's warning that the true artist should avoid society and Shaw's speech at the Tate likening the artist to the plumber, reverberate here. Even in Rex's fantasy landscapes these very real concerns continued to plague him. Staying at Faringdon, Gerald Berners's country house in Oxfordshire, beside his name in the visitors' book he wrote 'Peintre de luxe'. It was witty and suitably self-mocking, but it is what he had become.

Rex might have grown bored of his style but his work was in great demand. With the economic crisis at home, the rise of fascism and the threat of communism from abroad, and American influences beginning to infiltrate Europe, change once again loomed on the horizon. Society seemed to be in flux; there was an increasing sense of urgency, instability and unease. Now, at the beginning of the thirties, there were even whispered predictions of another war. In 1933, Edith would record in her diary that Sassoon had been with Winston Churchill at a house party. He reported that Churchill 'accepts the next War as a certainty and spoke coolly of a million Londoners being killed by bombs!'[3] 'Even Edith was now attending meetings of the League of Nations.

For some, especially among the aristocracy and the wealthy elite, the nationalistic and apprehensive mood of the time provoked an aesthetic nostalgia and renewed appreciation of Britain's heritage, as people sought reassurance in an ideal of old England. It was a mood heightened by scholarly work on historic buildings, by the National Trust and by magazines such as *Country Life*. And it was keeping Rex busy with such things as painting sun-bathed posters for Shell and designing a pretty toile de Jouy for the north Devon village of Clovelly. Exploiting the vogue in all things quaintly English, this pattern was to be used on fabrics and china to generate finances for the estate.

For its homes, this generation did not look to the cosy idiosyncrasies of the Arts and Crafts style, the 'olde England' of their parents with its 'honest' interiors drawn from a romanticized rural past, all inglenooks, stained-glass windows, exposed beams and oak panelling. And neither did it look to the knick-knacks, antimacassars and aspidistras of the Victorians. Instead it turned to the modern, sleek simplicity of Art Deco, or to the elegance of the eighteenth century or to a striking combination of the two. Georgian style was modern and rebellious in its restraint and rationality. In *The Fall and Rise of the Stately Home*, Peter Mandler writes that 'the Georgian could be prized precisely for its aloofness from modern life, its elegance, civility and grandeur contrasting sharply with the glutinous sentimentality and domesticity of bourgeois suburbia.'[4]

As the post-war aristocracy began to sell off its mansions and vast estates in order to face mounting financial pressures, the adoption of the Georgian style had a practical appeal:

> In high society . . . the further decay of rural society, the washing up in London of many old families, with money but with loosening ties to the land, caused a reaction against the philistinism and jolly ruralism of pre-war years. Country sports, huge country-house parties, the raffishness of the Edwardian court were out; dances and cocktail parties, the refurbishment and redesign of the town-house interiors, a certain stylishness and perky knowingness were in . . . Naturally it helped that there were plenty of genuine Georgian materials at hand. Fashionable London had never deserted its Georgian town houses in the West End, and since the 1880s these had gradually filled with country-house contents . . . these settings and antiques provided backdrops for the new creations of the fashionable interior decorators who flourished in the 1920s and 1930s.[5]

Edith witnessed this; she knew only too well from her friends how burdensome large estates could be. In *Dwarf's Blood* the Roxerby estate is a crumbling wreck until Nicholas arrives with his fortune from Australia. On a personal level Edith valued tradition and heritage while adapting herself to a brave new world. But she was fascinated by these changes in society, by the meeting of traditional, and the modern and the conservative and the liberal. They would be at the heart of her next novel, *The Seraphim Room*.

From its avant-garde, Sitwellian beginnings in the twenties, the historical inspiration for interior decoration became more mainstream in the thirties. The look, which became known as Vogue Regency, was introduced to London society by the new breed of interior decorators. The two grande dames of interior decoration of the period were Sybil Colefax, who created very English interiors with lashings of chintz, and Syrie Maugham, famous for her all-white schemes (inspiring Cecil at Ashcombe) and for juxtaposing gilded baroque furniture with Art Deco carpets.

It was Syrie Maugham to whom Stephen now turned. Inspired by Cecil's tempest of creativity at Ashcombe, he had begun to sweep away his mother's elegant Edwardian rusticity at Wilsford, although Pamela and her devotion to play, to an eternal childhood, remained the presiding spirit. In place of her Arts and Crafts charm came a neo-rococo extravaganza of swags, satin, sheepskin and seashells. Stephen needed none of Cecil's inexpensive invention; this was theatricality on a luxurious, operatic scale rather than the trickery and pantomime props of Ashcombe.

With its blend of the classical, the baroque and the modern, Vogue Regency was perhaps a more mature and sophisticated version of 'the Amusing' of the previous decade. Rex's work epitomized the style, being elegantly classical and seductively nostalgic but with theatricality and the requisite 'perky knowingness' that made it fashionable. Rex suited those wanting to put a modern but conservative stamp on an inherited property. And with its inherent illusory quality, Rex's work was the obvious choice for those who wanted to recreate the look of the country house in townhouses filled with the contents of their abandoned estates.

In 1930, Sir Philip Sassoon, an MP, Siegfried's cousin, cosmopolitan doyen of fashion and a discerning patron of the arts, commissioned Rex to paint an entire room at Port Lympne, the house he had built on the Kent–Sussex border, overlooking Romney Marsh to the sea. To Port Lympne Sassoon lured film stars, artists and politicians to frolic in his giant swimming pool or idle away the hours beside the fountain in his Moorish courtyard. He was 'an icon of new money' who liked 'his drainpipes gilded and his visitors glamorous'.[6] One such visitor was the American Henry 'Chips' Channon, the nouveau-riche grandson of a Chicago ship's chandler, an intimate of the future Edward VIII and an outrageously snobbish and poisonous society commentator. In his diaries he described Port Lympne as 'a triumph of beautiful bad taste and Babylonian luxury with terraces and flowering gardens, and jade green pools and swimming baths and rooms done up in silver, blue and orange' where guests were 'entertained with almost Oriental lavishness'.[7] That Rex should be commissioned by Sassoon, who was considered 'an arch social barometer' and who patronized some of the most fashionable artists of the day, including Sert and Glyn Philpott, was a sure sign that now Whistler was fashionable too.[8]

Rex had gone down to Lympne to see what was to be done and returned again with watercolour designs of the scheme he was proposing. 'His Majesty has commanded my presence down at Lympne. It's a <u>great bore</u>, but I shall be taking further drawings down with me, and I hope that <u>this</u> time the business will be settled – though there will be the <u>agony of saying the price</u>.'[9] Over supper with Cecil Beaton at the Savoy Grill a few weeks later, Rex had discussed his designs and his very large £800 fee for the Port Lympne room. Unfortunately for Rex they were within earshot of Tom Driberg, the notorious *Daily Express* gossip columnist, who naturally relayed the information in his column. The private and fastidious Sassoon was furious at this apparently vulgar disclosure and Rex dashed off to his house in Park Lane to apologize. For guileless Rex, it had been a foolish mistake and a lesson in discretion, but he was mortified. 'Rex feels everyone will think he authorised it and all his joy in that job is gone,' Edith wrote when they were together at Ashcombe in November.[10]

But Rex was forgiven and by the summer of 1931 he had begun work in situ. He was perfectly suited to adorn Port Lympne, already a temple of exoticism, whimsy and historical pastiche. The dining room was a gloomy, unprepossessing barrel-vaulted space. His plan was to transform it into the trompe l'œil interior of a tented Regency pavilion of blue and white striped silk to give the impression of ease and endless summertime. To this he applied real tent poles, tassels and curtains of identical stripes to make it more convincing still. In places the tent seems to sag and here and there the breeze appears to be sending ripples along the ceiling. Around the doors were classical arches with mounted trophies painted in grisaille, and a torn trompe l'œil map of the estate appears to hang on one wall. Three sides of the tent seem to have been pulled back to reveal an imagined riverside townscape beyond, composed of many of Rex's favourite buildings and some new ones: Bluecoat School, a Stowe Pavilion, St Martin-in-the-Fields, the Palladian Bridge at Wilton and the Eiffel Tower restaurant, where the beaming, large-bellied figure of the Austrian proprietor M. Stulik stands in the doorway. This was Rex's grandest, boldest scheme yet, the landscape a hive of activity, with people promenading on foot and in carriages along the tree-lined avenue, sailing on the river, sitting outside cafes, others begging, beckoning or standing contemplatively in the shadows. A procession of Church dignitaries, a bishop and cassocked priests, makes its way to the front door of the baroque church.

In another scene a long garden vista leads to a country house, Faringdon, Gerald Berners's house in Oxfordshire. A woman in widow's weeds laments beside a stone urn marked 'In Memoriam' on the lawn. In the foreground, a little boy waits for a paddle steamer, standing with a hoop, the trunk beside him on the quayside with a coroneted 'B' implying that this is the figure of Berners himself, seen by Rex and many others as an eternal child. Mysteries, in-jokes, a jumble of eras and architectural styles are all held together in the spell that Rex had woven.

Travelling up from Lympne on Friday 1 May, Rex arrived at the Daye House exhausted, with toothache and an inflamed eye. That night, clearly in some discomfort, he went with Edith to a ball at Wilton House given in honour of Caroline Paget, 'an angel in shell colour'.[11] The following day Rex was determined to dig a bathing pool for Edith and went searching for a romantic spot under the trees so that sunlight would play on the water: 'could there be anyone <u>less</u> like a Navvy?' she wondered.[12] Rex wrote to Edith back in London on the Monday:

> Thank you so much for that delightful weekend. It was lovely from the first minute to the last . . . <u>The Royal Ball</u> was great fun too. I simply loved it and you looked very much of the 'naughty nineties' in your long black gloves. <u>How</u> lovely that drive you took me on Sunday was. It is wonderful how you find new places every time we set out, after pretending at first that I have seen all there is to see. I suppose you do it to increase my delight with the new scenes which you intend presently to show me.[13]

But soon he was back at Port Lympne where he found the atmosphere challenging. At the Daye House and even at Ashcombe, he could be fun and relaxed, but in the sophisticated atmosphere of Port Lympne with its in-jokes and double meanings, Rex was expected to be sophisticated too. Instead he felt gauche. Sassoon entertained such disparate figures as Charlie Chaplin, Winston Churchill, Osbert Sitwell and the Prince of Wales, often with his mistress Freda Dudley Ward. Rex was invariably called upon to join in with the endless round of house parties, with bathing, picnics and cocktails before dinner. After another weekend at the Daye House the following year Rex wrote to thank Edith: 'it was such a deliciously peaceful, sightseeing, refreshing, <u>Heavenly</u>, visit as almost every visit to you always is. I am driving down to Lympne'. Sassoon had invited him to a house party and Rex was by then planning to put the finishing touches to his decorations. He wrote to Edith:

> Think of me and the agony I shall be in as I arrive. I shall put a brave face on it I hope but imagine the torture it is. Having to walk across the garden to a huge round table on the terrace (if it's hot) with lots of horrid people and strangers sitting about and having to eat sticky food with the sun in my eyes and be introduced and asked questions.[14]

After another Lympne house party where Rex's fellow guests had included Noël Coward, Anthony Eden and Gerald Berners, the latter complained to his host that Rex had failed to be amusing enough. And Marie Belloc Lowndes, in a letter to her daughter Elizabeth (of the Ellesmere Ball scandal), after a house party at Lympne in August 1935, said of Rex: 'He, of course, is rather "odd man out", though he is so quiet and unassuming that everyone likes him.'[15]

According to Sassoon's biographer, Peter Stansky, his subject 'was frequently assumed to be homosexual' and that he 'entertained without hesitation Osbert Sitwell, Gerald Berners, Glyn Philpot, and, though married, Malcolm Bullock and Chips Channon, figures who those "in the know" (and even those who were not) knew were homosexuals'.[16] It is possible that Rex found the aggressive air of homosexuality intimidating because it forced him to address his own sexuality. By August 1931, Edith was writing in her diary that she had talked with Stephen 'of Rex who seems lost to us both – between his . . . paintings and Malcolm Bullock!'[17] A Conservative MP and fifteen years older than Rex, Bullock was older, wealthy and powerful, and perhaps Rex was attracted – as he had been attracted to Siegfried Sassoon. Bullock took Rex to Paris, and to the *Folies Bèrgere* where, as Rex later confessed to his brother, he had been 'disgusted by the smell of female flesh'.[18] Perhaps Bullock intended to shock the sensitive Rex into acknowledging what many of his friends already thought: that he was homosexual. Chips Channon, writing in his diary, encapsulated Rex's sexual appeal: 'elegant, vague, gentle and strange, like an exquisite goat, he is a delightful satyr'.[19] But Laurence insisted that the relationship with Bullock was essentially platonic: 'No claim is made that any carnality ensued', albeit adding that Bullock later insisted that Rex had been 'provocative' towards him.[20]

Edith neither saw Rex nor received a letter from him for five months. Eventually, in an attempt at a rapprochement, she invited him to stay one weekend in October. He wrote in reply:

I am so looking forward to seeing you this weekend – it will be Heavenly. But I do so dread the visit to Ashcombe is there any chance of our getting out of it, do you think? Cecil told me on the telephone that there were going to be crowds and crowds of people . . . I want so much to see Cecil but I don't feel at all in the mood for a cocktail party and would so have loved a quiet weekend with you at Wilton or one of our delicious little picknicks in some lovely new-discovered country. I am extremely tired as I have been working up till 1 and later every night for several weeks and apart from the physical exhaustion, I feel rather flattened out by such a prolonged mental effort and you know with your writing (though writing probably needs even more concentration) how very tired one gets in getting through a very long continuous piece of work. Perhaps we could go just for <u>tea</u> only? Or for lunch and then have some good reason for leaving quickly afterwards? Can you think of something?[21]

Rex drove up from Lympne to London on the Friday and travelled to Wilton with Edith, who had been in town, on the Saturday. She thought he looked exhausted. The following month Rex and Bullock went on a weekend motor tour of Devon, Cornwall and Dorset and called in for luncheon with Edith at the Daye House. She made no comment about Bullock in her diary, an uncharacteristic silence. She was with Rex again at the end of November. Her brother Reginald had died suddenly of a stroke on All Saints' Day, leaving his wife Esther, his young son Tony and the rest of the family in horrified mourning. Less than three months later, on 21 January 1932, her brother Sidney would also die. Out of ten siblings only Henry, Mamie and Edith were still alive. On 25 November Edith travelled up to London to go through Reginald's papers. Later she dined at the Étoile with Rex and together they went to hear Walton's concert at the BBC, *Belshazzar's Feast*, 'Willy's magnificent work of genius':

We were all completely overwhelmed by its power and beauty. It is magnificent. The Vocalisation surprised me by its liquid loveliness, as I thought he could only write for orchestra. The <u>piano</u> passages wring the heart and the fortissimos sweep one off one's feet . . . Every interesting person in England was in the hall and Willy had a wild ovation, called six times and looking as white as a sheet, and very thin, as he bowed stiffly in all directions.[22]

Walton's gift of a piano arrived at the Daye House on 17 December. He was planning to come to stay with Edith in the New Year to begin work on his first symphony and she was delighted that, for the first time since Mildred's death, the sound of music would once again fill the house.

On 2 January 1932 Rex wrote to Edith to wish her many happy returns for her birthday two days earlier, to thank her for his Christmas gift, a book of Italian paper, and to accept her invitation for a weekend at the Daye House on the 17th. 'I've been engaged in the most awful correspondence with Malcolm B [Bullock] for some time now!' he told her. 'And the last horror has been that he sent me a very expensive book and I returned it to him. I am so longing to see you again and there is so much to talk about'.[23] Whatever the extent of his relationship with Bullock, Edith was appalled that Rex was being linked with a notorious homosexual, fearing that he would tarnish her darling friend's reputation:

Met Rex at 4.30. He is beset by Malcolm Bullock who insists on being his most monopolising friend. Gets seats for concerts, plays and operas . . . [and] tete a tete dinners. Takes him on tours of Paris and England and all the time Rex is <u>bored to death</u> and also finds his character <u>suspected</u> by being seen about with MB . . .We talked of this for hours. R has told M he doesn't want to see him so much and Malcolm won't accept dismissal. I am all for his breaking off totally because I hate R to be considered the kind of man which apparently MB's friends <u>are</u> considered – but Rex says gloomily that <u>that</u> harm is already done![24]

It is difficult to believe that Rex was 'bored to death' with this intimate and indulgent friendship which, after all, lasted for at least seven months. Edith's account of her conversation with Rex has the air of the confessional about it. He struggled to unite the two sides of his personality, the side that enjoyed submitting to Bullock and the other side, the melancholy romantic that Edith knew. 'He was, in a curious sense', Stephen later said, 'a purist and an idealist, always hesitating to violate the innermost shrine of his convictions.'[25] Edith's evident disapproval weighed on him and he excused the relationship by implying to her that it was only Bullock who wanted more than a platonic friendship. But in February Edith was still troubled: 'dined with Rex at the Savoy Grill where we feasted on Caviare [sic] and other delights', she wrote, adding: 'his pleasure spoilt by Malcolm Bullock who suddenly appeared at the next table and had his eye on R all the time!'[26] 'M B makes me <u>uneasy and unhappy</u>', she wrote a few weeks later.[27]

Edith clearly had a suspicion about Rex, of whom she had written only two years earlier; 'We can understand each other so entirely that the unsaid is said as well as the said'.[28] Now she was not so sure, but it comforted her to believe that Rex was the victim of the situation and Bullock the predator. Ironically, it was probably that dynamic which had attracted Rex to Bullock in the first place. The precise nature of the relationship and the nature of its end remains unclear but it seems that Malcolm Bullock became too demanding of Rex's time and affections and that he found it difficult to extricate himself from the situation. 'I know that I have a weak character in many ways', Rex would tell Edith. 'I try to be nice to <u>everyone</u> wether I like them or not and even when I dislike them.'[29]

Laurence Whistler was adamant that it was 'highly unlikely that as an adult [Rex] practiced homosexuality of any kind, if indeed he ever had', but Rex's friend Henry Paget, later Lord

Anglesey, acknowledged that there was a possibility that Rex was sexually attracted to men.[30] In seeking to explain his brother's many friendships with homosexual men, Laurence suggests that:

> He took to them, unconsciously because he had some degree of affinity with them, consciously because they did not challenge his masculinity with women . . . Hence the joy of his companionship with Stephen in which his feminine aspect could expand unsexually, and leave him free, one day, to be a man for a woman.[31]

Perhaps this was true, but speculation hovered around Rex as it always does for those of undefined sexuality, ever rushing to define the vagaries of the human heart. In a biography of the writer Beverley Nichols, whose nostalgic and hugely popular gardening books Rex had begun to illustrate in 1932,* a second-hand claim is made by one of Nichols's ex-boyfriends that he and Rex had 'a brief affair'.[32] Handsome and openly homosexual (as open as it was possible to be in the 1930s), Nichols makes no reference to an intimate relationship in his autobiography, but writes that he kept bundles of Rex's letters, that for a time were 'being daily delivered'.[33] Nichols was notoriously predatory and liked to boast about his conquests and supposed conquests, but whether it is true or not is beside the point; rumour followed him, and still does. Even his brother said that Rex 'knew that his homosexual friends always held that he was one of them, if only he would face it, and others thought he had no physical desire for girls'.[34]

Rex was, and would always be, confused about his sexuality. But what is certain is that he did not like being considered homosexual, especially by Edith, which perhaps explains the uncharacteristically waspish comments to her about a letter he had received from Cecil, who was frolicking in Hollywood with

---

* *Down the Garden Path*, published in 1932, was the first of a number of highly successful gardening books. Rex also illustrated *A Thatched Roof* (1933) and *A Village in a Valley* (1934).

William Randolph Hearst, Hedda Hopper and the Goldwyns. His letter boasted of relationships with women. 'How extraordinarily crude he is', Rex wrote. 'His one aim now is to advertise the fact that he is having affairs with women . . . the effect of it all is only, surely, to make it evident that this discovery of "his manhood!" is being as great a surprise to him as it is to everyone else!'[35]

Rex arrived at the Daye House on 18 January to stay with Edith. 'He has come here quite worn out by work and confesses he has been drawing every morning till 2.30 and 3!' Edith wrote in her diary:

> He tells me that unconsciously as he draws he fidgets and taps with hands and feet so that the people who live in the flat beneath asked if he would get his practising done earlier as they could never sleep until 3 o'clock. They said that of course we know being a professional you must practice your tapdancing but could you possibly do it at another time! . . . Rex is making drawings for some poems by a Mr James – the best drawings I have seen of his in some ways. Such a sure touch. An amusing one of New York – skyscrapers towering over a park in which the trees look like cabbages. It has great beauty.'[36]

Edward James was Edward VII's godson and amidst a complicated web of rumour it was suggested by some that he was also his illegitimate son and by others that his mother was the Prince's illegitimate daughter. James was a fabulously wealthy patron of the Surrealists and his house, West Dean in Sussex, was a shrine to their work. Rex illustrated a privately printed book of his verse, *The Next Volume*, and in 1935 he would design an Axminster carpet for James as well as painting an enormous equestrian portrait of his patron. Meanwhile Rex was working on urn designs for the Palladian drawing room of Sir Samuel Courtauld's house and a chinoiserie panel, commissioned by Courtauld to use as a rather unexpected frame for Picasso's *L'Enfant au Pigeon*. Rich clients and lucrative commissions abounded.

At the end of January William Walton arrived to plunge into work on his first symphony. Edith had put his piano into the dining room for the duration of his stay so that he could lock himself away. But it was not until the end of March that he finally began to make progress. On Sunday 20th Edith returned from early communion at Wilton to find that he had begun writing. He 'varies between thinking he is getting going and feeling sure that all he has done must be torn up', she wrote that night. That evening he had told her that he thought his latest work 'anaemic, sentimental, dull and worthless. Says he has never been inspired in his life – and can't think why he writes . . . I think all this is all right. It is <u>Birth-throes</u>.'[37]

Rex joined them for an Easter break and the trio had a happy few days together during which Walton celebrated his thirtieth birthday. They visited Diana (née Mitford) and Bryan Guinness at Biddesden, Edith commenting that 'Diana's beauty dazzled us all'. At the Daye House Rex drew whilst Walton played the piano: 'we have great fun we three but I like best to have Rex alone'.[38] They set off in Edith's car on a grand tour of Elizabethan stately homes in Somerset, first to Montacute and then to Barrington Court: 'it also belongs to the Trust who acquired it almost as a shell and the interior has been most lavishly <u>re-made</u> . . . a most expensive and perfect sham. I felt it <u>almost</u> spoilt our day! The boys thought it must be like America . . . It is well done but somehow so hateful.'[39]

The collision of tradition and modernity and the preservation of the past were at the centre of Edith's latest novel, which she had begun to write in earnest in January. *The Seraphim Room* tells the story of the tyrannical Reverend Mr Chilvester – another, more extreme, caricature of Dacres – who 'controlled his little world too completely for anything to occur in it which he had not foreseen and permitted'.[40] He lives with his two motherless daughters in a cathedral close inspired by Edith's own experience of life in Salisbury many years earlier. Most sacred to Chilvester, to the detriment of everything else in his life, is the Queen Anne

ch he lives; it is the source of all his joy, 'his only real
‌ it will be his downfall.[41] He boasts that it has
remained unchanged since his family acquired it 170 years earlier
and much of the novel is concerned with his battle to fight the
enforced addition of a drainage system in his beloved house. Like
Nicholas Roxerby in *Dwarf's Blood* he is obsessed by the idea of
inheritance. Chilvester fears and shuns change and distrusts the
modern spirit entirely, a position that life in the timeless, cloistered world of the close has allowed him to keep. In contrast,
modernity is represented by the monastically dressed and urbane
aesthete Clodia Bowerman, who buys an old house and proceeds
to fill it with bathrooms, lavatories, deep carpets, large soft arm-
chairs, electric lighting and heating, 'according to the newest
and most suffocating American plan'.[42] And when Christopher
Honythorne, a young architect, a respecter of heritage and history
but with a modern outlook on architecture and life in general,
enters the family's life, the carefully preserved and unchanging
equilibrium of their world is disrupted.

Edith dedicated the novel to Barbara Townsend, a ninety-year-
old woman she had known all her life. She lived in the beautiful
eighteenth-century Mompesson House in Cathedral Close, the
model for Chilvester House in Rex's drawing for the cover. Edith
was fascinated by the idea that place has the power to influence
people. Of living in the Close, she wrote: 'I was never tired of
observing how much the beauty and character of the houses there
affected the people who lived in them. This was the fundamental
idea of *The Seraphim Room*.'[43]

The book was Edith's last attempt at fiction: it is bizarre, funny
and perhaps, after *The Love-Child*, her finest novel. The most successful parts of the book are the moments of social comedy, the
Trollopian machinations and quarrelling of the civic and ecclesiastical circles within the little world of the Close. And though
Edith was passionate about preserving heritage and suspicious of
new-fangled American influences, she could see how ridiculous
were those sticklers for authenticity who avoided modernization.

'Only here, within the walls of this Close', declares Mr Chilvester, 'is it possible to keep intact the standards of the past. And even here we can only do so if we resolutely refuse all change'.[44] It was a sentiment she had known so well in her father and, as a result, determinedly shunned herself. 'I think you would be a happier man, you know,' the Bishop tells Chilvester, 'if you could love and understand the present, as well as you love and understand the past. We must live in our day and take our part in it, however much we might have preferred to be born in another.'[45] The novel was published in the autumn of 1932 to mixed reviews.*

At the end of April Edith had travelled to Paris as a guest of Lura Howard's American friend Mary Churchill Humphrey, a writer and a keen patron of the arts whose home attracted an eclectic mix of aristocrats, artists and Russian refugees. Edith finally visited Versailles, with Mr King Bull, a producer from the BBC who was intending to commission a play based on *An Adventure*. The original plan was for Edith to write the script but after their day at the palace Edith realized that she would never be able to work with him.

> His utterances are <u>unbelievable</u>. Such as '<u>Photographs are only a form of visual fetishism after all.</u>' (What <u>can</u> that mean?) and when Mary Churchill said she liked to have photographs of houses and architecture as they did recall what she had seen, he answered '<u>That which is purely cerebral can be communicated exactly.</u>' . . . I wandered alone, drinking it all in, as far as possible from Mr King Bull.[46]

Back at the Daye House in June, Edith invited Rex for a weekend away from Lympne where he was desperately trying to finish his paintings. He arrived midweek at the end of the month and they

---

* *The Seraphim Room* was generally considered to be less of a success than *Dwarf's Blood* but since the publication of her previous novel Edith had acquired a literary following which guaranteed her good, if not great, sales. In September she had even felt the need to employ a secretary, Ivy, a young friend of her housekeeper Violet.

set out on a sightseeing expedition, happy in each other's company and Malcolm Bullock, for Edith at least, now forgotten. 'Rex dashed down to answer a telephone call, his cheeks and chin covered with lather, as he was shaving, and looked like a distinguished grey beard. I see what he will be like when he is old – the only way I shall ever see it I'm glad to say', she wrote in her diary that weekend. David Herbert came over to join them and they walked in the park. Edith picked strawberries and flowers while the men made her a headdress to ward off the sun, crafting it out of Rex's bathing suit, some peonies and Edith's pearls. They drove to Stockton House to visit Lady Violet Asquith who was thinking of commissioning a mural and they drove back through a summer thunderstorm, 'Rex driving all over the pasture thro' great clumps of huge nettles as tall as the car which we crushed down.' That night, Midsummer's Eve, they strolled through the park until it went dark, 'everything softly sinking into a coloured twilight'.[47]

Rex's zeal for 'improving' houses was not to be confined to the grand homes of his patrons and during his stay he began to draw up plans to formalize the Long Room. Cornicing was to be added and a panel above the fireplace which he planned to paint. He wrote from his parents' house on the Sunday:

Darling Edith,

I did so love my mid-week visit to you and seeing those two lovely places Milton Abbas and Stockton. I think we went to see them both in quite the most perfect <u>time of day</u> don't you? And that amazingly beautiful valley round the Abbey was particularly lovely in that wonderful long-shadowed early night. What an extraordinary storm that was . . . that suddenly came on when we were at Stockton. The kind that I remember Lady Grey used to say often occurs when great spirits are dying – like at Cromwell's death . . . But it was so very heavy a storm and then cleared away so quickly. I've drawn out the cornice moulding for your long room . . .[48]

Late summer in Wilton was filled with parties and pageantry. In July Edith attended a charity costume pageant at Wilton and performed in a masque as Elizabeth I. A few days earlier at the Daye House Cecil had transformed her into the queen; he had made a crown and collar for her and Edith was astounded by his skill: 'an amazing creation. I was no longer myself in any feature, but entirely the Queen. He took several photographs then dashed on to London'.[49] On the day of the pageant Edith was delighted by all the compliments she received for her costume which she wore with effortless aplomb. She was bored by the masque itself, for which she rode a horse and was attended by two mounted retainers and which dragged on late into the afternoon, 'so dreary and monotonous and I feel the audience must hate it'.[50] There is a photograph of Edith as Elizabeth, clearly jaded at the end of the day, a marvellously haughty queen in a striped crimson and silver brocade dress, ermine-edged, a lace-winged collar, dangling pearl earrings and necklaces, with her white-painted face and a crown of pearls, her head tipped back as she draws on a cigarette.

Rex returned again for a brief visit in August, having been at Renishaw working on commissions for Osbert Sitwell. He went bathing and then they 'had a very Rex-like drive home – over virgin down and huge obstacles which we surmounted tankishly.'[51] Two nights later she wrote in her diary: 'Rex left to my sorrow. He was to have painted my panel this week but commissions from august patrons like Sir Philip Sassoon and the Duke of Rutland have supervened.'[52]

Rex had been commissioned by the Duke of Rutland to paint a mural at Haddon Hall, his enchanting Tudor house standing high above the River Wye in Derbyshire. It was the childhood home of Diana Cooper, soon to become Rex's patron herself, as well as a firm friend. Rex was to paint a panel for the Long Gallery to celebrate the Duke's restoration of the house and in September he drove up to Derbyshire to begin work. The panel he was to paint contained remnants of a Tudor painting which Rex merged seamlessly into his own. In it the viewer looks down onto the house from the vantage point of an opposite hill where the Duke and his son stand to one side with their guns and dogs. The house sits amidst acres of soft, verdant splendour and beneath billowing apricot clouds. In many ways it is a traditional portrait of an aristocratic house but his choice of perspective was unusual, although typical of Rex. Often Haddon is shown from below, its lofty stone walls rising high on the craggy escarpment on which it stands. In Rex's painting the house is nestled low in the trees, cradled within the unchanging refuge of the vast estate, in which it sits so securely. As with all the houses that Rex would paint, this is no more real than a landscape by Poussin; it is dreamlike, safe in its tranquil children's picture-book timelessness, shielded by its artificiality against the ravages of time.

It was around this time that Rex finally finished work on the Sassoon commission. Writing to Edith about the end of his time at Lympne he seemed to re-declare his devotion to her; perhaps it also served to close a chapter in his romantic life.

Thank you so much for your letters which I <u>loved</u> – they kept me in touch I felt, with the <u>people I love</u> while I was working at Lympne. I have at last finished my room there . . .

I have enjoyed my summer <u>so</u> much so far have you had a lovely time? Wilton must have been paradise in that hot weather. I have been very happy chiefly I think because I have been working well. I mean <u>hard</u> and then there have not been many people at Lympne and those mostly very nice . . . and I've had heavenly sea bathing, driving down alone to the shore everyday and having lovely sun bathes afterwards.

. . . How stupid of me not to have remembered, until there is no room left to say how I am <u>loving</u> 'The Seraphim Room' . . . it made me roar with laughter. You've certainly had Cecil in a lot of your creation of Christopher haven't you? Though it is not entirely him.

Best love, Rex.[53]

They now began to see each other frequently once again, Rex

coming to the Daye House for weekends and Edith travelling up
to London for cosy suppers and gallery visits.

Rex had designed a balustrade riverside terrace for Edith's
garden with a bench and steps leading down to the water and
Edith organized a ceremony to honour its completion with music
playing, paper hats, flags, balloons and the Pembroke family arriving in a procession along the river. Lady Pembroke christened the
terrace by smashing a glass bottle of cold tea. William Walton had
arrived the day before to play Edith the first two minutes of his
symphony. She thought it full of fervour and passionate beauty.
He told her how turbulent his relationship with Imma had become
since she had last seen them, both of them without money and
yet both desperately in love and determined to marry. It was this
very turbulence that he was beginning to pour into the symphony
and which would give it its extraordinarily vigorous, passionate
character.

On 6 November Edith and Rex went together to Cecil's
'Opposites' party at Ashcombe. Rex went as 'a pink-cheeked
curate' and Edith as one of the imaginary poetesses in Noël
Coward's *Anthology* in flowing red velvet trousers, a knee-length
black wig, a turban and ropes of beads and scarves around her
neck. One guest was dressed as a peer of the realm, another as an
angel with golden wings, and Diana Guinness arrived as a haloed
saint. Cecil was a sergeant, and later a ballet dancer in a cabaret.
At the end of the night there was a bonfire and fireworks. Edith
thought it a 'rollicking party . . . everyone dressed in any funny old
clothes they could find and in roaring spirits'.[54]

The night before they had been at another gathering, a fancy-
dress party with a 1750s theme thrown by the Guinnesses. At
the end of the previous month Edith had travelled up to London
to choose costumes for the party and had visited the National
Portrait Gallery for inspiration with Rex. Arriving at the party
Edith noted that some guests 'were not dressed up which put
Cecil into a fury and as we arrived at Biddesden he saw them
through the door and called out that he refused to speak to them!

Great cheek as it was Diana's party and she didn't mind a bit'. Among the guests were Cynthia Mosley, Zita Jungman, Robert Byron, Rosamond Lehmann, Olga Lynn and Prince Henry, Duke of Gloucester; 'all the gay young set'. Rex was 'quite beautiful' with a long train as Cardinal York and Diana was 'very lovely' in a 'wig of silvery green'.[55] In February the following year Diana would leave her husband for Oswald Mosley, whose mistress she had become and who had resigned from his position as an MP in 1930 and created the British Union of Fascists earlier in 1932. That December, however, after a dinner party with the Guinnesses, Edith observed that 'Diana's dazzling radiance is quite unclouded by storms of passion tho she is surrounded by love affairs and Bryan's face is tortured with hapless jealousy. He might kill her and himself except that <u>fundamentally</u> he is very law-abiding.'[56]

Edith was amused and appalled by the romantic antics of her young friends. But as 1932 drew to a close, she was most of all happy to have Rex back again and no longer in the thrall of an older man. It would be her sixtieth birthday on the last day of the year; and although she would never admit it, perhaps she hoped that Rex was at least a little bit in love with her as she was undoubtedly in love with him. At the Guinness party they had danced together. 'As the evening went on', she wrote in her diary in bed later that night, 'he took off his wig and danced with his own shapely head on view. His beauty unbelievable . . . it was a dream . . . it must remain a dazzling memory'.[57]

17: The 'Storm Touched Soul'

❖

> . . . all his powers go into his affection.

> Edith Olivier's Diary, January 1931

'Do tell me why you are anxious about Stephen?' Rex had asked Edith in early 1930. 'I had a letter from him – still from Syracuse – four or five days ago, in which he sounded very happy and quite himself. "My news is" – he writes – "purple anemones wild in the grass, – every tree in blossom – old Cappuccin convents – Etna – mosquitos at night – fatigue – narcissi – and sea like a floor of lapis lazuli"'.[1]

In Sicily since the end of the previous year Sassoon had been spending peaceful days with Stephen scouring the beach for shells to add to his collection at Wilsford. There he composed a strangely elegiac, melancholy poem, 'In Sicily'. Struck by the transience of youth and pleasure and of Stephen's beauty, and saddened despite the loveliness of the island, he sensed that this was the happiest that they would ever be. And he was right. So it was not only Rex's romantic troubles that kept Edith busy in those first years of the thirties. The demise of Stephen and Sassoon's relationship was a dramatic unravelling, at once farcical and tragic.

Returning to England through Italy and France they stopped in Paris, where Sassoon despaired of Stephen's possessive nature while at the same time disapproving of his enthusiastic leap into the whirligig of Parisian society. When they returned to England in May Sassoon stayed in London and Stephen returned to Wilsford alone.

A month later tests revealed that Stephen's tuberculosis had again become active, this time more virulently, and the devoted Sassoon moved into Wilsford and gave himself up entirely to caring for his lover. Edith drove over for luncheon with Sassoon in early July. She greatly admired his dedication: 'He says he <u>cannot</u> begin the next volume till he is free from Stephen and this he <u>won't</u> be till S is well . . . Stephen is his Crusade, his vocation, his life'.[2] Later she went to spend a few minutes with Stephen who was in bed upstairs. He was flushed and deadly pale but managing to amuse himself with his plans to redecorate the house. Later that month she wrote that 'Siegfried's love for S is unbounded. I would gladly die for him he said with great reality in his voice. Says people tell him S prevents his writing and says he would far rather have this affection in his life than write books'.[3]

For Edith, their relationship had taken on the tone of a Gothic romance: 'The greatness of their love, the unique beauty of Stephen's nature, the tragedy of this illness cutting across it, and the setting in the lovely meadows, that exquisite house, half-furnished and empty except for himself wandering about'.[4] No longer was Wilsford the setting for a *fête galante*; Stephen's life had become a melodrama. Sassoon began to see his lover in these terms too. He felt that Stephen should be isolated from the outside world and old friends were turned away. Rex was one of them. 'Saw Rex', Edith had written in May; 'he thinks Stephen's illness has been exaggerated so as to prevent his friends from butting in'.[5] She thought that Rex felt that Stephen had been '<u>quite</u> taken from him by Sassoon. So that he feels <u>on sufferance</u> there – quite an outsider and always shy and out of it at Wilsford. It is cruel of Siegfried who is really jealous and he ought to be above this'.[6] Edith could see that Rex was upset, but she justified Sassoon's actions by his apparently blinding love for Stephen: 'He always calls Rex "Dear Rex" and with his <u>mind</u> he loves him but his instincts make him keep him and Stephen apart. An overpowering and unconscious jealousy – Stephen is now Sieg's whole life – he can't write – all his powers go into his affection'.[7]

Throughout all this Stephen sat in his bed, the calm centre of the storm, rouging his cheeks and contentedly choosing silks for his drawing-room curtains. Characteristically capricious, he began to turn on Sassoon, whom he felt was becoming overbearing and, encouraged by a prudish and scheming nurse, Stephen eventually banished him from Wilsford, after months of arguments and recrimination. In his diary on 25 October 1930 Stephen wrote: 'Emerson says: "Today is a King in disguise." When I'm with Sieg there is nothing in disguise. I do miss him – but I'm better alone.'[8]

It was in effect the end of their relationship but for months Sassoon lived between London, where his *Memoirs of an Infantry Officer*, published in September, was being feted; the Avon Hotel at Amesbury, which he had established as a base for himself in Wiltshire, and Wilsford, where he was summoned by Stephen from time to time on a whim. On Boxing Day Edith drove over to Wilsford with Walton and Imma to lunch with Sassoon who was in residence, briefly, once again. They were not able to see Stephen in person but could only glimpse him through a window. Edith thought he looked less ill but seemed sad.

In February 1931, she was finally allowed to see Stephen, whom she found reclining on the loggia looking pale and yet 'his personality is like a radiant sky, dominating the landscape'. She was thrilled to learn that Rex had also been given permission to visit but was horrified to witness at first hand the malevolence of Stephen's nurse. Sassoon could now 'only come to the Avon Hotel at Amesbury and visit S from there . . . Nurse is jealous as nurses often are and Sieg sensitive as poets are.'[9] The following day Sassoon left Wilsford for his hotel without saying goodbye to Stephen because his nurse was in the room. 'Stephen in amused agony insisted on my telephoning to get him back', Edith wrote. 'He says Nurse will not even take a message to him, she hates him so. Stephen agrees and [says that] she keeps them both in bondage. But such a good nurse that he must keep her for the time. He has complete confidence in her in an emergency. We laughed a lot at the situation and he is so gay and like himself – taking it very lightly.'[10] Even Rex did not escape the nurse's malicious tongue; she complained to Edith of him '"lazing about talking in this absurd way – very modern I suppose"'. Edith immediately retorted 'that he was Stephen's <u>best</u> friend'.[11] Edith believed the root of the problem lay in the fact that rather than the nurse hating Sassoon she was actually in love with him. '<u>What</u> an effect he has!' she wrote in her diary.[12]

At the end of February Edith wrote a long letter to Sassoon telling him that she thought he must stay away from Wilsford. 'I so hope I am able to make him less unhappy, but I doubt it . . . I know this is the only way to give their friendship a good future'.[13] She quickly became their go-between and frantic letters flew back and forth between her and the two men. Edith kept them all, Stephen's impulsively scrawled, his huge, childlike writing in coloured inks slanting across pink or yellow paper and Sassoon's pained, anxious, but controlled.

Though she loved Stephen, Edith's loyalty now lay firmly with Sassoon. She found it hard to empathize with Stephen whom she could see was toying with his doggedly devoted lover: 'I feel wretched knowing how Siegfried will have been wounded but Stephen is quite irresponsible – he's like a half fairy creature – captivating and cruel'.[14] When Imma was staying at the Daye House in January, she had told Edith that she could read some-one's character in their handwriting. Edith was fascinated and immediately unearthed letters from Elinor Wylie and Sassoon. Imma was surprised by the latter's handwriting; she had 'only seen his exterior, determined, reserved, strong-willed'. But in it she observed 'his storm touched soul . . . his wish to be the <u>only</u> one with anyone he loves.'[15]

The following day Imma and Edith drove to a meet of the Wylye Valley Hounds to watch Sassoon ride out on a carriage horse of Stephen's. It was the first time he had hunted in eight years and he was exhilarated to be riding to hounds again. That night he arrived for dinner at the Daye House carrying pots of hyacinths, bottles of champagne and a bundle of sea kale. He was planning to spend the weekend with Edith and sleep at the Pembroke Arms in Wilton. According to one of his biographers, John Stuart Roberts, 'Sassoon spoke openly to [Edith] as he rarely did with women. She had an advantage in that she made no demands on him, sought nothing from him and offered herself as a listener. Above all she understood the depths of his feelings for Stephen.'[16]

In October 1931, Sassoon took a lease on Fitz House, Edith and Mildred's old home in Teffont Magna, which was not far from Wilsford and close enough to keep in what was now almost daily contact with Edith. Though it had been months since he had seen Stephen he found that he could not leave Wiltshire. He even stabled his horses at Wilsford and befriended the kindly Hunter sisters who tended to the gardens, in the hope that he might catch a glimpse of Stephen. But it was to no avail.

At the Daye House at Easter, William Walton and Rex discussed the situation between the two men with Edith:

> [They] talk sadly of Wilsford which they had walked round in the starlight feeling it a ghost and of Stephen – what will he be when – if he gets better – a deepened greater person? Willy thinks so but R and I feel he is losing more than he gains. Losing his interest in people, books, beauty, even in <u>fun</u> and only able to think of illness. Then of Siegfried. We all think the friendship can never be revived and they think that S may some day commit suicide. We were very sad as we talked of all this misery.'[17]

Edith was determined to keep Sassoon distracted. She invited him to dine with her at the Daye House, she introduced him to new people, she engineered invitations to luncheons and weekend parties at Ashcombe, which Sassoon accepted in spite of his reservations about Cecil, and she arranged for him to meet Henry Newbolt at tea one evening. 'He appreciates every inch, every scent and every birdsong here and not only those but the <u>something else</u> which is in them all', she wrote of Sassoon in her diary that night after the poets had left. 'He said to me "Do you know that you are one of the most blessed of people?" I do.'[18]

When Rex was allowed to visit Stephen at Wilsford he had found himself caught in the middle of their furious rows and was forced to intervene. 'The whole relation between these two men is strange and tragic', Edith wrote in her diary. 'Sieg wants to pour all his affection and his life at Stephen's feet – Stephen wants to have them but <u>at his feet</u> so that he can kick them when he likes! Sieg says he's both heavenly and inhuman. This is true'.[19] Rex too found his loyalty divided. Stephen was one of his dearest friends, but instinctively his support fell to Sassoon whose suffering was so painfully evident. 'I have been puzzled since I saw S, to really discover what <u>I thought myself about him</u>', Rex wrote to Edith after a visit in August.

> I don't know <u>why</u> it seemed a vaguely unsatisfactory visit; he looked well in a way and it was the first time I had seen him out of bed for – I think, nearly 2 years, and he was sweet and not in the kind of mood which I dislike him to be in. I think it is perhaps that one expects <u>so much</u> from a visit to Stephen don't you? So much more than one expects from any other invalid that one may go to visit. His whole manner was merely <u>passive</u> and I always (foolishly) expect him to meet me with <u>active</u> expressions of affection and charm and his lovely spirit. This is so badly expressed, for of course I don't mean <u>move-</u><u>ment</u> and the word 'active'! But you will understand. His face even, seemed to suggest a kind of negative turning attitude so so different from that wonderful <u>expenditure</u> of himself, that we know to be the real Stephen. It is beginning to dawn on me that he lost something by parting from Siegfried which nothing else and no-one could make up to him. Sieg nour-ished and kept living his <u>spirit</u> even if he tired and excited Stephen at stages in his illness when he oughtn't to have done . . . the tragedy is that Stephen thinks that he has lost <u>nothing</u> and that he is himself the same as he used to be.[20]

'Rex never ever writes or answers', Stephen would complain to Edith.[21] The following year, Rex did write a typically effusive letter seeking to reassure Stephen of his affection for him: 'Anyway, whether you know it or not, I have loved you all the time & I think I always Shall . . . I have thought of you continually during these months & sometimes felt very near to you'.[22] But that was later.

Eventually in August Stephen agreed to see Sassoon and it seemed that they had resurrected something of their old affection for one another. But it did not last. Though Stephen's tuberculosis had abated that autumn, in its place came a nervous breakdown, which the neurologist Sir Henry Head believed was both a result of his life-threatening illness and a delayed reaction to Pamela and Nannie's deaths. And so in October 1932 Stephen was sent to a private clinic in Kent, for nerve treatment. Though Sassoon visited him several times it soon became clear that the relationship was over for good. In May 1933, he received a letter from Stephen's doctor: 'He says you upset him and make him feel ill, and that he cannot see you again'.[23] This time Stephen was in earnest.

Edith had been with Sassoon on the day the letter arrived. She wrote that he was 'absolutely broken. It was a torture to see Sieg's anguish and I could not help him.'[24] She feared that he might be suicidal. Desperate to distract him she decided that he must come to a pageant at Wilton in the following week and invited him to stay at the Daye House along with her other guests, Rex and Richard Gatty and his sister Hester.

The pageant was Edith's idea, organized to celebrate the ter-centenary of the death of the metaphysical poet George Herbert. Sassoon was to play the part of a Jacobean nobleman and Rex that of a polymath like himself, Inigo Jones. He spent a whole day at the Daye House building a model church to carry in the tableau, constructing it out of an old box, paper, glass and bits of junk he found lying about. 'I sat by and did the ignorant apprentice's share', Edith wrote in her diary. 'From a heap of use-less scraps an exquisite elaborate Classical church grew up – a round church with portico and wings, pediment balustradings and

Italian windows standing on a broad pavement of coloured marble in squares. Nothing stopped him and he worked from after breakfast till after 2 in the morning.'[25] Edith later gave Rex's model pride of place under a glass dome in her anteroom.

The Gattys were the grandchildren of Alfred and Mabel Morrison of Fonthill, wealthy collectors and art patrons. Their uncle Hugh had become MP for Salisbury in 1918 and Edith had campaigned for him in many elections over the years. Hester's mother Katharine had married Stephen Herbert Gatty, a barrister who had become Chief Justice of Gibraltar. Edith had known Hester since she was a child; intelligent and sensitive, she had a lovely face with mournful downturned blue-grey eyes beneath thick, dark brows. Edith had a notion that she should throw Sassoon and Hester into each other's path that weekend at Wilton, even though he told her that his love for Stephen could only end with his death.

But Edith's plotting evidently worked, as not many weeks had passed before Sassoon was smitten. Though at forty-seven he was twenty years older than Hester, Sassoon, and indeed Edith and Rex, very quickly came to the conclusion that Hester was his salvation. With her he could put the tribulations of the Stephen episode behind him. 'O, Hester, you must redeem my life for me', he wrote imploringly in his diary before he proposed.[26]

Sassoon and Hester were married in a secret ceremony in December 1933, at Christchurch Priory near Bournemouth, with Edith standing in for Sassoon's mother who was too ill to attend. Hester looked serene in a white dress, lace veil and Russian crown and the church was filled with lilies and lily of the valley. There were only twenty or so guests at the wedding, Edith and Rex two of only a few friends of Sassoon including his former lover Glen Byam Shaw, who was best man, and his old friend T. E. Lawrence, then known as Aircraftsman Shaw.

In September Edith had visited Stephen in what Cecil would describe as his 'Fabergé fastness' at Wilsford.[27] She found him in the library which he had decorated in pink and white with rose-coloured curtains decorating the bookcases. 'He looks well in a way', she wrote, 'certainly fatter, but he's lost his air of dazzling other-worldliness when he seemed a transparent lamp holding a brilliant <u>shaking</u> flame.'[28] The next month she had consoled him as he sat 'weeping over Siegfried's engagement'.[29] He wept some more when the marriage was announced and scorned Edith and Rex for their lack of loyalty. But in her diary Edith concluded: 'it is very hard to be fair to both but I <u>know</u> it's better for them that the break was made – Stephen better in health and Siegfried radiant in a normal marriage'.[30] The relationship between Sassoon and Stephen was, she felt, for all its romance, fundamentally wrong. She wholeheartedly approved of this new 'normal' relationship.

Sassoon was thrilled to be married. He believed he could look after Hester, who was recovering from a nervous breakdown after a failed romance, as he had looked after Stephen. In turn Hester professed her understanding about the trauma of his relationship with Stephen and believed that she could look after her husband. Until then Sassoon had been unwaveringly homosexual and it seems strange that he sought happiness with a woman. Hester was almost the same age as Stephen, and both Edith and William Walton would later agree that she was very like Sassoon's former lover. Also she was part of a grand plan. For years he had nurtured a seemingly fanciful and yet oddly conservative domestic fantasy in which he played the part of a country squire. Ten years earlier, he had written in his diary: 'some day, when I have "settled down" and come into a fortune, I will buy a little manor-house in a good hunting country . . . play on a grand piano in a room full of books, with a window looking onto an old-fashioned garden . . . When I am forty-nine I will begin to look for that house, and when I am in it I will write wise books'.[31]

Marrying Hester in 1933 seems to have been the first step in fulfilling this dream. The following year, as he had predicted and at almost the same age as he had planned, he bought the house. Heytesbury was a monumental mansion in the Wylye Valley with hundreds of acres of parkland and woods and an extravagant number of windows punctuating its stark Georgian facade. It was a very masculine-looking house, as suited to Siegfried's character as Wilsford and Ashcombe suited Stephen and Cecil. He had fallen in love with Wiltshire and for Sassoon, whose heart brimmed with nostalgic longing for the lost world of his youth in the Weald of Kent, perhaps there was a feeling of paradise regained. And it was only a few miles from Wilton and his beloved Edith.

18: 'The Happy Heartbreak'

❖

. . . this love is almost all misery.

Edith Olivier's Diary, 22 June 1933

'My darling Edith,' Rex wrote to Edith in February 1933. 'How beastly you have been, haven't you? Of course I know you were within your <u>rights</u> in never writing to me as I owed you letters, but still, how cruel – priggish too, never to write a word of what was happening while you were abroad!' In January Edith had visited Rome for the first time, where she was ill and confined to her bed for some days. She then sailed from Naples to Gibraltar to stay with the Governor and his wife, friends of Lura Howard. 'And besides, you broke a kind of contract', Rex added, 'as you vowed you would write me lovely descriptive, detailed letters when you were in Rome and I said that I would answer them. Alas I had none to answer and you know in your heart of hearts that it is the duty of the person abroad, who is seeing all the lovely things to write to the bored and boring stay-at-home.'

In truth Rex was full of contrition for the letters he hadn't written to her. 'I had no news and I couldn't face the idea of writing a long apologetic letter which would have bored me to tears to write and you to read. But I have <u>felt</u> apologetic and miserable that I never wrote to thank you for that last lovely weekend at Wilton nor to thank you for that <u>wonderful present</u> of the set of Voltaire – nor to send you a present myself and wish you a happy Christmas – nor to say goodbye when you left for Rome.' Rex had been trying to finish his Haddon panel as well as painting Amazon queens and grisaille dolphins on the walls of the library at another of Philip Sassoon's houses, Trent Park in Hertfordshire.

> I know that I'm mostly in the wrong and humbly beg your forgiveness but your crime isn't small either – so there: <u>to be in ROME and your only pencilled note to me, from there, about a Charity Poster Competition in Wilton!</u> . . . how could you not have written from Rome (I mean to rub this in) even if you <u>were</u> ill? I wanted letters of Rome from you as you lay in bed just telling me what you heard even if you couldn't go out . . . Whether you heard rattling wheels on cobbles or that clanging bell of the trams . . . if there was heavy rain <u>splashing</u> on the great cornices and what silvery old domes you could see across the tiled roofs from your sickroom window . . .[1]

At the end of the month, however, they were reunited in London and Edith wrote happily in her diary that 'we are completely at one and can talk more easily than any two people.'[2] At the Wilton pageant on 7 and 8 June a photograph was taken of Rex, a handsome Inigo Jones in a black velvet doublet, a crisp white ruff and a fake moustache. Edith stands beside him in a Jacobean dress, holding his hand as she gazes at him adoringly. But his mind was elsewhere; he had fallen in love.

Earlier that year Rex had been commissioned by Freda Dudley Ward to paint a portrait of her daughters, nineteen-year-old Penelope, or Pempie as she was known, and her younger sister Angela. Freda was a close friend of Sir Philip Sassoon and Rex could well have met her at Port Lympne. She had divorced her husband the Right Hon. William Dudley Ward, a Liberal politician, and until recently had been the mistress of the Prince of Wales. She was still his close confidante but soon to be eclipsed by Wallis Simpson. Pempie had come out in the previous year and featured amongst the 'bevy of beautiful buds of 1932' in the *Queen*'s annual debutante issue.[3]

Just over a week after the Wilton pageant Edith was writing in her diary: 'Rex in a dream – absorbed by Penelope Dudley Ward with whom he drove down and fell in love – it was very cold at one time and she lent him her coat to put on his shoulders'.[4] Rex had driven Pempie to Oxford to join Laurence and Sassoon for dinner and then to watch a particularly romantic performance of *A Midsummer Night's Dream* directed by Max Reinhardt in the garden of Worcester College. Over the months that followed, this romance, as played out in detail in Edith's diaries, has the tragi-comic air of an *opera buffa*. Undoubtedly she was relieved that at last Rex was showing an interest in the opposite sex rather than his own. And if she can be believed, it took Rex no longer than a car journey from London to Wilton to fall in love with Penelope Dudley Ward. Only six days later, Edith found Rex 'half demented with love for Pempie': 'to Rex, in reply to his cry for help . . . <u>Desperate. Shattered.</u> Can think of nothing else. His hand shakes so that he can't paint. He thought that he had been in love before but now knows that this agony is quite another thing. He can't possibly marry as he has no money. She would let him be her lover', she added, 'but he knows he can't accept <u>that</u> from a girl of 19. If she had been married it would be another thing', an altogether practical comment that seems to belie her usual sense of rectitude. Perhaps she felt that different rules applied for Rex. 'It seems a terrible impasse . . . this love is almost <u>all</u> misery. He says she adores him (he can't think why!) . . . he <u>knows</u> she will marry someone else. I felt in the presence of a really great passion – for he has always been apart from such things and his is so supreme a nature that his love is indeed supreme.'[5]

Ten days later Rex arrived at the Daye House:

Absolutely deadbeat and looks it. This love tears him to the heart. He sees no prospect of marriage and in a way recoils [from it] . . . Does not think in itself that living together is wrong in God's sight but says he has too much honour to let Pempie do this tho she is willing to and knows that her mother couldn't throw stones! Yet it is another thing with a girl of 19. Rex says it is quite easy to seduce her and he <u>can't</u>. Yet he can't be with her without feeling that he can't <u>not</u>. It is a devastating passion stemmed by instinctive sense of <u>right</u> in a man.[6]

Rex tried to reassure Edith that their relationship would not change. 'Darling', he wrote to her, 'I think I shall soon become calmer and more used to this fantastic disease, then instead of feeling shattered by it, I shall be terribly happy and do wonderful things and everything will be the same as before between you and me . . . only much lovelier'.[7] But one night at the Daye House in July, Rex lay on the floor of Edith's room and told her that he longed to die for love. Edith, lying in bed in the darkness, can have been in no doubt that she was being called upon to act as his confidante, although 'the effect of his passion is that he clings to me and caresses me all the time – an outlet for his frenzy'.[8] Any romantic feelings that Edith might have harboured, even a whisper, could now never be acknowledged.

The news that Rex was in love with a girl dashed around his friends. But from the very start of his relationship with Pempie, Rex was miserable. Convinced that she would never accept a poor artist as a husband, he felt that it was 'hopeless'.[9] But Rex was making excuses. According to his brother Laurence, Rex exaggerated his lack of money. In the year 1933 to 1934 'his taxable income, with allowances for studio, car etc. already deducted was returned as £1,130 . . . He was poor only in the sense that he was spending all he earned'.[10] More importantly, perhaps, the idea of marriage horrified him, as Edith recognized: 'fundamentally Rex <u>doesn't want to marry</u> and he hates the thought of planning . . . and arranging a little nest! All this clashes with his wildly romantic love'.[11]

Rex's portrait of Pempie and Angela was completed in 1934 and selected for that year's Royal Academy Summer Exhibition. The sisters stand in the foreground, behind them a bosky Arcadian landscape and beside them, an elaborate picnic laid out by a black footman. But juxtaposing the eighteenth-century mood of the painting are the figures of the girls themselves, dressed à la mode in frilly, beribboned, white tea-dresses with waved, bobbed hair. It is a witty, knowing reinterpretation of Gainsborough, an aristocratic portrait for the Jazz Age. The tiny, almost Lilliputian, figures of the girls are curiously child-like; their faces like those of dainty porcelain dolls with vast limpid eyes, tiny noses, rosebud mouths and alabaster skin. Rex's likeness can also be seen on the fountainhead. He cast himself as the horned head of Pan, the son of Hermes and a nymph, half-goat, half-man, creator of beautiful music but too ugly for the Arcadian nymphs to fall in love with. With a wry expression on his face, he insolently but ineffectually squirts water at the two girls. His situation, the painting implies, is hopeless.

Edith dined with Juliet Duff in the summer. '"Rex is in love with Pempie isn't he?"' Juliet asked Edith. 'I said I don't want him to fall in love', Edith replied, to which Juliet responded: '"a little romance would do him good". I: "He can only have a big not a little one – and as he can't marry it would hurt him too much". Of course the silence can't be kept in that full gossiping world. All eyes, ears and tongues.'[12]

That world thought that Rex was making a lot of fuss about very little, that his headlong plunge into unhappiness had come too quickly. With characteristic bluntness Cecil, who had whee-dled the news of the relationship out of Rex, informed him that he was thought to be 'rather making capital out of the "affair" and rather <u>making the most of it</u>'. 'Cecil is a curiously insensitive friend in many ways, don't you agree?' he asked Edith.[13]

That month Ottoline Morrell visited Sassoon at Teffont Magna and he took her to meet Edith; 'a most wonderful woman', thought Ottoline, who, according to her biographer Miranda Seymour, constantly complained that 'she could never find a woman who really interested her'.[14] Sassoon thought that one *salonnière* might enjoy the company of another. Edith, who was only a few months younger than Ottoline, was fascinated by a woman who lived in

such a romantic way; her life seemed to be a kind of artistic performance and yet this was combined with a profound religious
sensibility. At Garsington, her manor house near Oxford, and at
44 Bedford Square in Bloomsbury, with her husband the Liberal
MP Philip Morrell, she had entertained amongst others Bertrand
Russell, D. H. Lawrence, Siegfried Sassoon, Lytton Strachey and
Aldous Huxley alongside a select group of undergraduates from
Oxford. The Morrells had left Garsington in 1927 and that year
moved to a more modest house in Gower Street. The following
year Ottoline had been diagnosed with cancer and her treatment
had entailed the removal of several teeth and a part of her jaw.

In July Edith invited her to the Daye House. Ottoline arrived
at Salisbury station 'in a garden party gown of flowered chiffon', as
Edith recorded with amusement.[15] That night Sassoon arrived to
dine and he stayed until after midnight. Ottoline had long harboured an unrequited passion for Sassoon and Edith was intrigued
to see the two of them together. The next day they were guests at
Ashcombe for lunch. In Ottoline's vast collection of albums there
are photographs, most likely taken by Cecil, in which the two
women pose together elegantly, on the lawn at Ashcombe and at
the Daye House. In one Ottoline stands in a floor-length chiffon
gown and large, wide-brimmed hat, while Edith sits on the grass
beside her, dressed in a simple tea-dress, with long beads and
bobbed hair and, perhaps in imitation of Ottoline, her own enormous picture hat. In another Edith and Ottoline look on as Gerald
Berners sits at an easel painting a portrait of Doris, Lady Castlerosse, who perches on a mattress beside him. Edith looks rather
tight-lipped beneath her hat in this photograph. She had recently
discovered that Cecil was having a relationship with Doris Castlerosse and she was most unimpressed; Doris was just the kind of
woman who made Edith so often scathing of her own sex.

Lithe, long-legged and beautiful, Doris was the wife of the
corpulent gossip columnist Lord Castlerosse and lived in Venice,
where Cecil had met her while on holiday the previous year. Doris
enjoyed a reputation as a convertor of even the most resolutely

homosexual of men and Cecil was delighted by the affair. That July night Edith wrote in her diary:

> Ottoline and I then lunched at Ashcombe . . . where Cecil said he was 'alone with Gerald', but no, we found them sitting in the courtyard – Gerald painting Lady Castlerosse . . . It is a liaison and 'we' always includes her. It makes me feel I can never go there again. There is nothing there but a common little demi-mondaine and why should one put oneself out for her. As Ottoline says, a woman like Mrs Keppel was on the grand scale – 'a King's mistress' – but this is nothing but a woman with physical attraction which she exploits in a mercenary way. It made me feel very depressed and quite unable to enjoy Cecil's society . . . Ottoline looked glorious trailing about in fluttering flowered chiffon and with a large green hat of enchanting angle. She and Cecil walked about together – she thus flowing and he in the shortest of shorts, legs bare to the thighs.'[16]

Edith liked Ottoline, and later said of her that her 'personality is sybilline'. She continued: 'When she talks, all that she says comes across with an added quality given by her beautiful figure, her noble features, her sombre eyes, and her deep emotional voice . . . She creates her own setting and speaks out of it.'[17] Perhaps most importantly Ottoline made Edith feel like a romantic character herself. 'She seems to have loved this place', Edith wrote in her diary after that first visit, 'and makes a little creation of its impression on her mind. The house, park, neighbourhood with the interesting people in it, and then me, and my past, and myself! She sees all this as in a book and makes it all seem very wonderful!'[18]

In late September 1933 Edith gave a dance at the Daye House for about thirty of her friends. It marked the pinnacle of her success as a salonnière. She hung Chinese lanterns about the garden, 'in all caverns under yew trees, very mysterious, flirting places'. A tent was constructed in the garden and a raft floated on the river laden with lamps and lanterns. The Pembrokes gave her a dozen bottles of champagne, whisky and cigarettes. As Edith was dressing for dinner Rex painted a beam above the door in the Long Room as a surprise for her. He had decorated it with green garlands, a red heart pierced by an arrow and 'Darling Edith' written in the centre. The entire party went for cocktails at Juliet Duff's house, Bulbridge, and then on to the Pembroke Arms where Juliet hosted 'a huge and merry' dinner. They returned to the Daye House for the dance, which was, Edith felt, 'a roaring success'. For supper she had set out four round tables lit with green candles. Green lanterns hung from the roof, potted palms had been placed here and there and ferns spilled out of hanging baskets. Rex told Edith that it looked like the Eiffel Tower restaurant. It was a great success but Edith was horrified by Evelyn Waugh, who became 'disgracefully gibberingly drunk'. Late that night Rex came to her room and talked for hours until 'the rain began to crash down'. Afterwards, she wrote in her diary: 'My one and only party.'[19]

That autumn Edith discussed Rex with David Herbert. He thought Pempie was beautiful but not enough for Rex – too trivial – though Rex didn't think so and neither did their friends. In December Edith had the opportunity to decide for herself. She drove to Salisbury station to collect Pempie and Rex who was 'in a state of heavenly bliss. He thinks her utterly unique and dazzling'. Pempie, with wide, heavy-lidded eyes and high, rounded cheekbones, was a classical aristocratic beauty, 'not pretty in the modern style'. That night Hester and Sassoon came to supper and Edith decided that Hester was 'far lovelier in spirit and body than Pempie' who she thought was 'a gay child and not I think . . . seriously in love'.[20] Pempie was not good enough for Rex, and perhaps Edith felt that Rex's ardour was not returned: 'I have a feeling that tho she loves him it isn't at all the same thing with her. She could and will easily marry someone else and I wish she would.'[21] By February, Edith believed that 'Pempie and poverty are killing him'.[22] Rex was spending too much money trying to impress the girl, who belonged to a grander, wealthier world than his own. He told Edith that he would often spend £5 taking her out for an evening '(and of course he wants to <u>every</u> evening . . .) . . . he has earned no big sum since Philip Sassoon. £100 for the Haddon Hall picture which took 8 months!'[23]

Edith vowed to support Rex and Pempie though she knew there was no future for the relationship. She was right. By March 1934, the affair, if it can be called that, was petering out.

> [Rex] said 'she doesn't love me as much as she did' but I always felt he was to her merely <u>one</u> of her many admirers. She had no idea of his nature. He only existed for her because <u>he</u> was in love not because <u>she</u> was. It is a very hard blow but I am glad it is over. It must only have meant other misery if they had married but my poor darling is suffering horribly now. He could not speak of it and we didn't'.[24]

Pempie sent a final letter to Rex in which she wrote that she hoped they could remain friends. Rex was with Edith in his studio and as he handed her the letter to read he scooped her into his arms and they danced for some time to the record that was playing. Edith thought it was a very Rex gesture. Just before Easter Rex was whisked away by his friend Kenneth Rae to drown his sorrows in Rome. On his return he wrote to Edith: 'I shall love other people before long – I trust so anyway – but I can't help feeling certain too, that sorrow for this love will never quite leave me – even though I stow it well away. It's something inexplicably beautiful lost to me, – a lovely lovely thing died and I was powerless to save it.'[25] Edith wrote generously that what he was suffering was worse than bereavement. Rex disagreed, believing death 'so much more <u>final</u>' and without that '<u>loving proximity</u>'. 'Besides', he added, 'there is always the barest <u>barest</u> chance that love may come back, isn't there?'[26]* Not long after this Rex fleetingly transferred

---

* Pempie became an actress and starred in several British films in the 1930s and 1940s. She married the actor Anthony Pelissier in 1939. They divorced in 1944 and she married the film director Carol Reed in 1948. She died in 1982.

his affections to Pempie's sister Angela but was kindly but firmly rejected by her. He painted her that year as 'St Toughy', a warrior saint in impenetrable armour, a halo above her head, lipstick and a wry expression on her face. It was not the last time Rex would find himself fixating on two women at once.

In March, Edith and Rex were together in his studio: 'we talked gravely of right and wrong, good and evil and of the horrible way in which <u>all</u> friendships are now presumed to be homo-sexual' adding, perhaps to reassure herself:

> Rex as ever has a very clear judgement and a very delicate conscience. He showed me Pempie's last letter to him – kind but final. She agrees that they had better not meet if it makes him unhappy but hopes he will come to see her again when he feels he can – it's definitely hopeless. She has never loved him really – this is a wise, sane, <u>heartbreaking</u> setting of the situation. My angel is deeply sad but again shows his character, his courage.[27]

They went to a party together that evening. 'Rex wanted to leave early', Edith wrote, 'and as I drove away I watched his figure looking very lonely as he walked down Belgrave Square'.[28]

Laurence said of Edith that 'there was not and never would be . . . a trace of jealousy in all the nightly doubts recorded by this faithful friend'.[29] True, there is nothing explicit, but there is a hint of relief that Rex was hers alone once more. Pempie, like David in *The Love-Child*, threatened to shatter the delicately constructed intimacy of her relationship with Rex. Clearly, in an abstract sense, she admired the 'wildly romantic' passion of her lovelorn friend, but she preferred having him to herself.[30]

For Rex, Pempie was perhaps no more real than the elfin girl in the portrait. That year he painted a self-portrait, reminiscent of Caspar David Friedrich's 1818 painting *Wanderer above the Sea of Fog*. Rex is dressed in a dark overcoat; with collar upturned and a red scarf bound around his neck like a stock, he stands against the wind, Byronic before a stormy sky. In the background stands one of the Boycott Pavilions at Stowe. The image is strikingly similar to one that he had drawn ten years earlier, in which he had cast himself as the adventurous Henry Brocken, standing on a wind-swept beach beside Poe's fated heroine Annabel Lee. With a very similar sky, an upturned collar and brooding expression, he huddles against the wind with the childlike girl who also, coincidentally, bears more than a passing resemblance to his later portrait of Pempie and her sister.

Rex had retreated into the romantic world of his imagination, a world that was informed by the poetry of his youth: Keats, de la Mare and Poe. 'I was a child and she was a child in the kingdom by the sea', recalls the narrator of 'Annabel Lee'.[31] In the poem, the lovers' passion is innocent and curtailed by the heroine's untimely death. In seeing Pempie as a child, Rex had rendered her similarly untouchable, echoing what he had told Edith, that Pempie was too young to be seduced by him. His vehement declarations of profound but futile desire call to mind the ritual and rhetoric of courtly love. This was a chaste passion that could never be consummated, with Rex, the suffering martyr to love, adoring from a distance, and Pempie, the untouchable maiden of higher status, comfortably out of reach on her lofty pedestal. For Rex, passion, like persona, was a kind of performance.

'Perhaps sexuality and heart were divided', his brother later pondered.[32] It is possible that, like Sassoon, Rex thought that he would find salvation in a woman. In 1932 he had painted *Ulysses' Farewell*, with naked youths frolicking in the foreground, for Malcolm Bullock. The next year, he painted Pempie as her classical namesake, Penelope, as Ulysses departs from Ithaca. Perhaps Rex identified with both Penelope and Ulysses, like the reversible faces he was drawing for children, visual tricks that could be inverted to reveal opposing faces: beautiful or ugly, benign or malevolent, jovial or miserable, adult or child, male or female.*

---

* Drawn in 1931–2 for Shell. Later published as *OHO!* (1946) and *AHA!* (1978).

Rex was troubled by these conflicting impulses. Returning to his studio late one night, he looked up to his window to see a vision of himself, staring out of the window, looking 'very pale, very woebegone', as he told Cecil Beaton.[33] In romantic literature, the double signifies the divided self, one part bound by its mortal existence whilst the other seeks a transcendental harmony with the infinite. Shelley saw a vision of himself just days before he died in 1822. In her diary, and increasingly as the years went by, Edith portrayed Rex as a romantic character, angst-ridden, disillusioned, inclined to melancholy and lovesickness, almost neurasthenic, lamenting the impossibility of love and perpetually dissatisfied with his life and his work. That Rex told Cecil Beaton and Osbert Sitwell of this vision and that he had recently completed a Byronic self-portrait suggests that he liked presenting himself as a romantic figure. He had told Edith he wanted to die for love and in 1934 he painted the head of a weeping girl beside a man's skull. Death remained a romantic concept for him.

In his 1813 essay on Beethoven, the romantic writer E. T. A. Hoffmann said that '*unendliche sehnsucht*' or 'endless longing' is 'the very essence of romanticism'.[34] The life of the romantic hero is overwhelmed by it; he is continually searching for an obscure and elusive aesthetic ideal that is perpetually and frustratingly out of reach. The endless search, simultaneously enchanting and enervating, ultimately inspires melancholy and disillusionment. Rex consciously cultivated his romantic image, but on another, unconscious level, his struggles with love and art and life suggest that he was dominated by a profound sense of *sehnsucht*.

Sehnsucht is difficult to define definitively; it is inherently personal. For C. S. Lewis it was 'that unnameable something, desire for which pierces us like a rapier at the smell of a bonfire, the sound of wild ducks flying overhead, the title of *The Well at the World's End*, the opening lines of *Kubla Khan*, the morning cobwebs in late summer, or the noise of falling waves'.[35] It is both nostalgia and anticipation, a memory, a promise, an almost transcendental longing for something that seems to remain tantalizingly out of reach; it is the sweet poignancy of *Et in Arcadia Ego*. Its mood is autumnal, inspired by damp, mossy woods; crumbling houses; twilight, transience and decay. The paintings of Poussin and the poetry of Walter de la Mare resound with it. For de la Mare, childhood was the perfect state, the richest reality, and he believed that in adulthood only the power of the imagination could help us to recover that vanished kingdom. For Rex it was 'that almost painful lovliness of longing or regret (which Stephen once called so well the "Happy Heartbreak")'.[36]

Rex's paintings were filled with nostalgia for the past, a lost world that he then created in his invented Arcadias. They are all essentially unobtainable – behind the lovely landscapes where nymphs frolic and unicorns roam, where the distant vistas trail off into infinity, was always a flat wall. And in life, too, it was the tugging between dream and reality that left him dissatisfied. He was forever imagining impossible things, his letters full of fanciful ideas, costumes, plans for pavilions he would never build, homes he would never own and women who would never marry him.

Stephen Tennant lyrically recalled his friend's 'love of shadowy beauty, firelight, new and moonlight, night scenes and twilight', which he thought 'expressed a profound tendency in his make-up to portray the indefinable in experience, the unavowed and transitory. Yes, he could paint with a uniquely personal talent'. Stephen called it 'the hinterlands of the enchanted imagination':

> The crowded animation of his terrain – its glitter and superabundance of fine detail, its never-ending, ever opening vista of romantic representation and fulfilment . . . He was a realist, who built his fancy on solid ground . . . Surely genius is the harnessing of the ineffable to visible, tangible achievement? The capturing of a vapour in design or music, a smoke wreath, an arabesque carved in stone.[37]

In 1929, Rex had written a revealing letter to Edith from Rome, in which he attempted to pin down the intangible effect that Italy had on his imagination:

This heart-breaking and exquisitely beautiful country. I say heartbreaking because, besides being so lovely, it is also to me so very <u>sad</u>. Only sad of course in the most <u>enjoyable</u> way! That kind of thin exquisite grief which so much poetry gives one, and which we have often discussed, and tried to analyse, haven't we? I don't think I feel melancholy when looking at some distant or beautiful Italian landscape; <u>but it is where people have lived</u>, (some old sleepy farmhouse out in the Campagna, or a little dark and boarded up palace in a side street), which moves me most deeply with their air of enchanted sadness. It is as though I am suddenly <u>reminded</u> of how we used to live in those long ago drowsy, pastoral centuaries, and I feel as though I was <u>an old man</u> full of sad longing for my vanished youth, and worried with a kind of regret for the way in which I must have wasted or not valued properly those wonderful and beautiful, and now irretreavable days! Staying in this country gives me agony emotionally of longing to be a poet or next best a writer but my painting can never express all the things that I feel . . . To say what one wishes to say is the almost impossible thing.[38]

For Laurence Whistler, this letter is the key to his brother's imagination. Although Rex might fill his paintings with scrolls and curlicues, classical columns and baroque churches, at heart he was a romantic. '[Rex] lived in two worlds with equal pleasure: visually in the Classical, poetically in the romantic', writes his brother. 'He looked at Classical art with the eyes of a Romantic'.[39]

Edith adored Rex's new melancholy self-portrait and, when it was exhibited at the French Gallery the year it was painted, she bought it. She granted it pride of place in the panel Rex had designed above the fireplace, opposite her daybed in the Long Room. She thought it 'enchanting and jocund . . . dazzling in its brilliancy of drawing', adding that 'it completely changes the room – filling it with audacious character . . . it's like a French 19th century painting.'[40]

The Rex of the self-portrait was the one that she loved and nurtured, not the man whom she had caught exchanging glances with Malcolm Bullock at the Savoy. This was the Rex of her diaries, the Rex who went up to her room at midnight to read poetry 'in a lovely deep sad voice', who would suddenly sweep her into his arms to dance to the music playing on the gramophone and whom Cecil Beaton had photographed, at Wilsford in 1927, in the manner of Watteau, dressed in stockings and breeches, love-lorn and strumming on a guitar while reclining on a leaf-strewn bank.[41] Perhaps Edith accepted Rex's artificial and chivalrous approach to love as a normal way of behaving because she had had no experience of it herself. Perhaps, to her, it seemed noble.

With an inherently romantic sensibility herself, Edith encouraged Rex's romantic instincts and this complicity was central to their relationship. 'We had amusing talk about Classic and Romantic art', she wrote in her diary in 1927, 'and agree we are both Romantics (which we fear means sentimental) much as we think we love the Classical. A thick fog and this set us off finding we like fog effects better than Gallic Clarity and Plein Air'.[42] He had written a long letter to Edith from Tivoli describing the exquisite sadness of the landscape; the 'enchanted dusk' and the 'light lingering in warm gold on the olives and ilex trees'.[43] To his mother, by comparison, he had written: 'we drove to Tivoli (well acoutered with painting things) on Monday afternoon . . . it was so heavenly there all the time and cooler too, being of course much higher than Rome'.[44]

The characters in Edith's novels – dwarves, adventurous footmen and imaginary children – could happily inhabit and animate the landscapes of Rex's paintings. They too spring from a place where fantasy spills into reality and the real world nudges into her fantasies, a spirit of magic realism, the 'dream condition' of the Tate mural. Rex's style lent itself easily to Edith's writing as the illustrations he drew for a number of her novels show. When Stephen offered to draw the frontispiece for her next novel, Edith confessed to her diary with words vehemently underlined:

'I want Rex in all my books'.[45] Edith's imagination, a gallimaufry of history, myths, legends and literature, reflects Rex's imagined and personalized version of history and lent a distinct atmosphere to her fiction. Edith's novels, like Rex's paintings, are quasi-historical and blend comedy and drama. *The Love-Child*, with its uncanny and unresolved interplay between insanity and the supernatural, calls to mind the Gothic and psychological terror in the tales of Rex's beloved Poe. For her characters fantasy is often more appealing than reality because it destroys limitations and opens life up to the endless possibilities of the imagination; suppression is a dangerous thing; heroes can re-shape their own destinies; and self-romanticizing is encouraged.

It was Edith who had seen a vision of Lyonesse off the coast of Cornwall and who had written the passionately defensive introduction to *An Adventure*. Perhaps her receptivity to the supernatural inspired Rex's vision of himself sitting at the window of his studio. Her belief in psychic phenomena, the fanciful nature of her own visions and her sensitivity to the primal energies of the landscape, reveal that she too sought to satisfy the hunger of a romantic imagination. From their first meeting alone in London in 1925 when they had explored the East End, Edith and Rex spent most of their time together on quests in search of beautiful places and scenes, sinking themselves into their shared fantasy of the past. It was at the heart of their friendship and it is what held them together, what drew Rex back to the Daye House; a sense of mutual understanding, a kind of *folie à deux*.

19: Sex

❖

O my darling. I must get him away.

Edith Olivier's Diary, 31 December 1934

'Rex looks very well. We went to a play and frolicked in a box', Stephen wrote to Edith in April 1934 from the Hyde Park Hotel in London. 'Rex laughing inordinately and being entirely characteristic and enchanting'.[1] Stephen had sulked alone at Wilsford since Sassoon's wedding in December and Edith had not seen him for weeks until a night in early April, when he had arrived at the Daye House after midnight shivering in the cold with only a coat and trousers over his pyjamas. She was struck by how bloated he looked but as they sat and gossiped into the night she was relieved to see that he was still 'so utterly his wayward self in spite of the disguise of fat'.[2] Stephen was soon roused from his misery and set off a few days later for London where he met Rex. Later in the summer he flew to Paris with Cecil and from there travelled south to Provence and to Marseille. The dirty, smoky, simmering city would awaken his senses and inspire him to write a book.

To assuage the lingering sadness of his failed love affair Rex had thrown himself into work designing sets for a production of *Fidelio* at Covent Garden. He was going to painstaking lengths to make the scenes, set in different locations in a baroque citadel, look as convincing as possible, be it the imposing arched entrance, a gloomy dungeon or an oppressive courtyard. While Rex grudgingly worked on a steady stream of book illustrations throughout the 1930s, his work for the theatre was gathering momentum. It seemed only natural that he should work in set and even costume design. The theatricality and illusory quality of his style lent itself perfectly to the stage. Rex already decorated interiors as if they were stage sets, creating a mood by pastiching and elaborating on historical styles. It was perhaps inevitable that with his mastery of perspective and his obsession for historical accuracy, his work should lead him in that direction. His attention to detail was staggering. When, three years later, he worked on a production of *Victoria Regina*, he accompanied his designs with comprehensive instructions. These, for roses:

> Mauvy pink roses (<u>cleaner</u> pink than I show) perhaps fairly light ice cream pink (not at all red or yellow) delicately sprayed with blue would get this effect. Old-fashioned cabbage rose . . . leaves very blue green and old-fashioned shaggy moss rose type as seen in old chintzes. They must all be bent when in position, to take graceful curves gently curling this way and that and no good at all wires straight out as they come from the shop. I know this is all <u>very tricky and difficult</u> and requires a lot of attention but I feel is most <u>important</u>.[3]

His sets were never radical or experimental, but they were acclaimed for their elegant restraint, historical accuracy and most of all, their charm: the sepulchral grandeur of Lady Catherine de Bourgh's Empire-inspired drawing room at Rosings Park in *Pride and Prejudice* and the moonlit ruins of a Gothic abbey for *Les Sylphides*. His set designs for the Vic-Wells Ballet production of *The Rake's Progress* in 1935 were particularly convincing, an *hommage* to Hogarth but swept clean of the Rabelaisian crowds that jostle for space in his pictures; instead they were on the stage. The house curtain was a Georgian street scene painted in grisaille with the tower of St Martin's to the left and a skull, a memento mori, hovering appropriately for the plot above the street. Each scene looked like a picture, with the backdrop changing but the side walls remaining the same, a proscenium containing the stage like a frame around a painting. The ballet's choreographer, Ninette de Valois, later recalled: 'Of course it was difficult for him, there was the period complete in itself, there was Hogarth the great figure of that period and yet he managed to produce something that was not a pastiche. It was the spirit of Hogarth'.[4]

At the beginning of May Rex was offered two more plays, one, for Cole Porter, set in pre-war Vienna, and another with a contemporary setting starring Tallulah Bankhead. Rex had met the notorious, flaxen-haired film star with Cecil, backstage at the Garrick after watching her performance in *The Lady of the Camellias* in 1930. Arriving back in England after an unsuccessful three-year stint in Hollywood she immediately called up her old friends and acquaintances. One of them was Rex.

In the twenties and thirties the name Tallulah Bankhead was a byword for iniquity. An Alabama senator's daughter, bisexual, chain-smoking, drug-taking and heavy-drinking, she represented the most devilish and decadent sophistication. Years earlier Reginald Herbert (later Lord Pembroke) had been sent by his family to work in the southern states of America and had befriended William Bankhead, Tallulah's father. When Bankhead first sent his precious daughter to England he had asked Reginald to act as a kind of guardian to her.

This proved no easy task. Very soon she was swept into the vortex of Bright Young London as one of its leading and most promiscuous lights. She had become great friends with David Herbert and through him she met Cecil, who thought she was magnificent. 'Cecil very impressed by the fundamental tragedy of a life like Tillulah's', Edith wrote in her diary in 1928 (she would always spell her name 'Tillulah'); 'she can't be alone for one minute. Lives in a succession of triumphs, rowdyism, drunkenness, furies and desperate fleeing from herself. He couldn't get this out of his mind.'[5] She was still in his mind the following year when he was writing his *Book of Beauty*:

> Tallulah Bankhead is a wicked archangel ... Hers is the most easily recognisable face I know and it is the most luscious ... Miss Bankhead's cheeks are like huge acid-pink peonies, her eyelashes are built out with hot liquid paint to look like burnt matches, and her sullen, discontented, rather evil, rosebud of a mouth is painted the brightest scarlet and is as shiny as Tiptree's strawberry jam.[6]

In 1934, two months after Pempie had sent her final letter to Rex, he began a liaison with Tallulah, with whom it is likely that he lost his virginity, at the age of twenty-nine. 'I have been having an affair with Tallulah Bankhead,' he boasted to his brother.[7] She was easy and magnetic company and an uncomplicated crash-course in sex. Stephen described Tallulah as 'a man-eating vampire', which is perhaps why she appealed to the instinctively submissive Rex.[8] In turn, as David Herbert later recalled, she found Rex 'gentle unlike so many of the brash bons vivants Tallulah knew'.[9] Not long before returning to England she had undergone an emergency hysterectomy as a result of a sexually transmitted disease and came out of hospital weighing only five stone and in a deep depression. Rex with all his gentle charm, his artistic nature, his reticence and his sexual inexperience, was an antidote to all that. She would later recall how she had 'steamed with indignation' when Rex stood her up for dinner one evening. 'But I thawed', she wrote, 'when, two hours late, he handed me two tulip bouquets. His delay', she discovered, 'was caused by the failure of the paint to dry. He had touched up the yellow tulips with black dots, the white ones with black stripes.'[10] David Herbert arrived at the door of her suite at the Hotel Splendide in Piccadilly to be informed: '"Miss Bankhead is in the bath with Mr Rex Whistler."'

'"I'm just trying to show Rex I'm definitely a blonde!"' shouted Tallulah from the bathroom.[11]

Another evening David Herbert arrived at Tallulah's suite to stay for the night only to find an unmade bed, Tallulah in a kimono and Rex in a dressing gown. 'How sweet', said Laurence

Whistler, 'to disabuse' those friends that thought he was homo-sexual or disinterested in women 'and get even with Cecil, by summoning as witness one who could be counted on to cater for that very curiosity he had denounced, only months before'.[12]

The previous year Rex had painted himself as a Byronic figure. In a self-portrait of 1934, he portrayed himself in a modern checked shirt, open at the collar. His face, as always, is more in the shade than in the light, his mouth is set and there are lines around his tired, averted eyes. Perhaps for Rex it marked his passage from innocence to experience. For a time at least, Pempie had shattered the romance leaving only the reality behind. And it is interesting that Rex did not paint Tallulah's portrait. Unlike Pempie, she was a woman rather than an elusive muse.

Edith didn't like the new Rex and noted sadly in her diary that they had passed most of the year apart from each other. Perhaps he found it difficult to reconcile the man that he was with Edith and the man who was enjoying a wild affair with Tallulah Bankhead. From Edith's point of view, though, it was the Pempie affair that had destroyed him. On 24 June she recorded in her diary that it was 'Darling Rex's birthday'. 'I feel anxious about him, he is so broken and yet I do trust his fine spirit'.[13] But when she saw him in London a few days later she thought that he looked 'thin and with his hair on end . . . his face has changed a little and is now a vizor'.[14]

To help him, although she was hardly in a position to do so, Edith gave Rex some of her share certificates and went with him to his solicitor to sign a guarantee for his overdraft. But of course she made no connection in her diary between his protestations of poverty and the 'smart new sports car', a convertible Swallow Special, bought in exchange for his Vauxhall saloon at the end of July.[15] At a bathing party at Bulbridge Edith sat with Stephen and talked of Rex:

> <u>Someone</u> abuses Rex to him. Who is it? Three separate times he has told me things against him (1) He speaks cruelly about people (2) sees <u>only</u> Tillulah (3) now, he has taken to

drink and is <u>carried drunk to bed</u>. I cannot believe these things, tho' he may have gone to the bottle instead of Pempie. But I feel sad and uneasy.[16]

In May Faber published Edith's latest book. From the time of Rex's obsession with Pempie Edith had been working on her first biography, a life of Alexander Cruden, the eccentric eighteenth-century biblical scholar who wrote a monumental and definitive concordance to the Bible. An 'enthusiast for whom it was no drudgery, but a sustained passion of delight, to creep conscientiously word by word through every chapter of the Bible, and then not once only, but again and again'.[17] His life was far more fascinating than this would imply, however, and Edith had been intrigued by Cruden since childhood:

> When I was a little girl, I was one day sitting on the floor in my father's study, when my mother came into the room and took from the shelf an enormous tome. She studied it for a few moments and as she pushed it back into the shelf, she said, with a dramatic gesture: 'Right as usual. That man never made a mistake. No wonder he went mad' I was profoundly impressed. Later on, I often remembered those words and wondered whether Cruden really had been mad, and if so, whether the *Concordance* had driven him out of his mind. At last I found his name by chance in the *Dictionary of National Biography*. There I learnt that Cruden did indeed go mad, not only once, but three times, and that each time it was a love affair which drove him demented.[18]

Cruden, the son of a merchant, was born in Aberdeen in 1699. As a young man, already of unsound mind, he became so obsessed with the daughter of a clergyman that he was placed in an asylum. Discovering that the object of his affection was his brother's mistress was the final straw. On his release from the asylum he travelled south to London where he found work as a tutor and as a 'corrector' or proofreader for the press, and was then employed as French Reader to the Earl of Derby. Edith amusingly recounts how unbearable it was for the Earl to listen to Cruden; he knew the French language but nothing of its pronunciation and was summarily dismissed. In the years that followed he tutored once more, opened a bookshop and worked on his concordance in a room at the back of his shop. He became bookseller to Queen Caroline and dedicated his book to her but when she died, soon after it was published, her promise of a financial reward never honoured, he slipped again into madness. And then his life became a sorry round of obsessions with women (one of them the daughter of the Lord Mayor of London), angry pamphlet writing in defence of his actions, and incarceration and ill treatment in asylums. Eventually he decided to become a champion of morality, appointing himself 'Alexander the Corrector', petitioning Parliament to make his appointment official and setting off on a provincial tour to do his work. Blasphemy and Sabbath breaking were high on his agenda and he wrote passionate articles decrying the treatment of criminals and the insane. He also wrote articles criticizing those women who had rejected his advances. He died at the age of sixty-nine in lodgings in Islington. His landlady entered his room and found him kneeling in prayer beside his bed, his head fallen onto the Bible open in front of him.

Cruden's life, coloured by puritanical morality, insanity and rejection and yet ultimately dominated by perseverance, religious and humanitarian conviction and dogged self-belief, was an inspired choice for Edith's first biography. The idea of veracity in madness and the power of obsession continued to fascinate her. She had researched tirelessly for the book, travelling to Aberdeen although she found no trace of him, trawling through his many pamphlets, his autobiographical accounts, his asylum journals and his indignant correspondence with the Earl of Derby. *Alexander the Corrector: The Eccentric Life of Alexander Cruden,* published with wrappers and frontispiece by Rex, received positive reviews from the *Observer, The Times,* the *Evening Standard* (which gave her a full-page review) and from Rex.

My darling Edith,

. . . I'm miserable not to have written also about <u>darling</u> Cruden which I really <u>adored</u>. I think it is a quite enchanting book sweetly sympathetic to the old boy and yet being divinely funny about him in a dry Osbertian way. How seldom one is made to actually laugh aloud while reading by oneself but I had to over this <u>merry</u> figure while somehow never feeling you were being <u>unkind</u> about Alexander.

Much love Rex.[19]

There is no doubt that Edith was inspired by Rex for her portrait of Cruden. She believed that his reckless behaviour was the tragic result of his disappointment in love and that, like Cruden, Rex needed to be saved. Naturally, she thought that she must be the one to do it.

But they spent the summer apart. Rex was at work on a conversation piece, a portrait of Valerian and Eliza Wellesley for their mother, the poet Dorothy Wellesley, later Duchess of Wellington. His father had had a stroke and was very ill and he spent time at home looking after his parents. Later, when his father began to recover he travelled to Italy with Kenneth Rae and in the autumn he started work designing sets and costumes for *The Marriage of Figaro* at Sadler's Wells.

Edith too was busy with her own life. She went to a luncheon at Ashcombe, and she drank cocktails at Bulbridge with Juliet Duff and her guests, after which Edith wrote in her diary: 'these crowds are too much. They take away all the character of Wiltshire – and they call <u>themselves Wilts . . .</u> They talk all the time of their orgies and live here as if it was London'.[20]

In London Edith was invited to first nights and private views. One diary entry, from 29 June, reveals that she visited her doctor in the morning to discuss her blood pressure, which was now lowering on a restrictive diet she called 'the Cure'. That afternoon she researched her latest book at the British Museum, a biography of Mary Magdalen for the publisher Peter Davies, who, nine days after the publication of the Cruden book, had commissioned her to write a short biography for a series he was developing. She then went to meet Osbert Sitwell at the Carlton Club. From there she went to a cocktail party given by Lady Colefax, where she met 'lots of litterateurs' including the novelists Margaret Kennedy and H. G. Wells '(I thought he was dead)'. Later, with Cecil Beaton's friend Peter Watson, she went to watch a Parliamentary Pageant arranged by the Conservative Central Office, which she didn't think very good, except for Cecil and Diana Cooper as Henry VII and Elizabeth of York. The day ended with a concert at Wimborne House which she attended with Watson to whom she was finally warming. 'Peter and I got on quite well. He has nothing in him but does love music. Hideously ugly.'[21]

The biography that Edith was writing was by her own account 'not really a biography at all, but a work built up from a number of the beautiful imaginative and poetic lives of the Saint written during the Middle Ages'.[22] Edith identified Mary Magdalen as Mary of Bethany, the sister of Lazarus. She did not want to write a definitive scholarly and historically accurate account but rather to recreate the image of the Magdalen passed down from the 'sacred Fairyland' of troubadours, mystery plays and *The Golden Legend*.[23] And so she pored over medieval jewels and tableware in the British Museum and drove up to Oxford to research in the Bodleian. While there, she stayed with Annie Moberly whom she found 'tragically changed and looks terrifying. A short bent thick humpbacked figure . . . she hobbles along like a witch'. Edith sat with her in the evening and listened to her recounting over and over again the events at Versailles. 'What a terrible thing this old age is', Edith wrote in her diary that night.[24] Annie Moberly died three years later on 5 May 1937 at the age of ninety.

In August Imma and Walton came to stay at the Daye House. They had been apart for several months and their relationship was more volatile than ever. After long discussions in the park at Wilton they decided that it was best for them not to get married; both were too poor, in spite of a legacy left to Walton by Elizabeth

Courtauld, wife of Sir Samuel Courtauld who had commissioned Rex in 1928. Imma believed that he should have no responsibilities to distract him from his work. Edith remarked that they both seemed visibly relaxed once the decision had been made. But it was the beginning of the end of their relationship.

Towards the end of the year, on 3 December, Edith went to the Queen's Hall in Langham Place with Imma, Cecil and the Sitwell brothers to a rehearsal and later a performance of Walton's Symphony No. 1 performed by the London Symphony Orchestra and conducted by Sir Hamilton Harty who had first commissioned the piece. Three of the four movements had been completed. Edith observed Walton sitting alone in the auditorium.

> . . . the orchestra worked away finding the music very difficult. The first glorious movement they have now <u>got</u> – but the scherzo is still beyond them and the yearning 3rd movement they took a bit too slow I thought. But one has no doubt that this is an immortal work – a classic – something which will be a landmark in English music. Its scale is stupendous and there sat Willy, pale and lean, smoking his interminable succession of bad thin cigarettes. Incredible that this great, complex, rich creation should have sprung from him.
> . . . <u>All</u> the musical world came and all the nicest people and the orchestra played <u>finely</u> – quite another thing from the morning. It sounded glorious and was gloriously received – Willy being called 5 or 6 times. A stupendous occasion.[25]

Walton had stayed at the Daye House at the genesis of his symphony and Edith felt almost like a midwife as she heard it played. She, along with only a few of his intimates, also knew that he had poured into it the passionate hurly-burly of his relationship with Imma, that it marked the passage of their love to its demise. The urgent, climactic first movement, the cruel scherzo, which he had marked 'presto, con malizia' and which was full of rows and anger, and the third marked 'con malinconia', the sadness after the anger had subsided. He felt so frustrated by the death throes of their relationship that he couldn't begin work on the final movement. Not long after this first performance, Imma finally left Walton and began a relationship with a dynamic Hungarian doctor, Tibor Csato, who was based in London.

When alone that summer Edith lunched on the River Terrace at the edge of the lawn, took tea by the dining-room window and had dinner in the Colonnade. Days were spent working at her book in the garden while pursuing shade and escaping midges in the summer heat:

> My garden is a maze of colour and scent. Larkspurs glorious, all colours, snap-dragons as yet all pale yellow and the tall evening primrose match them. The lavender a <u>deep</u> blue. Cluster roses every shade of pink, honeysuckle, tobacco plants, lilies and lots of herbaceous plants . . . Wonderful red clouds drifting over the sky after sunset and illuminating the garden. <u>I could not go in</u>.[26]

The lush sensuality of the Daye House garden seems to have worked its way into *Mary Magdalen*. The saint lives a life of sinful decadence in a beautiful pleasure pavilion, hunting, carousing, clothing herself in gorgeous robes, painting her already exquisite face and seducing men, before she sees the error of her ways and casts all this off for a life of simple virtue and repentance in a Provençal cave. Before then her world is one of courtly castles, formal gardens, banquets and tournaments, reminiscent of scenes from a tapestry or the *Roman de la Rose*. Mary is a princess, an exotic enchantress in ropes of pearls, heavy Egyptian earrings and peacock feathers, attended by dancing girls and slave boys; 'she seeks for love in the fever of lust, for joy in the drugging of wine, and for peace among the clatter of tournaments', her sister observes.[27] The book was published later in the year and dedicated to 'Billy [Hambleden]. Who told me to write the life of a saint'.[28]

In October Edith noted in her diary that Rex had not visited her at the Daye House since February: 'we have passed this Summer . . . apart but for London which doesn't count.'[29] Eventually he came to see her at the end of the month and they went to visit Sassoon at Heytesbury. '"I have not seen Siegfried since I lost Pempie"', he told her.[30] She accompanied him to the first night of *Figaro* in November and thought his sets beautiful, particularly a night scene with a dark wooded avenue leading to the Wilton Colonnade. Several days earlier, during a weekend party at Weston Hall, home of Sacheverell and Georgia Sitwell, Edith delighted, as ever, that Rex was 'seeing and appreciating the <u>quality</u> of everything. But how changed he is since last year. His youth is over and his face in repose is still, sad and very <u>reserved</u>: a quiet mask.'[31]

On New Year's Eve 1934, her sixty-second birthday, Edith dined at Wilton House and spent the evening drinking rum punch, singing drinking songs and playing games with the family. As the clock struck midnight she opened the door to welcome in the New Year and observed that a spider was the first creature to cross the threshold. But in her diary that night, the final entry of the year, she recounted a conversation from earlier that evening: 'talked of Rex who seems now associated with a bad rowdy drunken set – O my darling I must get him away'.[32]

Part Four

❖

LANDSCAPES

20: Distance

❖

He twice spoke of our distance from 'home' – meaning this place – I love that.

Edith Olivier's Diary, 27 June 1935

In London in March 1935, Rex and Edith celebrated the tenth anniversary of their friendship over a lunch of sausages and sauerkraut. Schmidt's, 'chosen because we neither of us have a penny', was a cavernous German restaurant on Charlotte Street, well known by the German community of north Soho for the cheap, *heimisch* food and surly waiters. 'Rather a sordid meal which distressed my angel', Edith wrote in her diary that night. After lunch they walked to his studio and Rex showed Edith his latest work. He felt that his technique was changing, he told her, that he had been 'a very "late developer"'. 'Certainly his style is changing and becoming stronger', she thought. 'He likes this new technique and I do think it shows he will be a freer artist but on the other hand he really developed <u>very young</u> and had a youthful genre which grew – reached its summit and is now passing away. He dislikes it now but in spite of his outgrowing it it has been a real living <u>thing in itself</u>.'[1]

Back in January Rex had stayed at the Daye House. The New Year had made him hopeful and he seemed happier. 'Rex adores my wireless', Edith wrote, 'and spends every spare moment chasing valse tunes all over Europe and when he catches one he makes me dance – great fun – but I nearly die of it.'[2] They sat in the Long Room and spoke of the future, 'a very lovely sympathetic talk'. Edith wondered if his renewed optimism was connected with Caroline or Elizabeth Paget, Lord Anglesey's daughters. 'I do want him to have a happy possible love as Pempie sent him all wrong', she wrote that night.[3]

The previous November Rex and Edith had been together at a concert and Edith wrote in her diary that Rex had left early to meet Caroline 'who is now his chief friend.'[4] He had first met Caroline in 1930 at Wilton but had recently been seeing more of her. She spent a lot of time with David Herbert, and Rex was by now also friendly with her aunt Diana Cooper and her husband Duff, whose drawing room at 99 Gower Street he decorated and for whom he designed an elaborate bed carved with gilded dolphins. With characteristic speed Rex had begun to fall in love with her. But from the start Edith was sceptical. She knew and admired Caroline, a frequent guest at Wilton, but she, like Pempie, was a rich socialite and Edith was convinced that she would never marry Rex. Edith despaired that his 'social world is that of expensive girls . . . only an exceptional one would be really happy giving up her fun!'[5]

Cochran had offered Rex the job of designing sets for a play written by James Barrie, famous as the creator of Peter Pan. It was a wonderful opportunity but meant that Rex would have to give up the idea of going to America where he had been offered work later in the year. Edith believed that he would have to do this anyway as he had little money and his father was still very ill after his stroke. 'I do think a <u>big work</u> is what he wants to give him free hold on life for his reputation and for his art', Edith said. 'The only doubtful thing is whether scene painting is food for the latter but Cochran says it won't be a whole time job and he can get on with pictures.'[6] Edith wanted Rex out of London and she worried that the Cochran commission would keep him there. But Rex wasn't keen to take the offer anyway: 'I do feel it bad for him to refuse a big piece of work because he doesn't want to risk "spoiling his summer" as he keeps saying . . . he wants to be free to go abroad at any moment. The temptation to <u>flaneur</u> is very strong as the reaction after those overpowering emotions.'[7]

In spite of the feeling of promise that had marked the New Year, to Edith at least, it seemed that Rex, as he worked on his designs for *The Rake's Progress*, was still bent on his own dissolution. Saving him seems to have become almost a religious vocation for her: 'Tea with Rex. He is beginning to illustrate Hans Andersen and wants to do 60 drawings before Easter! Of paintings he has done nothing lately. Lost in idleness, parties and drink. O my darling. How can I save him?'[8]

However, Rex was creating magical drawings for the Hans Andersen book, which was to be published by Cobden-Sanderson later that year. The language of the book was one that he was fluent in; the necessary blend of romance, terror, poignancy and humour came instinctively to him. When it came out, *The Times* commented that Rex's illustrations were 'curiously exact imitations of the eighteenth and early nineteenth centuries . . . except where he allows a certain facetiousness to appear in the faces'.[9] And so the Emperor, though puffed and pompous in his new clothes, has just a hint of misgiving on his jowly face as he processes along the road; and the bob-haired, perky-breasted Egyptian girl that the Marsh King surprises while bathing has the modish look of a flapper and throws the most disdainful of looks at the miry interloper. The book would become his most popular set of illustrations and was so beautiful, with its gilt edges and gilt rococo pattern that weaves over the cream buckram binding, that Elizabeth Paget would later carry it at her wedding instead of flowers.

'He says he is no more an earnest student but a <u>hedonist</u>', Edith reported when she saw Rex again in April.[10] He told her that he felt ill and tired and didn't know why, implying that he had descended into a kind of romantic malaise. Edith still blamed Rex's behaviour on the turmoil of his relationship with Pempie (she couldn't even bring herself to mention Tallulah Bankhead): 'He says his love affair has made living hard though he doesn't want it to be. He knows that he'd go back to her <u>at any moment</u> if she gave him a chance. Says she showed love to him before he betrayed his to her. It has made him unable to bear evenings alone in his studio.'[11] Was he making excuses for Edith's benefit to justify that he had changed, and, at twenty-nine, was no longer an innocent boy, that he was growing up and growing apart from her?

Rex was and would always be the focus of her love. His affection for Edith was strong, and in some ways perhaps he now cared for her more than he had ever done, but she did not claim the entirety of his heart as he did hers. Guilt and irritation thus nagged at him; doubly so, that he was irritated at all about one who was so devoted to him. Contrite letters laced with truly felt declarations of affection hurtled from London to Wiltshire. But he had other things on his mind and these things he could not share with her. And it pained Edith that she had learnt about his affair with Tallulah second-hand, that Cecil and even Stephen kept her up to date with Rex's life, rather than Rex himself.

Edith, though, would always delight at the faint whiff of impropriety about their relationship, an impropriety that perhaps she alone thought others perceived. One day in May she went to visit Rex at Fitzroy Street. She was tired and lay on the bed as he worked at his Hans Andersen pictures. She wrote that they 'had delicious talk until Edward James interrupted us', to discuss the equestrian portrait he had commissioned, and she added: 'Rex hastily (and guiltily) tidied the bed.'[12]

On 24 May Edith had cocktails at the Ritz with a friend, a 'tete-a-tete' luncheon with another friend ('good food and rather stupid talk, helped by some Mozart on the gramophone'), and then later she went to Kensington Palace to dine with 'the Athlones', Lord Athlone and Princess Alice. 'I was rather shy at this royal dinner', she admitted. Later the Athlones left for a Command Concert at the Albert Hall for which they had been 'sparkling with ornaments' at dinner. Edith and Imma then settled down to a 'terrific talk'. Since they had last met Walton had begun a liaison with Alice, Lady Wimborne, a music patroness and wife of the rich industrialist Ivor Guest, Viscount Wimborne. She was also twenty-two years older than the composer. Lady Wimborne and Osbert Sitwell had been great friends and Osbert Sitwell was horrified to discover the affair and felt deceived. 'Imma seems to have made him really happier about it. It has cured her of Willy', Edith thought. 'She sees his vulgar, snobbish-<u>coarse</u> side.'[13]

Edith's life remained divided between town and country, as it had always been, although perhaps the contrast was less marked now that many of her younger friends lived nearby. In November the previous year she had been elected to the Wilton Town Council, the first woman in the town's 900-year history. She sat on the Housing, Borough Lands and Rating Committees and would soon throw herself into plans for new housing schemes, inspecting tenants' homes and discussing domestic issues with the people of Wilton who seemed to enjoy the novelty and sympathetic ear of a woman councillor. Edith had been rather terrified by the idea of her first Council meeting, knowing that her fellow councillors, Lord Pembroke aside, thought her appointment rather farcical. She had bought herself a new dress, as armour, and would soon get into her stride. A year later at a committee meeting someone suggested, yet again, that Salisbury and Wilton should become one borough. 'I said "over my dead body". I can see <u>no</u> reason for this and it makes me most angry', she wrote in her diary that night.[14]

Edith had been thrilled with the American royalties from *Dwarf's Blood* but fiction had proved less lucrative than she had thought it would. She had hoped to make writing a career, one that would be financially sustaining, and yet she found herself floundering in the margins of the literary world. She was beginning to think that she would have to sell her beloved car if the situation didn't improve soon. 'Went through my Summer clothes which look too horrible', she wrote in her diary in late spring; 'things one would throw out as too bad for any Jumble Sale! – However Hilda [her new parlourmaid] is to iron and press and I am to wear them this year as I can buy nought else.'[15]

A few nights earlier she had spent the evening with Zita Jungman, whom she had always admired. Zita, whose marriage to
Arthur James Edith had attended in 1929, was now divorced.
That evening Edith and Zita discussed the possibility of living
together and pooling the few resources they both had. 'It looks
quite a lovely future but may not come off as she may have to go
back to her father.'[16] But it was a heartening conversation; they
planned how Edith could forge a career in journalism and Zita
said that she might buy Edith's car from her. A friend suggested
that Edith try writing for films, even proposing that she went to
Hollywood and write a screenplay for *Romeo and Juliet*. Considering that in the past she had said of cinema that it was 'as if
Shakespeare were re-written by a writer of headlines in the *Daily
Mail*', there was little chance that this would make her fortune.[17]
She did, however, write a script for an adaptation of J. Sheridan
Le Fanu's Victorian Gothic mystery *Uncle Silas*, a good choice for
Edith but evidently not good enough to tempt the film studios to
which she sent it. She then thought to ask Arthur Street if he
could help her make contact with editors on Fleet Street. It was
a strange turn of events as it was Edith, after all, who had persuaded Street to consider writing as a career in the first place.
Street had always been incredibly grateful to Edith for her help
and so it is unlikely that he ignored her request. But, either way,
nothing came of it.

She had more luck with Sassoon. In May she joined him for
tea at Heytesbury, 'driving via Yarnbro' Castle as when I have no
car', she wrote, 'I shan't see these out of the way places but at this
season the valleys excel the downs in beauty'. Heytesbury was
looking like a 'dream'; Siegfried had planted bays and the trees
and flower borders were in their summer fullness. She found Sassoon alone as Hester had gone up to London, so they could talk
freely. 'His happiness is great as his unhappiness was. He loves
and appreciates every hour of it. It is a wonderful love – a great
love – the love of a great man'.[18] Sassoon told her that he had
received a letter from Stephen, who 'evidently wants to come back

into his life. I counselled NOT', she wrote in her diary that night, 'as I know S has a prankish wickedness in him, and would rather like to try his power and see if he could break up their happiness. He has that inhuman hardness of a jewel or elf', she added. She had been with Stephen in the first week of January and wrote that he 'honestly thinks he <u>only</u> chucked Sieg because he felt it good for his health and this is true – tho' not <u>all</u> the truth. He often told Rex that Sieg had begun to bore him to death! And this because he <u>would</u> possess him entirely and keep everyone else away.'[19]

Sassoon promised to help Edith with her journalism. 'I told Sieg I must retrench and he was so darling and sympathetic . . . He knows how badly some pay. *Time and Tide* gave him 30s for a poem. *Harper's Bazaar* paid £25!'[20] In turn, a little later in the year Sassoon asked Edith if she would type out twenty-four new poems he had written to send to his publishers.

In June Edith went to stay with Patricia and William Hambleden at Greenlands. 'I alone with Billy who discussed my affairs', Edith wrote. 'This angel has already offered to "lend" me £500 saying he would hate it to be returned . . . he agrees I must try to muddle on with the knowledge that I can call on him for sums to this amount <u>if and when I want it</u> like a Bank . . . saying <u>I must not</u> be worried and frightened – and (as I am) I ought not to be – with such friends.' He offered her work with W. H. Smith's, including writing for their magazine, *Book Window*, and she wrote that 'this really does cheer me more than anything. It is what I could do and would be a regular help. Perhaps then I might not have to come down on him for extra money.'[21] Another job was to censor books for their moral content and soon books were falling through her letterbox in a steady stream. One which she was sent was the autobiography of a prostitute, 'dreary indeed and bare – business-like records of this dirty trade'.[22] She subsequently gave it to a friend to take back to London as she didn't want it in the house and had had to hide it from the servants.

Edith became a regular contributor to *Book Window*. Over the next few years, she reviewed C. W. Cunningham's *Feminine*

Attitudes in the Nineteenth Century, a book of Queen Victoria's letters, Amelia Earhart's *Last Flight* (published the year after Earhart's disappearance, in 1937) and a book about the state of Soviet Russia. She interviewed Sassoon, too. He asked to be allowed to write his own interview for her to clarify some points with the critics. She agreed, but insisted that the copy should be hers. Later, she also interviewed the novelist Margaret Kennedy, author of *The Constant Nymph*; this was her most successful novel which had been twice adapted into a film and for which she had written the screenplays. Edith, no doubt with her own failure in that field in mind, asked Kennedy to discuss the process of writing for film. 'I enjoy doing them', Kennedy told her, 'though I really think that scenario-writing should be a profession apart. I don't believe films will come into their own till that is recognised.' She added: 'I am a film fan, though I seldom see a completely satisfactory film, yet I sincerely believe in the cinema as an art form which will eventually become extremely subtle and intellectual.'[23]

In June Rex stayed at the Daye House and when he left Edith recorded that it had 'been an absolutely perfect weekend. R and I utterly happy together. He says it's the best we've ever had'.[24] Clearly, though, she was not blind to the distance between them. Her diary contains frequent self-reassuring references to his continuing affection. Driving with Rex to Wilton from London a few days earlier, 'he twice spoke of our distance from "home" – meaning this place. I love that.'[25] That weekend they drove to Cranborne Manor over the border in Dorset, a Jacobean house owned by David Cecil's family. While they were there Rex sketched the house and later painted it, half-obscured by an iron gate and a high dark wall beneath which a gardener creeps cautiously in the shadows. The house in the painting is the stuff of fairy tale. But for the lack of a ferny forest floor this could be the house that the traveller tries to rouse from slumber in de la Mare's 'The Listeners' or the godforsaken grange in Tennyson's 'Mariana': stricken, unyielding, uncannily still and cloaked in a strange twilight glow.

What secrets, it asks, lie unseen behind its mullioned windows? Pempie had not killed romance after all.

In July Cecil and his friend John Sutro, a film director, decided to make a film at Ashcombe and friends, neighbours and farm-hands were persuaded to join the crew. They planned to film David Garnett's *The Sailor's Return*, the story of a Victorian sailor who comes back home to his village, after years abroad, with a black wife and child and a parrot. Cecil was to play the sailor; John Betjeman was the parson; Caroline Paget, an aspiring actress, was cast as Tulip the wife; and a black child actress was recruited to play Sambo, the daughter. There were several other minor roles; Sutro played a village rustic and Edith was to play a village woman.

Caroline was in disgrace with her parents for agreeing to do the film and because Cecil, unsurprisingly, had told the papers all about his plans. 'It is odd that she should do all these *outré* things and get her reputation', Edith thought, 'for she has that lovely dreaming, aloof character always seeming apart from whatever is going on, and without enthusiasm or ardour.'

They planned to complete the film in one day. That night Edith concluded that it had been 'a very hot exhausting crowded time wasting sort of day'. Edith politely declined Cecil's offer to stay the night. She thought Caroline looked lovely made up as Tulip, 'though her black kept coming off and it is cruel to deprive her of that rich magnolia skin of hers'. She was fascinated to observe the 'little professional negress' playing Sambo being 'quite calm and business-like when performing and then rollicking about with the cook's child who adored her!'

The film was never cut and the soundtrack was never added but Cecil deemed the day a great success. Edith was less con-vinced and it had done nothing to improve her opinion of films and filmmaking. 'There is no acting in film-acting. It is only joining up bits of photographs.'[26]

Edith finally escaped Ashcombe after midnight bringing John Betjeman with her to stay the night. She had first met the young writer and poet in 1932. He was then writing for the *Architectural Review* (he called it the *Archie Rev*) and soon to be married to Penelope Chetwode, the daughter of a baronet whom Edith knew well. They had both come to stay for a weekend at the Daye House and Edith wrote on the first night of their visit that she found Betjeman 'cleaner than I expected . . . loves Georgian churches'.[27] She was surprised to learn that he had become a Quaker: 'as his temperament', she wrote, 'has not the clear simplicity of Quakers, but a most mocking, doubling-back-on-itself kind of humour, writing parodies on hymns and begging to see Henry Newbolt so that he can savour the out-of-date flavour of a literary man of the past'.[28] Even so, she decided she liked him more than she had expected to: 'His instincts are all right. He does not jar'.[29] Penelope's mother, Lady Chetwode, had been less than enthusiastic about her daughter's choice of husband. 'She says her parents want her to have a country place and shooting, but after all,' Edith concluded, 'these are less permanent even than marriage.'[30]

Now, three years later, Edith plied Betjeman for his contacts on Fleet Street. He seemed loath to oblige but instead made her an offer. He was then editing the *Shell Guides* to the counties of Britain, the idea of which he had developed with Jack Beddington at Shell. The travel writer Robert Byron was writing the guide to Wiltshire and Betjeman wondered if Edith might like to write the gazetteer, which was 'the real heart of the guide'.[31] Edith gladly accepted, not least because it would mean she had to keep her beloved car. *Wiltshire* was an opportunity for Edith to finally put to good use the knowledge and love of the county that had so captured Rex and Cecil's imaginations.

The gazetteer was perhaps the natural successor to Edith's fiction, imbued as it is with the same blend of fantasy and reality, with her belief in the elemental energies of the county that she loved and in the evocative and seamlessly interwoven bricolage of history, hauntings, geography, myth and folklore, invoking what she would later describe as 'the romance of a witch-haunted world'.[32] She had defended this approach when writing *Mary Magdalen*, the sources for which were:

> . . . written in the happy centuries before there had been drawn, between History and Legend, the artificial line which the present generation has been taught to accept. The two are of course distinct; but they differ as day differs from night, merging one into the other without the abrupt and hard distinction which has been created for us by the use of electric switches.[33]

And so there are ghosts and miracles and murders on almost every page. Edith writes of a folly that harbours highwaymen, Guinevere's abbey at Amesbury, a vicar entertaining James I with a masque composed by himself, hobgoblins in Bowerchalke, Dryden's refuge from the plague, an equestrian portrait that doles out curses, a sinister black basalt font where King John was baptized, mythical warriors defeating the Danes, and Charles II counting the stones at Stonehenge at night after his escape from the Battle of Worcester. Several years earlier Edith had advised A. G. Street to write about what he knew. Now she was taking her own advice and perhaps she was starting to realize where her strengths lay as a writer.

According to the architectural and landscape historian Timothy Mowl, *Wiltshire* broke the traditional mould of English travel writing, and not least because Edith's friend Gerald Berners was commissioned to design the cover, for which he created a surreal collage of photographs: the Palladian Bridge, Wilton House, Stonehenge whirling in the centre, a pack of hounds pursuing their unseen prey, farmers tending their sheep, pigs roaming all over the cover and a group of prim Victorian ladies sitting in a row.

Like Rex, Edith was profiting from the boom in Englishness. Their work tapped into the same wave of aesthetic nostalgia and nationalism. Both shared an ability to present and celebrate the spirit of place, the patterns and character of the English landscape and a fluency of reference to England's history.

Betjeman, whose own guide to Cornwall of the previous year had been conventional and dull, as he himself admitted, found in Edith's *Wiltshire* gazetteer the 'perfect model'.[34] By 1936, Betjeman had developed 'Edith Olivier instincts'.[35] His *Devon* of that year, unlike *Cornwall,* was 'positively elfish' and 'scattered with . . . whimsicalities'.[36] This was a new way of writing about the countryside and the guides would have a profound influence on the national appreciation of Englishness; as Mowl adds: 'an entire generation of the intelligent middle class and aspirant lower learnt to explore their counties from *Shell Guides*'.[37] Betjeman would later become an English icon for his affectionate celebration of English idiosyncrasy, rural quaintness and nostalgia. 'Strange indeed', begins Mowl's final note on Edith, 'that such a suggestive scribbler never made a wider reputation as the authoress of passionate historical romances.'[38] Strange indeed, but Edith would have considered them beneath her.

Now that the motorist had been inspired by Shell's advertising campaigns to escape the urban abyss for those enchanted places portrayed in the company's posters; now that he had filled his car with their petrol and motored out into the countryside with the promise of Elysian Fields, virgin downland and chocolate-box villages; he needed a guide to help him find them. By the 1930s roads were being tarmacked at an ever-increasing rate. The country was being explored and mapped. In the late 1920s the travel writer H. V. Morton had gone 'in search' of England and become a bestselling writer in the process. Now hundreds of books were being produced on similar subjects; heritage was becoming an industry. Those byways and bumpy tracks with grass growing along the middle that nudged against the underbelly of Edith's car on sightseeing expeditions were fast disappearing. And that contradiction was at the heart of the heritage industry. In writing about the county she loved, its secret places and its haunted houses, Edith, like Betjeman and their fellow writers, was seducing her readers, luring them to corners of England to shatter the peace and churn up the edges of the road with their cars. And so what she was preserving in words she was also destroying. Perhaps Edith loved driving too much to realize this. And she wanted to make money.

Wiltshire was not Edith's only new project. Earlier in the year she had approached Dick de la Mare with a proposal to write short stories. He suggested instead that she might consider writing her memoirs, an offer made infinitely more appealing by the promise of an advance. She grudgingly accepted the offer but the idea of writing about herself filled her with dread. In late summer Hester's mother, Katharine, Lady Gatty, asked Edith if she would be interested in helping her make sense of a collection of her mother's papers that she had just discovered, a jumble of notebooks and postcards which appeared to make up a kind of manuscript that her mother had written about ten years before. Mabel Morrison had died in 1933 at the age of ninety-three. Edith had known her all her life and had adored her, perhaps even seeing in Mabel, with her tireless joie de vivre, a role model. She and her husband Alfred, the celebrated collector, dedicated their lives together to the care and development of the collection as well as opening their homes to some of the most celebrated and liberal-minded people of the day like Robert Browning and George Eliot. Edith began to understand why Mabel Morrison herself had failed to finish the work and ultimately she too decided that the manuscript should be left incomplete. Edith gave the book the title *The Quest of Joy*, later writing of Mabel that: 'She wished to pass on what seemed to her to be the most precious thing which her long life had taught her – that sorrow is personal, and passes; while joy is universal, and remains.'[39]

In September Rex travelled up to Wilton for a weekend. On the Friday morning Edith walked along the river to the Palladian Bridge, which he had been painting all morning. She had crossed the river at the Dairy Bridge beside her house and taken a route that passed the Park School. There she had found Caroline Paget, David Herbert's guest for the weekend. They walked to the bridge together. 'Rex now loves her and this visit was a wonderful thing in his day', Edith observed. 'She is very sweet to him but always with that aloofness which is her chief character, as if her spirit were always elsewhere.'[40] In August Edith had taken the train up to north Wales to stay with Michael Duff and his new wife Joan at Vaynol.

Visiting Plas Newydd over the water Edith could observe Caroline Paget at close quarters. 'Caroline and Liz each looking lovely (Liz today the loveliest)', she wrote in her diary, although she added 'both rather ineffectual'.[41] She was inclined to admire Caroline but found her remoteness perplexing. That day at the Palladian Bridge, David Herbert, too, walked over from the Park School to join Caroline, Edith and Rex at his easel, causing Edith to comment: 'This spielmann (as we now call the malicious little charmer) alone has found his way in. When they left us, it was with arms round each other.' 'I minded terribly for Rex', Edith added, confusing friendship, and a mutual understanding, for romance. At a 'difficult' party at Ashcombe the following month she observed David and Caroline dancing a 'mad fandango', while Rex stood apart, alone. Edith fared little better herself. One guest 'laid his head on my shoulders and looked at me with an unrecognising drunken leer and at once fell to the floor. I had to escape his proximity.'[42]

In November Edith and Cecil went to the Queen's Hall for the premiere of Walton's completed Symphony No. 1. She thought Walton seemed calm and self-assured and that the orchestra played so much better than the last time she had heard it. The last movement, which Walton had struggled to write, was 'tremendous'. A shift from the tone of the previous three, full of joy and light, it suggested a sense of release from the malice and melancholy, *Maestoso – Allegro, brioso ed ardentemente – Vivacissimo* in the margins of the score. Later he would confess that it had been inspired by his new relationship with Lady Wimborne even though the piece as a whole had been dedicated to Imma. And ever loyal to her friends, it was the melancholy slow movement that Edith thought the loveliest. Later in the evening there was a party at

Wimborne House, at which Imma looked 'gay and charming' and Lady Wimborne was 'smart and brilliantly animated and pleased'. 'The symphony seems to be <u>her</u> child', Edith wrote, believing that it was at least in part her own.[43]

Rex on the other hand was giving her no such joy. She had been with him the night before in London. He told Edith that Pempie had telephoned to invite him to the first night of her film. 'He <u>can't</u> refuse her', she despaired; 'like a dog he must run if she whistles. But I feel angry (apart from myself losing him) because she has dropped him these years, broken him up and now she evidently feels dropped herself . . . she knows she can always put out her power on this faithful lover. I mind specially because on Sunday I thought him gayer and more his old self than he has been since she came into his life and went out. Now she means to begin it all again.'[44]

21: An 'Eventful Year'

❖

'Doesn't time pass?'

Edith Olivier's Diary, 12 October 1936

Edith had seen Rex rarely over the past few months; occasional hours snatched in his studio were no compensation for weekends alone at the Daye House. And then by late November he had sailed to New York on the *Aquitania* to work on the sets for Gilbert Miller's production of *Victoria Regina*. Joining him on the boat was Stephen, who had travelled alone to America for the first time in October of the previous year. 'Rex thinks they will think him <u>very odd</u>!' Edith had written then, adding that he was 'immensely aware of Stephen's effeminately absurd appearance weighing up the effect it has on different people and without bias of his own. No one else can speak of these things so dispassionately.'[1]

In recent years the two men's lives had diverged to such an extent that they barely saw one another, but since the demise of Stephen's relationship with Sassoon, Rex had been making gestures of reconciliation. He had written to Stephen thanking God that their relationship had not been sullied by sex, as well as apologizing that he wrote so infrequently and professing his constant and unchanging love for him. Both had been bitten by sexual liaisons and Rex was seeking to place their relationship on a higher, less temporal plane. And perhaps quite simply he missed Stephen and the comparative ease of their friendship. At the Slade they had whiled away hours dreaming of the land of fast cars, skyscrapers, Hollywood and jazz and it must have been with great excitement that they sailed towards that land together.

After they arrived, Stephen wrote frequently to Edith back in England. '5 minutes ago I was talking to Rex! – he in Baltimore in summer clothes, I, in Jefferson – New Hampshire – in winter wool . . . we return to New York for his play premiere'.[2] But a few days later he was telling her: 'I hate America . . . Rex was heavenly to me . . . I felt braced by his guidance and fineness. I am not fine: – like you are – he is: – yet I have wonderful thoughts . . . you know I'm not really changed it's just a sort of broken heart that disguises me'.[3] And in the spring Stephen wrote to Sassoon attempting to renew their relationship, which dismayed Edith: 'S would smash that happy marriage'.[4]

Rex wasn't unequivocally overjoyed by America either in the first few days. Dashing around his hotel room, which was awash with his designs, he frantically tried to finish his work before the opening of the play in Washington a few days later. One morning he thanked the paper boy too keenly; his effusive English politeness was mistaken for a pass, which mortified him.

Victoria Regina was written by Laurence Housman, brother of the poet A. E. Housman. The play was banned from British theatres; it was then against the law to portray a British monarch on stage until 100 years after their accession. Eventually it would be staged in London in 1937 for which Rex, having sold his designs in America, would have to begin again from scratch. In the New York production the American actress Helen Hayes played the Queen and Vincent Price her adored husband but though its stars were American it was wholly British in spirit. American audiences loved the play and it ran for three years on Broadway. But the trip ended Rex's love affair with America. He thought the idea of it better than the reality, despite the extraordinary difference in payment. According to Laurence, Rex was able to give his mother a cheque for £1,000 (around £60,000 today) on his return. Nonetheless, it was still not enough to tempt him, like Cecil, to return and make a fortune.

That December Edith's bedroom was so cold that she moved into the Trellis Room which was a few degrees warmer. Talking to Harry Bailey, the gardener, she said that she felt the cold more than she used to and wondered why. "'You're old'", he told her. 'I suppose it is', she wrote in her diary.[5] While Rex was away, she saw Caroline Paget again and began to believe that she loved Rex as much as he loved her. But she had heard that he was with 'Tillulah' in New York and indeed they had resumed their affair. 'I fear he will get drunk . . . and come back quite worn out. He had this autumn been recovering from that phase but now he and Tillulah have telegraphed telling David [Herbert] they are together and wish he was with them!'[6] But there was nothing she could do.

Christmas was as busy as ever. She went to Fordingbridge town hall to watch an entertainment put on by Augustus John and his family. 'All London was there. Everyone one ever heard of or knew of', she wrote, adding that Augustus John's drop scene had been widely advertised but that he had been too drunk to do it.[7] She spent Christmas Day at Wilton House and after dinner they played charades. One charade was 'Abyssinia', a reference to the Italian invasion of that country in October. David Herbert was 'very funny', Edith wrote, 'as the Emperor gabbling in Abyssinian'.[8]

At the Stresa Conference in April, Britain, France and Italy had met to discuss and unite against German rearmament. What was not discussed was the matter of Mussolini's territorial ambitions for Abyssinia. He took the silence as a tacit sanctioning of his plans and invaded on 2 October. Publicly Britain condemned his actions but privately, with France, agreed to a plan that would give Italy two-thirds of Abyssinia. Far from being the 'gabbling' fool mimicked in their charades that night, Haile Selassie, the Emperor of Abyssinia, would make an impassioned speech to the League of Nations in June of the following year which would win him universal approbation. *Time* magazine would name him its 'man of the year' in January 1936.

On New Year's Eve Edith celebrated her birthday, as usual, at Wilton House. They played bridge and mah-jongg and Edith opened the door at midnight to let in the New Year. Returning to the Daye House in the early hours of 1936 though, her thoughts were of the past rather than the future. Concluding her diary entry that night she wrote: 'So ends this year, a hard and frightening one for me'.[9]

Edith had begun to feel older. In the first week of January she went with Tony Herbert to the first night of Noël Coward's triple bill, *Tonight at 8.30*, which she thought 'terrific fun. The <u>occasion</u> more than the play – everyone in the world seemed there, flashlight photographs in every line of stalls, crowds and chatter between plays.' Later they went to supper at the Savoy Grill and after that her friends planned to go on to a nightclub, the Nest, 'where they would stay till 5am', she wrote. 'All begged me to go, but I got back at 1.15 saying I am no nestling but fledged too long ago'.[10] Some days later back at the Daye House, Edith was irritated to overhear her sister Mamie discussing her with David Herbert.

> . . . giving her favourite impression of being an adoring elder sister, quiet, wise and peaceful – while I am a mad, brainless, hysterical creature – wild for gaiety. I don't think this is true. She says it's <u>not fitting</u> that I should be friends with the young, but what am I to do? when I live among them. She does succeed in making me a fool.[11]

The following evening she sat listening to the wireless which announced that George V was dying. At 10 p.m. a committal service was broadcast across the Empire. 'One felt in the room and the whole world was there', she wrote; 'this has never happened before in all history.'[12] The next morning she learnt that the King had died just before midnight and that he was to lie in state in Westminster Hall. 'I am horrified to discover how much older I am than most writers', Edith was soon writing in her memoirs. 'I seem to be completely out of date. Almost everyone who wrote about the death of King George was either a child or a baby in arms when he succeeded; and none of them knew Queen Victoria except by hearsay.'[13] In her diary she wrote: 'The new King is to be called Edward – which I regret – as he has so many fresh names and Edward 8th is very dull.'[14]

She went up to London for the King's funeral and watched from Carlton House Terrace as the thousands slowly processed along the road in their dark outfits. She observed 'bunches of men swaying in the upper branches of trees' and the 'silent, immovable coffin, covered with standard, crown and sceptre'.[15] After the solemnity of the day Edith was delighted to be dining with Rex, who had just returned from New York. 'He is as exquisite as ever . . . completely heavenly', she wrote, in spite of the fact that he looked unwell, was suffering from toothache and that his 'favourite women' in New York had been Tallulah and Alice Moats, William Walton's friend.[16]

One thing that remained unchanged was Rex's workload. He had been commissioned to design sets and costumes for a new adaptation of *Pride and Prejudice* and had set to work creating painstakingly authentic Regency interiors. Edith had invited him for a weekend in February by which time he had hoped to have finished. But when he arrived by train at 7 p.m. he looked exhausted, having been working until the early hours every night, and Edith quickly realized that sleep and *Pride and Prejudice* were going to dominate their weekend. On the Sunday Rex slept after lunch, 'looking very pinched and white and tired', and it was only after tea that he sat down to begin work – fifteen dress designs that had to be completed and sent off the following morning. At 7.30 that night all the lights in the Daye House went out and they couldn't discover why. Rex was 'angelically sweet and unruffled but really in despair . . . he knew he must work all night.'[17] Edith gave him an Aladdin lamp but eventually realized that the electric generator had run out of petrol and the lights came back on. Edith sat up with him until after midnight and then woke every hour to see the lights still on downstairs. At four she got up to see him and by five he had at last finished; they packed the drawings away, filled their hot water bottles and got to bed by five o'clock.

The following evening Edith sat with Rex by the fire as he drew the frontispiece of her new visitors' book. They had been a long time apart and she tried to pretend that neither Rex nor their relationship had altered: '[he] is not <u>at all</u> changed by America – in fact it has made him love better all the cosy <u>un</u>-American things here'.[18] Though she willed it not to be so, things had changed. Rex sent her Valentine's Day greetings in a telegram that he had designed for the Post Office – 'Sweet Edith O. I love you so. You'd be divine as a Valentine' – but she received no letter to thank her for his stay or for her help.[19] And though she attended the first night of *Pride and Prejudice* at the end of the month they made no plans to meet again.

On 7 March Edith sat beside her wireless listening to reports that Hitler's troops had entered the de-militarized Rhineland, violating the terms of the Treaty of Versailles and the Locarno Pact. Edith noted that Hitler had offered a twenty-five-year pact of non-aggression alongside this move and that she believed he meant it 'but like a tactless German has done it in such a way as to queer his own pitch'.[20] Two days later the British Foreign Secretary Sir Anthony Eden spoke in Parliament to reprove Hitler's actions but it was generally felt in England that Hitler had done nothing dramatically wrong. This was certainly Edith's view. When the Council of the League of Nations met, only the Soviet Union wanted to impose sanctions on Germany and when the British Government further broached the idea of a treaty with Germany they had no response. 'We and all nations have a sense that we have come to the turning point of an age', Hitler declared in a speech that spring. For Winston Churchill, and the anti-appeasement faction, it was the start of a 'gathering storm'.

For Edith, more than anything else, it was a disruption to her travel plans. She had planned to go to Spain that Easter with her nephew Tony but had been advised by the British Ambassador in Madrid to go to France instead as it seemed likely that there would be a Communist uprising on the day of the Spanish elections, Easter Sunday. She worried that now her French trip had been scuppered too by the news from Germany but was assured by the Foreign Office that she could continue with her plans. They set off, Tony, who had just left school, at the wheel of Edith's new Ford, bought in part-exchange for her Austin. This was to be no languorous sightseeing trip; they dashed through the French countryside. Towns, villages and chateaux where she would have loved to linger whizzed past in the blink of an eye as they hurtled down to the Riviera and then back; only indulgent love for her nephew stopped her from reclaiming the driver's seat.

Edith returned to England with relief. She had an exhibition of pictures to organize for Wilton House. She planned to gather pictures from all the stately homes in the area and enrolled David Herbert to chauffeur her around the countryside from house to house. Helping her was her friend Tancred Borenius, a Finnish art historian who had lived in England since 1909, an expert on the Italian Renaissance as well as the art of his adopted country. In 1932 he had launched the archaeological exploration of Clarendon Palace, a medieval royal residence near Salisbury, and Edith often drove over to visit him.

For her first weekend home she had invited Ottoline and Philip Morrell to stay with her. Very soon they had come up with a plan to help Edith make money; they suggested that they might return later in the summer as Edith's paying guests. She thought this was a marvellous idea and they returned at the start of June in Philip's Rolls-Royce, which would not fit into the garage, and a heap of suitcases.

Only three nights later she was writing that they had spent a 'Red Letter evening' together. The Cecils drove over from Rockbourne to join them for dinner.

Such glorious talk . . . Memories of Lytton Strachey, Aldous Huxley and what not. Lytton with mumps and Ottoline talking up to him outside a window when he was first growing a beard. Aldous, very inspiring to David, very beautiful – and now his as yet unpublished book so coarse and horrible. 'Why is he a leader of the young?' Just because he stands for freedom to say <u>anything</u>. All the talk can't be reproduced. It remains as a <u>picture</u> in the mind. Ottoline her eyes set in those deep shadows, her hair, <u>cendré</u> curling all over her head. Her tangle of pearl chains and earrings, reading aloud in her deep voice, very full of meanings and emotions. David ardent, leaning forward, quickly breaking in with sensitive appreciation . . . Philip in the chair, proud of Ottoline, commenting in his rich voice – rather amused. I <u>could not</u> have enjoyed anything more. Talk is always good when David comes, but this was Ottoline's night.[21]*

The 'dear Paying Guests' made lovely companions. They and Edith slipped into step with each other. Philip and Edith drank morning coffee together and talked about religion and reminisced about their pasts. Ottoline was at work on her study of Katherine Mansfield and Edith wrote articles for the *Book Window* and worked on her memoirs. In the afternoon they went on sightseeing trips together, Edith introduced them to her countless friends and Ottoline opened the Fugglestone fete with a graceful speech about George Herbert, church building and beauty. When they left towards the end of June, '<u>embedded</u> in despatch cases and parcels', Edith was sorry to see them go. She went up to London that afternoon on the train to see Evelyn Waugh receive the Hawthornden Prize for his biography of the Elizabethan Jesuit martyr Edmund Campion. 'Evelyn looked shy', she thought. 'The book is good but I hate him getting this. He is so <u>horrid</u>.'[22]

For the rest of the summer Edith shut up the Daye House to save money and spent the next two months on what she called her 'annual tour of Britain's country houses'.[23] From Greenlands, where the Hambledens now had three young children to keep her

---

* Ottoline's friend Aldous Huxley had wounded her deeply by pillorying her and her Garsington guests in his 1921 satirical novel, *Crome Yellow*, a parody of a house party at Ottoline's Oxfordshire home. Edith thought him 'possessed of a very low devil'. (EO Diary, 13 June 1936.)

entertained, she was to travel up to Vaynol. Michael Duff sent his small Leopard Moth down to Henley to collect her. It was her first proper trip in an aeroplane, discounting a brief loop at a fete with Rex, and she found the fifty-minute flight through high winds marvellously exciting. At Vaynol Edith and Michael went walking in the mountains, and picnicked by a high, hidden lake where they swam, Edith having borrowed the cook's wool bathing costume. Michael's wife had left him after less than a year complaining of mistreatment. Perhaps she had discovered that he was homosexual, but Edith did not know this, thinking him only a little mad.

Marriages were on her mind. In July she had attended Sidney Herbert's wedding at Westminster Abbey, where the seat given to her was only two rows behind the Pembrokes, which gave her great pleasure. The bride was Mary Hope, daughter of the First Marquess of Linlithgow and lady-in-waiting to Princess Marina. The Duke of York was best man and Caroline Paget, with red roses in her hair, was one of the bridesmaids.

Edith hadn't seen Rex that summer; instead she had spent time with Cecil who was busily at work on theatre and ballet designs that she thought pretty but far inferior to Rex or Oliver Messel's work. They finally met for tea in October. '"Doesn't time pass?"' he declared as they met. '"I've just found some trowsers on approval sent 2 years ago and have returned them to the shop"'.[24] It had been almost nine months since she had seen him. He was as lovely, as busy and as troubled by love as ever. Edith had come to the conclusion that Rex's eternal longing for some elusive thing could only be satisfied by marriage. She was convinced that it would give him purpose and drag him out of his malaise. Now that he was in his thirties, she thought it was time for him to settle down; after all, if it could work for Sassoon then it would surely work for Rex.

Sassoon and Hester were still basking in their newly wedded happiness and she felt proudly responsible for the marriage. A photograph taken by Ottoline Morrell shows the couple on a bench at Heytesbury, Edith sitting beside them, their satisfied matchmaker. She was delighted when Sassoon asked her to be godmother to his son who was born on 31 October. Edmund Blunden and Max Beerbohm were the godfathers. The child was christened George, like the hero of Sassoon's literary alter ego. It was a resolutely English name and perhaps George's birth marked the final chapter of Sassoon's domestic fantasy. But the happiness would be short lived.

In London, Rex was working harder than ever, on commissions for the theatre, illustrations and murals. He was in love with Caroline Paget but she gave him little joy in return. Wild girls like Tallulah and privileged society girls like Caroline and Pempie would not do, thought Edith. She decided to introduce Rex to Henry Newbolt's winsome nineteen-year-old granddaughter Jill Furse, an aspiring actress, whom she admired a great deal. Jill, she felt, would make a far more realistic wife for Rex. Edith had obviously been emboldened by her success with the Sassoons and the introduction was engineered one weekend in late November 1936, when Rex and Edith had returned to the Daye House from George Sassoon's christening in London. Edith also arranged for the two to meet again on Valentine's Day the following February, the date no doubt chosen in the hope that it might inspire passion. But though Rex admired Jill's elfin beauty, and wanted to paint her, telling Edith he loved 'her profile and her primness', Edith's plan failed.[25] For it was to be Laurence, Rex's brother, now a prize-winning poet and also at the Daye House that day, who would marry Jill Furse three years later. And there was little chance of Rex falling in love with anyone else whilst the raven-haired Caroline filled his thoughts.

At the end of 1936, Edith concluded in her diary that it had been a 'sad turbulent eventful year'.[26] Perhaps she was thinking not only of her friends' romances, but of the Spanish Civil War. At Christmas she dined at Wilton House with the Duke and Duchess of Alba whose palace in Madrid had been destroyed. The couple had been given refuge at the British Embassy, escaping

with only a few of their treasures, including Christopher Colum-
bus's diary, which the Duke had brought with him to Wilton. No
doubt she also was referring, in part, to the abdication crisis
which she had been chronicling in her diary that month. Rex
was not the only man at the mercy of a woman's affections that
winter. Edith thought the King 'as mad as George III'.[27] Patricia
Hambleden told her that he had been given fertility-boosting
injections that had altered his mental state. 'We think and speak
of the King all day', she had written on 5 December. 'At night it is
announced that he has cancelled all his engagements. This looks
like abdication. It is <u>incredible</u> that the great British Empire
should be shattered by an American tart!'[28] And on 10 December,
she wrote:

> The King has abdicated. A week ago the idea was impossible
> – but these days have brought everyone to thinking it <u>is</u> the
> best thing . . . The King must however have lost all respect,
> and would be setting an example of immorality to the Empire
> for the sake of a worthless American Co-ed. I lunched with
> Osbert and we went to Westminster together and saw the
> seedy, quiet crowds waiting for the announcement in Parlia-
> ment.[29]

The following night she sat with her servants in the Long Room
listening to Edward's abdication speech on the wireless. 'It brings
tears but he had nothing to say except that he "couldn't go on
without the woman I love", said he was a loyal subject of King
George and ended with "God Save the King" in a loud voice. It's a
sad admission of weakness', she wrote, 'but perhaps better to
admit it and go than to stay and bring the monarchy into disre-
pute'.[30]

But undoubtedly, as she lamented the sad year that had
passed, Edith was also thinking about her friendship with Rex. He
had stayed at the Daye House only twice and no letters survive
from 1936. Perhaps he resented Edith meddling in his love life.
And it seems that she was no longer in his confidence. At the

end of November, with Rex staying at the Daye House, she had confessed disappointedly in her diary: 'I felt that he had something to confide and <u>wouldn't</u> as he came to my bedroom and waited about till 12 then left saying nothing'.[31]

22: *La Belle Dame*

❖

... there hasn't really ever been a beginning, has there?

Rex to Caroline, 1936

Back in April 1936, Caroline had taken the sleeper train from Euston with Rex for a weekend to Plas Newydd, the vast, grey, Gothic mansion that was her family home on Anglesey. Sybil Colefax was redecorating the interiors and Charles, Lord Anglesey, had decided to commission Rex to paint a mural on the huge empty wall of the newly created dining room. He had no doubt been recommended to Anglesey by his wife Marjorie's brother, the Duke of Rutland, for whom Rex had painted the Haddon Hall panel, and by Diana Cooper, her sister.

Rex received Anglesey's commissioning letter at Easter, along with a generous £200 advance. They agreed that he should receive £1,000 in total. It all made for an enticing proposition. Rex was struggling to complete a mural at 36 Hill Street, in Mayfair, for Baroness Porcelli. The architect Sir Edwin Lutyens, who admired Rex's work, had organized the commission but it had become an arduous task. He loathed 'the old cat Porcelli', who interfered with his work, insisted on altering his designs and quibbled over his £600 fee.[1] And so he was delighted at the prospect of one day escaping London for that graceful mansion on the banks of the Menai Strait and the delightful family who lived there: good-natured Charley, artistic Marjorie and their five children: Caroline, of course, the eldest; Liz, and their younger sisters Rose, Mary and Kitty. Henry, Lord Uxbridge, aged thirteen, was their youngest child and only son. As Rex began work on the mural, chatty, charming letters with amusing illustrations to keep his patron updated with his progress would soon be winging their way to Wales.

That summer Rex accompanied Caroline and Liz, along with David Herbert and Cecil, in a fleet of cars to Schloss Kammer in Austria, as guests of Raimund von Hofmannsthal and his wife Alice Astor. Rex had stayed with them for some days at their house on the Hudson River. Raimund, the son of Hugo von Hofmannsthal, the Austrian poet and librettist, was worldly and sophisticated and Liz Paget had fallen deeply in love with him.

It had not been a happy trip for Rex. A photograph of him sitting beside Caroline al fresco at a cafe tells of friction and distance in spite of their proximity. Two faces, both beautiful and both with melancholy eyes and set mouths, look off into the distance. Caroline, with a ribbon tied in a bow around her curls, clutches a wine glass; Rex's arms rest on the table. 'I feel rather extra unhappy because things are so wrong between us, aren't they', he wrote to Caroline on their return. 'I suppose I have hoped for more affection from you than I have any right to expect . . . I do realize that this is not a case in which I can say: "I knew at the beginning that it wouldn't last long" because there hasn't really ever been a beginning, has there?'[2]

'Caroline was a dream of physical beauty, long classic legs, brief modern pants, Garibaldi shirt, her beautiful sulky yet smiling face very small in a Zulu shock of hair', her aunt Diana Cooper later wrote.[3] In Cecil's photographs of Caroline and her sister Liz, it is the latter who firsts catches the eye: more classically beautiful, perfectly coiffed, more at ease with the patrician hauteur and insouciance required for Beaton's lens. Beside her, Caroline, with her unruly shock of curls, her petulant mouth and her sad eyes, though quite as beautiful, looks coltish, uneasy, as if she is itching to bolt. In another, formal photograph, dressed in a slippery satin evening gown and pearls, she seems only bored, a wisp of curls escaping her marcelled bob: the reluctant socialite. In snapshot photographs on the other hand, she strides out in shorts, strolls with her mother beside the Menai Strait in a trench coat and trousers or rolls around amongst hens on the lawn at Ashcombe. 'Clothes were of little importance to her', Caroline's son later recalled:

> . . . her dress was discreet but always expensive. In the country or casually in London she had a weakness for slacks and men's sweaters. There was an incomparable stillness about her. She always listened beautifully (although I'm not sure she often heard much). Her movements were lithe and sexy. She was very much of the present, in the moment.[4]

As a teenager Caroline had fallen in love with Antony Knebworth, eldest son of the Earl of Lytton and widely praised for his brilliance and promise. They were engaged in early 1933, when she was nearly twenty, but he died in a flying accident in May that year. Caroline was fetched out of her box at Covent Garden during the first act of *Der Rosenkavalier* to be informed of his death.

Society bored her: 'even after my first "season"', she later wrote, she 'had escaped it and gone to Munich'. She loved the theatre and decided to become an actress, 'an opportunity of burying myself in a completely different life'.[5] And so she began to escape her destiny, even adopting a stage name to avoid detection. Around the time she starred as Tulip in *The Sailor's Return* at Ashcombe, she had found work with the Oxford Repertory Theatre. It was not long before her real identity was revealed and announced gleefully in several newspapers. She had wanted to begin a new life, to lose herself in the theatre, but now she no longer sought to escape into a new persona. Her acting continued, and she began to live a double life.

One weekend, in the autumn of 1935, at the beginning of their relationship, Rex had painted an intimate portrait of Caroline at David Herbert's house on the Wilton estate. In the painting, which Edith thought should be called 'Dressing in

Lodgings', she stands before a mirror sweeping up some of her hair which cascades in curls beside her face. Her eyes are downcast as she looks at her reflection. The pale skin of her face, her bare shoulders and arms are the focus of the portrait, rendered paler still by the vivid acidic yellow of her petticoat, her dark hair and the black glove on her right hand. The only warmth is the deep red of her lips and the rose at her chest. The portrait's impressionistic style was a new departure for Rex; it was a more sophisticated technique than his usual one and no doubt he used it to reflect the maturity of the relationship. It is a far cry from his portrait of Pempie and Angela Dudley Ward. Edith and Lady Pembroke went to see the portrait exhibited at Tooth's Gallery, in Mayfair, in December 1935. Caroline's aunt was shocked, thinking it indecorous to paint the daughter of a Marquess *en déshabillé* and Edith heard her mutter '"that black glove"', in disgust. Edith, however, thought it had 'great beauty and character'; later it would hang above the Regency sofa in the Long Room.[6]

But though Rex had chosen to signify the comparative sophistication of his relationship by painting Caroline's portrait in this new style, it was still essentially, as with Pempie, a love that sprang from his imagination. If Pempie was the childlike Annabel Lee, then Caroline Paget was another favourite, Rex's *belle dame sans merci*. He was therefore, by default, the poor deluded knight.

'Rex adores Caroline', Edith had written in her diary in the month that he had painted the portrait, 'she has a <u>tendresse</u> for him but at any moment leaves him'.[7] To their friends it seemed clear that Caroline was fond of him and enjoyed his adoration but she never seemed to be ready to commit to him. As with Pempie, this was an unrealistic kind of love. For Rex, Caroline, like her predecessor, was a *'princesse lointaine'*, the faraway princess of courtly love. Pempie was unattainable because of her youth, Caroline because she was aloof, secretive and non-committal. Edith liked her; she was fascinated by her 'withdrawing character' and agreed with David Cecil that she was 'like the moon, cold and out of reach' and though Rex's portrait of her is an intimate one, she appears cool and withdrawn like the goddess Diana and, like Narcissus, wholly absorbed by her own reflection.[8]

And Caroline had secrets. She 'was the first girl I really loved', David Herbert said in his memoirs. 'When we played "Sardines", my intention was always to find her first and kiss her in the linen cupboard. Everybody loved Caroline, and perhaps this has been her trouble in life, for she has had to take it for granted that many people of all shapes, sizes and sexes would willingly kill themselves for her.'[9] Sometimes she responded to these devotees, at times with love and at times without. One of her most persistent and adoring admirers was the Conservative politician Duff Cooper, husband of her charismatic and universally loved aunt, Diana, to whom he was continually unfaithful. 'The only excuse for restaurants or parties at my age [forty-seven] is, in my opinion, love', Duff Cooper wrote in his diary in early January 1938. 'Now at present so far as I can be said to be in love with anybody I suppose I am in love with Caroline but it is as vague, as shadowy and as one-sided an affair as Dante's love for Beatrice. It consists solely of an occasional luncheon in Soho.'[10] Caroline was as elusive with him as she was with Rex. After she cancelled a lunch, he was 'determined to take no further pains with her. It is only disturbing, wrong and ridiculous.'[11] However, it seems he did take further pains as at some point they became lovers and their affair continued until his death in 1954.

But Caroline's biggest secret was that, since September 1934, just over a year after Antony Knebworth's death, she had been in love with someone. Audry Carten had been an actress and was now an aspiring playwright, and was introduced to Caroline by Tallulah Bankhead. She became her 'dearest and most beloved friend' as Caroline wrote many years later.[12] Tallulah had been Caroline's first female lover and Audry had been Tallulah's lover too. Curiously, in spite of this tangled web, all three remained friends. Caroline's son, Charles Duff, later recalled that 'Tallu had warned Caroline that Audry was an inverted snob and this, I imagine, Caroline found refreshing. Audry was iconoclastic, wild, rebellious, insecure and wonderful fun.'[13] Their relationship remained clandestine and so did the life that they shared in London.

Her heart therefore was elsewhere, even in the autumn of 1934 when Edith wrote that Caroline had become Rex's 'chief friend'. And yet she courted Rex's love and relished his attentions and at some point they became lovers. 'But it does not seem to have made a radical difference', Laurence wrote. 'His letters never speak of fulfilment, and it would be strange if she chose to keep only those of longing or of sad reproach'. He adds that 'years afterwards she said, as proof of understanding, that she had not minded the occasional failure that occurred, but she did not seem to have set much store by the success'.[14] Caroline's brother, the 7th Marquess of Anglesey, admitted that his sister 'was never in love with Rex . . . she never reciprocated his love eagerly'.[15] What attracted her to Rex was his artistic talent. Perhaps too, he reminded her of the dashing Antony Knebworth whose photograph she carried, almost like a talisman against marriage. And so, perhaps selfishly, Rex became a decoy, of whom she was very fond but to whom she could never fully commit. Writing to a female friend in France, who was also deeply in love with her, Caroline lamented the impossibility of making everyone happy.

Did Rex know about Audry? He must have done. But then Caroline might have been less appealing to him if she had made herself wholly available. Perhaps Rex, with his unflagging devotion and continual dissatisfaction, was difficult too, as moody and emotional as the girl he loved. It seems that for Rex, the reality of sex with women was never as good as the promise of it. '"Sex takes so much time, doesn't it?"' he said to his brother. 'He was no instant seducer', Laurence wrote. 'His mind was like a subtle key which would not fit a simple lock, yet knew how very sweetly it might turn.'[16] It is perhaps no coincidence that a nude portrait he painted of Caroline is his weakest painting. In it she sprawls on the bed in Rex's studio, her pose awkward; the crumpled sheets around her are better realized than her body. This was the artist who, in life-drawing classes, had turned his back on the model so that he could draw her from his imagination. For Rex, as far as women were concerned, obliquity was invariably better than reality.

At New Year 1937 Edith stayed at Greenlands with the Hambledens where she was diagnosed with a recurrence of high blood pressure and forced to take to her bed for a week. At the age of sixty-five, with the Council and other numerous committees and associations to which she belonged, her life was busier than it had ever been. She was attending Red Cross air-raid precaution lectures, writing her memoirs, helping Cecil to write his *Scrapbook* (a collection of essays, photographs and drawings), writing book reviews, reading books to censor and, later in the year, she was invited to become a governor of Southampton University College. And when she wasn't working she was entertaining guests at home, sightseeing, visiting friends or dashing up to town to slip into the hurry-scurry.

When she returned home she went to see Stephen at Wilsford; he had summoned her to admire his new nautically themed decorations. He had long been fascinated by the romance of the Mediterranean, the beauty of its shell-laden beaches and the seediness of its sprawling ports where sailors loitered in alleys and smoky harbourside bars. For several summers now he had been travelling, to the Balearics, to Rhodes, and to the South of France, and it was the spirit of the south that he was determined to evoke at Wilsford. Gradually he turned the white Syrie Maugham shrine into a rococo mermaid's grotto. Scallop shells studded the dining-room ceiling; there were nautilus shells, rope swags, draped fishermen's nets and lobster baskets. Edith found it rather amusing and returned home with arum lilies and £100 for her medical expenses. Less amusing was the book Stephen had been reading, which he insisted that Edith should read too. René Guyon's *Sex Life and Sex Ethics*, published in 1933, was a Freudian psychoanalytical study of sexual phenomena, psychosexual development, repression and neurosis, which sought to liberate sexuality from the fetters of morality. It dealt not only with homosexuality but also incest, necrophilia, paedophilia and other variants. Though she was fascinated by the mysterious depths of the brain and by the impact of childhood influences on the formation of personality, unsurprisingly, Edith was not persuaded.

Stephen was on a quest for novelty but Rex began the year nostalgic for an earlier time. According to Edith, 'he looks back on his life . . . to a period of sustained happiness to which he wants to return. Perhaps the Slade School time of lectures and painting.'[17] He had been a carefree student then, spending his days reading poetry and designing fancy-dress costumes with Stephen. For Rex that period had taken on a prelapsarian hue, before he began to feel the burden of responsibility and when women, with few exceptions, really did lurk only in his imagination.

Perhaps it was this nostalgia that drew Rex back to Edith in 1937. She was the one person who would always respond to his self-romanticism, always sympathized about his love life, and loved him unreservedly, without making any physical demands. Once again, the Daye House became a retreat for Rex; Edith was again in his confidence and the romantic tribulations of her beloved boy began to reappear on the pages of her diary. Those tribulations were all he could talk about, but Edith doesn't seem to have minded.

On 6 January she received a letter from him telling her that he was 'now faintly in love with Patricia Douglas' to which Edith added: 'and she (by her letter to me today) rather more than faintly in love with him.'[18] Patricia was the unhappy eighteen-year-old daughter of the Marquess of Queensberry, great-niece of Oscar Wilde's beloved Bosey, and perhaps the most beautiful of Rex's girls. Her mother had abandoned her father for another man and then in turn been abandoned, leaving herself and her daughter penniless. Now, Patricia sought the refuge of the Daye House rather than returning to live with her angry, abusive father and Edith welcomed her as a paying guest. Rex had met Patricia briefly at the Daye House the previous year and they had become friends. At the end of the month, after seeing Rex in London, Edith wrote in her diary: 'He can't keep out of love but always loves 2 people at once. Pempie and Angie, Caroline and Liz now Patricia loves him he is fascinated but <u>not</u> in love he says. She wants him to come here whilst she's with me. He thinks not lest he should go too far!'[19]

At the Daye House, melancholy had been replaced by love-sickness in the susceptible heart of the lonely girl staying with Edith. She bit her nails and stared longingly at Rex's portrait. 'Poor little Patricia is pining for love of Rex – can't sleep at night, can't fix her attention on anything, feels utterly miserable. She says she has never been so much in love before and thinks she will never get over it.'[20] In February Rex and Laurence came to stay. Rex kept Edith in his room after midnight, 'talking of his complicated love affairs. Caroline whom he adores and who <u>says</u> she loves him but seems to forget that she has. Patricia – whom he feels guilty about as he flirted with her to make Caroline jealous and so fears he has hurt her. He <u>has</u>', she added, 'but I think she . . . will soon love someone else.'[21]

It was not many weeks before he was back at the Daye House again. 'Wrote at my book and then drove to Salisbury at 12.30 to meet my beloved Rex', Edith wrote in her diary on 10 April. They walked in the park amongst daffodils. 'I've never seen him <u>enjoy</u> a piece of work so ardently as the big diningroom for the Angleseys. His face lights up when he speaks of it, tired as he looks', she wrote.[22] Rex had now begun work on his commission for Plas Newydd. The wall that Rex was to decorate was fifty-eight feet long and faced four high windows. The mural was not to be painted onto the wall directly but onto stretched canvas, woven in France. This had arrived in the New Year and Rex had been work-ing on it in a theatre workshop in Lambeth that he had rented specifically for the job. By June, when it was more or less com-pleted, it would be taken to Plas Newydd and glued onto the plaster.

On 12 May King George VI was crowned in Westminster

Abbey; Walton had been commissioned to compose the corona-
tion march. Edith listened to the service on the wireless: 'The
King spoke very slowly as he took his oath and his pauses added
to his emphasis and did not sound like a stammer. Very good
enunciation and musical voice. It was thrilling to hear the Westminster boys and then the shouts in the Abbey as he was
presented. It must have sounded so in Saxon days.' She was firmly
on the side of the new King, 'this unassuming man' who had
'taken up the job his brother dropped'. That night she went up to
the Race Plain at Netherhampton to see the bonfires that had
been lit and the fireworks bursting in the sky; '. . . we were in the
midst of peace, a crescent moon to the West and in the East
the floodlit spire moonlight colour. A nightingale singing.'[23]

It was quite another matter later in the month at a dinner
party at Ashcombe with Cecil, Rex, Juliet Duff, the composer
Constant Lambert and Grand Duchess Marie of Luxembourg.
The only topic of conversation that night was Mrs Simpson, or the
Duchess of Windsor as she was about to become. 'Everyone
loathes Mrs Simpson and grudges her her "place in history"',
Edith wrote. But she was comforted by the thought that Mrs
Simpson's particular place would be 'a very small hole'.[24] Two
weeks later Cecil came to dine at the Daye House having just
returned from France where he had photographed the Windsor
wedding four days earlier at the Chateau de Candé, south of
Tours. Edith relished every detail just as Cecil, no doubt, relished
the telling.

> Says she is the hardest woman he ever saw. No emotion, no
> feeling at this crisis, but the Duke is in radiant spirits, like a
> schoolboy. They made a 'Chapel' for the religious service. It
> was like getting a charade ready – dragging bits of furniture
> about, the Duke on his hands and knees laying the carpet.
> The 'Altar' was an oak chest with caryatides. Said Mrs War-
> field, 'We must cover up those other women.' The servant
> had to get out a tea cloth from the bottom of the linen box

which she had just packed and said in very cockney lingo, 'If being married is always like this, I shan't marry.' Whereat Mrs W [replied] 'No, it's not always like this, unless you marry the ex-King of England.'[25]

On 21 June, with Zita, Edith attended the premiere of *Victoria Regina*, which had finally been allowed on the British stage and for which Rex had made new designs. It was the centenary of Queen Victoria's accession to the throne and the Lyric Theatre was full of a most enthusiastic audience. Edith marvelled at the set: 'Rex's décor creates the whole world of the Queen. They are more than brilliant – a really 3 dimensional creation.' After the play there were celebrations at the Savoy: 'Rex in a dream with Caroline, who for the first time seemed a part of his life – as if she shared his triumph. They are a perfect pair, both quite unfit for marriage', she wrote. 'What can they make of it?'[26] Two days later Edith had a late supper with Rex whose birthday dawned as they sat together in a new restaurant that he had discovered. Edith gave him a biography of Wren and asked if Caroline was being nice; 'only Nicer', he replied.[27]

That summer Sassoon, ever generous and knowing of Edith's financial struggles, began giving her an annual allowance of £200 (about £11,500) telling her that she had given him much more by way of friendship in return. 'I am overwhelmed', she wrote, 'but feel immensely relieved. Anxiety is all lifted off'.[28] She continued working at her memoirs and reviews for the *Book Window, Country Life,* the *Observer* and other publications. In July she was flown up to Vaynol to stay with Michael Duff whose marriage was to be annulled. While she was there she attended the Royal visit to Caernarvon and thought the Queen looked 'not only very pretty, but most dignified'. 'They both look so young and touching with the solemn old castle walls around them', she wrote.[29] She was flown home in Michael Duff's plane through a violent storm and was 'for some time lost in whirling clouds'. After a brief emergency landing at an aerodrome near Worcester they headed south to 'the smiling spaces of Salisbury Plain'.[30]

Earlier that month Cecil had organized an Arcadian extravaganza, a fête champêtre at Ashcombe to which he invited all his friends. Edith swept down to the house in the omnibus that Cecil had hired to transport his guests. Ashcombe was aglow with the light from flares, torches and fireworks, and the facade was festooned with ribbons and paper flowers. Garlands of flowers and swags hung in the studio. Sheep were penned on the lawn, goats were shepherded by young boys and rustics danced around a maypole. Some guests came as characters from Greek mythology, others from *The Beggar's Opera*, and David Cecil's party dressed as jaunty picnicking Victorians. Edith went as a seventeenth-century countrywoman; Stephen as a sailor in blue satin shorts; Patricia Douglas, with a partner, a young barrister 'whose name she hardly knows', was a dainty French soldier in tight trousers and cutaway coat with epaulettes; Juliet Duff dressed as a Watteau shepherdess; and Rachel Cecil in a green velvet Victorian riding habit that Rex had selected for her. Later in the evening Edith and others performed in what she described as a 'Burlesque Restoration play' written in mock-Shakespearean verse by John Sutro. At the rehearsal the night before she'd been relieved to hear that Gerald Berners was taking John Sutro's place: 'I think on the whole I like his lap to sit on better than John's, though they are both frightful to look at'.[31] The following morning Cecil's guests ate breakfast as the sun rose over the valley. Marie Antoinette herself would have been pleased with the success of this legendary party.

Caroline had also been there, in a costume that Rex (a moustachioed Victorian sportsman in a suit, cravat and spats) had designed for her. It was a dress inspired by Renoir, with scarlet and white stripes, a tight bodice with a row of white buttons, a bustle, a little boater on her head and a tiny striped parasol in her hand. In a photograph she poses demurely beside a bush from which the grinning face of David Herbert emerges. She barely spoke to Rex that night.

'Rex . . . bared his agonised heart . . . he breaks <u>my</u> heart', Edith wrote two days later after he had called in for lunch at the Daye House.

> He is full of love for Caroline who has given no reply – says she loves him then does nothing about it when he asks her to dine she just says she <u>can't</u> and that's all. He sees that she really only cares for him at moments when he is having a big success. That excites her then it goes. He can't work because of this and he has to <u>work so hard</u> to win her. Knows he could be . . . happy married <u>if she loved him</u> but also knows she never will. And then this complication that he is also physically in love with Patricia . . . when she is with him he always <u>knows</u> he can have her. This attracts him . . . I told him I now think he <u>wants to marry</u> and <u>must</u> but neither of these. He says if his marriage failed it would break him and either of these might fail.[32]

Again Edith urged him to marry, to find someone more suitable than Caroline Paget, 'but no one can eclipse that moonlike miracle'.[33] He needed someone who would meet with her approbation and, more importantly, who would not take him away from her. 'I want him to marry Jill Furse or someone like that. He says he was attracted but Laurie is <u>in love</u> so he can do nothing there'.[34]

Rex travelled up to Plas Newydd in August to add the finishing touches to the mural as well as overseeing the decoration he had devised for the rest of the dining room. He was charmed by Plas Newydd and the Pagets, and his friendships with the other members of the family weathered the storms of his relationship with Caroline. That year he painted a sensitive portrait of Lord Anglesey and a picture of the house with the teenage Henry Uxbridge, with whom he became great friends, cycling along a path in the distance. In another painting, a conversation piece of the family in the music room, the figure of Caroline is a faceless caryatid in the doorway, as the painting was left unfinished in 1939, the year he painted it.

And so the artist-in-residence set to work on completing his mural. He was left to work when he felt like it and made to feel quite at home. One morning, he reassured the amused 'Charley', as he now called Lord Anglesey, that if he did not like the tower that he had painted the night before, it could easily be dismantled as he had left the scaffolding attached.

The tall windows of the dining room at Plas Newydd look out over the Menai Strait and, beyond the water, to the grey, looming, cloud-capped peaks of Snowdonia. Rex's mural, on the facing wall, is a fantastical, panoramic reflection. The grey stretch of water and the dark mountains of the Welsh landscape are transformed into a warm, lively Mediterranean scene, with the clarity of a dreamscape and the luminosity of a Canaletto.

Here are menacing mountains but rendered in shades of viridian and teal beneath a tumultuous sky. The townscape, at first glance Italianate, perhaps Neapolitan, is another invented kingdom. Trajan's Column, a helter-skelter, a Roman baroque basilica, the onion dome of an Austrian church and St Martin-in-the-Fields stand alongside houses typical of Weymouth, Brighton and Amalfi. The Plas Newydd mural, more than any other, is an allegorical summation of Rex's experiences and travels. But, probably coincidentally, it also reflects a real place: Portmeirion, Clough Williams-Ellis's whimsical, Mediterranean fantasia, begun in 1925, lay just across the water.

Everywhere there are amusing, irreverent details. A washing line runs from a window to the mast of a ship, a small boy can be seen urinating surreptitiously, whilst another steals apples from a stall. At right angles to the mural Rex painted colonnades that seem to extend along the harbour wall. To the right, the Anglesey daughters' pampered pug and French bulldogs frolic on the steps and smoke wafts from an abandoned cigarette.

Beyond the harbour lies an island with the Round Tower of Windsor Castle at its peak. The breeze crests the waves and whips the sails of boats in the harbour and the scudding clouds overhead, as seagulls circle eagerly around a fisherman's catch. In the foreground stands a quayside; here there is no loggia to divide the real world from the imagined one but a harbour wall where a fisherman has laid his nets and his lobster basket. It appears that Neptune has climbed the steps out of the sea, walked across the quayside and out of the fantasy world into the house, leaving only his wet footprints, his golden crown and trident propped against the harbour wall.

And as Neptune had escaped the picture, Caroline had entered into it and serenely sails past the harbour in a gondola. The reality was rather different; things had taken a passionate turn and if Neptune had walked into the house he might have wished to keep on walking. It was not long before Edith received a phone call from Patricia Douglas, also at Plas Newydd, telling her how riotously happy she suddenly felt. The cause of her joy was Caroline. With Rex, the two girls became a tangled triangle of affections with much kissing and cuddling and high emotion in those heady August days. Patricia left, but was soon writing to declare her love for Caroline who, unnerved by the intensity of feeling she had inspired, headed back to London herself. Later that month, according to Laurence, Patricia, who was still desperately in love with Rex, came to his studio, there to make love with him for the first time. Rex began but then 'cried and said he felt sick, apologized abjectly, and took her home in a taxi'.[35]

In September, Edith lunched with Rex at the Café Royal. They talked about his work at Plas Newydd and at Brook House on Park Lane where he was decorating a sitting room for the Mountbattens.* 'He . . . has adored his visits to Plas Newydd and the whole family there . . . saying several times "it's been an extraordinary summer"', she wrote.[36] Rex had not quite completed

---

* Edwina Mountbatten insisted on Rex painting onto canvas rather than directly onto the wall. This proved fortuitous as the flat was destroyed by a bomb in 1940, by which time the canvases had been removed to Broadlands, her house in Hampshire.

the mural, and planned to return to finish it, when he sent the final bill to Lord Anglesey in December 1938, writing:

> . . . of course there's such a bill you could send in <u>against</u> me as could wipe out any claim of <u>mine</u>. How could I hope ever to repay for all those lovely days of fun and bathing and sunshine and moonlight and luxurious nights and enormous delicious meals. I couldn't even pay the worth alone of those visits to the bay – the Bill gets higher and higher – lovely dear friends – and rows and rows of champagne cocktails [drawing of a long row of champagne glasses] <u>pyramids</u> of potted shrimps and absolutely countless bottles (all told) of heavenly claret.

The letter was illustrated with a hand holding scales, on one side of which is a bowl of potted shrimps and a wine glass and, on the other, Rex's paintbrushes.[37]

It had not been quite as simple as that. But as reality coloured Rex's work, so the fantasy, artificiality, exaggeration and romance of his work seemed to colour his life more and more, as if he himself were living a kind of mannered trompe l'œil existence. There is a small but significant relic of this, now encased in a glass cabinet at Plas Newydd. On the night that Caroline told him she was returning to London, Rex had written her a note, surrounded by a delicately drawn cartouche, topped by a heart and crown. 'To Beautiful Darling Caroline', it reads, 'a petition to beg her to reconsider her decision to leave Plas Newydd on the evening of August 22nd 1937 and to defer such departure until it shall have (if ever) the approval of the undersigned'.[38] It is signed by Rex and Henry, Caroline's younger brother. For Rex, it was a typical gesture, like a billet-doux between lovers on a Sèvres vase or a painting by Fragonard. But it did not have the desired effect: Caroline left Plas Newydd and Rex was left to his painting.

Beside his mural, on a side wall, Rex had painted a self-portrait. Standing at the far end of a shaded colonnade, dressed as a gardener in garters and neckerchief, this is Rex the spurned lover, trapped in a world of allegory and symbol, the humble, devoted 'servus' of courtly love, sweeping away scattered rose petals as his capricious mistress sails by in a stately gondola. His sense of himself as a romantic figure seems only to have increased with age. 'I do feel year by year an increase of melancholy', he wrote to Edith two years later, 'and it is not, I really believe, of a selfish kind mostly. But the result of an always increasing power of loving – this world and all the things in it that take me more and more by the heart.'[39]

A perpetual yearning for the unobtainable increasingly dominated his life. His melancholia began to verge on the tragic and became his chief characteristic, veiled diaphanously though it was, by wit and charm. To women, this was an irresistible combination. In May, Rex had lunched with Jill Furse, his future sister-in-law. She recorded her impressions of him in her diary. 'He is a darling, one of the most attractive and fascinating people in the world. But he has a sad face and his hair is going grey. He works much too hard and has I believe been always fond of people who wouldn't marry him . . . I always fall for sad people. I always think they are the kind I should like to marry and make happy for ever after.'[40] Of course, it seemed that Rex's unreciprocated love for Caroline and her waxing and waning had become the principal source of this misery. 'Please please PLEASE darling Caroline, don't chuck me, you know you are such a chucker – in fact an absolute chucker queen', he wrote to her from Fitzroy Street.[41] The Plas Newydd mural remains unfinished to this day.

That year Rex painted *Conversation Piece at the Daye House,* a small watercolour of the Long Room for the frontispiece of Edith's memoirs. Edith reclines on her daybed beneath a blanket, reading aloud from a manuscript, a book on the floor beside her. At the end of her daybed and facing her, in profile, perches an elfin David Cecil ('don't show it to David before publication!' Rex begged Edith), beside him on a chair, Ottoline Morrell, both sitting in rapt attention as she reads to them. Opposite Edith, Rex leans against the mantelpiece in front of a roaring fire and

332

beneath his self-portrait, smoking wistfully. The painting, which he gave to Edith, was a nostalgic reverie and a tribute to her loyalty. It was his favourite work. 'Darling Edith if you die before me', he told her, 'will you leave this picture to me as I shall love it as a "Long Room" souvenir. If I die first please bring it with you when you come'.[42]

23: 'Out of the Ordinary'

❖

> . . . the Mayor-Elect said she would be known as 'Madame-
> Mayor' and not 'Mr. Mayor'.
>
> *Western Gazette*, 5 October 1938

On 12 March 1938 German troops entered Austria to cheering
crowds, flowers and Nazi salutes. The Treaty of Versailles had
forbidden the union of the two countries but when Austrian Nazis
staged angry demonstrations in Vienna and other major cities, the
Chancellor Kurt Schuschnigg announced a plebiscite to decide
the matter. Hitler decided to make a move before this could take
place and Schuschnigg was forced to resign. Not long afterwards
German troops flooded over the border and the Anschluss, the
'connection', was declared the following day.

On 20 April Edith received a letter from Margaret Newbolt
telling her that Henry had died the previous day. He was seventy-
five and had been ill for some time but to Edith it was the end
of an era. Newbolt had belonged to a different age and there
would be no place for his famous poem 'Vitaï Lambada', with its
summons to valiantly 'Play up! play up! and play the game!' in the
coming conflict.

The following day Ottoline Morrell died, too. Ottoline had
been at a clinic in Tunbridge Wells suffering from a mysterious
illness for which her doctor had injected her with an untested
drug. Realizing that he had made a dreadful error, the doctor committed suicide on 19 April and Ottoline died two days later. She
was sixty-five. Virginia Woolf wrote her obituary in *The Times* and

Edith wept at the memorial service at St Martin-in-the-Fields. Philip Morrell had discovered in her journal a 'Farewell Message' that Ottoline had written two years before. At the end of the year he sent bound copies to Ottoline's friends with a photograph of her beside it.

> Don't mourn for me, dear friends. When you are quiet and alone remember me kindly, and when you are in lovely country – in England or Italy or Greece – give an affectionate thought to one who drank the beauty to the dregs and poured back there a full measure of happiness and gratitude, the perfume of which may reach you as you pass by.[1]

But Edith did mourn her. 'O darling Ottoline what a changed world without you', Edith wrote in her diary on the day she heard that her friend had died.[2]

With the success of the Shell *Wiltshire* guide Edith had begun to develop a niche for herself writing about Englishness, heritage and landscape. In November she had been invited to make the first of countless radio broadcasts and two months later she drove to the BBC in Bristol in January to make the programme, on Wiltshire dialect. Pleased with the result, her producer Mr Stucley invited her to return in the summer to record a series on local lore, country themes and historic buildings, to be called 'Out of the Ordinary'. When Edith heard a recording of her first broadcasts she was appalled by the sound of her own voice: 'very <u>refeened</u> and elegant, like the most ladylike governess'.[3] Perhaps though, Mr Stucley and the BBC thought that Edith's was just the kind of conservative voice that was needed on the radio at a time when the sanctity of 'this sceptred isle' was under threat. Her stories about history and the landscape were a retreat into Englishness, a nostalgic and timely reminder of what was at stake.

Edith's work was at its strongest when she wrote about place, history and personal experience. The characters in her fiction either yearn for liberation or shy away from it, retreating into the security of the past and its unchanging values. There is always an autobiographical subtext, as Edith implicitly comments on her own modernity and adaptability to change. But her fictional writing style has none of the fresh, jaunty ease and pace of her diaries; instead it is prim and rather forced. 'You won't write your best book till you <u>unbutton</u>!' Rex had told her years before.[4] When she wrote about landscape and place, the buttons had always started to come undone.

Edith felt the insinuation and insistence of history, and particularly that of her beloved Wiltshire, as she felt the primitive energies of its landscape beneath her feet. Her ears were attuned to the echoes of the past and those ancient voices inspired her. Salvaging memories, traditions and 'legends which still haunt the countryside' – old recipes, Mummers' plays, tales of hauntings – she shored them up against change.[5] 'I truly believe that there are certain people to whom or through whom the territory, the place, the past speaks', the writer Peter Ackroyd would later claim.[6] This he calls 'the territorial imperative' and nowhere in the world, he argues, is it more powerful than in England:

> English writers and artists, English composers and folk-singers, have been haunted by this sense of place, in which the echoic simplicities of past use and tradition sanctify a certain spot of ground. These forces are no doubt to be found in other regions and countries of the earth; but in England the reverence for the past and the affinity with the natural landscape join together in a mutual embrace. So we owe much to the ground on which we dwell. It is the landscape and the dreamscape. It encourages a sense of longing and belonging. It is Albion.[7]

Edith had become a professional moonraker and it was fast becoming a patriotic act.

On Saturday 7 May Edith's memoirs were published, with Rex's *Conversation Piece at the Daye House* as the frontispiece. She had finally finished writing the book the previous August with the help of her niece Rosemary. Back in June 1936 she had read some of her manuscript to Ottoline and Philip Morrell, both of whom had encouraged her to make the focus far more personal. 'I see their point and I think them good critics', she had written, 'but I know not if I can do it . . . lots of people probably dislike my angle and this would give them the chance of hating me'.[8]

But she had done it. She had gone back to her childhood and the man who exerted the greatest influence on her: Dacres, her father. The title she had chosen, *Without Knowing Mr Walkley*, with its implication of a circumscribed life, was entirely characteristic of Edith and her writing. Mr Walkley, the theatre critic of *The Times*, who she would never meet because her father refused to allow her on the stage, became a symbolic gatekeeper to the world of her imagination. The life she recalls is one lived under the shadow of his influence; it is what she forged for herself, both because, and in spite of, that influence and without ever knowing Mr Walkley. Her theatricality and love of performance and spectacle lay dormant but never died. Instead it had entirely underpinned her life.

At times in the memoir Dacres is almost reduced to a caricature: an eminent Victorian monolith in the Lytton Strachey mould, a character Edith evidently relished portraying in her fiction. But the portrait of her father is also written with the greatest respect and love; there is humour in it, but it is never vicious, rather it is tinged with fond irony. Edith had plundered her own childhood and early life for her fiction; now she plundered and recycled aspects of those novels for *Walkley*, particularly when writing about the Ivy Compton-Burnett world of her childhood and her tyrannical father. Perhaps this is suggestive of the unreliable nature of memory itself, in which stories are recalled, reinterpreted, smoothed or entirely invented. It was something she wondered about herself.

Papa often thrilled us with the story of his first visit to the Lakes, when he saw the poet himself at the gate of his house at Ambleside and found him not at all forthcoming. Then one day, when we were looking at Wordsworth's grave in Grasmere churchyard and saw written upon it the date '1850', Papa suddenly exclaimed: 'Why, he died years before I ever came here.' So ended a legend; and I wonder how many of the memories in this book are as imaginary as my father's recollection of the poet Wordsworth.[9]

And so when she writes that 'it is always summer in one's childhood, and in the summer the garden door stood open, and people sat both inside and out of it, in the hall or on the steps', it is with the knowledge that although fiction might colour the facts it does not detract from the telling.

Perhaps the loveliest moments in the book are Edith's extraordinarily evocative reminiscences of her childhood imagination, that world that she created in the hidden spaces of her life.

Then there were numbers of cupboards in the walls, in which we spent our afternoons when it was too wet to go out. In every house, an immense amount of space is lost to the grown-up people who never sit in cupboards. We had first of all the big nursery cupboard where Mildred and I played houses, each on her own shelf, for we were not sophisticated enough to call them flats. There was the vast cupboard in Mamma's room where one could walk about on the floor, as well as clamber on the shelves among her hats. In the attic was the Bird Cupboard, called from a painting of magpies which surrounded it. It was like a long low room, and we heaped pillows at its two ends and pretended to go to sleep in it. And then there was the tiny cupboard high up in the dark wall on the back stairs. It could only be reached by someone who was very small and very agile. I was both, and so I often got into it, and remained lost for hours. When I remember Wilton Rectory, I think of it as larger by all these cupboards than it ever could have been for my parents, who only sat in the rooms.[10]

The tiny cupboard on the dark stairs has never been found; perhaps it never existed.

Second only to her father, the other great presence in *Walkley* is that of Wilton. The book is divided into three sections, 'Wilton Rectory', 'Away from Wilton' and 'Wilton Once More'. It was how she had divided her life. And *Walkley* tells much more than the story of her own life and plunges off into myriad digressions about the old Wiltshire she had known. There are stories, both commonplace and fantastical, of clocks, calendars, floods, seasons, houses, rooms, processions, the realities of rural poverty, the peculiarities of the Wiltshire landscape and her fascination with the 'revenants of the plain'.[11] And the characters that people these stories are recalled with Hardy-esque charm, a combination of affection, amusement, honesty and romance. She recalls her time in Oxford, her memories of Queen Victoria, the First World War, the Land Army and, more recently, the death of George V.

Edith had unbuttoned as she had been told to. She writes with endearing honesty and warmth, and her voice echoes both the formality of the past and the ease of the present, drawing comparisons between her Victorian childhood and her progressive conservatism. She uses modish terms like 'sex-appeal', and takes pride in her modernity, the oscillation of her life between Wilton and London, and her friendships with younger people. There are portrait sketches of Stephen, Cecil, Sassoon, Walton, Zita Jungman and David Cecil. There are her friendships with Ottoline, Osbert, Sybil Colefax and others. She writes about the start of her career as an author and about the act of writing; she discusses her personal and highly romantic brushes with the supernatural and lovingly recalls her sightseeing expeditions with Rex. The vignettes are not all glowing and there are some moments when the secret voice of her diaries comes through. She writes, for example, of Stephen's sparkling way of talking, of his mercurial and joyful nature, but adds: 'when Stephen is alone with one friend he is often drawn to speak of very grave and profound subjects, and then he becomes unhappy, for he is never sure about what he loves and believes in, and he would like to love and believe in so much.'[12] It reads like a school report written by a fond but exasperated headmistress. What Stephen thought of it has not been recorded.

Edith presents herself as a *salonnière* and the Daye House as a bucolic haven for her friends where 'conversation has always been the chief amusement'.[13] 'Some of my happiest memories', she writes, 'are memories of voices – the birds outside and conversation within.'[14] It was how she liked to imagine herself and no doubt why she chose Rex's painting for the cover. 'I glow with gratitude for Rex Whistler, whose drawing perpetuates, far better than any writing, the memory of delightful talks in my Long Room', she writes.[15] Edith dedicated the book to Kitty and Evelyn Rawlence 'and other friends who remember with me the old Wilton days'. Edith had dined with the sisters in the summer of 1934 after the 'braying' of crowds at Juliet Duff's cocktail party. Returning home she had sat in her garden with the sisters and felt entirely at peace. 'They are dull things', she had written, 'but they leave the beauty of the country undisturbed'.[16]

In *Walkley* Edith writes:

> I rather shared my father's fancy for the unattainable in bridegrooms, and the consequences of various 'inhibitions' (as they call them to-day) which he laid upon our youthful ambitions, has been for me a happy life. Spent, not upon the stage or in any of the other professions which presented themselves, not as a wife, mother, mother-in-law, and grandmother (the fate of most of my friends), but as a lifelong inhabitant of Wiltshire, which is in my eyes, the most beautiful of the English counties.[17]

This majestic explanation has something of Elizabeth I about it. Edith's friend Edith Sitwell quite consciously identified herself with Elizabeth, whom she resembled and about whom she wrote two books. Perhaps Edith Olivier, who had 'become' the Queen for the Wilton pageant, also identified with her as a woman who had lived and triumphed in a man's world, who had sacrificed marriage and motherhood for something greater. Although Edith presents herself as a victim of her father, ultimately there is a triumphant note in her memoirs: she has become a grande dame. Set apart from a conventional life by her father, and because of that, unburdened by the confining and defining bonds of matrimony and motherhood, her greatest loyalty is to her county and, implicitly, to her country.

The Times review on 6 May read:

> The charm of this book, and it has a charm which should endear it to many readers, lies in the accurate and unostentatious picture of those golden years before the War which Miss Olivier has conjured up . . . At an early age Miss Olivier decided that her life would have been lived in vain if she never knew the famous dramatic critic of this journal. She never did. It may be hoped that other celebrities were some compensation for that disappointment.'[18]

On 29 May Edith dined at Heytesbury with Sassoon and Hester and drank to 'Walkley's health' with a bottle of pink champagne. They 'talked a good deal of foreign affairs and the hovering horror of war'. They discussed Mussolini, still publicly nurturing his reputation as a peacemaker although now privately aligning Italy's destiny with Germany. Sassoon and Hester had seen Mussolini in Italy and told Edith that he had 'a magnificent face, and very grand personality. No charlatan at all.'[19]

By the end of August Edith was writing in her diary that 'this peaceful world may end this week as the Czech-German situation gets worse. Why should we fight for this corner of the world?'[20] 'Still can't visualise War, though I indeed remember it', she wrote two days later.[21] Within Czechoslovakia unrest was growing. A fifth of its multicultural population was made up of Sudeten Germans who were responding warmly to Nazi propaganda and pushing for Hitler to annex Czechoslovakia to the Fatherland. Hitler announced his plans to do just that and in turn Britain announced that they would be obliged to defend Czechoslovakia in the event of an invasion. In the following weeks as the crisis played out Edith sat anxiously beside the wireless listening to news from the continent, relayed by the BBC. Her diaries were entirely given over to politics. 'All Europe begging for calm and peace while Hitler, Göring and Goebbels tell the Nazi party assembled at Nuremberg that they <u>must fight</u> and that there is glorious honour to live so as to do so', she wrote on 10 September.[22]

> Newspapers and Broadcasts all day about the crisis. The world quite puzzled. <u>Everyone</u> against war and yet feeling they can't let Hitler seize country after country and treat the inhabitants as he treats Jews, aristocrats, and learned men in Germany. I suppose he thinks our hatred of war so great that we shall shut our eyes to what he does. But I suppose we can't do this.[23]

Three days later Edith dined with Rachel and David Cecil and they found themselves talking as if war had already begun. David thought it was inevitable and that the sooner it began the better, before Hitler had made Germany any stronger than it already was. The next day, 14 September, was one of 'great anxiety'. Edith had been busy with air-raid precaution inspections and had decided that in the event of an invasion the school could be taken over as a hospital. That night at 9.40 'came the astounding news that Chamberlain will fly to Germany tomorrow morning to see Hitler. Quite unprecedented and most dramatic, all England must accompany him with prayer.'[24]

As talks continued in Germany, on 21 September Imma arrived at the Daye House. As a German she was expecting to be taken to an internment camp as soon as war was declared. She was afraid of returning to Germany but felt that she must, although she knew that if she did so she would be forced to act against England. Imma worried that her presence at the Daye House was bad for Edith and offered to leave. 'I tell her we are not yet at war and she has given the police her address, so she <u>ought</u> to keep still and wait for her instructions . . . She is heart-broken', Edith wrote; 'she sees her country first disgraced, then ruined.'[25]

That night Edith wrote:

> Chamberlain seems to be climbing down and making terms with Hitler, throwing the Czechs to the wolves and tho' no one likes the Versailles arrangement <u>we have given our word to Czechoslovakia</u> . . . Imma and I went sadly to bed after hearing the last news. Winston Churchill and Anthony Eden have both protested against this surrender to <u>bluff</u>![26]

By 25 September it seemed that Hitler was on the brink of declaring war. The following day trenches were being dug in Salisbury. In London bomb shelters were hurriedly erected, gas masks were handed out and there were reports of people fleeing the city. Edith went to an ARP meeting to discuss digging their own trenches 'and <u>how</u> we were to choose the 10 per cent of the population for whom we were to provide'.[27] That day she returned home to find Imma translating Hitler's speeches and Phyllis, her cook, taking notes.

Negotiations continued in Munich between the four powers represented by Chamberlain, Hitler, Mussolini and Daladier of France. But everywhere Britain prepared for war. Plans for the immediate evacuation of over two million people from the centre of London were ready to take effect. At Munich it was agreed that the Sudetenland should be joined with Germany and Chamberlain returned to England in triumph. Czechoslovakia, like Russia, had not been invited to the conference and was told that if it resisted the Munich decision it would receive no assistance from Britain or France.

> It is Peace. The 4 Powers reached agreement. The Czechs must give in . . . Phyllis made a dish she has long wanted to try and she begged to cook it to commemorate peace –

orange in a pigeon, pigeon in a chicken, chicken in a duck. We called it the Four Powers Compote.[28]

Rex dined with Edith the following night and 'was heavenly'. The night before, he had been at dinner with Winston Churchill and Duff Cooper, who had resigned from his post as First Lord of the Admiralty the day after the Munich Agreement.* Chamberlain naively held to the belief that despite his territorial aims Hitler was an honourable statesman. 'D.C. thinks Chamberlain has <u>gone down</u> before the dictators. He and Winston have <u>rapproche</u> and W. was dining last night too,' Edith wrote.[29] And so the country clung to Chamberlain's promise of 'peace for our time' but at the back of everybody's mind was the fear that Hitler was not going to stop there. It was peace, for now.

At a council meeting back in June the idea of Wilton, with its population of 2,322, being swallowed up by Salisbury Council was once again mooted. This was something that Edith could never allow. 'Canon Brabent chaffed me for becoming very <u>bellicose</u>', she had written, 'and I did rise up in my wrath and say we must fight rather than let our government be annexed, as the Austrian was by a nation which would do such horrors as the Germans do to Jews and Scientists. I took the room with me!!'[30] It was little surprise to the people of Wilton when Edith was elected as Mayor of the town by unanimous vote on 4 October 1938. She was the first woman Mayor in the town's history. That night the *Daily Mail* telephoned for an interview and the next day the BBC asked for a broadcast. The *Mail* ran a photograph of her alongside its article, a photograph that, to a reader who didn't know Edith, shows a woman wearing large hooped earrings and a wide necklace looking little like the conventional idea of a civic elder. The *Western Gazette* reported that 'the Mayor-Elect said she would be known as "Madame-Mayor" and not "Mr. Mayor"'.[31] Pasted into Edith's scrapbook are letters and telegrams congratulating her as well as

---

* To which he had been promoted in 1937.

articles about her appointment in the *Daily Herald*, the *Daily Express*, the *Evening Standard*, the *Manchester Guardian* and several local papers. She was astounded by the publicity.

Just over a month later on 9 November Edith was sworn in as Mayor of Wilton, wearing a crown that Rex and Cecil had designed, her mayoral chain and the long scarlet robes of her office. That Sunday, Remembrance Day, she made the traditional mayoral procession from the town hall to the church in full regalia and torrential rain. 'From Wiltshire', reported the *Evening Standard*'s correspondent, 'a friend sends news of week-end house-parties of guests who flocked to Wilton Church to see the mayoral procession headed by Miss Edith Olivier, the new mayor.'[32] Those guests included Juliet Duff, Rex, Caroline Paget, Conrad Russell, Diana Cooper, Sybil Colefax, Lord and Lady Pembroke and several Herberts. Rex later made a drawing of this blustery ceremony as the headpiece of Edith's 1939 visitors' book. In it the little imperious figure of Edith is seen processing past the town hall in her sweeping mayoral robes beneath the canopy of an umbrella, behind her a line of civic dignitaries huddled beneath their umbrellas, the Union flag whipping violently in the wind as a dog barks angrily at the jubilant strains of the brass band. The church service was followed by an At Home at the town hall and then a luncheon at the Daye House for her friends.

David Herbert had decorated the dining room with tubs of roses and platters of fruit. Rex had written name cards, the menu and the seating plan and a poster on which he had written 'Homage à Mademoiselle ma Mère!' David Cecil and his wife Rachel were guests, along with Juliet Duff; Sybil Colefax; Edith's sister Mamie; Lady Carter; Rex and Caroline; Edith's nephew Tony and niece Rosemary; Imma; Laurence Whistler; and a couple of Herberts. Rex sat at her right hand. Phyllis had outdone herself with a menu of Merluche Polonaise (hake garnished with buttered breadcrumbs and hard-boiled eggs), Gigot Pravaz (which involved injecting burnt brandy and orange juice into the lamb with a syringe), Poires Belle Dijonaise (pears poached in white wine with a blackcurrant sauce) and Stilton. That night in her diary Edith wrote that it was as if she had married Wilton that day, just as the Doge of Venice was married to the sea.

Since her youth, as her father's daughter, Edith had taken her role in the community very seriously. Though in many respects she was a very different woman now, her fervent loyalty to Wilton remained unchanged. She took to the job with zeal and a characteristic blend of romanticism and practicality. It was the old Tory sense of paternalism that inspired her; it was why the rector's daughter lived on the aristocratic estate and why that daughter was now the town's Mayor. Certainly she was the first Mayor of Wilton to have her official portraits taken by the society photographer Cecil Beaton. In the photographs, for which she posed in the grandiose surroundings of the church of St Mary and St Nicholas, Edith stands in stately profile (or 'profeel' as Cecil pronounced it), resplendent in her long robes of office, her mayoral chain and her rather Arthurian crown, along with enormous gold earrings. This regal portrait stands out amongst those of her predecessors and successors lining the wall of the town hall in Wilton. It is still the source of some wry amusement amongst the councillors.

As Mayor, economical and well-designed housing with decent sanitation was at the forefront of Edith's agenda. It had been decided that Wilton was overcrowded and a quantity of houses had been condemned. With like-minded friends Edith had recently founded and become the chairman of the Rural Cottage Improvement Society for Wiltshire which aimed to safeguard old buildings against demolition and assure that newly built houses were sensitive to their surroundings. In the New Year she would write an article for the *Evening News* entitled 'Fun of Being a Woman Mayor' which opened with a quote about mock turtle soup from *Alice's Adventures in Wonderland*. In it she likened the Mayor of London's role to turtle soup (the turtle being the emblem of Mansion House) and her own role as mock turtle. She said that as Mayor of a rural town she delighted in having 'a finger in every pie'. She wrote about the awkward amusement at official banquets, at which the previously exclusively male guests felt obliged to curb their language for the sake of the lady now present. 'There's no doubt about it', she concluded, 'politicians may talk of democracy and community life, and sociologists may write books about them; but to see these things in practice, you must come to a small town. There, individuals still count, and each can pull his weight in the general life of the place. Give me the Mock turtle every time.'[33]

Entrenched as she was in Arcadian ideas of community, tradition and responsibility, that winter Edith wrote to Wilton's elderly residents telling them that they had been selected to receive bread at New Year. It was an old Wilton custom dating back to the beginning of the nineteenth century. 'I am, as you know, the first Lady Mayor of Wilton; and the word "<u>Lady</u>" comes from a very ancient word meaning <u>Loaf-giver</u>', she said in the letter.[34] No doubt this gesture was inspired by her father who had taken a very practical and engaged interest in the well-being of his parishioners, often helping them out of his own pocket. He made sure no one was ever without a fire. On New Year's Day, Cecil joined Edith at the door of the church and, with his camera, captured her as a beaming lady bountiful handing out loaves to the chosen recipients, who in the photographs are clearly enjoying themselves too, untroubled, it seems, by the modern connotations of charity. It was a romantic gesture from the old world, that which Edith had celebrated in her memoirs, a gesture perhaps more poignant than before, now that, as 1939 dawned, the threat of war loomed ever larger.

24: 'Another Season'

❖

'Charm is the great English blight . . . It spots and kills anything
it touches. It kills love; it kills art; I greatly fear, my dear
Charles, it has killed you.'

Anthony Blanche in Evelyn Waugh's *Brideshead Revisited*

In May 1938 Edith had met Rex for supper at the Gourmet restaurant in London. In his pocket was a letter from the Queen to
whom he had sent photographs of his Plas Newydd mural. 'She is
glad to know we have so brilliant an artist in our time and she
"longs" to see the picture – underlined. He is very pleased with
this', Edith wrote.[1] In the letter the Queen had written: 'I am
happy to know that in this generation we have an artist of such
genius and good taste as yourself '.[2]

It was their mutual friend Osbert Sitwell who had brought Rex
to the attention of Elizabeth, then Duchess of York, in 1936. She
commissioned him to design a bookplate which Rex never actually produced – fortuitously, as by the following year she was no
longer Duchess of York but Queen. She then commissioned Rex
to design ciphers for herself and the new King. He also painted
various portraits of the new Royal Family arranged informally in
domestic settings, Rex having been chosen specifically to help
present the new King's image as an honourable, and reliable,
family man, unlike his elder brother. Rex had taken Laurence to
the first levee of the new reign; he was presented by Euan Wallace
and Laurence by Lutyens.

In September 1937, Rex was invited, along with Osbert Sit-

15. Rex photographed in his studio by Howard Coster, 1936.
'Elegant, vague, gentle and strange, like an exquisite goat, he is
a delightful satyr', wrote Chips Channon.

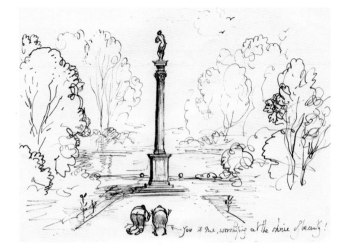

16. Rex's illustration at the bottom of a letter sent to Edith after his first visit to Wilton in June 1925. 'The lovliness of Wilton was so soaked into me during my stay with you, that I can quite clearly see in my mind all the intoxicatingly beautiful spots that you showed me', he told her.

17. Edith's desk in the Long Room at the Daye House, photographed by Cecil Beaton. A row of portraits of those most dear to her, including Rex, William Walton, Siegfried Sassoon, her father Dacres Olivier and a drawing by Stephen of her sister Mildred, are ranged along the back.

18. Rex and Edith on the stone terrace of the Villa Natalia in San Remo, 1925. Edith hiding her newly bingled hair under her hat.

19. Edith with Siegfried photographed by Lady Ottoline Morrell at Fitz House. Sassoon took a lease on Edith's old house in October 1931 when he was banished from Wilsford by Stephen. 'Do you know that you are one of the most blessed of people? I do', Sassoon told Edith in the following year.

20. Edith playing Elizabeth I (with a little help from Cecil Beaton) at the Wilton Pageant in July 1932. 'I was no longer myself in any feature, but entirely the Queen', she wrote in her diary.

21. *Edith Olivier seated on a Day Bed*, 12 September 1942. Painted by Rex in the summer that he was stationed nearby at Codford. Petrol rationing had put an end to sightseeing. Instead they spent their days together in the garden at the Daye House, Edith reading aloud as Rex painted at his easel. 'The sun chased us about and we had to move again and again', Edith wrote that night.

22. Rex and Caroline Paget in Austria, 1936.

23. 'Mayor Edith Olivier hosting a party for British soldiers 1 January 1940' in *LIFE* magazine.

24. *Self-Portrait*, May 1940. Painted by Rex at 27 York Terrace on the day his uniform arrived. He sits pensively in the shade but behind him Regent's Park is bathed in early summer sun.

Lt: Rex Whistler.
2nd Bn: Welsh Guards.
B.N.E.F.
July 9. 1944

My darling Edith
a little present from
Normandy with much love.
Writing to you to day, with what
news I can give. Thank you
darling for your dear letters.
Wonder if this will be
allowed to reach you
Rex.

25. Rex sent this note and three cheeses from Normandy a few days before going into battle in 1944. Edith received the parcel on 18 July; she later discovered Rex had died that day.

26. Edith's last letter to Rex, returned unopened some time after his death.

27. A note with a drawing of Edith sent by Stephen to Cecil some time after her death.

28. Edith photographed by Cecil Beaton in the late 1940s. During the war Edith had stopped dyeing her hair. 'She appears more of a conventional old lady and less the violent character that her conversation still proves her to be', Cecil wrote in his diary.

well, to join the Royal Family for a weekend at Balmoral. Some days before his departure he had met Edith at the Café Royal and after lunch they had gone to Simpson's to buy 'very grave pyjamas and shoes to stay next week at <u>Balmoral</u>! He is thrilled and terrified!' She added: 'He goes for weekend and as Osbert will also be there he has a protector. <u>What</u> progress for a king and queen to have such guests!'[3] Rex, not known for his punctuality, had gone to the length of borrowing a wristwatch from his brother to ensure that he would be on time for meals. Once he got to Balmoral, though, he realized that the equerries were very efficient time-keepers, discreetly tapping on the doors to invite the guests down. He had been intrigued by the untouched Victoriana of the castle, a kaleidoscope of colourful tartans, its rooms filled with huge vases of flowers, objets d'art and plaid carpets, his *Victoria Regina* sets brought to life. He attended a Ghillies Ball and was delighted to observe the King and Queen dancing breathless reels amongst the people of the estate.

It seemed that Rex had left his former life behind. The circles he now moved in were loftier than Edith's. In April 1938 he took new rooms behind the elegant, white, Adam facades of Fitzroy Square, at the upper end of Fitzroy Street. In May Edith was his first guest and arrived to find it 'all in wild confusion still. We found an old ham breakfast roll which we ate between us.' She thought it 'a great improvement on Fitzroy Street'.[4] Rex was renting two middle floors. Downstairs his studio had large windows; upstairs were his bedroom, sitting room and bathroom. By now too, he could afford to take the lease on a house for his parents. His father was becoming increasingly infirm and Rex planned to move them from north Buckinghamshire to Wiltshire; he discussed possible houses with Edith. Shortly after her visit to Fitzroy Square, they headed to Salisbury in Edith's car. 'We set out for a picnic at about 11 with a list of possible houses for Rex's parents and [went] to the Close to sit there and study our maps'. He had soon set his heart upon the Walton Canonry, in the heart of the hushed Close, a large, perfectly proportioned, early-Georgian house of pinkish brick with a long garden at the back stretching down to the Avon and a view over to the water meadows on the far side of the river. 'Rex crazy for it', Edith wrote; 'he says in 3 years he would give up his studio and make this his headquarters.'[5] The house looked out onto the majestic west front of Salisbury Cathedral and the perfectly mown sweep of lawn in front of it. It was a choice inspired by Edith. And it was a long way from Eltham.

By June he had secured the house and made plans to move his parents up to Wiltshire. The following month he telephoned Edith, 'a very long call', she wrote, 'distracted and tortured by his father become much worse just as they are trying to move to Salisbury . . . poor darling Rex is heartbroken'.[6]

Rex's parents were eventually installed in the Canonry but it was not just his father's health that broke his heart that summer. At a ball at Buckingham Palace on 6 June, Duff Cooper observed his beloved niece from afar: 'Caroline was looking very beautiful in a red satin dress that I had given her for the occasion. She is plainly in love with Rex Whistler now. He has no money and a lot of hungry relations. He is however a charming man and would be delightful to live with.'[7] She might have appeared to be in love with Rex but things remained as complicated and indistinct between them as ever. At the beginning of the year he had written to her in London from Plas Newydd, saying 'I would die for you' and suggesting that they should go away together that summer, perhaps to Provence: 'think of the white dusty roads and delicious meals at little cafes and dancing and reading and painting.'[8] But she continued to vacillate and he continued to despair.

Sitting alone at the Eiffel Tower restaurant one 'Gloomy Sunday' he wrote to her:

> I can see you standing in the hall and hurriedly reading this with a bored expression and thinking – Blast him, another invitation for me to have to wriggle out of, or chuck. But you'll be wrong, it <u>isn't</u> another invitation and whats more,

there ain't going to be no more neither, so there. I've been thinking about you young Lady, ever since last Wednesday (and before that ever since last – whenever it was) and I consider you done me wrong – or rather, you never done me right. So you see you ain't my girlfriend no longer. You never really were, were you? but you pretended to be and I pretended you were too. Well it's going to be sad for me, but perhaps less worrying and less disappointing and so no more sad than it has been and so far as <u>seeing</u> you goes, it can't make the slightest difference ... I've <u>loved you</u>, you see Caroline, while you have never loved me at all.[9]

He had even lost the other girl in his life too. Patricia Douglas had finally given up hope of Rex. In January she had married John de Bendern, a rich golfing enthusiast and the son of a count. Rex had attended the wedding at the Brompton Oratory to be greeted by the bride 'among the wedding guests with tears in her eyes'.[10] In August Edith had visited Rex at his studio where he was hard at work on a triptych for Brompton Oratory. 'He won't leave it', she wrote, 'but ate sandwiches to sustain him and had slices of ham ready for the night.' They talked of Liz Paget and Raimund von Hofmannsthal who were now quite openly in love. Raimund's wife Alice had decided to divorce him and Liz hoped to marry him. 'Hateful for the Angleseys and a disaster for Liz', thought Edith.[11] Towards the end of August Caroline, friendly once again, and Rex travelled together to join Liz and Raimund at Schloss Kammer in Austria. 'Rex sees misery ahead if they marry', Edith wrote in her diary, adding: 'and yet Caroline thinks she must side with them because they are anti-authority!'[12]

From Austria Rex sent Kenneth Rae a telegram: 'Terrible confusions in the schloss lots of love hate tears fun and truckin at nights': cryptic, and 'designed to arouse envy', writes Laurence.[13] The party then took the train to Milan where they transferred to Raimund's car and headed to Venice. There they stayed with Juliet Duff, who had rented the Palazzo Vendramin and had Cecil

Beaton and David Herbert staying too. Together they attended a ball given by Lady Castlerosse at the Palazzo Venier dei Leoni on the Grand Canal, which had previously belonged to the Marchesa Casati and where once lions had prowled in the gardens.* They danced under the stars and took to the water in gondolas. But as the night went on they suddenly received news that war over Czechoslovakia was imminent and that Duff Cooper had mobilized the British Fleet. The four lovers dashed for the Swiss border, the girls still in their evening gowns. As an Austrian Jew, if Raimund had been caught on the wrong side of the frontier in pro-Nazi Italy, he could well have been interned.

After the furore of Munich, life seemed to return to normal at the end of 1938. But the country was still holding its breath. Despite this, Edith leapt into the New Year of 1939 with a ball in the Michael Herbert Hall at Wilton to celebrate Twelfth Night. The dancing was led by Edith with David Herbert as her partner, and she had also invited Patricia and John de Bendern, Lady Pembroke, the Hambledens, the Jungman sisters and Juliet Duff. There were mummers mumming in traditional dress, a Twelfth Night cake was carried in and after the cotillion they danced the Lambeth Walk. Rex did not come to the ball but instead arrived for a weekend alone with Edith at the end of the month. He wrote to her when he returned to London:

My darling Edith,

Thank you for that delicious cozy peaceful weekend which I did _so_ love. It is a great happiness and comfort to me always, to stay with you as we are such good friends. I was very tired – physically but more I think mentally, during my stay with you and I feel, as a result, that I wasted your company and council. I couldn't quite raise the <u>energy</u> to explain and think over my troubles and so you had nothing to go upon and consequently, your advice was based on a wrong

---

* Now the Guggenheim Museum. Doris Castlerosse died of an overdose of sleeping pills in London in December 1942.

supposition. The last thing in the world that I want to do is just marry for the <u>sake of marriage</u>. I am not looking for a wife <u>any</u>where and marriage without love or without enough love is infinitely less preferable to me than staying as I am.

I have a very full life and a very busy one and so much of my unhappiness comes from the accident of most of my love being attracted to one person (and that second magnet is always there as well) who doesn't return it.[14]

In March Hitler annexed the rest of Czechoslovakia. 'The world looks on not knowing what to do', Edith wrote in her diary; 'attack him now, and plunge Europe into war? or wait till he is much stronger and attacks us?'[15] Edith once again sat listening to the hourly reports on the wireless. The British Ambassador was recalled from Berlin and the German Ambassador returned to Germany. Edith lunched with Juliet Duff who had had Duff Cooper to stay for the weekend. 'Of course he (and Juliet too) says Chamberlain should not have taken Hitler's word', Edith recorded, 'but if Statesmen <u>start</u> on the presumption that the other man is a liar there is the end of negotiation, force is the only weapon and we are back in barbarism. We probably shall be in a week's time! – but we are bound to try the other first.'[16]

At the end of the month Britain ended its policy of appeasement by announcing that if Poland was invaded it would be forced to act. The government began to prepare for war and conscription was introduced the following month. The Italians marched into Albania. Edith began to prepare for the evacuated children that she believed would soon start to arrive from London and had the Trellis Room made ready. She wept to hear that her nephew Charlie had been recalled from leave to be sent to Egypt, thinking of his father, her brother Harold, who had died at the beginning of the previous war with Germany only twenty-five years earlier. She went to the cinema to watch a propaganda film which 'was supposed to help shew me how to run a Control Centre. It <u>didn't</u>! Far too confused, but the whole thing was a ghastly scene of ruins'.[17]

Back in 1936 Rex had been photographed in his studio by Howard Coster, the self-proclaimed photographer of 'men of consequence and achievement',[18]* among them, to name a few: Somerset Maugham, G. K. Chesterton, Walter de la Mare, H. G. Wells, Bertrand Russell and Augustus John. In the pictures Rex looks wistfully out of the window, smoking or talking on the telephone, with his head always slightly turned aside, guardedly. His address book overflowed with the names of film stars, playwrights and aristocrats, including Noël Coward, Robert Donat and the Duchess of Kent. He was a fixture in London society, his name often appearing in the Court Circular, as a guest at dances, aristocratic weddings and private views. He decorated society's drawing rooms, painted portraits of its children, designed its letterheadings and bookplates. He was a welcome and entertaining guest at dinners, house parties and on continental holidays. 'The name *Rex*', Osbert Sitwell later recalled, 'spelt an infinite charm to which all responded.'[19] In this he was echoing Edith, who had written in 1935: 'everyone loves Rex. There's no one who has such unfailing charm'.[20] Rex and his work had become synonymous, a successful brand, one that Edith had helped to cultivate from the beginning of their friendship. But beyond the debonair gloss, to many Rex remained an enigmatic figure, with a mystique of course that only added to his charm. Increasingly forgetful and inaccessible, he was continually writing letters of apology to hostesses whose parties he had forgotten about. In their letters to Edith, mutual friends asked after Rex, complaining about his lack of communication and sending him their love.

'Dinner with Rex', Cecil had written in his diary in September 1937. 'There could scarcely be a nicer way of spending time. More than any among all my friends, Rex has an aura which improves the more you are with him and the older he becomes. His sense of repose, no doubt, springs from an unruffled, poetic

---

* Now at the National Portrait Gallery.

and calm interior world.' However, Cecil knew quite the opposite to be true. He continued:

> Rex has a tawny elegance; though he may sum up contemporary situations and passing foibles with understanding and wit, his atmosphere is nevertheless that of an older man of another century.
>
> Perhaps this anachronistic solidity is the very reason for Rex's being more laurel-crowned than almost any young painter today, especially by the older generation of cultured aristocrats. And recognition has come to him in spite of his putting every obstacle in his way: Rex makes himself almost impregnable, hardly ever answering letters or the telephone.[21]

But although the last years of the 1930s were undoubtedly the most successful of Rex's career, they also marked the lowest depths of his melancholy. In June 1939, Rex confessed to Edith:

> I have a great sense of failure upon me, darling Edith and have had for some long time now, which keeps me dispirited and unhappy. But looking back on all the work I have done in the last 10 or 12 years there is <u>nothing</u> that has even <u>approached</u> the standard of beauty and fineness of taste, in conception and execution, which every real artist sets himself, and which, oddly enough, I too have always set myself – though no one would think it to look at my laboured overworked productions. This is not said that I might have the pleasure of hearing you contradict it, but it is a <u>confidence</u> sweet Edith, which it relieves me to make.[22]

Rex was as troubled by doubts about the validity of his work as he had been at the start of his career fourteen years earlier. Now, though, he was more and more dissatisfied with his style. There was a growing contrast between his commissioned work, which he continued to paint in the elegant style for which he was known, and the increasingly experimental naturalism of his private work. He had painted perhaps his finest portrait in 1936. Sonny Grant was a young black boy who lived down the road from his studio. Rex painted a sensitive, gentle portrait of the boy's head and shoulders, warm light softly illuminating his face with its averted eyes. The style is loose and confident, arresting in its simplicity. Here was no grand patron expecting a 'Rex Whistler'; here there were no expectations at all, and it shows.

Edith had noticed the change in Rex. Writing in her diary in 1938 she said: 'he grows diviner – a new kind of heavenliness – a mature judgement. But more and more he can't arrange his life even as to whether he will telephone or telegraph to his char-woman'.[23]

Back in 1925, when Rex was working on his first mural in Shadwell with Mary Adshead, Henry Tonks had written to Ads-head, complaining that he could not contact Rex: 'social engagements play so large a part in the artist's life now, that it is only the old artists who escape them. Make it a rule, if you can,' he advised her, 'never to let anything interfere with your work. I think it was Balzac who talked of the divine selfishness of the artist and selfish he must be if he wants to get things done.'[24] And Cynthia Asquith, friend of both Tonks and Rex, recalled the former telling her that 'all artists . . . should eat disgustingly or else have some equally effective social disqualification that will prevent them being asked out. See too many people, become an amiable member of Society, and the mind goes out of your art'.[25] Perhaps Tonks had sensed that Rex would be seduced by the society life. 'If only we can save him from the Pit, because directly he is launched he will be an amazing success', he had written in 1926 to a friend.[26]

But Rex had been seduced. His plight calls to mind Anthony Blanche's warning to Charles Ryder of the dangers of 'creamy English charm' in *Brideshead Revisited*.[27] In the novel, Ryder becomes an architectural painter:

> The financial slump of the period, which left many painters without employment, served to enhance my success, which

was, indeed, itself a symptom of the decline. When the water-holes were dry people sought to drink at the mirage. After my first exhibition I was called to all parts of the country to make portraits of houses that were soon to be deserted or debased.[28]

Like Rex, Charles's success is symptomatic of the decline of the aristocracy and the nostalgia this inspired. Charles too has developed a successful brand: 'I seldom failed to please, for there was no conflict between myself and my patrons; we both wanted the same thing . . . But as the years passed', he adds, 'I began to mourn the loss of something I had known in the drawing-room of Marchmain House and once or twice since, the intensity and singleness and the belief that it was not all done by hand – in a word, the inspiration'.[29]

On 24 June 1939 Rex celebrated his thirty-fourth birthday. He was working on a mural for Gilbert and Maud Russell at Mottisfont Abbey for which he had originally planned a neo-Gothic design to suit the medieval origins of the house. But Maud Russell had rejected the proposed scheme of Gothic sylvan landscapes against palest pink walls in favour of a more restrained and impersonal design of trompe l'œil Gothic plasterwork, with ermine swags at the windows and formal classical trophies on the walls. Edith thought Mrs Russell 'a feeble little woman – afraid of her own taste and trying to be in the correct <u>art</u> fashion'.[30] Her tastes ran more in the Matisse, Picasso and Modigliani line. She thought of Rex as an interior decorator and having agreed to the commission, he was grudgingly obliged to suffer her complaints and indecision.

'Went to the Close and picked up my darling Rex and drove him to Mottisfont', Edith had written in May. 'He has not licensed his car this quarter – can't he is too poor . . . they keep changing R's design . . . drove back to luncheon at Heytesbury. The strain of war talk is very bad for Siegfried who is in a shocking state of nerves.'[31]

The coming of the new war reminded Sassoon of the last: 'Happy are those who are too busy to think! It all makes me wish that the July 1918 bullet had finished me. I can do nothing now except endure this nightmare.'[32] He retreated into the seclusion of Heytesbury to wrestle with his memories: 'All I want to do is to forget – and forget – and have no arc-lights of practical minded-ness turned onto my loathing of the Second Great War, by which I am being reduced to an impotent absurdity.'[33] Though he adored his son and was fond of, if no longer in love with, his wife, he wanted to be alone. He even moved his study from the ground floor at Heytesbury to a smaller room tucked away in the attic. Later that year he began writing the second volume of his auto-biography and withdrew into memories of the Weald of Kent of 1909 and his cricket-playing youth.

Edith often drove to Mottisfont that summer to visit Rex whilst he worked, and witnessed his predicament. One day in June she arrived to find him 'painting away on ladder and scaffold and discussing with his workmen how he can best carry out the ignorant changes demanded by Mrs Russell in the finished part. This means days of extra work for the workmen and Rex himself and as the men cost him £20 a week, he is being financially ruined'.[34] The tyrannical Mrs Russell would fail to recognize the symbolism of a pair of limp, bound hands, incorporated into one of the trophies on her wall.

But soon Rex would be liberated by events far beyond the elegant drawing rooms of Hampshire. 'I was painting this ermine curtain when Britain declared war on the Nazi tyrants. Sunday, September 3rd, R.W.', reads a painted message concealed above the cornice at Mottisfont and only discovered many years later. On 1 September German forces had invaded Poland and two days later Britain declared war on Germany.

'Rex came and we had a long agonising talk', Edith wrote a few days later; 'he is miserable. His love affair at an impasse. He says Caroline does not love him and carries Antony's photograph with her everywhere. She is as elusive with Rex as with everyone', then moving onto another subject always dear to her heart, she added: 'financially he is shattered. All painting over the Mottisfont work has brought less than £300 . . . He's overdrawn and is responsible for rent of his studio and of his parents' house – thinks he will go bankrupt. Longs to go to the Front and be killed. He looks very ill it is utterly heartbreaking.'[35] And in October, Rex wrote to Henry Uxbridge, Caroline's younger brother:

> I have been <u>petrified</u> – in its real sense, not scared to death but turned to stone – by this long drawn out <u>intensely boring</u> nightmare . . . it's a curious feeling, being turned to stone; one doesn't feel hot or cold, just very <u>very</u> cool with no inter- est in oneself and not much in anyone else. One is left with no sense of living or urgency (I'll say it first: I never had much) and as it takes millions of years to petrify the feeling is that one will last a good many more which is quite a dreary prospect . . . I am just finishing this wretched room . . . it has been the longest and most arduous and boring of any that I have done. Well, there will be no more which is a pleasant relief.[36]

He had been considering military service since February. 'I'm trying to get myself all mixed up in the Territl: army', he had written to Henry Uxbridge that month.[37] Rex's undoubtedly genuine desire to fight for his country was no doubt influenced by the anti- appeasement views of Duff Cooper and Winston Churchill, from whom he had received artistic guidance while they were out paint- ing landscapes together. After Duff's resignation from the Admiralty in 1938, Rex had responded vehemently to a fellow guest's com- ment doubting that the country was well armed enough to go to war: 'Surely that's nothing to do with it! We should go to war if we think it right to do so – not because we're sure we're going to win.'[38] But by September 1939, the idea of joining up had a dual purpose. It was an opportunity to escape from the stagnancy of his work and his life. But, as Edith's diary entry reveals, it was also a gesture imbued with a characteristically chivalrous heroism and, for her, a worrying fatalism.

In August Edith had taken a brief respite from her mayoral duties and the town's preparations for the coming war and travelled up to Chatsworth in Derbyshire to stay with the Duchess of Devonshire, an old friend. The Duke left urgently for London and a meeting of the House of Lords. Once there, he sent for an estate lorry to take valuable paintings back to Chatsworth from the Devonshires' house in Carlton Gardens, saying that he had learnt that London was to be bombed within the next few days. And then the lorry was cancelled and it seemed that Hitler was backing down. And so rumour and uncertainty coloured the days. No wonder then that Edith sensed a charged poignancy in the peaceful late-summer beauty of the Peaks: 'There seemed to be something ominous in the air', she later recalled, 'as if a snow-storm should suddenly sweep across a harvest field. The sheaves would still be standing in their hyles; the greater part of the heavens would still have the brilliant blue of an August day, yet a cloud would have hastened by, portending the coming of another season.'[39]

Part Five

❖

PAINTING FROM LIFE

25: *Commission*

❖

It is thrilling & magnificent & lovely to know that you are being actually heroic isn't it? That what you are doing is really fine & absolutely the top as a way of behaving.

Rex to Caroline, October 1940

Edith hurried back to Wilton from Derbyshire in her car and saw not a single soldier on the journey home. 'There seemed to be more war on the wireless than in the world', she observed.[1] But on 1 September 1939 as German tanks rolled into Poland the first consignment of evacuated schoolchildren rolled into Wilton in a fleet of buses. Edith, the other ARP officers and the families that were to host the children were waiting to receive an entire junior school, including its teachers and caretakers. The buses started to arrive in the evening and a stream of chattering, excited children clutching bundles of luggage and gas masks poured out into the Wilton school yard. 'They looked very gay and evidently treated this as an extended "children's country holiday excursion" and as great fun', Edith later wrote.[2] After a rather chaotic start the Chief Billeting Officer encouraged the children into an orderly queue and established a system of registration and distribution. After several hours of driving children to their new homes Edith returned home to meet her own evacuees, three little girls, all under the age of eight and the youngest only five. She went upstairs to find them in the Trellis Room which had been converted into a dormitory, dressed in their nightgowns and kneeling beside their beds saying their prayers, as Phyllis sat beside them in a chair.

For the next few days evacuees continued to arrive and a Welfare Committee was established to oversee the process of finding homes for them. By the end of the week about 500 children and teachers had arrived in Wilton. Now gas masks became mandatory, the blackout was strictly observed from dusk until dawn and church bells across the country were silenced. The Pembrokes' chauffeur came to paint white stripes along Edith's car so that it would show up in the blackout. Her sister-in-law Esther arrived two days later from London, as war was officially declared. Edith cared little for Esther with her cockney accent and vulgar ways, and the thought that she might now be with her for the duration of the war depressed Edith immensely; her diary, perhaps more than ever, became her refuge.

As in many journals written during the war, Edith's diary entries oscillate between the details of her daily life, her observations about nature, the countryside, the seasons, comments about herself, her work and her friends and news of the world at war. The wireless, as for most of the country, was her chief source of information; it was a lifeline to events beyond the little Wiltshire town. At the beginning of the war regional branches of the BBC closed so that there was one national service and each programme now began with the words: 'This is the BBC Home Service'. Edith followed the day-to-day unfolding of the war and relayed it to her diary: Chamberlain's resignation in May 1940 (a 'brave and patriotic man'[3]), in the following year Hess's defection ('stupendous news'[4]) and the German assault on Moscow ('terrifying'[5]). Significant political figures were inevitably subjected to character analysis. She particularly admired Churchill: 'Heard Winston address the French people in v. amusing 18th Century accent', she wrote in October 1940; 'I mean like the French of the 1st Duke of Marlborough when English ambassadors despised foreign languages too much to speak them, and wilfully mispronounced; anglicising everything'.[6]

At the beginning of the new term it was decided that the Daye House was too far from the school and that Edith's girls would have to be moved closer to town. 'They howled as they went, and my cook and I nearly did the same.'[7] To distract them, she took them en route to see Arthur Street's cows being milked. The city girls were fascinated by the strange mechanical process and the steaming, noisy beasts jostling one another in the parlour. Edith returned to the Daye House and was saddened by the sight of the empty dormitory. Her little charges had stayed for less than a week. By the end of the month Edith was still dealing with the impact of the huge influx of people on the town. 'The children are now all happily settled but the mothers with children under school age can <u>never</u> be.' The plan was that these mothers should be allowed access to their hostesses' kitchens to cook for them-selves. But as Edith noted, 'Only a very impractical man could have thought of 2 women cooking 2 separate meals on a tiny range in a tiny kitchen. It can't be, and if the guest mothers <u>don't</u> cook, they have nothing to do. They walk out with their children morning, noon and night and criticise their Hostesses. Having had a house of their own they are now on the edge of someone else's housekeeping.'[8] These were the things keeping Edith on her toes in the first month of the war.

Rex had decided to apply for a commission soon after war was declared. But his first application was rejected in spite of a letter of recommendation from Duff Cooper. At the beginning of Octo-ber Edith arranged for him to meet Lieutenant General Alan Brooke, then in charge of Southern Command and stationed at Wilton. 'I have arranged a rapprochement for him with the C in C who thinks his drawing will be wanted in a special post.'[9] The following day Edith and Rex walked along the river onto the Palladian Bridge and for a moment there was no discussion of war as they silently 'absorbed in the beauty of the park'.[10] Later that day Rex met with Brooke and made it clear to him that he wanted to be at the front, not painting propaganda. Brooke conceded that it was 'a question of conscience' and that he wouldn't force him to change his mind.[11]

Eventually Rex applied to the Welsh Guards and was accepted.

But as it turned out, he was not granted an emergency commission until the following March and was not ordered to join his regiment as a second lieutenant until the beginning of June 1940. 'R can't decide . . . Kenneth Clark says the artist should [be] providing art <u>regardless of the war</u> in order to preserve civilisation for which the soldiers fight or whether he ought to fight too', Edith wrote in November. 'R has joined Welsh Guards but is not sure if this is cowardice or not. <u>It is not.</u> It's his sincere and right conviction.'[12] For Rex it was a typically quixotic gesture; at the age of thirty-four, he threw himself into war as quickly and as passionately as into a love affair. 'I know I shall make an idiotic soldier, but then what else could I do', he wrote to Lord Anglesey. 'I expect I've been an awful fool, but I <u>had</u> to make up my mind for once and quickly'.[13]

Had he waited, it is possible that he might have been selected as an Official War Artist but by the time his name appeared on a list he was already committed to his regiment. At some point before he joined his unit, Rex was offered work in the Camouflage Department but he declined the job. He wanted to be a part of the action and Edith admired his noble stance. 'To accept any other job would be impossible', he told Cecil Beaton, who was himself planning to join the Camouflage Department, hoping, like many in the art world, to find work for which his talents would be useful.[14] Others, who knew Rex less well, were surprised by his decision and considered it rather ridiculous: 'anyone more unsuitable I cannot imagine', Chips Channon wrote in his diary.[15]

In September 1939 Laurence married Jill Furse at Salisbury Cathedral. Despite Edith's disappointment that he, not Rex, had fallen in love with Jill, she was enchanted by the romance of a hurried wartime wedding, later recalling that: 'the bride had appeared, floating up that long reach of nave, like a spirit form. Her wedding dress seemed to be made of pale mist . . . her face spoke dazzled wonder, as though, in this dark week of the world's history, she hardly dared to be so happy.'[16]

At the beginning of 1940 Rex travelled north to stay with

Lutyens's handsome daughter Ursula, Viscountess Ridley, at Blagdon in Northumberland to paint portraits of her children. With heavy snow falling on the estate in a soothing, silencing shroud, Rex spent his time skating with Ursula's children and painting with them beside the fire. There he painted what he considered his finest portrait to date, of Ursula's five-year-old adopted daughter Laura, pink-cheeked, dressed in a miniature hussars uniform and beating a drum.

In another portrait Laura sits surrounded by paint pots beside a glowing fire contemplating the picture she is about to begin. The painting is a window onto a domestic scene of which Rex was only temporarily a part. Perhaps he was seduced by the family atmosphere at Blagdon. Whilst staying there Rex began a relationship with Ursula who was a year older than he was and unhappily married. Some years earlier Laurence had had an affair with her too. Rex knew this but not, perhaps, that she had also then miscarried his brother's baby. Years later, Ursula wrote to Laurence offering a refreshingly frank account of her relationship with his brother and her insightful thoughts about Rex's sexuality:

> He and I would sit up for hours talking in the firelight, talking until we went to bed – together. We were not either of us in love, and we were both making love to a dream or trying to lay a ghost: he of Caroline and I of you. We both wept a good deal – for ourselves and for each other. He wanted me to have a child by him . . . Caroline kept him in an agony of unfulfilled desire – and yet I don't think he could ever have given real happiness to a woman. He was infinitely loving, but could neither find nor give the love he longed for with his imagination, which was greater than his emotions, or desires could ever attain. He had such a strong streak of homosexuality in him, which his imagination wouldn't admit, but I am sure that speaking purely erotically he might have been happier. He was like a child or another woman as a lover. I think the only reason I ever went to bed with him was to try to give him confidence and reassurance sexually.[17]

Rex had decided to give up his studio not long after the war had begun. 'I have parted from my darling Fitzroy Square for ever and aye', he had written sadly to his brother as his carpets were taken up and his urns bundled off in boxes.[18] He had then gone to stay with his parents at the Walton Canonry and for some peaceful weeks lived a cosy life of painting and reading with 'deep sleepy quiet all day long, with yellow leaves drifting down and an occasional bell tolling', as he told Henry Uxbridge.[19] It was a glimpse of a possible future, a longed-for future. But he knew that his days there were numbered. In April 1940 the army requisitioned the Canonry and his parents went to stay with relations at Bierton in Buckinghamshire. Rex would never return to live in the Close.

Now essentially homeless, Rex wrote to Edith: 'It was agony to leave that delicious house and the garden with the swans sailing gently past at its foot . . . still more painful was the feeling of having once again no <u>home</u> which – though you may not know it – is a terribly important feeling for me . . . the future is so <u>completely</u> obscured isn't it'.[20]

Rex painted a self-portrait wearing his uniform on the day that it arrived in the summer of 1940. At the beginning of March he had been offered the drawing room of a flat belonging to Liz Paget, now married to Raimund von Hofmannsthal. In a letter to Henry Uxbridge he wrote that he had 'just the minimum ingredients – easels, a chair, table and bed. The painting light is <u>wonderful</u>.'[21] There he continued his affair with Ursula Ridley, terrified that Caroline, whom he still saw from time to time, would find out. And there he painted himself as a second lieutenant, on the balcony of 27 York Terrace with Regent's Park behind him. In the painting he sits on the balustrade, the shoes and buttons of his new uniform shining, with one hand in his pocket, the other clutching a glass of gin and Dubonnet. To his right, a tray of drinks and a bundle of paintbrushes; to his left, his cap, gloves, Sam Browne belt and walking stick beside him on the chair. Behind Rex the sky is blue and people saunter through the sunny park below. He sits in the shadow of the building, a sombre, diffident, contemplative figure in his dark service dress, belying the informal, debonair pose, with his mouth set and his eyes obscured by the shade. This is the same Byronic Rex of earlier portraits but older and imbued with a new sense of purpose. Edith thought the portrait 'enchanting'.[22]

In those last weeks before he joined the guards Rex worked on designs for a new ballet for Sadler's Wells, *The Wise Virgins*, choreographed by Frederick Ashton, with music by Bach arranged by William Walton. Staying with Edith for his last weekend of freedom in May, Rex painted her dressed in pink, perched on the wall beside the Daye House gate, in the shade of the yew trees. She sits with a hand on her hip, as if waiting impatiently for him to join her on a sightseeing expedition. Sunlight glints through gaps between the leaves and the open gate beckons the friends out towards the sunlit road and into the landscape beyond it. It was his most impressionistic painting to date, soft, loose, lacking focus; it is the essence of *dolce far niente*, the days of which Rex knew were numbered.

With Edith he discussed his 'unhappiness over love'.[23] But it seems that he didn't tell her of his new relationship with Ursula Ridley and he could never discuss with her the sexual anxieties and desires, which, as Ursula suggested, he could barely acknowledge to himself. To Edith, Caroline remained the focus of Rex's love and the chief source of his sorrow. To reveal anything more would have been to shatter her romantic vision of him. To Edith, Rex was a hero, and when he left the Daye House before joining his regiment, she wrote: 'I know not when I shall see him again', sounding in turn, rather like his anguished heroine.[24]

'I am certainly not <u>resolved</u> against marriage, and <u>might</u>, of course, marry,' Rex confessed to his brother, 'but frankly I think now that I shall probably never do so. It is rather late in the day'.[25] He realized that he would never be able to achieve the contentment his brother had found, telling a friend: 'now I've seen real happiness I know for certain I could never find it.'[26]

By now Caroline and Audry were working as drivers for the Auxiliary Rescue Service and living together in a flat in Chelsea. When the Blitz began Caroline worked tirelessly, driving four men and their stretchers to wherever bombs had fallen, seeing horrific sights, the memories of which would never leave her. 'You do not know how proud I am of you', wrote Rex to Caroline that year:

> & how much it makes me love & admire you for the way you continue with your perilous job in London & it is all the finer & more wonderful for your being able to give it up & retire to comparative safety (at Plas Newydd) if you chose. But it is thrilling & magnificent & lovely to know that you are being actually heroic isn't it? that what you are doing is really fine & absolutely the top as a way of behaving. Even though nobody <u>says</u> it (for so many are doing the same) still it must be a lovely warm, happy feeling to <u>know</u> that you are being unselfish & truly courageous.[27]

Later, after the Blitz had ended, Caroline drove secret papers around London and towards the end of the war she would work in a factory soldering wires for radios. 'She loved the working girls that she sat alongside, who all talked of sex as a fine art', her son remembered, 'with a delicacy and humour far removed from the usual upper-class's assumption of the lower orders just rutting and sleeping.'[28] For Rex and Caroline, though, there was no definitive ending to a relationship that had never really been a relationship in the fullest sense. They continued to meet occasionally throughout the war, but Rex eventually accepted that she would never marry him, and he told his brother that he knew he could never make her happy.

Rex and Ursula spent a final weekend together before he set off for training. They went to Brighton, that favoured getaway for countless adulterous lovers, so close and yet so far from London. They walked and lay upon the Downs; Rex read Keats and Kipling's 'If' to her. 'Poor Rex went off to the Army like a boy to school', Ursula wrote to her mother in June; 'I helped him buy

his equipment . . . He seemed so helpless and hopeless'.[29] Rex
too felt as if he was going back to school as he headed off to
the Training Battalion at Colchester, writing to Henry Uxbridge:
'I don't know any of the "new boys" in my draft and have had that
awful feeling in the tummy for days now that one had when waiting for a tanning'.[30]

One of Rex's first lectures gave the new recruits instructions
for operating against tanks and he dutifully began to write the
'5 Rules against the Tank' in his army notebook. But reality had
always nudged into fantasy in his work and in the margins, and
taking over most of the page, he drew a baroque tank with a turret
like the cupola of a basilica, rumbling over a bridge. Beneath it
flows a river that falls into the mouth of a mythical beast, as if at
Tivoli. A bucolic shepherd sits beneath a tree playing pan pipes
and a gondola sails languidly beneath the bridge. It was entirely
instinctive for Rex to retreat into classical fantasy. But though he
would fill his notebooks with doodles beside his lecture notes as
he had as a bored schoolboy, it seems that in the scholastic atmosphere of discipline, uniformity and male camaraderie, Rex began
to feel a new sense of freedom and of the present rather than the
past.

Setting out one day with an easel and canvas to East Mersea,
a little village near the Essex coast, he had begun a small painting
of a sunny landscape with various buildings, a church tower
amongst trees and a small brick cottage with outbuildings clad
in corrugated iron. It is an ordinary little scene and painted in a
soft, impressionist style. But despite, or perhaps because of, the
ordinariness of the subject there is a feeling of summer and of
freedom. Rex placed himself in the foreground of his picture,
painting at an easel. No longer would he have to paint from his
imagination unless he chose to; released from the demands of
patrons, he was now free to paint from reality. Another painting
from this time, *Portrait Group at Colchester*, is a view of a subaltern's dormitory. Rex sits on his bed tying a shoelace; two other

men are in the room, one writing and the other reading. At last Rex had become the action rather than the spectator. And there would be no more solitary, brooding self-portraits.

26: 'The Conditional'

❖

> Mayors are not combatants but I shall have to use my powers of
> control and the feeding and protection of my people will be my
> concern. I pray I may be able to do it rightly.
>
> Edith Olivier's Diary, 1 February 1941

In the months after war had been declared and once the fear of
imminent attack began to subside, in its place came uncertainty,
a sense of anti-climax. The air-raid shelters stood waiting, barrage
balloons hung in a sky marred only by clouds, gas masks came
out of their boxes and parents wondered why they had sent their
children away to unknown people in unknown places. Submar-
ines and ships sank far away at sea, someone tried, and failed, to
assassinate Hitler and the only reality at home was the blackout
and the many other inconveniences this unseen war had wrought.
But the war was getting closer. German troops massed on the
Dutch and Belgian borders. Holland flooded its defences and put
out its lights. Russia invaded Finland. In Edith's fiction, the First
World War represents a turning point in the lives of her characters, a paradigm shift that forces them out of the microcosm of
their world, beyond the narrative of their lives, into something
bigger than themselves. So it had been for Edith herself, and it
was again.

Edith had no time to contemplate the uncertainty that winter
of 1939. She had been re-elected as Mayor. Now that the dust
had settled after the novelty of the evacuees' arrival had worn off,

it was a full-time job to keep the peace between the town and country contingents who were learning to live amongst each other, as well as maintaining the welfare of the evacuee schoolchildren. To bring everyone together Edith started an afternoon club for mothers and babies, both from Wilton and those who had been evacuated. Later she organized concerts with visiting artistes such as Jelly d'Aranyi, Beatrice Lillie and Olga Lynn. From time to time a small crisis would occur. Once an expectant mother arrived howling for her children who had been billeted in a different place from her, and Edith warned the Billeting Officer that if he didn't resolve the situation swiftly the woman would be expectant no more. The situation became even more complicated in November when refugees began to arrive from Czechoslovakia and Vienna having fled just in time, as well as 500 soldiers and medical staff from a hospital train.

At Christmas Edith threw a party for these arrivals from abroad. Knowing that they would be homesick for Christmas trees, Edith found one, decorated it with candles and placed it on the tea table. As so few of her guests could speak English, Imma, soon to marry and move to Canada, was recruited to act as translator. One Viennese lady told them of Christmases at home, of the illuminated trees in the squares, of Christmas markets, of coffee and pastries filled with fruit and almonds, of Midnight Mass and Tyrolean snow. All now lost to them.

On Christmas Day Edith went to the Michael Herbert Hall to visit the soldiers at the Christmas dinner she had organized and to which her guests had been allowed to invite a friend from home, 'a most rollicking roysterous meal'. She listened to the King's broadcast and admired the bravery with which he persevered after '2 <u>very</u> bad stammering break-downs when one felt he must throw up the sponge and hand it over to someone else'. That evening Esther opened a bottle of champagne and they sat in the Long Room listening to Gracie Fields singing at a concert for the Air Force in France. 'The noise she makes is hideous but her gay good humour and spirit and vitality gets it across and it's marvellous to hear her, knowing she is really desperately ill.'[1]*

A slew of articles about Edith began to appear in magazines and newspapers and her celebrity was the subject of some awkward exchanges at the Town Hall. *Queen* hailed her as 'the moving spirit in Wilton's war work' and 'the right woman in the right place'. 'Under the leadership of their Mayoress, Miss Edith Olivier, M.B.E., the people of this West Country town are setting a fine example in every kind of war-work', it continued, featuring a photograph, taken by Cecil, of Edith and Lady Pembroke with her consignment of forty children from Kentish Town, all under five, on the lawn at Wilton.[2] 'Their language was appalling, and a great surprise to us country people', wrote Edith, 'but I often wonder what the effect will be on those slum babies of the memory in after life of those months in one of the famous great houses of England'.[3]

There had even been articles published about Edith as far away as Australia. In the New Year an article appeared in *Vogue* entitled 'Wiltshire in Wartime' about the grand ladies of the county and their war effort. It described Lady Pembroke and Juliet Duff doling out coffee and doughnuts to the soldiers, and others whose houses had been taken over by evacuated boarding schools or children's hospitals. Also mentioned and much praised was 'Miss Edith Olivier . . . the life and soul of the town'. It spoke of the 'quiet charm and dignity' with which Edith had led the procession on Armistice Day and featured a photograph of Edith at the Wilton war memorial. '. . . Oh yes', the article concluded, 'after touring Wiltshire, there is no doubt at all there's a war on.' *Vogue's* entire issue that month was dedicated, unsurprisingly, to women at war. It opened with a manifesto, 'Faith in Fashion', which implored its readers to dress well for the sake of the country. It featured 'The Diary of a War Bride', recipes for stew ('stew has the sturdy peasant virtues which win wars')

---

*   She was recovering after surgery for cervical cancer.

and an article headed 'Fashions and Crisis', which looked back at fashion in the Great War and the French Revolution. A Moss Bros advertisement with a model in an ATS (Auxiliary Territorial Service) uniform promised that 'your uniform can satisfy your own preconceived notions of elegance as well as the critical eye of the Commandant.'[4]

Edith had lost none of her faith in fashion. There is a photograph of her entertaining officers at a dinner in January 1940. She sits at a table, flanked by two of them, looking elegantly diminutive in the enormous mayoral throne, dressed in a slim-fitting, dark velvet evening dress with narrow white straps. Her arms and shoulders are bare. She appears to wear her mayoral tiara and chain more like chic accessories than the formal trappings of office. One arm rests casually on the arm of the chair, the other holds aloft a long cigarette holder and she smiles, almost provocatively, at the camera. The person in the photograph looks confident and feminine, as she holds court in a room full of men. Even at sixty-seven, Edith did not dress, or act, like an old maid.

Before the war began, in March 1938, Edith had gone to see Cecil at Ashcombe and talked with him as he walked about in a black-and-white dressing gown. He told her that he was bored with photography and that he wanted to become a writer. 'He will never be other than a secondrate journalist in that line', wrote Edith; 'he must go on with the visual arts.'[5] What Cecil may not have told her, and what, no doubt, precipitated this change of heart, beyond a certain feeling of weariness about his career, was that his New York bubble had burst and he had returned from America in disgrace. He had filled an illustration for *Vogue's* society pages with anti-Semitic remarks that could only be seen with a magnifying glass. Unfortunately for Cecil someone had used one and the news, at a time when the Nazi treatment of Jews was horrifying the Western world, did not go well for him. He had been warned to remove them by his editor but had refused, claiming that they were about certain New York circles he disliked rather than Judaism generally. Condé Nast sacked him and his American career was in ruins. He would still be feeling the reverberations in the 1960s.

The war, when it came, was a liberation for Cecil, as it was for Rex, and it marked a turning point in his career. But it didn't happen at once. While he waited to see if the Camouflage department would accept him he worked as the telephone operator on the control switchboard at Fugglestone House in Wilton. Then at the end of the year he went to London to discuss the possibility of taking photographs for the war effort and was soon at work taking portraits of generals with eye patches and ministers at their desks, no frills, no cellophane and no doe-eyed debutantes in sight. The following year he was granted official War Photographer status, which took him all over the world.

But before that, in December 1939, Cecil decided to put on a charity pantomime to entertain the troops and with John Sutro to help him write it, and Simon Carnes, Juliet Duff's constant companion, to produce it, his plans were quickly under way. *Heil Cinderella* starred, amongst others, Olga Lynn and Cecil as the Ugly Sisters, Lady Pembroke as the Queen, Lady Margaret Drummond Hay as Prince Charming, David Herbert as the Page and Edith as the Witch. Cecil designed the sets and Rex drove over from Salisbury to help paint the scenery. The preparations quickly descended into farce. Rehearsals, for which Edith dashed from Council meetings, were not taken quite as seriously as Cecil had hoped. The first night should have been New Year's Eve but it had to be postponed when Cecil lost his voice. Later, Cecil and David fell out over a wig and Edith overheard them saying spiteful things to one another. On the new first night, 2 January, Lady Pembroke bowed out with laryngitis and Juliet Duff stepped in as the Queen but Cecil offended Olga Lynn who had to be lured back onto the stage with compliments. Lady Pembroke resigned in disgust as President of the company. On the second night Augustus John was in the audience and drunkenly mistook his daughter Vivien, dancing alone onstage to Chopin, for a row of pretty ballerinas. The audience was oblivious to the unintentional dramas on stage and the play, in which an Ugly Sister's clothes hung from the Siegfried Line and Prince Charming kept a brandy flask in her gas mask, was deemed a great success. Articles appeared in *Country Life*, the *Tatler,* the *Bystander,* and the *Daily Express* under the headline: 'Mayfair-in-the-Shires gives the troops a Cinderella pantomime'. 'The lady mayor of Wilton (Miss Edith Olivier)', it stated, 'painted her face blue, wore a double scroll of blackout paper for a hat, and nearly stole the show with unearthly cackles as the Wicked Witch.'[6] There was a certain irony in the tone of *The Times*'s coverage: '*Heil Cinderella*, the pantomime produced by Mr. Cecil Beaton and rehearsed at Wilton House, where Shakespeare may have acted . . .'[7] Cecil planned to take the pantomime on tour to various coastal theatres and then on to London. Edith was most relieved that her duties in Wilton meant that she wouldn't be joining them but she sent them on their way to Brighton with a scroll for the 'Mayor of Brighthelmstone' begging his welcome to her 'travelling players'.

Summer time began early, on 25 February, allowing an extra hour of light in the evening to make the blackout less dangerous. On 9 April Germany invaded Denmark, which surrendered after two days. From there it invaded Norway and met with the resistance of the Norwegian army along with British and French troops. That day Edith went up to London to lunch with Rex at the Astoria and for him to paint her portrait. He still had two months to wait before joining his regiment at the beginning of June. One consequence of the war, now that he no longer had rooms to decorate, was that Rex began to paint more and more portraits and his technique grew ever more confident. Perhaps he had a vague idea of pursuing a career as a portraitist once the war was over. Now he was painting a picture of Liz Paget at her desk and another of her wearing a daffodil dress and stretched out against scarlet cushions on her sofa, perhaps in thanks for the loan of her drawing room, as well as a beautiful portrait of Ursula Ridley, a bow at her neck, her head tipped forward, her painted mouth slightly pursed and her eyes, carrying sadness, looking down into the distance. It is not a lover's portrait, but those of Caroline pale in comparison; he saw the woman rather than the idea of one. According to Laurence, Rex frequently asked Ursula to join him on leave during the war. But she never did. 'I have a sense of guilt because I didn't fall in love with him', Ursula later told Laurence. 'I thought it was bound to happen . . . But I couldn't. I was never really at ease with him'.[8]

In London, at the von Hofmannsthals' flat, Edith found Rex frantically at work on his sets for *The Wise Virgins*, due to open on the 24th, and she sat with him while he worked. They had seen little of each other; his father's illness (and Ursula Ridley) had kept him away from Wilton. That day they could talk only of the war but the next morning Edith arrived to sit for her portrait. The painting is perhaps a companion in mood to Rex's sober self-portrait in uniform. She sits in an armchair, wearing an old, dark pinstriped suit. The cool palette of dark brown and grey, pale blue and ivory, is warmed only by the glimpses of red in her shirt, scarf, lips and drop earrings.* The pale, rather grave face Edith thought looked 'severe'. But as with his own portrait, Rex wanted to portray his old friend with a new air of sobriety and seriousness. 'He says I do look stern, tho' my friends know I'm not so', she reassured herself in her diary.[9]

On 24 April Edith went to the first night of *The Wise Virgins* and thought Rex's designs better than the ballet itself. At the curtain call Rex was asked to appear. Suddenly the curtain fell behind him and he panicked in the solitude of the footlights and leapt off the stage into the auditorium. Perhaps to compensate for this embarrassment he drank too much at the after party and met Edith for lunch at Antoine's with a hangover and a 'violent headache'.[10]

Edith awoke to the news that Germany had invaded Holland and Belgium on 10 May. All day she listened to bulletins on the

---

* This portrait of Edith is owned by Wilton Town Council and is on display in the council chamber at Wilton Town Hall.

wireless and at 9 o'clock the news informed her that Chamberlain had resigned and that Winston Churchill was now Prime Minister. She was moved to hear Chamberlain's 'steady voice, with the breath coming quickly beneath it'. 'He has shown that he <u>is</u> great – and Hitler who thought to catch us squabbling, has got a united Govt. under the man he hates most.'[11] Hitler now had his sights on France and Edith spent her time organizing volunteer sharp-shooters to combat the German parachutists when they arrived. There were more evacuees to house and mothers of missing airmen to comfort. 'I am very bad at this', she wrote, 'as when I saw Mrs Parsons I could only weep <u>with</u> her, not comfort at all'.[12]

The German army crept ever closer to the French coast. 'Germans at Boulogne', she wrote, 'so was Napoleon once.'[13] Sybil Colefax came for the weekend and was light relief with all her gossip about the King and Queen and the Duchess of Windsor, whose friend she had once been before the abdication. Three days later, though, the Belgian army collapsed leaving half a million British troops cut off in France. On 30 May Edith listened to reports on the wireless of the extraordinary evacuation from Dunkirk when destroyers and a fleet of little ships manned by volunteers sailed for France to rescue the trapped men. On the 4th she heard that 'the last man has been taken off Dunkirk. It's the most magnificent and <u>moving</u> episode', she wrote, but then added: 'there are 30,000 casualties'.[14] Next day she was horrified to discover that the decontamination room at the Town Hall was not gas proof and that work on it would have to begin again, urgently. Italy declared war on 10 June and by the 13th she was writing that 'Paris seems doomed'. That day at a meeting the Council discussed how best to advise the townspeople about suspected fifth columnists. 'It's a duty to tell the Police <u>anything you know</u>. They can follow up and act', she wrote, 'but to spread unfounded rumours is damnable and also libellous. Regy backed me well, saying rumour-mongers may soon be shot!'[15] The next day Edith heard the one o'clock news and learnt that the Germans had reached Paris. 'I couldn't help crying for a long time', she wrote. She was moved to hear the Queen speaking in French to the women of France. An 'SOS' took her out of her reverie and to the County Bench where, as magistrate, she had to deal with a prostitute who had disobeyed orders to keep away from the camps. 'She had a nice face and a bad record. Imprisoned for 2 months', she concluded.[16] Later, in October, Edith was the only magistrate on a murder case.

> Before me came a short, little soldier, with very black hair and eyes who yesterday shot his Sergeant. I asked if it could be an accident. The Police said No. They only gave evidence of arrest and thought the man had made a statement, this was not read, as he had no lawyer to defend him. So I heard nothing of the circumstances. But I looked on a man who yesterday killed someone. He looked a low type, but not a murderer – and his expression neither defiant, frightened nor desperate. He might have been up for being late on duty. But all day I could not forget him – and the man he killed and that he will doubtless die for it.[17]

In early June Rex had begun his training at Colchester, where he was taught how to read maps and how to use weapons. On 9 June he was happily painting at East Mersea on a few days' leave. From Colchester he moved to Sandown Park at Esher where the officers had quarters in the Royal Box. From there he wrote to Edith while sitting in the grandstand overlooking the famous racecourse, drawing a picture at the top of the letter to illustrate the point. On 23 June General Pétain's government capitulated to the Germans and France was divided in half. Edith wrote of 'a French General, de Gaulle', who in England was forming an army of French servicemen outside France that was being backed by the British government. 'Courage and faith in God alone can carry us thro' these dark perplexing days', she wrote in her diary,[18] while Rex wrote to her:

My darling Edith,

. . . I feel more loathing and disgust for that little group of craven self-seeking traitors at Bordeaux than I do for Hitler himself, don't you? – though none at all for France and only admiration and pity for her. Not because they found it necessary to give up in a desperate and overwhelming fight, but because these despicable creatures (without the smallest authority) are betraying their country without a thought or provision for the way in which it may be redeemed in the future, and without apparently any effort to hand over to us what little they can to help continue the struggle.

When one recalls that it was <u>they</u> who were so insistent upon the agreement between us, that neither ally should ever make terms with the enemy without the other's permission, it nearly brings on what Philip Sassoon would have called a 'bile storm'.

I'm afraid I haven't got much news darling Edith with which to make a letter and there is <u>so much</u> to be said about 'the situation' that I feel unable to touch on any part of it, except to say how deeply I feel with you, the <u>truth</u> of what is everywhere written, that our nation is tremendously strengthened and steeled in its determination to conquer in the end by this present catastrophe. It really has been so curiously marked with almost <u>everyone</u> this general sense of being stronger from now on, instead of weaker – as though the entire nation had started with a gasp of horror and ended with a great sigh of relief. Thank God we have <u>at last</u> got rid of all our allies! goes up the cry, which must seem madly funny to the rest of the world – and it does make me laugh too – but I think we also all realise now with a thrill of delight that we have at last reached strength and wisdom as well as what is funny and glorious . . .

Goodbye darling Edith, Much love to you from Rex.[19]

At Sandown Rex was given a studio in the grandstand and there painted several portraits. One of these, of Lieutenant Gilbert

Ryle, an Oxford philosopher in peacetime, shows a well-modelled, brooding and somewhat grimy face rendered in murky shades of sage and brown. It was perhaps a little too self-consciously militaristic but another portrait, of the regiment's cook, would remain the pride of the Sergeants' Mess for many years after the war. Sergeant Isaacs sits formally, facing outward, his legs apart and his head turned to one side. The fleshy, gleaming face and the bulky body straining in the white cook's suit were painted in a neutral palette that is almost monochrome, and with strong areas of light and shade in the creases and contours of the clothes. Perhaps Rex had the austere style of Vermeer in mind. Certainly, the use of natural light, the simple interior setting and the domestic scene glimpsed in the doorway behind the cook, of a figure washing dishes, suggest it. Though Rex still struggled to paint hands (those in the painting are unrealistically small, feminine and ill-formed), this portrait is one of his finest.

It is perhaps unsurprising that Sir Kenneth Clark, Director of the National Gallery and chair of the War Artists' Advisory Committee, should have overlooked Rex for a war artist's commission in the early days of the war. Rex's pre-war work in the public domain included book illustrations, and commercial and theatre design. Of his murals, only the Tate refreshment room was on display to the public; the others, along with his portraits, were privately owned. Even so, Clark would have known his work and perhaps dismissed Rex as a society interior decorator, stuck in a fictional golden age without any interest in the present. But the Commission, according to art historian Frances Spalding, 'transformed war artists into a privileged breed: they were made honorary Captains, given the use of cars and other forms of travel. For them it was . . . a cosy war'.[20] And, as Spalding says, 'Even Kenneth Clark later admitted that the general level of work was mediocre and tame'.[21]

Rex's painting of the subaltern's dormitory, in which he had included himself sitting on a bed and tying his shoelace, is an intimate glimpse into a scene of men at war. It portrays something of the camaraderie but also the homogeneity, austerity and lack of privacy associated with life in the army. It was one of a number of studies of soldiers and of army life that Rex would paint during the war. These paintings are never visceral; rather they are imbued with a gentle sensitivity and affection, but without nostalgia or elaboration. They represent his maturing style and his desire to paint scenes from life without imaginative or illusory gloss. As an officer in the Guards Armoured Division, Rex was not destined to see combat for some years. But from June 1940, he was one of the many who trained tirelessly in preparation for the planned invasion. It is ironic that Rex, dismissed as a whimsical fantasist, was ultimately in closer contact with the realities of the war than many official war artists.

On 1 July Rex came up to London to take Edith out for dinner. 'He looks beautiful in uniform and much better in health tho this may be by being sunburnt', she wrote. 'I thought his mind a little <u>fettered</u> as if he had been checked in his lovely natural free way of thinking and speaking. Says it's less bad than he expected. I asked him if he much liked any of the other officers. He says he quite likes most of them and <u>absolutely hates</u> none!' That night he returned to Sandown Park after dinner at Antoine's.[22]

'Rex Whistler and Caroline came to dinner last night, Rex with a tough military moustache. He says there are not so many hairs, but each one is as thick as a hedge, so they make a brave show', Diana Cooper wrote to her son that month (Caroline was evidently having an affectionate moment).

> He was funny about his agonies as an inexperienced subal-
> tern in the Guards. He was told suddenly to form his men up
> and march them to church. Every order he shouted produced
> greater chaos, soldiers scuttling in opposite directions, form-
> ing sixes and sevens instead of fours (or is it threes now?). At
> last he found himself isolated in the middle of the parade-
> ground. One day's more experience would have taught him
> when in doubt to say 'Carry on, Sergeant-Major.' Standing in

a row to be inspected, he realised that he had forgotten his collar. The Colonel inspecting felt this so apoplectically that he was robbed of speech, which did not return to him until he came to the next officer, who got the full blast of blimp rage for having a loose shoelace. Poor Rex, he's not suited to the life.[23]

After his initial blunder there were no more notable ones and Rex settled into the intensive months of training. And it was not long before his artistic skills were being put to use. Soon he was making military drawings, maps, panoramas for target practice, and later even a new design for the regimental badge of the Welsh Guards. He also drew an illustration of the correct layout of kit for inspections. It is technically accurate, but of course, it is more than a diagram. The brushes, polishes, gloves and shoes of the kit are drawn with the same charm and character of his peacetime work and he could not resist surrounding the title of the drawing with an elaborate, albeit military-themed, baroque cartouche.

With France fallen England expected to be the next target. 'This is said to be the week in which we are to be invaded', Edith wrote in her diary on 30 June.[24] Edith had posters pinned up to encourage volunteers to give blood for the Army Blood Volunteer Service, which included a personal appeal from the Mayor to her townspeople. On 6 June she sent a letter to the people of Wilton calling on them to face the coming days with 'COURAGE and CONFIDENCE'. She reminded them of King Alfred's victory over the Danes at Wilton in 871 and asked that they be prepared to defend Wilton with the same fighting spirit. She concluded the letter:

LIFT UP YOUR HEARTS
HOLD UP YOUR HEADS
And ENGLAND will never go under.[25]

Some weeks later the Battle of Britain began and though the German Luftwaffe greatly outnumbered the RAF it soon became clear that the RAF was holding its own. By 17 September, after a day of huge losses for the Luftwaffe, Hitler decided to postpone the invasion; he had other tactics to try. Ten days earlier the Blitz had begun and London was subjected to fifty-seven consecutive nights of bombing.

In June Wilton House had been requisitioned and was now the Headquarters of Southern Command and with this came the entire staff of an evacuated ministry. 'The neighbourhood became alive with military activity', Cecil would later write.

> The peaceful side-walks were crowded with soldiers carrying mugs on their way to and from the various canteens, the roads were jammed with traffic, the air filled with fumes of lorries and the motor-bicycle roaring of despatch riders. The Pembroke family lived in three rooms of their house. The Kent furniture was taken from the other rooms, the cloisters were emptied of statuary and the cube-rooms were boarded up with plywood while the innermost secrets of war were plotted within their walls. In the Park asphalt paths were laid down and hundreds of wooden huts sprang up, dark-green mushrooms under the cedars of Lebanon, and in all the formal flower beds, vegetables were planted.[26]

It horrified Edith that her beloved Wilton House was a potential target for German bombs and that the Double Cube, emptied of its masterpieces, was now a general's office, filled with maps. Worse, perhaps, was that a sentry now stood at her gate.

Six months later, Edith was having dinner in the Long Room with her niece Rosemary. Suddenly they heard two loud bangs as incendiary bombs fell to the north of the Daye House. 'None touched us but fires blazed along the river bank, red, orange, lurid, evil, garish and glittering', she wrote; 'some were greenish white – notably the only one on this side of the water.'[27] The plane continued to fly overhead and they heard bombs dropping further away. Edith rushed to the bridge to check that Wilton House was unharmed.

Not since the Civil War had the peace of this particular Arcadia been interrupted. Until the war the Daye House had always been enclosed in silence, something Edith's London friends always remarked upon. There was the rustling of wind in the trees, the occasional lowing of a cow and the call of birds in the woods, the owls at night and the throaty commotion of pheasants rootling about in the undergrowth. Now the sound of a pheasant meant distant bombs falling on Southampton whose vibrations they felt in the earth. At night the sky filled with the roar of German bombers en route to the Midlands or RAF planes heading to France or Germany. Now convoys of tanks trundled down the lane that ran beyond the Daye House gate. 'I believe that the word "<u>Park</u>" and "<u>Paradise</u>" have the same origin, and this was formerly easy to believe', Edith wrote. 'Now it seems that our paradise has been invaded, not by one devil in the silent slippery disguise of a serpent; but by the whole Hosts of Satan'.[28]

It was these changes to her little world that, towards the end of 1940, prompted Edith to begin writing a new book. In November she had been approached by Charles Fry, a friend of Cecil and a publisher at Batsford, to write a book about life in the country. For this he was offering £70, which she quickly accepted. The result was *Country Moods and Tenses – A Non-Grammarian's Chapbook*, a paean to the countryside, to its people and their way of life.* She described it as 'The Grammar of Country Life' and divided the book into five moods.[29] 'The Infinitive' relates to 'Nature's primal mood', the timelessness of the landscape, the lie of the land, so evident in Wiltshire and 'so entirely the countryman's atmosphere that he is hardly aware of it . . . It is the air he breathes, the serene silence falling ever on his ears.'[30] 'The Imperative' is dedicated to the weather, to 'the powers of Nature', the fruits and flowers of the seasons and the solace of a cosy fireside in winter.[31] 'The Indicative' is about travelling in the countryside,

---

* A chapbook was a small pamphlet containing tales, ballads, or tracts, usually sold by pedlars.

its roads and its signposts and sightseeing. 'In a sense it is true that a country house and garden create a world apart', she writes, 'yet country people always seem to be going somewhere.'[32] The Indicative, she laments, had been banished from the countryside; now no signs show the way and no villagers direct strangers for fear of fifth columnists in their midst. 'The Subjunctive' engages with human relationships and 'The Conditional', the last mood of the book, is about the changing countryside, modernity and her fears for the future. She describes the effect of war on her hitherto peaceful home. She laments the dying out of trades, the approach of universal education and the slipping away of local customs. She fears for the future of architecture but then, rather surprisingly, looks forward to the day when 'an enormous concrete viaduct – a line of solemn arches – might without incongruity carry a modern motor road over a valley from one down summit to another'; this no doubt written with the true heart of a sightseer.[33]

Edith wrote *Country Moods* in the classic Town versus Country mode with the latter the undoubted winner. At the close of the book she invokes an old fable, 'The Town Mouse and the Country Mouse': 'Le Rat de Ville doubtless thought his Turkey carpet set him several steps higher in the social scale than the Rat des Champs with his buttercups and daisies; but there came a common danger, which sent them both in search of country peace. Does not this recall memories of past months?'[34]

'The Past is a long road', she writes, 'vanishing into a distance veiled in rose-coloured mists. The Future is a short lane which very soon reaches a turning beyond which one cannot see. So a book written in the Present must draw its material mainly from the Past.'[35] And so Edith layers anecdotes, memories – the sound of birds, the scent of flowers, the flitting of moths – like sandbags against the ravages of time and war. The book is filled with photographs by Cecil and others. Rex illustrated the dust jacket with a cornucopia of wheat sheaves, barrels, apples, scythes, Ceres with her bounty, a mill wheel, a cockerel, a Gypsy caravan and, because death is a part of that infinite cycle of life and perhaps the final imperative, he added a gravestone and a skull. Edith sent a copy to the Queen, hand decorated by Rex and inscribed in her own hand: 'To Her Majesty the Queen with Humble Duty from the Author November 1941'. After all, the book was Edith's contribution to the war effort.

Amongst the fan letters she would receive in the years after the book's publication in 1941 are two written in praise of the curative value of Edith's brand of pastoral nostalgia. One is from an American woman, Katharine Allison Gurley, writing from New Jersey in 1944: 'It was only the other day I was glancing idly over the shelves of one of the Fourth Avenue bookshops, that I espied COUNTRY MOODS AND TENSES . . . in these troubled times those of us who find in books our release from sorrow and anxiety turn to them more than ever before'.[36] The other, a small note written on a postcard in 1943 and stamped 'Kriegsgefangenen-lager' is from a man called Malcolm Fry, an English prisoner of war being held at a camp in Germany: 'Dear Madam, I have just read *Country Moods and Tenses*. May I say how much I enjoyed your book. Having been in captivity since May 1940 I can assure you one is overwhelmed by a nostalgic craving for the beloved old things'.[37] Like much of her writing of the previous decade, the books that Edith wrote during the war represented stability, tradition, stoicism and gentility. They served to remind people what they were fighting to preserve.

The dawning of 1941 set the old way of life into even sharper relief. Edith was now Director of the County ARP Executive; she was attending Executive Emergency Meetings about fire watching and recruiting volunteers, and German raids were coming ever closer. A Luftwaffe plane strafed the streets of Salisbury and Wilton with machine-gun fire and the noise of guns practising near the Daye House had brought down the ceiling of the Long Room. Nonetheless, on New Year's Day, she again handed out bread to the parishioners, believing that now, more than ever, tradition was what kept the country from falling into the quagmire.

27: *Home*

❖

. . . the enchanting ideal longed-for country.

Rex to Edith, 19 May 1941

In October 1940 Rex's father had died after a long period of illness. On the day of his funeral Edith arrived at Salisbury Cathedral to find the casket containing his ashes standing in the choir, covered with a red silk pall and with candles burning around it. Beside it, alone, stood Rex, 'a rigid still figure in guard's officer's uniform'. His mother was too ill to attend and Laurence was not given leave, so Edith followed the ashes to the grave with Rex. 'His manners never fail him . . . He told me some of what he is enduring – all the small tortures which accompany bereavement', she wrote. 'Emptying pockets and drawers of the little treasures. But as we stood together I felt that though I think there are between our minds fewer barriers than exist between most people yet I am outside the pain of what he was holding within his pale impassive face. I <u>believe</u> he felt less desolate because I was there.'[1] Back at Sandown Park, Rex wrote to Caroline, telling her of his father's death and writing, emphatically, that 'my heart bleeds for poor darling Mother who loved him with an <u>extraordinary</u> singleness of heart far beyond everything else in the world.'[2]

Laurence now spent every leave with his wife Jill and their first baby in a Devon cottage.* Without a home of his own, Rex

---

* Simon, born on 10 September 1940. A sister, Caroline, known as Robin, was born four years later.

passed much of his leave as the guest of his friends. The time that he had stayed at Blagdon with the Ridley family would be echoed, although with less emotional intensity, many times throughout the war, at different homes and with different families. Rex delighted in the company of children. He loved to entertain them with rebus letters, reversible faces and picture games. He loved their spontaneity and responded to it in kind; he enjoyed their games and their emotional simplicity. Many of his friends' children would later remember him vividly; perhaps Rex's imagination allowed him to pass beyond the seemingly impenetrable barrier between adulthood and childhood and to connect with them.

Rex stayed several times with Christabel McLaren at Bodnant, an elegant, wisteria-clad Victorian house set in terraced gardens sloping down to the River Conwy, in North Wales. There he painted Christabel's young daughter Anne several times and to entertain her he drew impromptu illustrations for a story that her mother had written.* Another friend, Daphne, Viscountess Weymouth, who lived on the Longleat estate, later recalled Rex painting a portrait of her son, the future Marquess of Bath: '[Rex] taught my other children to draw fantastic faces, played drawing games with them and gave them caricatures of almost everybody they knew. I could hardly ever entice him out of the schoolroom, and when he did appear in the drawing-room it was always with two small boys at his heels'.[3]

Perhaps his loveliest portrait of a child was the one he painted of the eight-year-old John Jolliffe at his home at Mells in Somerset in 1941. 'All that I can remember of the occasion', Jolliffe later wrote, 'is how Whistler teased me by pretending to encourage me to have a swig at the turpentine in which he was about to clean his brushes'.[4] In the portrait the little boy is sitting on the stairs with his red setter beside him; the hall below is filled with the paraphernalia of family life, riding boots and a bank of coats hanging from hooks. Perhaps for Rex, this affectionate, poignant

---

* *The Story of Mr Korah,* published in 1954 by Michael Joseph.

portrait was an enticing glimpse of an intimate domestic world, a way of life that was closed to him.

But there was one place that would always be a home for him. 'I had a telephone call from Rex who has vanished from my life since the day of his father's funeral', Edith wrote in March 1941.[5] Driving home with him, she thought that 'it was new life to have Rex in the car seeing all that was beautiful as we came along in the car and valuing <u>that</u> more than anything still'.[6]

The Daye House was no longer Edith's alone though. It had become a lodging house. As well as Edith, Esther, the new cook Ethel and her baby, and those many friends who came for fleeting visits, Edith had begun to take paying guests, mostly officers working at Wilton House. And so she became a landlady, albeit with rather grand lodgers, her first the grandest of all, the Commander-in-Chief of the Home Forces, General Sir Alan Brooke. With his wife and young children Brooke had stayed at the Daye House for some weeks at the beginning of the war. 'It was a happiness to me to have this little family in my house', Edith later wrote.[7] Early in 1941 Major Tom Henn, a Cambridge English don in peacetime, now working in Intelligence, moved into the bedroom that Edith called the Canary Room, on the ground floor beneath her own room. He kept her abreast, in vague terms, of the actual progress of the war. A keen fisherman, Henn would disappear off to the river at night and Edith would hear him returning in the early hours, his waders squelching on the lawn outside her window. The household would wake the next morning to a catch of trout or grayling which they would grill for breakfast or have 'lurking in lettuce as a mayonnaise for luncheon', as Edith wrote.[8]

Throughout the first months of 1941 Edith's diary tells of nightly bombing in London. 'Barbarism has indeed returned', she wrote; 'the Germans can never again be part of the Commonwealth of Nations'.[9] A few days later, after one of the heaviest raids, Rex called Edith from Caterham where he been sent for further training. He told her that his studio had been bombed and that he wanted to bring the pictures that he had salvaged up to the Daye House for safekeeping. He arrived on 10 June with the paintings and new commissions to work on. As much as he disliked doing illustrations, when he was offered them he could not afford to refuse. *Königsmark*, published in 1938, was a historical romance set in the seventeenth century. Rex had been commissioned by the author, A. E. W. Mason, to make illustrations for a private copy for an advance of £100. Mason had sent him the full payment but it was several months before Rex acknowledged it, nudged into action by their mutual friend Christabel McLaren, and it was several months after that when Mason received his illustrations, drawn in a sensual, baroque style, in sepia touched with pink. Rex finished them, hurriedly, in unprepossessing digs in Caterham and perhaps they were rendered all the more beautiful by the aesthetic contrast of his surroundings. Rex continued to accept and complete commissions for the theatre and ballet, book illustrations and even designs for a film, often puzzling over the bizarre juxtaposition between his designs and the world of war.

At the Daye House that week in early May, Rex and Edith spent a day in the garden. Rex scythed the long, unkempt grass while Edith read aloud to him. 'Talked more easily with Rex than I have ever heard him talk with anyone', Edith wrote in her diary the following night.'[10] Once again, sixteen years after they had met, Edith and her house behind the high park wall at Wilton had become a sanctuary for Rex. 'I don't remember ever having been so astounded before by the beauty of Wiltshire', he wrote to her some days later. 'It seemed – seriously – to be scarcely credible – like the enchanting ideal longed-for country which one usually only sees so clearly in dreams or is conjured in the mind by Poetry.'[11]

Edith had invited Rex's mother to join them at the Daye House for a few days. But even now rivalry hung about the pages of her diary. Helen was 'still rather silly' she thought,[12] and walking with Rex and his mother in the park, she concluded that he 'doesn't admit that he finds her trying, but he <u>does</u>'.[13] Edith must have been delighted by Rex's admission to her in a letter, a few days later, that she, and not his mother, took pole position in his affections: 'I often feel', he wrote to her, 'that I understand and am closer to you than her'.[14]

That month Edith held a party to welcome an American hospital unit. 'The Bishop tried to make out that Wilton was quite eclipsed by Salisbury from the 13th Century till I put it back on the map! I begged him to read his history', she wrote in her diary. She returned home to lunch on trout mayonnaise with Sybil Colefax who was staying for the weekend. On the Saturday evening she gave a supper party for Sybil and invited David Herbert, now a wireless operator in the Merchant Navy. 'Sybil held the party with her London – political and other – gossip', she wrote.[15] That night the conversation was all about the defection of Hess. But news tired quickly these days. On 22 June Germany invaded Russia, which until this point had been maintaining a pro-German neutrality. Edith couldn't believe that such good news came with no ulterior motive on Hitler's part. 'This was the one subject of conversation all day', she wrote, 'though a sham fight came off here and Wilton House was unsuccessfully attacked. I came out of church at 12 into a cannonade at the gates. Regy P. rushing about at the head of his Home Guards and the Wilton people adoring the fun.'[16]

That summer Brian Howard visited Edith. She had not seen him for years and his behaviour was stranger and more mercurial than ever. He was then working for MI5 although he only told Edith that it was top-secret work. Though he had passionately denounced Nazism since long before the war Edith still couldn't bring herself to trust him. When a sentry was shot one night in the park while Brian was staying at the Daye House her suspicions grew even stronger and she was happy when he left Wilton.[*]

---

[*] Brian was working for MI5 but was dismissed in 1942. He then worked as a clerk for the RAF from which he was dismissed in 1944. After the war he began writing a biography of the writer Norman Douglas but his approach to

A more welcome visitor was Cecil, who now frequented the Daye House for help writing the text of his latest book. When he was not travelling the country or going abroad for his work for the Ministry of Information, he returned to Ashcombe where his mother and aunt still lived and where vegetables now grew in the flower beds. The photographs he was taking would become some of the most iconic of the war, his vision was maturing and, after years catering to the whims of society hostesses and fashion editors, he found the work exhilarating. Edith had received presentation copies of all his books but she was never as impressed by his writing as she was by his pictures, which made her all the more determined to help him. When later in the year he sent her a copy of *History under Fire* she was genuinely impressed by the images inside it. She wrote to tell him that it was 'a most moving creation. It is a real work of art, not the work of the camera which we have been so wearyingly told "cannot lie" but something really vital, seen by an artist, and made alive by him. Great tragedy must always have great beauty', she added. 'You make the sordid heaps of masonry which were once Wren buildings into something with a new beauty which they did not possess before. I don't mean that I prefer the ruins . . . but you have made these ruins <u>bearable</u> and <u>beautiful</u>!'[17]

Back in May Rex's battalion, the 2nd (Armoured) Battalion Welsh Guards, was sent to the camp at Codford St Mary near Warminster on the Salisbury road, about twelve miles from Wilton. Rex was given the command of a tank troop comprising three tanks and about fifteen men including his batman who was also a gunner on his own tank. After the months of training, mess life offered unexpected ease and days of leisure, ease which embarrassed him when he thought of Caroline driving ambulances in London.

---

work was no more dedicated than it had ever been. He spent the next few years drifting around Europe with his young lover and they were expelled from several countries for immorality. His health was failing and he was increasingly reliant on drugs and alcohol. Brian committed suicide on 15 January 1958 at the age of fifty-two, some days after the accidental death of his lover.

But then he found a way to keep himself occupied. The huts at Codford were miserably unprepossessing and after one particularly unsuccessful mess dinner, Rex, with his eye for creating an ideal world out of an inferior one, drew a pair of humorous cartoons entitled *The Dining-Room as it was* and *The Dining-Room as it might be*. In the 'before' drawing, the mess is a squalid, chaotic shack lit by viciously bright overhead lights. At one side, officers huddle around a small table and in the centre of the room, tray, glass and bottle are sent flying as a waiter trips over another man crouching on the floor as he writes a letter. In the improved version, Roman-style, oval portrait plaques of the Squadron Leaders line the walls of what appears to be an elegant tent with red-and-white-striped tent poles, as at Port Lympne. The room is lit by table lamps and the officers sit at spacious tables or recline in comfortable chairs as the waiters go niftily about their work. So persuasive were Rex's suggestions that the Commanding Officer allowed him to carry them out, although his scheme was applied instead to the anteroom which was kept off-limits for ten days as he transformed it into something Napoleon might have felt at home in on campaign. Some months later, Rex painted the walls of the dining room green which he then adorned with frames that he slowly filled with amusing pastiches of surrealist paintings and Old Masters including a Holbein Henry VIII, a sleeping Venus with 'Colonel Blimp' as a peeping Tom behind a curtain, and an Arcadian nymph dancing to a shepherd's pipes in the manner of Poussin and a Titian Bacchanalia.

Edith was overjoyed at the news of his arrival in Wiltshire. 'Rex has reached Codford', she wrote with purpose in her diary at the end of September.[18] But she was tired. In October she decided not to stand for a third year as Mayor. 'I <u>could not</u> refuse if asked, as War is going on, but I am quite ready to retire into the Council and indeed I do want a rest'.[19] Ethel's baby screamed at night and kept the house awake: 'It never sleeps, tho' it seems well and we think its brain too active . . . How can we stop it from thinking?'[20] She could bear the yelling as the baby was her 'safeguard' against the loss of her precious cook: 'As the wife of a serving soldier who has a child under 5 will not be called up.'[21]

On 17 October Tom Henn moved out of the Daye House. At dinner the night before he told Edith that the Germans would probably invade after February and before May 1942. In the last days of her mayoralty Edith recorded that she was 'chaffed by the Bench for my various "Records". The first woman councillor of Wilton and its first woman Mayor. Col. Maitland said I wrote and told him that in 6 months I had doubled the population of my Boro' – a record for a Woman Mayor – and then Mr Jackson, the Clerk, said I was the only Woman Magistrate who had sat alone, and committed a murderer for trial. I had felt that this was a terrific thing from my own point of view but I had not known that it was a unique thing to have done.'[22]

It was not long after Edith had relinquished her mayoral chain before new lodgers came to the Daye House. One, 'a young man whose beauty made me dizzy', had a telephone line installed in his room and Edith could hear him talking through the night.[23] And Edith still sat on the Invasion Committee as Chief of the Information Bureau, she coordinated the local Women's Volunteer Services and she was President of the local Order of St John Ambulance, these on top of her Council duties. Rationing had begun at the start of the war but since the spring it had become even tighter. By August 1942 almost all foods apart from vegetables and bread were rationed. But with Ethel's help, Edith made the most of it. She still dressed for dinner (a photograph shows her chatting with Esther and a lodger in the Long Room, Edith on her daybed in a satin evening gown) and favoured 'Champagne Ruby, the wonderful drink I buy in Elliot the Tailor's Shop in a Champagne bottle, so it looks most festive, and is merely fizzy fruit juice'.[24] And there was always food from friends to supplement the meagre rations. Fish caught in the river, the occasional duck shot on the estate, local mushrooms gathered in the woods, or gifts from friends. Imma sent dried minced lamb from Australia where she was now living and David Herbert arrived with pressed beef, tinned butter and raspberry jam from South Africa.

With Rex stationed nearby, Edith was able to spend more time with him than she had for years. When he had been staying in the summer, another guest had been watching over his shoulder as he worked on his *Königsmark* illustrations. Patricia Douglas, de Bendern, as she now was, had fled England for America with her baby at the beginning of the war but had now returned alone to spend time with her husband, of whom she was fond but did not love, before his embarkation. That weekend in October she had returned to the Daye House for a few days before going back to America and her baby. Rex tried to dissuade her from returning as it was a dangerous journey and she was equally unenthusiastic about the prospect. Edith was torn between love of Rex and belief in the sanctity of marriage. Not to return to America 'might smash their marriage', she wrote, adding: 'Rex sees it differently. I think he thinks that if it was smashed he would comfort and marry her!'[25] Perhaps Edith secretly hoped that he would.

Patricia decided to return after all but the week before she was due to sail, she invited Rex to join her at Claridge's. He shared her room and, according to Laurence, spent a happy few days with her, mostly in bed, wishing she was free to marry him. But Patricia was yet another woman with whom Rex fell in love but who was out of his reach. She sailed for America and never saw him again. Later, like Ursula Ridley, Patricia told Laurence that she thought Rex was instinctively homosexual, either not really interested in sex or 'that some special need never found expression'.[26]*

It was at the Daye House that Rex now usually spent his leave. When he was staying with Edith one weekend she wrote: 'it is delicious to be with people like this – pre-war – who talk the

---

* In December 1941 Rex heard rumours that Patricia's husband, John de Bendern, was missing in action. He did return from the war and they divorced in 1950.

same language'. She liked his moustache, grown at the suggestion of his commanding officer to mark his transformation into a military man, and wrote that it 'alters him less than people say . . . It's very short and I think good – like a Crusader.'[27] Cecil agreed, thinking it made him look like a 'czarist nobleman'.[28] To Henry Uxbridge Rex wrote that he had been growing his moustache 'for something to do between meals'.[29] Some time that year Edith had stopped dyeing her hair with henna, perhaps because she thought it too frivolous for the time or that, at sixty-eight, she should give up trying to maintain the illusion of youth. Cecil Beaton wrote about this with his usual candour: 'Edith Olivier's hair has become white. We shall soon forget that she was all these years the dark-haired gipsy for ever on the move, laughing and scratching her scalp. The white hair', he added, 'while being more becoming, is not so striking. She appears more of a conventional little old lady and less the violent character that her conversation still proves her to be.'[30]

But, though Rex and Edith had both changed, their relationship during the war was as it had been in the early years. They felt a new enthusiasm for each other. Writing from 'A Blasted Heath near Imber', on exercise in Wiltshire, Rex told Cecil that he had dined with 'darling Edith' who 'seems so well and vigorous and charming to be with – as much as she has ever been – for me – perhaps more so'.[31]

On 7 December the Japanese attacked the American fleet at Pearl Harbor and America entered the war to the immense relief of the British. Soon millions of men and tanks and planes were heading for Britain. When she heard the news, Edith had been lunching with Violet Bonham Carter who she drove immediately to Westminster to hear Churchill speak in Parliament. Later that day she met a friend for tea at the Dorchester and was asked to write and present a series of radio broadcasts to India and the Empire.

At Christmas as the German army retreated from the devastated ruins of Moscow, Edith and Rex sat by the fire in the Long

Room. Rex illustrated the 1942 page of Edith's visitors' book with a drawing of a huge Japanese head, flames pouring out of it as it devours an army in its mouth. It was a sharp contrast to the putti and flowers of earlier years. That night Edith wrote that it had been a 'very delicious day with Rex tho' he is changed by the war. Has less ardour and misses the beauty of life which means so much to him.'[32]

Edith was asked to write an article on 'Village Life During Wartime' for the *Geographical* magazine and she went up to see Cecil in London at his new house at Pelham Place for advice about the photographs she would use. He was about to be sent to the Middle East 'which thrills him', Edith wrote.[33] Not long after Singapore had surrendered to the Japanese in February she was off to the BBC to record one of her broadcasts, 'An Old-Fashioned Country Education'.

That spring the basic civilian petrol ration was abolished and fuel was now only available to official users like the military, bus companies and farmers. Germany began its Baedeker Raids over England and Edith was filled with 'trepidation as to what damage these barbarians have done'.[34] The Wilton fire engine was sent to help fight the flames when Bath was attacked and Edith learnt that bombs had fallen on 'a working-class part of the town and killed many people'.[35]

At Codford, Rex 'craved time to devote to painting', according to Cecil, who went on: 'he said he was only just beginning to feel how to use oil paint. As he examined somewhat wistfully his pre-war paintings, he said: "I can do much better than that now."'[36] But despite this, Rex did find time. In one painting that he executed at the camp, two soldiers are at rest under canvas. Through the opening of the tent the landscape is bathed in bright sunlight. In the dark shade of the tent, the men recline in deckchairs, one, with his legs casually crossed, the other, in the foreground, reading with his head resting indolently on the arm of his chair. The apparent ease and contentment of the scene with its bucolic setting and its deckchairs, is at odds with the officers' uniforms, a reminder that these men are not merely whiling away a warm and peaceful afternoon. Rex captured the unease and the ennui felt by those waiting for the action to begin, a feeling he shared.

Comradeship gave Rex a feeling of equanimity as spring turned into a stifling summer. But he could still feel a pang of nostalgia for the old world and for a home of his own. After visiting Ashcombe, as lovely as ever, he wrote to Cecil: 'I know I could never tell you how much real delight that visit gave me – how profoundly moved I was by the loveliness of the place which I really had quite forgotten. I mean the beauty of it . . . How infinitely pleasant and civilised days spent like that in such a place are. It was really painful to have to leave this morning.'[37]

In June Edith wrote in her diary, 'A joyous telephone from Rex saying he got back today from his course and his car is out of action,' adding: 'I used my last gallon of Basic Petrol (almost the last!) and drove to Codford to fetch him.'[38] The following day they used the very last of her petrol: 'This will probably be my last drive with Rex', she wrote; 'our drives together and seeing things together have been so much of our lives'.[39]

Without a car they stayed within the confines of the park that summer and Rex began to paint Edith and the Daye House almost compulsively, as if he was attempting to make memories of this 'longed for' place. In the paintings the house and the park are peaceful, dreamlike places, enclosed by soft, billowing trees and bathed in a balmy sunshine. These landscapes are as Arcadian in mood as those of his murals, but their style is loose and impressionistic, with strong contrasts of light and dark and a richer, warmer palette, imbuing them with an almost Mediterranean atmosphere. There were no more brooding mountains or Claudian mists; now all was bathed in golden sunlight. Symbolic of this – and indeed Rex considered this a major development – was his painting of the Palladian Bridge, most dear of inspirations. This he painted from the Dairy Bridge beside the Daye House, the Palladian in the background, partly obscured by trees while swans glide peacefully on the river in the foreground. The scene is serene, still, almost bleached by the morning sun. Edith considered it his 'loveliest landscape'.[40] The day that Rex painted it Tobruk in Libya had fallen to the German army led by Rommel, who took more than 30,000 prisoners and pushed the British into retreat.

But it was not to the Palladian Bridge or to Wilton House or to the follies on the estate that Rex returned to paint each weekend; it was to the Daye House. Though he had always loved Edith's house he had never before felt inclined to paint its exterior. And so there is another painting, composed from the riverside, that shows Edith in the foreground, standing in the long grass with the Daye House behind her, its grey stone rendered a pale apricot by the warm sunlight. And another, with Edith standing beside the drive, to the left; his shiny black American car, a Hudson Terraplane, is cosily tucked away beneath a tree and in the background stands the Daye House, covered in roses. 'My darling Edith', Rex wrote to her, 'I also want so much to thank you for those two delightful "sojourns" at the Daye House – (I would have said "stays" only thought you might think I meant . . .).'[41] At the side of the letter he had drawn a corset.

In July Laurence's wife Jill came to convalesce at the Daye House. She had been about to play the lead in a production of *Rebecca* but had become seriously ill. Laurence, stationed at Tidworth some miles away in Wiltshire, took the late bus to Wilton and then the early bus back to camp the next day. Edith sat listening as Rex and Laurence talked about soldiering and the war: 'R brings a <u>current of life</u> into the talk', she decided, and she still wished that Rex, rather than Laurence, had married Jill.[42]

As Rex whiled away his leave at his easel in the bucolic peace of the park that summer, a short walk away, in the Double Cube at Wilton, at the heart of Sir Philip's pastoral paradise, plans were being drawn up for the invasion of Europe. In the months leading up to the D-Day landings, visitors to Wilton House included King George VI, Winston Churchill, and Generals Eisenhower, Bradley and de Gaulle. Edith and Rex did not need the presence of Southern Command to remind them of what lay ahead. One night bombs fell in the park but no one was hurt and Edith walked out into the still, starlit night. But in August her latest lodger told her that 'the Guards Armoured Division will be spearhead of 2nd Front'. 'This is Rex', she realized. 'He will be killed. <u>I cannot look on at all</u>'.[43] A few days later Rex arrived on a new motorbike. 'He loathes it but loves its power of bringing him here', wrote Edith, adding, 'they say the <u>Guards</u> will be the <u>Vanguard</u> when we do attack and I feel R is destined for Doom'.[44]

In September Rex did a final painting of the Daye House, and of Edith, in her paved garden, wearing a sundress, reclining on a daybed and shaded from the sun by her enormous straw hat. 'The sun blazed on us', she wrote in her diary that night, 'and I had to get my huge muslin hat, which looked very funny and turned the picture – with its blazing light – into a mid-19th-century "Plein-air" Impressionist. The sun chased us about and we had to move again and again.'[45] Books and papers are scattered on a table beside her. Behind her lies a bed of flaming nasturtiums and a neat row of tomatoes ripening beneath the arched windows of the Daye House.*

'Simmering in my mind a book called "Night Thoughts of a Landlady in Wartime". The Landlady will be called "Miss Emma Nightingale". I <u>may</u> be able to do it', Edith wrote in her diary that month.[46] The book she wrote is a gentle, amusing and thinly veiled autobiographical account of Edith's life in wartime. It offers readers a glimpse at the diaries of Miss Emma Nightingale, a spinster who, each night in bed, writes about the day that has passed. When Miss Nightingale dies, the 'narrator', Miss Edith Olivier, to whom Miss Nightingale had entrusted her diaries the night before her death, decides to publish what she had found within their pages. 'I believe that in the future, we shall often have to look back to see what we did in the past,' Edith tells Miss Nightingale, 'and your diary has generally been our only book of

---

* Edith bequeathed this group of five paintings to her niece Rosemary, for her lifetime, and then to the Salisbury and South Wiltshire Museum.

reference.' Like Edith, Miss Nightingale is said to be 'one of those cultivated and "county" old ladies to be met with in most villages supremely interested in local affairs, generous to the poor, stern to the evil doer, pardoning to the penitent.' More importantly, perhaps, 'She was a leading spirit in all local activities . . . She also "lived her own life", as they say, for she did not consider herself to be altogether *of the village*. She had moved in wider circles.'[47]

Unlike the real Miss Olivier's diaries though, Miss Nightingale's journals were merely dull, functional minute books. That is until the war began. Edith, the 'narrator', writes that Miss Nightingale's journey from Derbyshire in the last days of 1939 proved a 'watershed'.

> It was to cut the landscape of her life in two, and now I saw that it had also cut in two the character of her diaries . . . instead of the curt notes recording merely each day's engagements, she now described in some detail what had actually happened. She wrote what she thought about what she did. This writing is like Miss Nightingale's private talk with her friends. Sometimes she was a rather racy conversationalist, and now her records of the coming of the lodgers, and the way in which the village entertained them, reproduced some of the spice of her personality.[48]

It sounds familiar. For the book Edith drew heavily from her diaries, the observations she had made and the memories she enjoyed; in some parts of the book she was almost quoting verbatim. The plot centres on Miss Nightingale's experience as a landlady. 'Only a European War could have driven her to such a revolution' as to take paying guests.[49] Edith dwelt on the duality of her life: her daytime practicality and her night-time imagination. She was a Mayor and a landlady by day and a writer by night. The book is a record of rural life on the Home Front. Edith writes of blackouts, food queues, evacuated children, rationing, of the strange sounds of men in her house, the sound of German planes flying overhead en route to the Black Country and of tanks and military lorries passing down the lane. She writes about her lodgers and decides that there is nothing uniform about men in uniform. She gives a rather ambiguous compliment to her 'soignée' sister-in-law Esther, her superlative cocktail-making skills and her perfectly made-up lips.[50]

The book is a tribute to the war efforts of many of her young friends and Edith recounts their extraordinary adventures, tales that they had brought to her at the Daye House. Zita James driving a Polish ambulance in war-torn France and making a narrow escape before the Germans arrived in the summer of 1940, 'the painter torn from his easel to view the landscape from a tank and to discover an unexpected new beauty in the world as he watched the dawn rise over a column of these monstrous black engines of war, after a dark night spent in a wood during manoeuvres'.[51]

Edith dedicated the book to 'The Strangers within My Gates' and in contrast with *Country Moods and Tenses*, the tone is optimistic. Edith no longer expressed her fears for the future of the countryside. Rather, the perennial workings and the enduring beauty of nature had, for her, come to represent England's resilience, continuity and immutability.

> That is the happiness of living in this place, and indeed in any country place in England to-day. We are not cut off from the life-and-death struggle of our country, for has not this been called "a war of little groups", in which the Home Guards and the housewives take their place behind the aircraft and the tanks? Yet we still live on in our own homes, and if other homes are like mine (as I am sure they are) it is still possible for a visitor to say, as he enters our doors, "Here, one can hardly realise the war". And that is perhaps the best thing we can ever give to the strangers within our gates.[52]

One reviewer of *Night Thoughts* called Edith 'the village spinster in excelsis'.[53] And that is what she was. 'Not once during the war did she allow herself a respite from her altruistic activities', Cecil later wrote. 'She managed, without ever mentioning the difficulties of rationing, to give hospitality to all friends, acquaintances and lame dogs, who came flocking to her with their troubles. Through the most rigorous winters she would turn out at night, in her small rickety car, to drive in the black-out to some meeting, or to perform some act of charity.'[54]

In September Rex went to Warminster to meet his mother and came back to the Daye House 'breathless with the news that she is going to marry a Mr Turner . . . retired . . . quite well off'. Rex wasn't much taken by Mr Turner even though it made him happy to see how much he cared for his mother. He 'does really feel relieved that there's someone to take care of her', added Edith, 'now he himself must expect to be killed – Oh God.'[55] Rex had long been fascinated by the idea of romantic death but now it was a real possibility. He wrote a new will leaving everything to his brother including nearly £2,000 in investments. And he was reassured by the idea that his mother's marriage meant that she would not grow old alone.

Though Edith still hoped that Rex would find happiness with a wife and family, undoubtedly these feelings were in conflict with the urge to have him to herself, not as her lover of course, though she would often wish that she was thirty years younger, and not as her son. For Edith, Rex was still a kind of idealized synthesis of the two. One weekend in March, when Rex had arrived at the Daye House, 'he looked lovely . . . in his dark blue Guards uniform, lovely buttons, brilliant broad red stripe down leg. Such a joy after this desert of khaki'.[56] He and Edith had walked together in the water meadows where, Edith wrote, Rex wanted to build a house. 'It would sink thro' to the Antipodes, but as there is no chance of building <u>anything</u> till after the war one is free to indulge one's fancy . . . Rex's natural ardour came back to him as we revelled in these impossible plans'.[57] With no experience of sex and the realities of romantic love, it was perhaps easy for Edith to fantasize about an uncomplicated, pastoral and platonic existence with Rex, sheltered in the unreality of the park at Wilton.

28: 'In the Long Ago'

❖

Vast distances . . . stretch away on every hand until lost in a
thin melancholy mist . . . instead of that lovely soft green of our
beloved Plain . . .

Rex to Edith, 21 February 1944

Rex had written to Siegfried Sassoon as soon as his regiment had
arrived in Wiltshire back in September 1941. Codford was only
three and a half miles or so from Heytesbury and he begged Sassoon to put down his pen and the new book that he was writing
and descend from his eyrie so that he could visit him. As fond of
Rex as Sassoon was, his presence only reminded Sassoon of the
war. Later, in June, Rex had spent a weekend at Heytesbury and
the following Monday he telephoned, 'very upset', asking if he
could come and see her. 'The marriage seems going on the rocks
thro' the adored baby,' Edith wrote. 'He's very naughty, maddens
Sieg by always being in the way and because Hester can't manage
him, but if she ever corrects him Sieg takes his side and is against
Hester. Rex thinks her <u>very stupid indeed</u> about it but he says he
couldn't have stayed there another hour.'[1] Two months later, Edith
went to Heytesbury to visit Sassoon herself. 'He has a crazy letter
from Stephen', she noted, 'who writes like a jilted woman and says
he contemplates suicide because their friendship ended', adding:
'it is hard to know whether he is demented or posing – both I
believe. He wants to break up this marriage and he won't although
it is in danger but <u>not from him</u>'.[2] The danger, Edith implied, was
in fact from Hester but she wasn't sure why. That month Stephen

appeared at Heytesbury and Sassoon wondered how he had ever loved the bloated boy who sat eating boiled eggs and talking about books in his house.

In September, at the Daye House, Rex confessed to Edith that Sassoon had told him that Hester was in love with him. Rex wasn't sure what to do. 'He isn't in love but is fascinated and would make love to her if it made things happier for her. I beg him not to. She would ask him to take her away and Sieg might be glad of the chance to push her off onto Rex for life. This R couldn't stand', she added. 'He is still in love with Caroline tho she will give no love back and he says he'd rather marry Patricia than anyone and now wishes he had. He has so many entanglements and none to make him happy.'[3]

As the war had progressed Sassoon had begun to focus all his frustrations on his bewildered young wife. In the solipsistic solitude of his attic study he despaired of the war, of his wife's possessiveness, of the claustrophobic domestic life that he had laboured so hard to create. He wanted to sleep alone, to live alone with his books for company, while Hester longed for him to love her and told him so. Inherently misogynistic, he took her demands as a sign that she was hysterical. In the early days of their relationship Hester had naively believed that she could change him; Sassoon, equally naively, had believed it too. Now they were both unhappy and lonely in that vast house with its many windows and its lovely garden. For Sassoon only his son George was a source of joy.

Hester, forlorn, had turned to Rex and at some point, despite his initial protests to Edith, it seems likely that they had begun an affair. Perhaps Hester was drawn to Rex's air of tragic romance, as earlier she had been drawn to Sassoon. It is easy to imagine that Rex felt a vicarious pleasure in attracting the wife of the man who had rejected his own advances twelve years earlier. But this is unlikely; Rex harboured no ill will towards Sassoon. Perhaps quite simply, like Hester, he was lonely too.

A few months later Rex wrote to Hester asking her to join him for a weekend in London, where he intended to spend his leave working on scenery and costume designs for, ironically, a production of *An Ideal Husband*. She accepted the invitation and returned to Heytesbury more youthful and exuberant. She told Sassoon that she had fallen in love with Rex. What Edith had dismissed as little more than a joyless 'entanglement', continued, in some form or another, until 1944. That year, 'Hester was still pursuing Rex' even though she admitted to Sassoon that she wanted to have another child with him and had no desire to marry Rex.[4]

That Edith mentions nothing in her diaries of Rex's weekend in London with Hester suggests that he had not told her. When in March 1943, Jill Whistler was staying again at the Daye House, Edith naively suggested to her that she and Laurence might share the house in the Close at Salisbury with Rex after the war. She seemed to be implying that the brothers should share Jill as well. Laurence later wrote about this conversation with baffled amusement: '"I don't mean as lovers, of course"', Edith had said to his wife, '"but you are the only person who can take care of him". She certainly meant no harm to a marriage she had brought about. But then, physical love was outside her reckoning – not very important perhaps.'[5]

At the end of November 1942, the 2nd Welsh Guards, now the 'Armoured Reconnaissance Battalion', had moved camp to Fonthill Gifford a few miles away and Rex went out on tank exercises where William Beckford had once wandered as he conjured up visions of fantastical follies to build on his estate. In the New Year he went to stay with Edith and sat by the fire, painting as she read aloud. On the Sunday he went to Wilton House and drank gin and Dubonnet with Lady Pembroke and then sat and talked with David Herbert as he lay in the bath regaling Rex with his adventurous escape from a sinking ship a few weeks earlier. It was one of the last weekends Rex would spend at the Daye House before his battalion left Wiltshire. A few days later he wrote:

My darling Edith,

. . . On Saturday we have another exercise starting at
3a.m. so if you wake at 4 say, think of me looking out of my
little iron tower, rolling along through the darkness across the
plain. If it's a fine day I shall enjoy the dawn . . . It has so
often made the dreary hours of darkness seem worth while as
I have looked at that unearthly lovliness and the glory of it.
The curious keen purity of the air at that hour and the beauty
and <u>strangeness</u> of everything (even of scenes with which one
is really quite familiar) never fail – however often experienced, to fill one with wonder and a glorious delight – almost
as though one had seen God's face for a fleeting moment . . .
Good night my darling Edith and thank you again for these
<u>lovely</u> contenting visits . . .[6]

At the end of February, the night before his battalion left, Rex
went to dinner at the Daye House. He arrived with 'two car loads
of pictures, canvasses, books, hats, his lovely . . . overcoat and all
sorts of possessions', Edith wrote, delighted that he considered
her home the place to store his belongings.[7] He left his car at
Heytesbury with Sassoon and Hester. That night, Edith wrote:
'Gave R the best dinner I could – turbot, pheasant and choufleur
au gratin'. She added that he was going on a 'very secret Exercise
called Spartan which seems to mean mobilising the whole army
. . . I know it means abroad after this'.[8]

But it did not. Instead, Rex set off with his battalion in a slow
convoy of tanks to a camp near Thetford in Norfolk. On leave one
weekend in the spring he went up to London and there dined
in uniform with John Gielgud at the Ivy. Gielgud had proposed
that Rex do the set design for a production of Congreve's *Love
for Love* at the Phoenix Theatre and Rex had accepted. They discussed plans for the production late into the night, Rex scribbling
sketches on the backs of envelopes as they talked. Later Gielgud
would ask Rex to design a production of *A Midsummer Night's
Dream* and Rex made some initial sketches. He had in mind cur-

tains to sweep across the stage to give the effect of branches in a leafy glade.

On 1 May Rex and some fellow officers were invited to an informal dinner at Sandringham with the King and Queen and their seventeen-year-old daughter, Princess Elizabeth. 'I sat next to sweet little Princess Elizabeth and we had a great deal of talk throughout dinner', Rex told Edith:

> . . . She seems such a sweet-natured <u>charming</u> child, gentle and a little demure from shyness but not <u>too</u> shy, and a delicious way of gazing – very serious and solemn – into your eyes while talking but all breaking up into enchanting laughter if we came to anything funny. After dinner I had a most enjoyable talk with the Queen about a great many things: paintings she had bought, – and painters – and books – and poets . . . we bellowed with laughter and had a lot of very good jokes . . .[9]

Not far from Thetford was Breccles Hall, home of Rex's friend Venetia Montagu. While Rex's battalion was stationed in Norfolk Venetia decided to give a ball for the officers. Rex decorated the ballroom and wrote to Caroline begging her to come: 'We can have lovely waltzes, and walks under the stars . . . How glorious if you could find that striped dress I loved so much, do you remember it? If you come I will paint another head of you on Sunday much better than the previous ones'.[10] Beside it he had drawn a sketch of them whirling around in each other's arms, and in perfect synchrony, Caroline in her billowing striped dress, Rex in his red-striped dress uniform, as if in a scene from War and Peace. For Rex, Caroline remained an idol, a beautiful creature to dress and to paint. She joined him that weekend but it made no difference. 'In those days', Laurence recalled, 'he accepted that Caroline did not love him, never would, yet he could not free himself.'[11]

In March Edith's first article for Vogue was published. 'Country Occupations' was accompanied by a biographical feature about her and a page of photographs taken by Cecil to illustrate her life in Wilton: Edith 'cowled monkishly against the cold' in a cloak with an elfin pointed hood, walking 'abroad' in a fur coat beside a mist-cloaked Palladian Bridge, looking earnest in a Council meeting and entertaining her guests in the Long Room. The mood of the magazine was rather less brisk and blithe than it had been when Edith featured in it before at the beginning of the war. Now there was an article about the reality of life for women in Occupied France, fashion ideas were presented as 'A Portfolio of Wartime Economies' and the food section gave tips on how to entertain in 'Rations for One – Dinner for Two'. Edith's article was once again written in the tone of the Country Mouse as she entertained readers with tales of her busy, varied life. 'Who can say', she asked readers at the close of her article, 'that to live in the country is not to live in the world of adventure?'

'She is that rare, yet typical Englishwoman who is, before all else, entirely individual . . . a woman of achievement,' declared *Vogue*; '. . . she combines those attributes of wit, learning, detail and perspective which place her among the best contemporary writers.'[12] Clearly the magazine considered the writer and civic leader an inspiring example of the way a capable woman could adapt in wartime, a resourceful Mrs Miniver for the chattering classes.

Though Edith's diary still bristled with the daily progress of the war gleaned from the wireless, her days were now more leisurely than before. In April she attended a poetry reading at Aeolian Hall in New Bond Street. There she met Osbert Sitwell, who found her a seat at the 'very crowded and <u>chic</u>' event. She admired Vita Sackville-West's powerful reading and thought Edith Sitwell 'looked really too odd in a flowing cassock of stiff silk'. Walter de la Mare gave a reading which Edith considered 'really <u>too</u> matter of fact tho' that does give quality to his elusiveness but he seems to <u>want</u> to omit the <u>music</u>'.[13]

On the 30th she was back in London for a meeting at the Ministry of Health about housing issues. Edith held a particularly passionate view that water and drainage should be paid by taxes rather than by rates, believing that they were a national rather than a local responsibility. After the meeting she walked out into Whitehall in search of a taxi and by the time she found one in Pall Mall she was drenched by the rain. At Batsford Charles Fry lit a fire to dry her wet clothes. Later they had lunch at the Savoy, Edith chatting with the film director Anthony Asquith who sat at the next table, and discussing with Charles the illustrations for *Night Thoughts*. 'He wants to get my book out quickly', she wrote, 'and Cecil to illustrate if Rex can't. I do hope R will consent – tho' Cecil is very kind and gentlemanly saying he will do it if R does have to give up.'[14]

Rex returned to the Daye House with heaps of luggage one evening in early June. He was tired after the long journey from Norfolk but taking advantage of the double summer time, they walked in the park and 'saw wonderful delicate sky and cloud effects – colours never seen before – one particular grey-brown-silver-rose, we christened "Wilton"', Edith wrote.[15] Rex had brought frames with him for the paintings he had already brought to the Daye House, which meant that Edith could create a 'Whistler Gallery' in the Long Room. He spent all of the following day on illustrations for Edith's book. 'It was much against the grain', she wrote. 'He really doesn't like illustrating and feels ashamed of his work in that genre', adding that he 'has only done it out of love for me'.[16] They sat for a while in the garden the next day until it began to rain and then Rex returned to the gentle, humorous illustrations for Edith's book. To remove Edith even further from the 'author' of the book, Miss Nightingale became a tall old lady with bony limbs and a sharp, pointed nose. That night he worked until three o'clock in the morning to complete them. 'It nearly killed him', Edith wrote. 'He knows these days are the only ones he can give. I read to him a bit, talked to him a bit. Sat with him till 12.30 and went down at 3 to drag him to bed. I felt guilty at holding him to this job which I know will make my stupid book, but at all this cost to himself. It has prevented this leave from being a leave at all.'[17]

A few days later Rex's battalion moved north to the small Yorkshire market town of Pickering for the last period of training. 'It is a most dreary waste, this part of the wolds', he wrote to Edith. 'Vast distances . . . stretch away on every hand until lost in a thin melancholy mist . . . instead of that lovely soft green of <u>our</u> beloved Plain'.[18]

Back in January Edith had received a letter from Stephen written in black and sepia ink on candy-pink notepaper with a yellow letterhead, and stuffed into a pink envelope lined with yellow tissue paper. 'I'm home in this beautiful bedroom with white polar bearskins, arum lilies, and tall white velvet curtains', he had written.[19] Wilsford had been requisitioned by the Red Cross as a military hospital early in the war and Stephen, considered unfit for active service, was living in the nursery flat. No longer a golden boy, but a lonely, somewhat depressed and directionless middle-aged man, Stephen was contemplating plastic surgery on his nose and spent his time entertaining friends, flirting with American soldiers from the nearby camp, redecorating his flat and attempting to attract the attentions of his old love at Heytesbury.

Later that month Edith had lunched with him at the Red Lion in Amesbury. 'Most of the "clients" were officers who I thought would see S's painted face and demand his dismissal from the Hotel!' she wrote. 'But they took him quite calmly and I think they thought him only a red-faced boy . . . especially', she added, 'as he wore his flying hood, so his dyed hair was hidden. That is far more conspicuous than the paint on his face which is put on well'.[20] After lunch, Edith returned with him to Wilsford and was 'astounded' by his flat, which, she wrote, 'looks like a tent, but the tent of Lady Hester Stanhope', with 'baroque columns . . . mirrors everywhere . . . Tables and shelves <u>cluttered</u> with nick-nacks'. There were so many 'makeup pots and bottles' that it was 'almost impossible to squeeze into the bathroom. Sham roses thrown <u>partout</u> . . . the most fantastic establishment I ever saw'.[21] There were clothes in boxes 'jumbled about and he threw them on the floor, saying he must hang up three golden balls as the room looked like a Pawnbrokers! But these balls would never be seen among the jumble', she wrote. Louis Ford, a stablehand in Pamela's day, was now his only servant. That night Edith stayed at Wilsford and Stephen talked with her about 'nine short stories which he says he <u>has</u> written, then he <u>has not</u>, then he <u>is</u> writing'.[22] She knew that Stephen was a dilettante. Though she acknowledged that he had originality she feared, rightly, that he did not have the self-discipline to get anything done. And yet, she remained loyal to him. In January of the following year, driving around London with Stephen in a 'luxurious pre-war hired Daimler', they would visit 'Chemists, coiffeurs and the London Library'. 'He is child-like in adoring all these things and has no vice in him, whatever his painted appearance may lead the common-place to suspect!' she wrote, still wanting to set herself apart from conventional opinion.[23]

At the beginning of 1944 Rex would also hear from his erstwhile friend. 'I was much interested to hear Stephen had visited you . . . and then came this amusing and wildly personal letter from him', he wrote to Edith. '[It] reminded me so of some of those heavenly winter days we used to have together in bitter weather in the long ago', Rex told her, adding, 'what a truly <u>magical</u> touch comes to him whenever he speaks or writes of nature. For me he has only to mention a particular flower for its whole "personality", its scent, its colour and texture to be brought vividly to my senses'. 'I rather feel', he added, 'all the fantastic confusions of his mind and character – the subtleties and crudities – the loving heart and ice cold reason – the crazy pernicious immaturity and the wisdom, come pouring in in glittering overcoloured streams and <u>alloy</u> the whole mixture so often.'[24]

It was many years since they had truly been friends in spite of protesting letters to the contrary and the time they had spent together in New York. As Rex had escaped a life that he had begun to find constricting, Stephen had retreated into the gaudy, artificial fantasy he had created for himself at Wilsford. The breakdown of their friendship was irrevocable. But for Rex, at

Pickering in the final stages of preparing for the invasion of France, the letter inspired nostalgic thoughts about the early days of their friendship and about the Stephen he had known, that outrageous, beguiling, beautiful, sensual, flawed and self-obsessed aesthete who had welcomed him into his charmed world. Nearly twenty years later, as Rex sailed for France in early summer 1944, Stephen was in Scotland for psychological treatment, having had a severe mental breakdown.*

Rex hated the war. He worried that he was a useless troop commander, even dangerous. But he was popular in his regiment and his men found him fair, of good judgement, generous and entertaining. They were intrigued by this gentle artist who was always sketching and painting; even the gun covers on the tanks were decorated. Rex was much older than the other officers of his lowly rank. But it seems that he had found a kind of unexpected peace: 'I was surprised that anyone with his essentially artistic nature should be so happy in the army, as he clearly was', his friend Daphne Weymouth wrote in her memoirs. 'He seemed to take his military duties far more seriously than my other friends, and whenever he came to Sturford Mead would devote hours to preparing regimental training schemes, studying maps and making notes', she added.[25] From the start of his career as an artist Rex had shared with Edith his unease about the relevance of his work, a paranoia which no doubt sprang, in part, from his early success. Fifteen years earlier, Edith had recorded in her diary that Rex was having a crisis of conscience during which he broke down and decided to give up his art to go and work in the slums. And, although this never happened, it seems that his decision to sign up was another manifestation of this instinct. Perhaps his happiness sprang from being in the action, a sense that he was finally achieving something after years of inertia. Twice he refused the

---

* Stephen had fallen into a deep gloom. Philip Hoare writes that this was in part because he was lonely and in part because he was trying and failing to lure Sassoon back into a relationship.

offer of desk jobs because he was adamant that he should remain an active soldier, even though many of his fellow artists, like Cecil Beaton and Oliver Messel at the School of Camouflage, were not. He wanted to go into battle alongside his men. Back in December 1941, Rex had a long talk with Edith about his new life: 'He thinks it good for him and has found the value and admirable side of what many artists deride – the ordinary man's point of view so scoffed at by highbrows in the *New Statesman* or *Horizon*'.[26]

Ultimately, though, the army was another escape for Rex, into a world of order and action, of mud, men and machines, a retreat from the chaos of his romantic entanglements and troublesome clients. Army life sidelined the trappings of civilian life, wives, children, domesticity and careers, in favour of comradeship and single-minded purpose. And so, in a way, Rex returned to a way of life that he had known during his friendship with Stephen.

By the last Book of *Brideshead Revisited*, Charles and Sebastian have grown apart. Sebastian is an alcoholic living in self-imposed exile; Charles is 'homeless, childless, middle-aged, loveless' and his art has grown stagnant.[27] The end of the novel, like the beginning, sees Charles billeted at Brideshead Castle, now an army camp, in the Second World War. The story that he tells is an elegy to his past, to 'those distant Arcadian days'[28] and to his 'lost friend'.[29] And yet, despite the loss, the sadness and the destruction, at the end of the novel, Charles finds a kind of peace.

Though Rex would write from Pickering in the summer of 1943: 'oh Edith darling how my heart <u>aches</u> for peace and I really loathe the endless roar of engines and stink of petrol and the coarse loutishness of soldiers', he had found in the army a measure of contentment that he had been yearning for, escaping from the troubles of his life and liberating his art from its elegant shackles.[30]

That winter, Rex's training intensified but he also decided that the battalion should throw a Christmas party. From 'Wits End, Pickering, Yorkshire', he wrote to Edith: 'like an idiot I suggested a Children's Party to the infants of Pickering. The idea was approved so now I find myself mostly responsible for organising the whole treat, decorating the Hall, engaging conjurors etc: and generally making preparations to entertain about 250 little troglodytes on Christmas Eve. So I ain't got much time and no wits left at all by the evening.'[31] In the Memorial Hall where the party was to be held he painted two Welsh Guardsmen, Father Christmas, a group of children greedily devouring cakes and others skating on thin ice. He had found a Christmas tree which he covered in lights, strung bunting and flags to the ceiling and adorned the tables with candles and Christmas crackers. There were bags of sweets to take away, a Punch and Judy show and a conjuror. The party was long remembered by the children of Pickering and the following morning Rex was up before dawn for firing practice on Fylingdales Moor.

That year Edith made more broadcasts for the BBC, she still had lodgers at the Daye House, and she still had Council meetings and countless other meetings to attend, as ever. It was, no doubt, with some irony and perhaps a little envy, that she began writing a book about leisure. *Four Victorian Ladies of Wiltshire* was comprised of pen portraits of four women: Miss Annie Moberly; Miss Barbara Townsend of Mompesson House in Salisbury, to whom she had dedicated *The Seraphim Room*; Pamela Grey's mother, Mrs Percy Wyndham, of Clouds; and Mrs Alfred Morrison of Fonthill.* Edith wanted to record a way of life that she knew had been lost forever. She knew, too, that the world would have changed again when it finally emerged from the war. These were the ladies who had inhabited her childhood and the safe, certain, Victorian, country-house world she had known as a child, 'days when Leisure bordered Life like the margin of a well-printed page'.[32]

A fleeting holiday with Zita James at Dawlish aside, where their view and ease had been marred by the defensive barbed wire that ran along the beach, Edith's greatest pleasure at the end of

---

* Published by Faber & Faber in 1945.

that year was a commission to write a book about Wiltshire for a new county series. 'I feel this, if I could do it well, would be the achievement of my life, something I would love to leave behind'.[33] Now people sent their 'literary attempts' to Edith for advice, 'hoping', she wrote, 'that I shall make them into <u>A. G. Streets</u>, not realising that he made himself, as all must do'.[34]

Weary at the end of that fourth dark year of war, Edith found the thought of starting work on a book about Wiltshire a spur; it filled her with a new sense of purpose. 'Worked for 3 and a half hours in morning', she wrote on 10 December, 'and all the time the thought of that Wiltshire book clangs in my mind like a Church bell – a lovely distant sound calls me. I do hope I shall be able to do it – to live to write it and to write it well'.[35] And at the end of December she wrote: 'The pace quickens as the year's end approaches, like a bell sent spinning on the edge of a cliff which will leap off into space when the last hour sounds . . . War news gets better and better.'[36] On 26 January 1944 Edith went to London to meet her publisher. Her book was to be finished by autumn 1945 and published the following spring. On the last day of 1943 she had celebrated her seventy-first birthday. 'I feel I can't live as long as that', she wrote in her diary.[37]

In February she ate an orange for breakfast, memorable as it was her first since the Italians had entered the war: 'it was so good and refreshing'.[38] Her cousin Laurence Olivier came to visit bringing his wife Vivien Leigh with him, 'a pretty little thing', Edith thought, but added: 'Esther's prophecy is that she won't stick with him. "Mark my words."'[39] But for the present, the war eclipsed everything in her life. That month she was informed that, in the event of an invasion, it seemed likely that paratroopers would land on Salisbury Plain and that Wilton House would be in the firing line. 'It is all most logical and yet seems quite impossible', she wrote; 'the American loudspeaker will be trebled in loudness when the Germans begin attacking us and will say again and again – Attention. Attention. Attention. Defend Wilton. Defend Wilton. Defend Wilton.'[40]

Happier news came in the form of a mud-stained letter from Rex written while sitting beneath the tarpaulin covers of his tank on exercise in Yorkshire. In December he had promised to write to her three times a week and apologized that his resolve had not lasted quite so long. He described in graphic detail the noisy, dirty misery of the mock-battle he was engaged in and drew a sketch of himself huddling beside his tank as the desolate moors stretch out behind him. It marked the climax of his training in preparation for France. That same month, at the New Theatre in London, a sigh had arisen from the audience as the curtain went up on the first night of *Le Spectre de la Rose*. It had revealed Rex's backdrop of an enormous, glistening, voluptuous, pink rose, with the spirit of the rose asleep at its heart and a star-filled night sky behind it.

In March Rex visited Edith at the Daye House. They had not met since the previous June. He arrived before lunch and they sat talking in the Long Room. In January he had written to her: 'Did I ever write to you to say how much I love that photograph of you in the Long room by Cecil which you sent me so long ago? It gives me continual pleasure and I feel so easily when I look at it that I am with you again in that loved room'.[41]

Later that day they walked to the temple across a park blanketed with snowdrops. That night, after he had left, Edith wrote in her diary: 'Rex says he has seen much beauty in the War which he would not have seen otherwise, dawn twilight and evening twilight on downs and in deep woods among his tanks. He loves his crew of 15 men and his 3 tanks and they love him'.[42] She would not see him again.

29: Action

❖

My darling Rex,

Outwardly your life has drifted from me, but not inwardly for I think of you every day – not once but often – and I know you think of me when you can. You can think of this darling little house, unchanged as far as its structure goes, and also as far as its heart lives and beats, but becoming more and more romantically weathered and lost in weeds . . .

Edith to Rex, 2 June 1944

Rex's division began its slow passage south on 1 May, the tanks slowly rumbling along the 300-or-so miles of roads and country lanes from Pickering to Brighton, to join the thousands of troops gathering near the Channel ports, in preparation for the invasion. The battalion arrived in Brighton on 3 May.

That spring Laurence wrote to tell Rex that Jill was pregnant with their second child. Rex was delighted: 'First of all (though I used to think once that being poor made it unwise to have a family) I do now feel so __strongly__ that you and Jill must have as many as you can & I really don't think the money makes much odds . . . remember', he added, 'you have got to have the children I ought to have had & to produce my share of little Whistlers, which I shall love just as if they were my own'.[1]

At the end of April, Edith had received a letter from Helen Whistler. 'Dearest Edith', Rex's mother began, 'the trial of my faith has come'. Rex had called her to tell her that his new address from then on was simply 'Army Post Office England' and Edith (wrongly) assumed this meant that he had already sailed for France. 'I know how he adores staying with you and always has . . . the next few weeks will be hard to live through, for many reasons, won't they? It is a comfort to me to know that your prayers for him join with mine, dear Edith.'[2]

At Brighton the battalion waited. The Cromwell tanks of the 2nd Welsh Guards had to be brought up to field specification and waterproofed for landing on the beach at Normandy, which meant that they could be no longer be used for training. Rex worked on sets for a play put on by the Welsh Guards at the Hippodrome at Eastbourne, *Strictly Between Ourselves*. He wrote to Hugh 'Binkie' Beaumont, the theatre producer for whom he had planned to design John Gielgud's *A Midsummer Night's Dream*, to apologize for not being able to carry out the commission: '. . . will you <u>believe</u> how sad I am about it & make John believe too? There's nothing I would have loved more to do for the theatre & feel I would have done nothing else so well; if you haven't done it by the time I am free again remember that I shall still be <u>longing</u> to do it.'[3] He travelled up to London to meet his mother. They went to the cinema and to Selfridge's and then sat in a park, after which Rex took her to Paddington to meet her train. From Brighton he also visited Sacheverell and Georgia Sitwell, Cynthia Asquith, and the Gages at Firle Place. 'When is this war going to start!' he wrote to his mother. 'It had better get going soon or I shall be broke. Champagne suppers and a great deal of gaiety are the order of the day here.'[4] 'How had the war years affected him?' Cynthia Asquith later wrote. 'In place of his usual extreme pallor, there was a new appearance of sun-bronzed health. I was also struck by a noticeably carefree look – a look that goes with complete "acceptance". His smile was as intensely amused as ever; his wit had the same quality of unexpectedness. He spoke a little, not much, of the past', she continued, 'still less of the war, only once and then with characteristic lightness of touch referring to his own impending initiation. "I don't know that I exactly look forward to it, but at least it will be going ABROAD."'[5]

Inevitably Rex couldn't resist the urge to decorate his billet, a cheerless red-brick Victorian villa in Preston Park Avenue. A fellow officer later recalled that one rowdy evening, somebody suggested that Rex should paint a Varga girl on one of the empty walls. Rex proceeded to sketch and then paint his idea of a pin-up. Instead of a sexy modern girl, in stockings and lipstick and bursting out of her corset, Rex painted the naked figure of a sleeping nymph, the Spirit of Brighton, a girdle around her waist with 'Brighthelmstone' written on it. Beside her kneels the winged, pot-bellied figure of the Prince Regent, naked but for his patent pumps and the Order of the Garter slung around his torso, its star resting on his buttock. With a keen face and a lascivious, beady eye, the Regent is in the act of unveiling the nymph's beauty. Behind the figures, clouds are buffeted by the wind in a stormy seascape and below the painting, within a cartouche, the title: *Allegory. HRH The Prince Regent awakening the Spirit of Brighton.* Somewhere Rex must have heard the story that the Prince Regent, on a visit to Brighton, had spotted a comely wench reclining on the beach and was evidently impressed enough to build a palace.

Instinctively, in those last few days before he sailed for France, Rex had returned to fantasy. *The Spirit of Brighton* is a *jeu d'esprit,* satirical in the manner of Rowlandson and Gillray, camp, knowing, and yet ultimately innocent. This was Rex's kind of woman, an ideal, a dream of woman, so much more successful than the nude he had painted of Caroline Paget. And perhaps he saw himself in the pathetic figure of the Prince Regent, worshipping and yet impotent, forever kneeling beside the beautiful, sleeping nymph.

Listening to the wireless on the evening of 6 June, Edith heard that the invasion had finally begun. That day 150,000 troops had landed on the beaches of Normandy. It was a vast operation with hundreds of ships, and immense air support. Behind the lines in France the French Resistance were sabotaging rail networks and communication systems and Allied paratroopers were seizing strategic targets. By the end of the day the Allies had a foothold in France.

That night Edith lay in bed watching through the window as hundreds of planes in perfect formation, 'lit by red and blue lights and looking most beautiful', flew over Wilton en route for France.[6] Illuminated by a full moon, she thought them 'like a celestial Army going into war . . . The stars paled in the background'.[7] 'All my life I shall remember lying in bed throughout the night . . . and watching the unending armies of planes flying over . . . It was the grandest sight of the war', she wrote to Cecil.[8]

The following day Edith's diary entry is less whimsical, as the reality of what was happening across the Channel dawned on her. 'News coming all day by newspapers and wireless', she wrote, and that news reported that the German army had begun to retaliate. 'O Rex', she wrote, underlining the words for emphasis.[9] On 9 June she wrote to him, thinking that by then he was in action. And then, a few days later, she received a letter from him:

> My darling,
>   A frantic line from the freedom of [a friend's house] . . . (to whom I have most illegally escaped) to tell you that I love you and am just going to write from my seaside home when I get back.
>   I expect to 'travel' about Thurs: or Fri: of next week, but of course do not know, and cannot when writing from there mention the matter owing to censorship etc: I will write when I know, and say that 'I hope to dine with Charley tomorrow' . . .
>   Please don't fail to burn this and never mention to anyone until papers mention.
>   Much love, Rex.[10]

On 13 June the first 'doodlebug', an unmanned bomb, landed on Mile End in London killing eight people. 'Esther amusingly says we need have no more blackout as the robots won't see our lights!' Edith wrote in her diary on 16 June.[11] Four days later she received the coded letter that Rex had promised to write. In the brief note, 'in great haste' three days earlier, he had written: 'This is dashed off to assure you – of what you already know so well – my lasting deep love for you my darling Edith. Tomorrow I dine with Charlie! I will write and tell you about it when I can . . . Good-bye my sweet darling Edith and may God grant that I will have the great joy of seeing you again before a great while'.[12] In her diary, Edith wrote: 'That means my darling left England on Sunday. His letter is very tender and loving. O God keep him safe'.[13]

On 18 June, Rex's battalion had been moved from Brighton to a marshalling area at Hambledon, near Portsmouth, for embarkation the following day. It was not until the afternoon of 28 June (four days after Rex's thirty-ninth birthday) that the men were sent to Gosport. That evening the ships arrived in the harbour. At one o'clock in the morning on Thursday 29 June, twenty-three days after D-Day, Rex sailed for France in rough seas, carrying a pocket edition of *Palgrave's Golden Treasury* that he had bought to take with him.

With Rex in France, Edith's life returned to a semblance of normality. *Four Victorian Ladies of Wiltshire* went to print; she drove to Heytesbury for lunch with Sassoon and came away with five chapters of his autobiography to type up. She spent other days with Hester trying to untangle the Gordian knot of her marriage. She dined with the Army Commander at Bulbridge, who told her that 'no officer has ever given <u>more</u> to his Regt. than Rex, of ideas, interests, and tastes. His men love him, so do his brother officers'.[14] Every night Edith walked into Wilton to pray for Rex at the old church in the Market Place.

On 18 July she received a parcel from Rex containing a circular card written and decorated in coloured Indian inks, and three cheeses.[15] 'A little present from Normandy with <u>much</u> love. Writing to you today with what news I can give. Thank you for your dear letters. Wonder if this will be allowed to reach you . . .' he wrote on the card. 'So enchanting to get this from him on the Battlefield', Edith wrote in her diary, and she replied with a letter reassuring him that his cheeses had passed the censor and hoping that the *Country Life* she had sent him, with an article by Laurence, would reach him in France.[16]

The next day she was delighted to hear from Tom Henn, her former lodger who worked in Intelligence, that the war would end, at the very latest, by 1 October. *The Times* printed a despatch, sent the previous day, from its Special Correspondent on the Caen front, hailing the first day of Operation Goodwood, General Montgomery's attempt to break through into eastern France, a success: 'Let it suffice for the moment', he wrote, 'that the Germans on the Orne have been dealt a mighty blow and that victorious British arms are in full cry'.[17] No doubt Edith was also encouraged by this news, although she would not then have realized its significance. The day after that came the equally thrilling news on the wireless that there had been an assassination attempt on Hitler's life. Perhaps it gave her hope. But it was too late. Rex had died on 18 July, the day that Edith received his letter.

Six days later, on the evening of 25 July, after a WVS meeting in Trowbridge, Edith wearily drove the thirty miles back to the Daye House where her sister Mamie was staying with her for a few days. She was too tired to put her car in the garage and left it parked in the drive, thinking to do it later. Mamie was waiting for Edith at the door and beckoned her in to sit beside the fire with a hot cup of tea. And then she told her the news. The message had been passed on by Kenneth Rae, who worked at the Ministry of Information, via a whispered trail of telephone calls. Edith sat staring into space and her sister suggested that perhaps they might put away the car. Then Mamie took Edith upstairs to lie down on her bed. Later that night she took up her diary:

> When I got back Mamie (poor darling) had to tell me that my beloved Rex is killed. Since Mildred's death he has been the whole happiness of my life. Such companionship, sharing of

interests, sense of humour in common. Everything which I
like to do he likes. Everything that I would like to do he can
do. He creates enjoyment of life wherever he is . . . He is a
Gift of God . . . I must thank God that he is not blinded or
maimed but taken in his vigour of mind and body. England
and the world has lost <u>much</u> – so what is my loss – only a few
more years here with the memory of our love to help me . . .
I could not see anyone. To try to speak makes me cry. O Rex,
Rex.[18]

That night, in pencil, she wrote beside her diary entry for 18 July,
'this is the day Rex was killed'.[19]

Rex's battalion had disembarked at Arromanches beach in
Normandy and his squadron had set up camp in the orchard of an
ancient farmhouse. There the men waited idly for the start of
Operation Goodwood. Writing to his mother, while sitting
amongst overgrown old apple trees in the twilight, he told her that
'everything looks the picture of peace . . . only the almost cease-
less gunfire contradicts'.[20]

There he waited. Welded to the back of his tank was a metal
box containing his paints and canvases. Inside the tank were
about twenty little white boxwood crosses; Rex had been
appointed the battalion's burial officer. There were brief unofficial
sorties to Cherbourg, now abandoned by the Germans, and to
Bayeux to see the cathedral and visit a lace factory. One evening
he set off for a walk from the orchard with a comrade and 'passed
the grave of an airman recently shot down'. Rex said that 'he
wanted to be left just so, where he was killed, not taken to an
enormous cemetery. With his old blend of the romantic and self-
mocking, he enlarged on this: it would mean so much more to
anyone who visited the grave, not that anyone would, to find a
beret with its tarnished leek hanging from a little cross, just where
it happened'.[21]

Two and a half weeks later, on 16 July, he posted his final
letters, with sprigs of mistletoe threaded into them, to Edith, his

mother, his friend Imogen Gage, and also to Caroline.* Then he
set out with several officers to dine at the Lion d'Or in Bayeux.
On their return to the orchard they stopped at a ruined sanctuary.
As the other officers prayed in the dark, Rex sketched a Madonna
and Child in charcoal on a patch of white wall.

> . . . My darling sweet Edith, [he had written that night] you
> know how much I love you without my writing to tell you so,
> but in spite of the long silences remember always that I am
> thinking of you continually.
>
> Till now nothing much has happened, we have been pre-
> paring and waiting and only the continuous thunder of guns
> has disturbed our overgrown countryside where we lie
> hidden. We live in little holes dug on the ground in an
> orchard and covered with mackintosh sheets near the tanks,
> and eat plenty of butter from the farm – but no bread – only
> biscuits! Now my darling we are on the verge of battle from
> what I understand. I know you will pray for me and for my
> particular little troop too, and it will be a comfort to me to
> think that you are doing so. Forgive this letter for giving so
> little news, and there are so many things in your recent dear
> letters to which I want to reply. I will write I <u>promise</u> when
> next I can – but it may be a long period now – I cannot tell.
> God bless you darling Edith.
>
> My fondest love Rex.
>
> I am writing this outside my 'bivvy', and enclose a sprig of
> mistletoe growing on the old apple tree above me.[22]

After four years' training at last it was to begin. On the morning of 18 July the battalion began its advance through open
country bathed in summer sunlight, Rex's troop heading for the

---

* Laurence Whistler later wrote emphatically that Rex hadn't sent a letter to
Caroline on the eve of battle. On the contrary, Charles Duff recalls his mother
telling him that she had received a letter from Normandy with mistletoe
attached.

village of Giberville. At some point in the afternoon, when they were attempting to cross a railway embankment, the wheels of his tank became tangled in trailing telegraph wires. As it was a hot day, he ordered all his men out of the tank, to wait for the wire to be cut. A few mortar bombs landed in a distant field, then, suddenly, they came under attack and found themselves unable to get back into the tank. Rex needed to contact the other tank under his command for help, but without a radio, he made the decision to make a dash for it himself, across sixty yards or so. This he managed to do, but as he jumped back down from the tank a mortar blew up beside him, throwing him up into the air and breaking his neck, killing him instantly. His body, seemingly untouched by the blast, was laid out beside a hedge dressed in shirtsleeves and wellingtons, 'looking as though he were asleep'.[23]

AFTER

'The Loving Spirit'

❖

I feel I am living with him. Yet he is always out of reach.

Edith Olivier's Diary, 27 February 1948

Edith was alone again. 'There's a deep darkness over the house and yet I do not realise that Rex will never again come into it. Blessed am I to be so old. I <u>must</u> die soon', she wrote the day after she had heard that Rex was dead.[1] That afternoon she worked on a lecture and attended a welfare meeting about refugees.

It was another day before Rex's mother and brother learnt of his death, another day after that before Helen was officially informed. Sitting on a train at Waterloo station on his way to spend his leave with Jill and their children in Devon, Laurence opened his copy of the *Daily Telegraph* and immediately recognized one of Rex's sketches on the Diary page. Below it he read: 'One of Rex Whistler's last sketches. Art and the stage suffer a considerable loss'.[2] 'Laurie darling. We can say nothing to each other. I guess.' Edith wrote to him on the 28th. 'I share your feelings . . . for though I was not born his sister – as you were his brother – for the past 19 years he has been growing more and more closely into my life and he had made practically all the happiness of it. I am so glad that you have Jill and Simon and soon another child. They will be consolation I hope. Especially dearest Jill.'[3]

Stephen received the news at Wilsford and, even four years later, he could not accept it: 'His death was something I could never learn. There are some things the ear rejects'.[4] Sassoon read of Rex's death in the paper. 'It was the worst pain I've felt since the war began', he wrote in his diary.[5] That evening he had been invited by Edith to stay at the Daye House and to dine with her other guest, Sir Frederick Morgan, Chief of Staff to the Supreme Allied Command. 'For Sieg too the sun has gone out', Edith wrote in her diary that night after dinner. 'No one can hear of Rex's loss unshaken and everyone feels that the loss to the world is infinitely more than our personal loss. Yet our personal loss makes the world seem small. Everyone seems to know what R. and I are to each other. In spite of this', she wrote, 'the dinner was strangely a success and the two guests liked each other . . . Siegfried put his arm round me and said I am always and ever your friend. Be brave – you are – and live for us'.[6]

In New York, Cecil was told of Rex's death by a friend some time later. 'My nerves, long pent up, suddenly snapped . . . tears, lamentations, and hysterical cries of self-condemnation', he later wrote. 'Rex, a natural talent if ever there was one, would now never be able to develop the art of painting, which, he said, he felt he was just beginning to learn. Now his potentials were all unfulfilled, and Rex the person, suffused with effortless charm, so romantic and youthful of appearance, with his bold ram-like profile and pale, tired eyes, would never grow old.'[7] Edith had written to Cecil three days after she had heard, but he had been in Connecticut, with friends:

> I know not where you are but wherever it may be you will need comfort such as I cannot give but I want it so much myself that I must hold out my hand to you.
>
> Rex's death is the worst thing that has ever happened to me – and not to me only – but to the world to which he was so precious. So much work remained for him to do and to do with that <u>lighthearted power</u> which he possessed as a unique characteristic he ought not to have been <u>allowed to go</u>. Everyone feels this but no one seems to have had the position to stop it . . . Rex wrote his last letter to me on a 'Sunday' . . .

but I believe he was killed the next Saturday. He said 'you may have to wait a long time before my next'. Yes – yes. It is a long time. Bless you Cecil and may we all find comfort some day . . . Come back to me soon.⁸

'Everyone speaking to me about Rex and it's <u>agony</u> to save myself from crying all the time', Edith wrote a few days later.⁹ She immediately suggested to Rex's mother that there should be a memorial service at Salisbury Cathedral and in return she received a warm and generous letter from Helen. 'Oh Edith darling what we so dreaded has come upon us, in spite of our prayers', she wrote. She was pleased by the suggestion of a memorial service: 'Rex so loved the Cathedral and Salisbury and Wilton. I think they were more to him than any other places on earth'.¹⁰

In the archive of Edith's papers, there are boxes filled with letters of condolence written to her after Rex's death. 'I got a great many letters about Rex', she wrote, 'agonising <u>for me</u> but making me proud <u>for him</u>'.¹¹ In some she is treated like a proud mother, in others like a widow, reassured of Rex's devotion to her. It was a great comfort for Edith to hear how loved and admired Rex had been. On 31 July, Edith read a tribute to Rex in *The Times*, written by John Gielgud. His production of *A Midsummer Night's Dream,* designed by Rex, would now never come to pass. Edith thought Gielgud's tribute 'a most true and beautiful appreciation of Rex' but the words, in black and white on the printed page, were the final proof that her dear friend of nineteen years had gone: 'O that it should have come to this – "<u>personal tribute</u>" to the <u>late Lieut Rex Whistler</u> – so that's the end'.¹² Some time later Edith's last letter to Rex, thanking him for the Normandy cheeses and fretting about his copy of *Country Life*, was returned to her unopened, on it stamped: 'it is regretted that this item could not be delivered because the addressee is reported deceased'.¹³

The night before Rex's memorial service Laurence arrived at the Daye House. 'It was about midnight when I arrived', he later recalled, 'and opening the gate found Edith Olivier waiting in the leafy tunnel, silent, in zebra-striped moonlight.'[14] The next day they went to the cathedral. Later there was tea at the Daye House.

Sassoon was horrified when Hester began to act like Rex's grieving widow, telling him that now she had no one to live for but George. A few days later she arrived at the Daye House 'looking very striking in black and white' and bearing a letter with an eye-witness account of Rex's death that she had received from her friend Francis Portal, one of Rex's fellow officers.[15] It addresses Hester in an intimate way, suggesting that at least one of Rex's friends considered her to be, in effect, his widow. Edith knew very little about Rex's affair with Hester but she refused to believe that it had been serious. Later, in October, after Hester had sat with her at the Daye House weeping over Rex's death, Edith wondered: 'How many hearts have been broken by his going.'[16]

The following year she wrote that Hester had said to her: 'I am fond of Siegfried but I loved Rex', to which Edith added in her diary: 'Rex did not love her'.[17] How much of this was an attempt to provoke Sassoon and how much was real affection remains unclear. But for Edith, that day in early August, the letter that Hester bore was some comfort. It said that Rex had died without pain, that he was not disfigured by the blast, that his 'expression was perfectly calm and happy' and that he had been temporarily buried on the spot. It also said that Rex's manservant was 'inconsolable'.[18]

Rex was buried beside the hedge where his men had laid his body, as he had wished. Later it was disinterred and moved to Banneville-la-Campagne, a war cemetery near Caen, to be buried beside 2,174 other men killed in the Normandy fighting. It was as he had feared, but Banneville is relatively small compared to others; red roses grow near his grave and nearby, at the entrance to the cemetery, stands a wood with a Gothic ruin at its heart.

Portal had spent much of his time with Rex in the two days before his death. He told Hester:

Rex had no illusions about the danger of his job. The one thing that used to worry him was the fear that – being not very military by nature – he might fail to do the best thing for his troop. He will be relieved now, to know that this fear was groundless. He is one of the best friends I have ever had – so I miss him . . . I suppose the war will come to an end soon now – though still too late for so much that matters.[19]

Edith's diary was still full of war news: the allies landing on the Riviera and the German defeat in Normandy. Later that month she began writing an article about Rex commissioned by Christopher Hussey for *Country Life*. She cried as she worked at it and wrote in her diary that she could no longer understand who it was she was writing about. She had never been in any doubt, though, that Rex was a genius, and she felt it her duty to write it: 'One's own grief is nothing compared with the loss to the world'.[20] When the artist Henry Lamb came for tea that month, Edith showed him Rex's pictures which he had never seen before. He commented upon 'his great gift for seeing and producing light', Edith wrote later, adding: 'I think that symbolises what he was throughout – a god-like creature creating light'.[21]

To Edith's delight, Sassoon and Charles Fry of Batsford had suggested that she should write 'a splendid memorial volume' about Rex. This, then, was to be her tribute to him, her final vocation. In September a notice appeared in the press announcing her plans. David Cecil came to lunch and talked with Edith about her plans for the book. 'I want to sit the personal story in the universal – but how. The artist's character – Rex standing out'.[22] Stephen brought letters from Rex for her to use in the book. 'I think 'em too personal', she wrote, 'chiefly shewing R's great love for Stephen when they were boys – but naturally that does appeal to S'.[23]

When her niece Rosemary arrived from 'the world of active living and doing', Edith suddenly panicked at her own inactivity. 'This house becomes a back-water. It will be – unless I can be alone and can find again Rex's creative power helping me to make the book about him from the letters and memories which I am receiving from his friends. How often', she wrote, 'I have seen his pen create a completely new and vivid <u>thing</u> out of uninspired material – as when he was illustrating a book. It suddenly came to life and something was born, living with his life.'[24]

For the present, however, although she was doing some preliminary research for the Rex book, Edith had her Wiltshire project to focus on and, of course, beyond her own tragedy, the war rumbled on and with it her official work. But it now seemed that the end was in sight. At a meeting in September, the council discussed proposals for the way in which Wilton would celebrate the end of the war in Europe. Edith wanted a royal proclamation to be read, church bells to ring, the national anthem to be sung, a band to play and a bonfire to be lit. 'All will be spontaneous', she wrote.[25]

At the end of August, Laurence had arrived at the Daye House to sort through all the paintings and personal items that Rex had left with Edith for safekeeping. 'Going thro darling Rex's paintings and things – making lists of all his work, partly for the book and partly because they must be <u>placed</u>', she wrote.[26] Laurence was a comfort: 'says I must not think my life is over with Rex's . . . I am a <u>shrine</u> and he was a pilgrim to it! I say NO – he was the priest who made it a shrine!' she wrote in her diary that night.[27]

The next few months of Laurence's life were coloured by joy and then yet more sorrow, in quick succession. In November Jill died suddenly, a week after giving birth to a baby girl. She had suffered from a recurring blood disorder. Edith was staying with friends when she heard the news. 'This to me is the worst tragedy of all', she wrote. 'What <u>can</u> Laurie do? . . . Nothing can make it any better – and that exquisite little spirit vanished.'[28]

'I think the Daye House one of the muses' favourite lodges; so much has been painted and written and composed . . . and planned and spoken there', Laurence would later write to Edith, after a month's stay at the Daye House in April 1946.[29] They grew closer after Rex's death and even more so, it seems, after Jill had died. Undoubtedly they were united by their grief and a mutual sympathy, each of them a link for the other to those that they had lost and, at least for Edith perhaps, a kind of substitute, as Rex had been for Mildred in 1925. 'He has loved being here and I have loved him', Edith wrote in her diary after Laurence left at the end of April 1946, in words reminiscent of those she had so often written about Rex.[30] In turn, Laurence's letters to Edith, which arrived more frequently in these years, sound increasingly Rex-like, increasingly affectionate. From the heat of London in July, he wrote: 'I thought of my cool, rain-drifted days with you, and the colours of sunlight spinning over the water, and that was refreshing'.[31] And at the beginning of 1947, he would write, again from London: 'Beloved Edith, This is to say that I love you – and why not say it for once instead of always thinking it, and leaving it at that . . . I want to be with you darling Edith . . . Darling I think of you so much, and your gallantry is always an inspiration to me.'[32] Even Laurence's mother Helen, worrying that her son was lonely and seemed ill, wrote to Edith in a letter from Maidenhead where she now lived with her new husband: 'if he were with you it would be a real tonic for him, and he would write all the more delightfully in your exquisite Wilton atmosphere'.[33] Laurence too encouraged Edith to write the Rex memorial book. It 'would be a solace', he wrote, and he agreed with many of their friends that Edith might find it cathartic, in much the same way as *Mildred* had been, nineteen years earlier.[34]

In the autumn her cousin Lally, Laurence Olivier, sent her tickets, 'the 2 best seats in the house', to see him play Richard III at the Old Vic. She asked Zita to join her. She thought he was 'marvellous . . . He was not a bad or cruel man but a terrible Force of Sin.'[35] After the performance Edith went to visit him backstage; he could barely speak and was about to go on duty as a fire watcher in the theatre that night. Later that month Cecil came to see her at the Daye House. She observed that he had 'grown very bald and now looks more and more a dignified

Ambassador. No one would recognise the hated and despised feminine boy of 20 years ago'.[36]

At Christmas Edith wrote in her diary that she had made a festive arrangement out of bamboo with red glass balls. 'Rex and I agreed to hate bamboo – and now I have brought it in', she wrote. 'After all it doesn't look too bad.'[37] On Christmas Eve, the day the country was told that there was no longer any need to dim the lights on cars, Edith received a parcel of her own letters to Rex, sent to her by his mother. She had sent with it a note to Edith: 'I found this bundle with darling Rex's things & seeing your handwriting, Edith darling, I return them to you – unread by anyone of course.'[38] Reading through the letters Edith wept; there was 'no one now to whom I can write like that', she wrote in her diary that night. She was overjoyed to realize that a number of the letters had been sent to Rex some weeks before he sailed for France and that he had taken them with him on the boat: 'O how wonderful'.[39] On New Year's Eve, her seventy-second birthday, Edith lay in bed listening to the passing of the old year on the wireless and wrote in her diary:

> How unbroken is the silence of the dead – Far worse as the months go on – because at first they don't seem gone at all, but nearer than before and now it grows more and more acute. This is the devil tempting us to believe that death is a reality when all the time it is a deceit. Yet the deadly silence is here. No response. None.[40]

Over the next few months as the war drew to a close, Edith began to gather information about Rex's life from people they knew and received many offers of help from his friends. In March one told her that 'Rex was full of plans as to what he would do after the war'. 'I was in every one of them', she wrote with delight.[41] She received a letter from Stephen in Bournemouth about Rex and their time together at the Slade: 'what a unique gift his was! How we shall miss him. Perhaps one of the most beautiful elements in the immortality of the artist, is the unspoken burden of what he might have done.'[42]

By the end of April German forces were all but defeated. Hitler committed suicide in his bunker in Berlin on 30 April as the Russian army poured into the city. On 7 May Admiral Karl Dönitz surrendered to the Allied General Dwight Eisenhower in France. The surrender was signed by General Jodl (on behalf of Dönitz) and Walter Bedell Smith, Eisenower's chief of staff. The Germans also surrendered to the Soviets, represented by General Susloparov. That day Edith sat by the wireless waiting for the news of victory. The following day she wrote 'Victory Day' in her diary, 'called officially V.E. Day . . . and tomorrow is also a Public Holiday V.E. Day 2. These names shew the lack of imagination engendered by nearly 6 years of war.' There were thunderstorms in Wiltshire as the country came to a standstill. Later Edith joined the celebrations around a bonfire built by German prisoners of war on Grovely Hill. 'They must have hated doing this', she wrote.[43] The next day she was delighted to get into her car again with the promise that petrol would be available at the beginning of June. She drove to Heytesbury to lunch with Sassoon and his son George, and saw, at first hand, that Sassoon's marriage was all but over. 'He really hates her but still would love her if she would only be a bit more clever', Edith wrote of Hester. 'She talks as if she and Rex had been lovers. Says she wanted him to come home blinded so that she could do everything for him!' she added.[44] Edith's loyalty inclined towards Sassoon even though she pitied Hester's predicament. But Sassoon did not see it like that, believing that she had taken his wife's side, and though Edith would continue to see him, they were never again as close as they once had been.

Apart from Sassoon who remained in semi-seclusion at Heytesbury, as he had throughout the war, it seemed to Edith that her circle of male friends had all but dissolved. There had been a brief and happy time when all of Edith's most cherished friends lived nearby: Rex at Salisbury, Stephen at Wilsford, Cecil at Ashcombe and Sassoon at Heytesbury. Now, although so many of the war-scarred men that she had prayed about over the years were returning home, and the country returned to a semblance of normality, her old world was changed irrevocably.

Later, in June, she attended the unveiling of Rex's painted room, which included his *Allegory* of the Prince Regent at the regimental mess at Brighton. She was shocked by the nude which, until now, she had only seen in a photograph. She thought it 'loud and <u>lascivious</u>' and realized that she had never known Rex completely.[45] On 24 June she returned home from Brighton; it would have been Rex's fortieth birthday and she decided that she was glad he had only seen his thirties. 'He could not have been an old middle-aged man and now he is <u>forever young</u>'.[46]

Another disaster (to Edith it was such) befell her at the end of July. 'Labour swept the Polls and has an enormous majority. The Coalition ends. We face the world a divided nation and tho' the War is practically over the safety of the peace is in the hands of a Party Govt. and one which has no knowledge of international affairs.'[47] And then two months after the war in Europe had ended, Edith visited Cecil at Ashcombe: 'Borley's [the landlord] son is taking it away from Cecil in Sept. We shall none of us see it again', she wrote, adding: 'it will be a ghostly memory of a creation which has lived for 15 amazing years'.[48]

Edith was Cecil's last guest before he left Ashcombe in September. She took a taxi up the steep, slippery, chalky road and down into the valley, that road which she had driven so many times with Rex beside her in the car or once, in an omnibus, en route to a fête champêtre, the house lit by torches and adorned with ribbons and paper flowers. It was fitting that she should be his last guest. Edith had first told him about the house; they had set off in search of it together and discovered it together, that 'Grand Meaulnes sort of place', on a magical day back in the spring of 1930. Now it had truly become a lost domain, a symbol of another age, of fantasy, and all that had gone.

When Edith Olivier came over to visit me in the house that

she had helped me to create, the past surged to the surface. There had been so many Arcadian meetings here: many scenes that were important to us had been staged here: so much had happened during fifteen years. During that time the world we knew had come to an end. We looked back amazedly at the albums of photographs and at the silhouettes of the hands scrawled upon the bathroom walls to discover how many of those names now belonged to the dead . . . the loss of Rex creating an unbridgeable chasm. Now those who had survived would meet here no more.

As I walked with Edith, now white-haired, for the last times across the lawns towards the studio, to the archway and to the attendant car, neither of us were able to speak. I felt a constriction of the throat and my eyes overflowed with hot tears.[49]

'I cried all the way home', Edith wrote to Cecil the next day. 'It is the end of a wonderful creation . . . giving to us all a new world in which to find all this fun, all this beauty . . . it is impossible to believe that Ashcombe is over but then the houses on High Ground in Wiltshire are always evanescent – Clarendon Palace, Beckford's Fonthill and now Cecil Beaton's Ashcombe . . .'[50] Cecil planned to write a book about the house and spent the days before he left haunting its rooms and walking in the garden with his camera as if to capture every aspect of the world he had created there.

In her diary, Edith's life appears much the same after the war as before it began. She continued to attend daily communion, she was secretary of the Wilton WI, she sat on committees and was invited to join new ones. She worked on her Wiltshire book and received fan mail from her readers. She recorded a series of broadcasts for the BBC and, one Sunday afternoon in September 1947, *The Love-Child* was broadcast by the Home Service. She went up to London, to visit friends, to watch plays, and to dine at the Savoy. She entertained at the Daye House and stayed with friends in the country, the Angleseys at Plas Newydd and Michael Duff at Vaynol. She was there in August 1945 when news came that an atomic bomb had been dropped on Hiroshima. She heard Clement Attlee on the wireless announcing peace and wrote how much she missed the sound of Churchill's voice. Later she travelled to The Hague to stay with an old friend and there met Dutch Resistance fighters who had sheltered British servicemen. She made new friends out of the children of her older friends. Old friends died, including Caroline Paget's mother, Lady Anglesey, for whom Edith wrote the obituary in *The Times*.* Only a few months later Lord Anglesey died too. David Herbert brought Caroline and Liz to see Edith: 'in spite of all, Caroline keeps her wry, <u>withdrawing</u> character, which completely carries me away'.[51]

And then there was Rex. In November 1945 she had written in her diary:

> I had a very clear vivid dream, heard a bell ring. Told the servant . . . to go to the door. She returned and announced <u>Mr Rex Whistler</u>. He came in, only one eye and one cheek could be seen for bandages . . . his arm tied up and his leg. He looked well. I said <u>my darling Rex</u>. He looked at me with great love – and did not speak. We kissed and stood embraced. I knew we had thought him dead and I thought this had been a mistake . . . we <u>felt great love</u>. I woke happy and then cried.[52]

In January 1946, Edith was overjoyed to learn that forty-two of her friends, including Siegfried Sassoon, Cecil Beaton, Laurence Whistler, the Duchess of Devonshire and Lord and Lady Pembroke, had grouped together to buy Rex's 1940 portrait of her wearing a striped suit. Their names were listed on the back of the frame. Imma suddenly appeared at the Daye House with a basket of strawberries that summer. Edith had not seen her for six years. She had left her husband, Neil McEachern, whom she had discovered to be homosexual and a violent alcoholic after only

---

* She died on 3 November 1946.

a few months of marriage. She had returned to England with a young Dutch officer called Kees with whom she was in love. Imma stayed at the Daye House for almost a month; she was planning to divorce her husband, and although this was against her Catholic instincts she saw no other option. Edith sympathized.

Edith continued to research the Wiltshire book through 1946, but the fibrositis that had troubled her for years became so bad that her doctor told her not to write or type anything. This was exacerbated later in the year by a sudden loss of vision in one eye.* In August, at Vaynol, she wrote in her diary that she had 'an extraordinary <u>blur</u>' in her eye. 'I am quite blind', she added.[53] Edith's high blood pressure, probably caused by years of smoking and which she had been trying to keep down with a restrictive diet, had caused a blood vessel to break in her eye.

In December she wrote to Cecil, just returned from America from where he had brought unobtainable luxuries:

> A most wonderful present came from you yesterday. A parcel containing not only what we once thought were <u>necessities</u> but now know are <u>impossibilities</u>. That is the concrete side – but Cecil dearest it means such affection on your part, such consideration, such understanding and such generosity, all those things are even more precious and rare, and it is for those which I thank you most of all . . . I have had a rather bad Autumn. I was at first <u>completely blind</u> and in front of me there seemed to be hanging a screen composed of sea-weed, scorpions, hairy caterpillars and woodlice with red tails.

When this had happened, Edith's doctor had banned her from driving. It had been a great day when he told her that she could drive again. The next day Stephen presented her with the latest Rover Twelve, 'heavenly to drive when I have mastered the mysteries of the complicated dashboard!' she told Cecil.[54]

---

* Fibrositis, or fibromyalgia as it is now known, is an inflammation of joints and connective tissue which causes chronic and debilitating muscle pain.

That month Edith rejoiced at the melting of the snow and the return of green fields and realized that that was how it was to be old. As a child the disappearance of snow before Christmas meant an end to skating and festive fun. Her boiler broke in the New Year and she went to stay at Wilsford until it was mended. Stephen was full of new plans for the house; he had made the terrace outside into a Mediterranean garden with urns and fountains and exotic plants, all at odds with the bitterly cold weather and the frost that covered it all in a crystalline coating. He also told her that he was friendly with Sassoon again.

Early in the New Year the snow returned. Edith learnt that Patricia Hambleden's beloved husband William had a brain tumour. He died in the following year leaving a family of five children, the youngest being only two and a half.

In March Edith went to visit Cecil at the new home she had found for him, Reddish House, where once the artist Christopher Wood's parents had lived, an exquisite manor house in Broad Chalke. One day in October she had driven him to Dinton to see a house that was for sale there. It would not do, they soon realized, being far too grand and too expensive for Cecil's taste. They dejectedly returned to the car, skidding along icy roads as they made their way back to Wilton. They drove through Broad Chalke and there Edith had abruptly stopped the car in front of a house with an early-eighteenth-century, pink-brick facade. Reddish was lovely, perhaps even more perfectly proportioned than his last home; it was not Ashcombe though. But for Cecil it was the start of a new phase in his life. 'Of course Reddish House did not possess the wayward romantic remoteness of Ashcombe. Instead of hiding in folds of wooded downland, it presented its extremely formal exterior on to a village street . . . Moreover, the house was a real house – not a fantasy, makeshift pretence like Ashcombe. This was the abode of an adult person: perhaps it would be a good thing if I started living up to my swiftly advancing age.'[55]

When she returned home from visiting Cecil that day she received a call from Imma's landlady telling her that Imma was seriously ill in London. She was also alone. Kees was on the continent; only weeks before, Imma had heard from her husband that he would not oppose a divorce and she planned to marry her lover. Arriving at Imma's flat at Buckingham Gate, having struggled across London in a taxi through heavy snow, Edith found her unable to talk or move. Her doctor had diagnosed pernicious anaemia, a condition in which the immune system attacks the stomach cells. It was then incurable. Edith stayed in London that night and returned home as Imma, almost unconscious, was taken to hospital the next day. Edith desperately tried to contact Kees and William Walton but had no luck with either of them. She returned once to London to see Imma as she lay dying. Two days later she was gone, without regaining consciousness. Edith organized the funeral, at Netherhampton. The Daye House had been the only place in England that Imma considered a home. Two days later Edith had anguished telephone calls, first from Kees and later from Walton. Neither of them had known Imma was ill.

Edith struggled on with the Wiltshire book, the thought of which had been a kernel of joy for her throughout the war, and eventually, by October, it was finally finished. That month Cecil sent her the manuscript of *Ashcombe* to read. 'I love the way in which the house grows into you', she wrote to him.

> . . . the charm and magic of its first appearance, the gaiety of the years until 1938, the courage, the danger and the hard daily life of the wartime and then the renunciation and loss of today. It is all very near one's heart. But now my darling I must thank you for the heavenly way you write of <u>me</u>. Tears came from my eyes so much that for ages I couldn't read at all. I do feel that you write so sincerely that I can indeed be proud of what you say. I long for the book to be published!! I jumped from page to page at first to find every mention of darling Rex and it will be one of the worthy monuments to his darling memory. A long time hence people will read it and will know that the most precious thing about him was not his genius (great as it was) but his unique loveableness.[56]

The winter of 1947 was one of the most severe on record. Edith spent Christmas Day at home and lunched with her housekeeper in the kitchen. A few weeks after the New Year and her seventy-fifth birthday, she had a meeting with her bank manager at Lloyd's who told her that she was £187 overdrawn 'and no hope of getting it right, and no publishers can issue new editions so I get no royalties and my new books are delayed for the same reason – lack of paper', she wrote. 'I have been living on capital for 3 years and shall go on doing it. He advises me to buy an Annuity with some of my money and I am doing this which will ease matters.'[57]

'What a beloved letter you wrote me and I cling to it and its writer the more because I am now very lonely – so I <u>do thank you</u>', Edith had written to Cecil in December. 'Laurie Whistler is here for a few days as he is trying to get the material for the Rex book into order they want it in the spring but make no promise of it ever being published. Laurie is very helpful in arranging the papers but there could not be two more <u>unlike</u> brothers. Rex glowing with youth till the end while I chiefly see Laurie as a <u>nice old gentleman</u>!!'[58]

There was still other work to do. She was asked to write an essay for a book to be published by Faber, *A Tribute to Walter de la Mare on His Seventy-Fifth Birthday*. Other contributors were T. S. Eliot, Edmund Blunden, Cecil Day Lewis, Graham Greene, Edith Sitwell, John Masefield, J. B. Priestley, Vita Sackville-West and Siegfried Sassoon. She was in grand company. She decided to write about 'The Wiltshire homes of two poets', Henry Newbolt's Netherhampton House and Pamela Grey's Wilsford. They had been two of de la Mare's closest friends, and two of Edith's closest friends as well.

Though she had fainted for the first time some months earlier and been advised by her doctor to take care of her weary heart, and though the roof of the Long Room now leaked in heavy rain, there was some comfort. At the beginning of 1948 she could finally dedicate all of her time to the Rex book. 'I sometimes think

I can't go on bearing it – this long lonely life without him', she had written to Laurence.[59]

Back in January 1945 Sassoon had written to her from Heytesbury. 'The important thing about the Rex book is to collect material', he told her, adding: 'I feel that you could get it written better when the war is over. There is no hurry about it, and all our minds are hindered and devitalised by present conditions'.[60] As it happened, she would not begin work on it for some time after the war had ended. But Edith failed to recognize that the hint of caution in Sassoon's letter was a veiled suggestion that she should not, after all, write the book at all. Laurence agreed. He had promised to help her with information about his brother's childhood, as soon as he had finished his own book on festivals, but it seems that he never did. After reading Edith's *Country Life* article in 1944, both Sassoon and Laurence had become convinced, although they could not tell her, that her book would be a hagiography. 'Beginning at last the Rex book', she wrote on the 11th; 'only did childhood and Haileybury and can't get on far without seeing pictures he did at those times as I do want the whole story to be told by his own work . . . the problem will be to get these. If Helen won't send them here I must go to [her] and this journey will kill me. At the moment the book feels heavy and unlike me but then I haven't really got into it'.[61]

Charles Fry, Edith's publisher at Batsford, told her that he had envisioned the book as 'a patchwork of contributions' with about one hundred illustrations.[62] Edith wanted to write it exclusively, with the friends' contributions going into her research rather than into the final text and for Rex's pictures to be the focus. 'It will not be good', she wrote.[63] But researching Rex's life brought him closer to her once more. 'Another steady day of work on Rex – transcribing several of his letters', she wrote in February; 'I feel like I am <u>living with him</u>. Yet he is always out of reach. But how alive and vivid his letters are'.[64] Reading them was harrowing, but she felt that they were 'so overflowing with life and youth that I believe <u>less than ever</u> that he is dead.'[65] She worked on the book

...ost every day in early 1948, collecting material, conducting interviews and writing to Rex's friends for information. But she was struggling to write as her fingers were becoming too stiff to type. And she was feeling increasingly tired.

Then, in March, Edith drove to Wilsford where she hoped to glean contributions from Stephen. Instead, ever to the point, he told Edith of Laurence and Sassoon's fears: 'Drove to Wilsford trying to get something from Stephen for Rex book', she wrote in her diary that night. 'He depressed me having heard from Laurie and Siegfried that it <u>won't be good</u>. Asked me if we could find someone else to do it instead of me'.[66]

But she persevered. A few days later she went up to London to meet Rex's old friend Oliver Messel for tea. She enjoyed his company and was heartened by their discussion about Rex: 'O and I were busy till 12 making his contributions to the Rex book which will be just what I want and quite unlike all the others'.[67]

But Edith never wrote the Rex book.* And she would not live to see the publication of the Wiltshire book.** On 16 April, she had a small stroke and found that she couldn't write. Two days later she noted that she had struggled to hold her cup at a party earlier that day. She also wrote that she had heard the first cuckoo. It was the last time she wrote in her diary. On the 19th, she had a second, stronger stroke, which left her semi-paralysed and she asked for her niece Rosemary to be with her. Edith continued with her diary by dictating to Rosemary, but by the 22nd she could no longer speak and her diary ends abruptly on that day. Over the next few weeks, as visitors came and went and the daffodils bloomed and faded in the park, Edith's condition slowly deteriorated. And, on the evening of 10 May, she died in her sleep.

---

* It appears from her diaries that Edith was still in the preparatory stage of her work on the Rex book when she died.

** *Wiltshire* was published in 1951. When Edith died the proofs had not yet been corrected and she had not selected the illustrations. Her niece Rosemary edited the text and wrote the foreword, thanking those who had helped Edith with the book towards the end of her life, when she was almost blind.

Edith's obituary appeared in *The Times* two days later. She 'spent', it reads, 'almost the whole of her life at Wilton, in Wiltshire' and 'drew the motive of almost everything she wrote from her knowledge and love of her native county'.[68] Her funeral was held on Friday 14 May at St Mary and St Nicholas. In a tribute written for the *Salisbury Journal* Cecil gave an account of the service:

> The perfection of May – the beauty of architecture – and the smell of flowers. And the stillness beyond feeling. This was the day on which we took our leave of a very gracious lady. Slowly the Church filled with her friends – young and old, those who had shared in her widely differing interests, those who had helped her, and those whom she had helped. Steadily they came, some in processions, others alone, all with their own reasons for their grief. At the back, unnoticed, a great poet; across the aisle, a man of letters, whose voice is known across the world.
>
> The dignity of Church and government was there to pay her honour, as was fitting.
>
> But that was only part of what was in our hearts. There was honour, indeed, for what she had done; but there was love for what she was and is. We were there because we loved her: we owe her so.[69]

Later Cecil walked with David Herbert and others to the grave. 'As they lowered the coffin', David wrote, 'with a swish of wings a pigeon flew straight up into the sky. Cecil and I gasped and in one breath said: "Edith soaring through tracks unknown!"'[70]

When it was published the following year, Cecil dedicated his book, *Ashcombe: The Story of a Fifteen-Year Lease*, to 'the memory of EDITH OLIVIER who brought me to Wiltshire'.[71] 'Darling Edith, how I miss her', Stephen later wrote to Cecil, beside a sketch he had drawn of Edith, a vital, sharp-nosed little woman, tugging at her beads, a pen in her hand and stars at her feet. 'Her genius for loving her friends set her apart', he wrote; 'she was a practitioner of the loving spirit – She made of friendship a fine art – a <u>miracle</u>.'[72]

'How time slips by', Arthur Street wrote in the autumn:

> I drove Edith to a party one evening last Christmastide. There she was the centre of attention, a magnet that drew old and young to her side, to pay homage to a sparkling personality. In short she was the Edith Olivier we all knew and admired and loved.
>
> It was not until I conveyed her down the garden path to my car that I realised that her great heart had now become too big for her body. Indoors, Edith had been as ever, the life and soul of the party; outdoors I suddenly realised that on my arm was a very fragile old lady.
>
> But still her great heart kept her going at full speed. Shortly after that party she flew to Belgium. Every week I read somewhere that she had travelled here, taken the chair there, or spoken somewhere else. And each time I read of such activities I felt ashamed of my own laziness by comparison.
>
> Then, with such little warning, in May of this year Edith Olivier quietly slipped away from us, leaving a gap in the life of Wessex that will require many lesser people to fill. Honestly, it was not until I found myself at her funeral that I realised that my fairy godmother was indeed a mortal.[73]

Edith was buried beside her sister Mildred in the shadow of the church of St Mary and St Nicholas at Wilton. A simple wooden cross marks the grave, curiously rustic amongst the stones and wrought iron. It stands, as if symbolic of Edith herself, halfway between the flamboyant church and the conservative rectory beside it.

Legacies

❖

'What do we any of us live for but our illusions and what can we ask of others but that they should allow us to keep them?'

Somerset Maugham, *The Sacred Flame*, Act III

'"Rex Whistler!" . . . To those who knew him the name <u>Rex</u> could signify only one person', wrote Osbert Sitwell in 1949;* 'a young man of great and lovable character, and possessed of such various talents in the arts and decoration as in their sum to approach genius'. For Sitwell, writing five years after the event, Rex's death still provoked 'anger at the waste in war of so valuable and irreplaceable a life'.[1]

In the wake of Rex's death, Laurence Whistler claimed, *The Times* received a larger mailbag about his brother than for any other person killed in the war.** To John Gielgud's tribute in *The Times* was added one by Osbert Sitwell in August and another, in September, by Rex's commanding officer, who wrote that he 'possessed a rich sense of the ridiculous, a strong sense of duty, and his character was simple and clean', adding that he 'was one of the most delightful men the Welsh Guards has ever carried on its roll

---

* *Noble Essences or Courteous Revelations*, published in 1950, is made up of a number of pen portraits of people that Sitwell had known and admired. Rex is amongst a group that includes Wilfred Owen, Gabriele d'Annunzio and Arnold Bennett.

** If this is true, it is extraordinary. As Laurence does not support this with any evidence and *The Times* keeps no record of this kind of information, it is not possible to verify this claim.

and he died a hero.'[2] In an article in the *Daily Telegraph* written by his friend Lady Eleanor Smith, Rex was compared to Rupert Brooke; in a poem written by another friend, the Duchess of Wellington, he was compared to Shelley. To Caroline Paget in August, Christabel McLaren wrote: 'To me his death is the greatest tragedy of the war: indeed, I haven't minded anything so much for over a quarter of a century: I really feel I cannot bear it. That proud tilt to his head – that lovely . . . white face – his smile – gaiety, – wit – the look on his face when he was teased – oh, it is unendurable that all that should be swept away, – finished. Dear, dear Rex.'[3]

Diana Cooper, writing her memoirs many years later, recalled that she had found the news of Rex's death 'heartbreaking', 'the saddest that the war brought me', she wrote.

> I minded desperately and Duff was sobbing like a child. Rex was one of the few younger men I really loved, and I'll miss him, his charm and his art, his sympathy and affection. There is pathos about it that compels tears. Rex was like Fortinbras – fair, dedicated and physically most refinedly made. His spare figure and pale face, the texture of his skin, the fit of his finger-nails, his shining well-set teeth and sweeping hair were those of a delicate and tender prince . . . What was touching was his fervour, his frame too frail for so much armour but wearing it erectly though it was much too heavy. He'll be mourned indeed, sweet Rex.[4]

There were far more famous casualties of the war, far braver men and many more dramatic and heroic deaths than this one. Obviously Rex was loved. But, for some, he had also become a symbolic figure: he represented the waste and brutality of war and to an extent he would represent the 'in-between time' as Rupert Brooke had come to represent his own, the 'Lost Generation', that which had gladly gone off to fight and planned to be home by Christmas. After his death in April 1915, Brooke's short life was spun into a romantic myth, one that, it has since been revealed, was at odds

with reality. But the myth persisted, that of the young and beautiful fallen hero who had naively defended the war: a poet; a
golden-haired Apollo; punting on the Cam on a mellow, Edwardian afternoon.

It is interesting that after the Second World War no iconic
military martyrs captured the British imagination as they had after
the First. In military terms, World War Two was a war of heroes,
not martyrs; its victims had gone into battle knowingly, not inno-
cently. Rex was not directly associated in the British consciousness
with war, as the author of 'The Soldier' had been. He was not the
Rupert Brooke of the Second World War. And yet, for some perhaps, an image of Rex, his face painted and dressed in a frilly
white shirt and breeches for a tableau vivant, came to represent
this second lost generation and the seemingly carefree frivolity of
the Bright Young People of the twenties, who themselves had
been identified as a reaction to the previous war. The historical
inspiration, the elegance and charm of his work, had always
provoked nostalgia, an idealized reminder of an earlier time, it
represented a dream of England that now, more than ever, was
lost. Rex's persona lent itself easily to the role of the fallen hero.
He had appeared as charming and old-fashioned as his work.
Perhaps for his friends, the exaggerated innocence of his work,
coupled with his romantic persona and his perceived eternal boy-
ishness (this, despite the fact that Rex was thirty-nine when he
died), were akin to Brooke's idealism and the innocence of the
Lost Generation. His decision, in 1939, to sign up, though seen
by some as foolhardy, was considered by many who knew him to
be a noble gesture. That he continued to resist the lure of the
desk jobs offered to him made him appear nobler still. Those
close to Rex had recognized the melancholy and loneliness concealed behind his charming facade, the causes of which, it
seemed, were his unhappiness in love and his lack of children. To
many of his friends he was a tragic figure, who seemed destined
to die in battle. 'Somehow, instinct told me Rex would be killed',
wrote Cecil Beaton in his memoirs. 'There was something so

indefinite and vague about him the last time he came on leave and stayed in my London house. He didn't know what he would do after the war: he didn't even know what to do with his leave.'[5]

Writing in her diary on the eve of D-Day in 1944, Diana Cooper confessed that 'the dread of landings' was upon her. 'So many to pray for . . . Rex. Rex worries me most. They can't all survive.'[6] And Siegfried Sassoon, on reading the news that Rex had died, wrote in his diary: 'I somehow felt he would be killed'.[7] Even Rex's death was romantic, in as much as any death can be described as such. He died on his first day on the battlefield. His body had seemed untouched by the blast that had killed him and he was laid to rest in a 'foreign field'.

And Rex reminded his friends of their own lost youth. Though they had grown up and embraced the responsibilities, burdens and bonds of adulthood, Rex remained, it appeared to them, a Peter Pan figure, tragically sacrificed on the altar of war. But this was based on a misconception. Rex had grown up. Far from being an unwitting victim of the war, Rex's time in the army had been one of liberation, both for himself and for his art. And far from making a feeble soldier, he had been a responsible and capable officer, held in high esteem by his men and fellow officers.

Laurence Whistler would later write that he was alarmed by the reaction to Rex's death and the analogy with Rupert Brooke. There was, he wrote, 'the same risk that if a myth were substituted for a man, some harm might be done, by reaction, to the true assessment of a talent'.[8] The *Country Life* article that Edith had written in August 1944, 'Memories of Rex Whistler', went a step further, opening with a reference to Sir Philip Sidney. 'Each of their deaths in battle evoked from his contemporaries something of the same emotion'; she added: 'after the death of Sir Philip, the Dutch Minister wrote: "What perfection he was grown unto, and how able to serve her Majesty and his country, all men here almost wondered at".'[9] 'Already the fond legend-spinners were at work', wrote Laurence.[10] 'No doubt', he conjectured, 'it was hard for a friend, clearly more than a friend . . . not to falsify slightly'.[11] Unquestionably, the tone of Edith's article was excessive. Her romantic idealization of Rex seems quaint and malapropos set against its wartime backdrop. But she had written the article less than a month after Rex's death, in the first flush of her grief.

So much of Rex was fashioned by Edith; she shared, and had helped to shape, his imagination, an imagination that coloured his life as it had coloured his art. Edith inhabited Rex's interior world and their lives were inextricably interwoven. Her *Country Life* article was a fantasy of Rex, but then fantasy was at the very heart of their friendship. Edith had likened Rex to Sir Philip Sidney because to her and indeed to others, Rex was a talented renaissance man, an artist as Sidney was a poet, and then a soldier. Like Sidney, Rex died in a war and was greatly mourned by his contemporaries. But it was not only that. The Daye House, at the edge of woods that had inspired Sidney's *Arcadia*, became a spiritual home for Rex. It became an Arcadia for him, too, an escape, first from his family home and later from his life in London. Like Sidney before him, Rex was profoundly inspired by the estate at Wilton; it was there that much of his aesthetic re-education took place, with Edith at the Daye House or joyfully exploring the surrounding countryside in her car, amongst the old masters at Wilton House or gazing in awe at the Palladian Bridge that spanned the river nearby.

Edith transformed Rex, socially and intellectually, and she believed in her invention unswervingly, as Agatha in *The Love-Child* believed in her imaginary friend, Clarissa. Rex helped to transform Edith, too, both physically and socially, and she in turn educated him and doted on him, unreservedly and uncritically. She was perhaps the reflective stream for Rex. This is also true, to an extent, of her relationships with Cecil Beaton, Stephen Tennant and Siegfried Sassoon and also, to a degree, her friendships with Brian Howard and William Walton.

Edith and Rex's friendship was intimate, symbiotic and exclusive. In her company he could satisfy his instinct for fantasy, their days spent exploring Wiltshire, visiting the grand houses of Edith's aristocratic friends, writing stories together and inspiring each other's work. For Rex, Edith's world within the high walls of Wilton Park was not only an escape from the demands of family, friends and clients, it was a retreat from the reality of his life. The man that Rex was for Edith didn't struggle with his sexuality and it did not matter that he was unmarried and childless; she allowed Rex to be a fantasy version of himself, one that was often at odds with the reality of his life. With Edith he was chivalrous, old-fashioned, Byronic. She would not question the courtliness of his dealings with women. This is the Rex she portrayed in her diaries and the Rex that his friends knew, mourned and memorialized. Even after his death, she remained loyal to Rex, presenting him as he would have wanted to be portrayed.

Rex, though, was as much a mirror for Edith as she was for him. Because, like the fictional friends in *The Love-Child*, the dynamic of their relationship was artificial, a courtly romance, a collaborative fantasy in which Edith became Rex's 'society' mother and a kind of platonic wife, while for Edith, Rex became a substitute for both the son and the husband she had never possessed. But there was an inherent sadness, an impotence, in their relationship. Behind the elaborate latticework of illusions that held them together, lurked frustration, unspoken desire and loneliness, and though it was both a loving and creatively inspiring relationship, perhaps, in different ways, it was never quite enough for either of them.

Perhaps the biography that Edith was planning would have been a hagiography, a memorial book, as *Mildred* had been. But that is not entirely fair. Years of writing books and reviewing them, had taught her objectivity. Years, too, of writing her diary, was proof that she was not without insight, even though she was the first to acknowledge that there was much of Rex's life that was unknown to her. It would never have been the definitive life of Rex Whistler but it would have been a loving tribute to him from Edith and all the friends that were helping her to write it.

By the time that Laurence Whistler came to write his life of Rex, *The Laughter and the Urn,* published in 1985, the business of biography was an entirely different entity. After the publication in 1967 of Michael Holroyd's *Lytton Strachey,* with its ground-breakingly candid revelations about his subject's homosexuality, nothing was off limits to the biographer. *The Laughter and the Urn* has a lapidary quality, as finely wrought and painstaking as the glass Laurence was by then engraving and as lyrical as the best of his poems. It is as much his autobiography as it is the story of his brother's life. And it is the accumulation of years spent protecting and preserving Rex's memory, an effort to dismantle the myths that 'the fond legend spinners' so lovingly wound around Rex's memory and an attempt to haul Rex's posthumous reputation out of the realms of whimsy and decoration and into the canon of fine art. It is a worthy tribute and a beautiful, poignant book.

But though Edith's plan to write Rex's biography had been thwarted, after her death she would, in a way, reclaim him. To the Tate she bequeathed the romantic self-portrait of Rex that she had owned and cherished, the portrait which best epitomized the man she knew. She kept his letters, the sprig of mistletoe still woven into his last, faded and mottled, but still green. And to her niece Rosemary, she left the many volumes of her diary, in the hope no doubt, that they would one day shed light not only on Rex's life, but also, perhaps more importantly, on her own.*

If the Edwardian period is often characterized as a prelapsarian Golden Age, then the time between the wars was perhaps silver: elegant, cool, elusive. The tough, tarnished world that emerged from the ruins in 1945 was a changed one. Some plunged into it, adapted, even thrived in this brave new world. Others retreated from it.

Like a phoenix, or a chameleon perhaps, Cecil Beaton

---

* Rosemary left Edith's archive to the Wiltshire Record Office after her death in 2002.

embraced each new age as it came; his eye for beauty and thirst for novelty never left him. He continued to take photographs and to write, and he headed for Broadway where he designed sets and costumes for the stage. Later he moved into film, as Rex might well have done, designing for *Gigi* in 1958 and *My Fair Lady* in 1964 and winning the Academy Awards for Costume Design for both films. Eventually America forgave him for his misdemeanour at *Vogue*. He was knighted in 1972. Cecil lived at Reddish for the rest of his life; there he courted and sheltered the reclusive Greta Garbo, and there he died in the first days of a new decade on 18 January 1980.

Ashcombe later became the locus of another's fantasy, a distinctly English one, when the pop star Madonna purchased it in 2001. Once again the house was to become the stage set for a pastoral performance. Tim Walker photographed her for *Vogue* wearing a tea dress and pearls and feeding hens on the lawn where once Beaton had rushed from the house to welcome his guests in a Tyrolean suit.

During the war William Walton had been exempted from military service in order to compose music for propaganda films, one of them Laurence Olivier's rousing adaptation of *Henry V*. Alice Wimborne died of cancer in 1948. Grief-stricken, Walton travelled to Argentina where he met Susana Gil Passo, an Argentinian woman twenty-four years his junior. They married later that year and bought a house on Ischia, La Mortella, where they created a celebrated exotic garden. Walton, who was knighted in 1951, loved the isolation of the island. He lived and composed there for the next thirty-five years until his death at the age of eighty in 1983.

Laurence Whistler continued to write poetry but it was for his glass engravings that he became well known and he was later credited as having revived the art of point engraving. He carried out a number of prestigious commissions, including work for the Royal Family. He was awarded an OBE, then a CBE and was knighted not long before his death in 2000 at the age of eighty-eight. Initially encouraged by Lutyens and Rex to engrave glass, Laurence developed an innovative technique whereby he engraved both sides of the glass to give an illusion of perspective to his spellbinding depictions of the English landscape. Laurence always felt that he lived in Rex's shadow, and perhaps his glass engraving is something of a response to that; subtle, self-effacing and yet audacious, using light, rather than paint, with an echoic affinity to the work of a brother he adored. Laurence later married Jill's younger sister Theresa with whom he had two children. A third marriage was dissolved some years before his death.

In 1949 Caroline Paget had discovered that she was pregnant. Who the father was is unclear, but many then thought that it was Sir Anthony Eden, with whom she had had an affair. Stepping into the breach, her old friend and neighbour Sir Michael Duff offered to marry her and she accepted. Just before Christmas that year she miscarried a boy. Some few weeks later she adopted a ten-week-old baby boy and christened him Charles. Audry Carten remained Caroline's life partner until Audry's mental illness became too extreme in 1960. Much of the final two decades of her life Caroline spent with the American artist and photographer Marguerite McBey. Caroline died in 1976 at the age of sixty-two. 'Growing up I felt as if I knew him', Charles Duff said later of Rex. 'He had been truly mourned, truly loved by Caroline.'[12] He also said of his mother and Rex: 'Her inability to return his love as he would have wished was the great sadness of Rex's life. But she told me that, just after she last saw him, she had decided that she was going to tell him, next time he came home on leave, that she would marry him.'[13] Caroline kept the scarlet-and-white Renoir dress and its matching parasol, which Rex had designed for her for the Ashcombe fête champêtre of 1937, until the end of her life. It was perhaps symbolic that she kept it in the dressing-up box.

After Rex's death his other love, Hester Sassoon, inherited his car, still at Heytesbury where he had left it in 1943. She separated from Sassoon in 1945 and in the following year moved to the Isle of Mull, taking Rex's car with her. She found it too frightening to drive and, in a turn of events that Rex more than most might have enjoyed, the Hudson Terraplane was relegated to a cave on the shore at Lochbuie. The Sassoons never divorced. Siegfried lived on alone at Heytesbury and his son George continued to be a great joy in his life. But there was little else, besides friends and cricket, until, at the age of seventy, he was received into the Catholic Church. Perhaps it was another escape but it provided the solace he required. His final decade was marked by a sense of peace, after a lifetime spent in pursuit of it. He died on 1 September 1967 at the age of eighty.

And then there was Stephen Tennant. Stephen, whose life had always hung in the balance, lived on, at Wilsford, until he died in his eighty-first year in 1987, Margaret Thatcher having just won her third term in office. The eddies of clutter that lapped at Edith's feet when she had visited him at home in 1943 would swell over the years into a tide of detritus. In the last years of his life Cecil Beaton returned to photograph his old friend and to capture final glimpses of the faded, gaudy glory of that house which once had been a paradise. 'This is a lovely place – beautiful, peaceful – not too grand – but just too calm and easy – it would kill the soul', had written Elinor Wylie in 1926, when a guest at Wilsford.[14] Photographs, mostly by Beaton, and mostly of Stephen as a golden-haired youth, lay scattered on the floor amidst a chaos of shells, pebbles, potions, drawings, frames, books, letters and trinkets. As if on a raft, bobbing about on this sea of memory and nostalgia, lay Stephen in a coil of clothes and blankets on his bed, overweight, orange-haired, fantasizing about the Mediterranean, clutching at the pearls around his neck, cooling himself with a fan or reaching out for those relics of the past that lay scattered all about him. There he too became an indolent, reclusive relic, his house a shrine to an earlier age that drew pilgrims to perch at the end of his bed: the director Derek Jarman, the artist David Hockney, the writers Hugo Vickers and Philip Hoare, who would become his biographer. Admission was selective, sometimes fleeting and always worthwhile. One might wonder why he didn't leave for the South of France, to gather shells and walk on sand that hadn't been imported. But Stephen was eternally bound to Wilsford, still tethered to the memory of his mother. And perhaps it would have been too literal. It was the incongruity he loved, the idea of a thing rather than the reality. And perhaps he was too lazy. Afterwards he was said to haunt the place.

Into this midst, in Stephen's last years, had come a stranger to Wiltshire, a foreigner, the writer V. S. Naipaul who rented a house on the Wilsford estate. He was fascinated by his unseen, reclusive landlord and by the house itself, redolent of 'something more complete, more ideal'.[15] Naipaul arrived with the idea of a time-less, unchangeable England; what he had found was decay and decline. But as he set off on walks, seeking out the ancient, well-trodden paths over the downs and into the valleys, it began to dawn on him that what he observed was merely part of a cycle of decay and renewal playing out in this most immemorial of land-scapes. Years before, Edith had recognized and celebrated this continuity too; it had given her comfort in a time of war. Youths dressed as shepherds, a Palladian Bridge, woods that inspired Arcadia: all a part of the continuum. The casket of Stephen's ashes is buried by the chancel wall of Wilsford church, the modest flat headstone marking his grave is all but covered in grass, his name obscured.

But some things remain unchanged. After Edith's death her niece Rosemary retained the lease of the Daye House and became the custodian of her aunt's papers. She lived there until the 1980s when she moved into a cottage in the centre of Wilton. Though the Long Room has gone, the Daye House still stands behind the high wall that runs along the road to Netherhampton, tucked away in a corner of the Wilton estate and veiled in 'green silence . . . within a "Charm of birds"'.[16]

Acknowledgements

My first thanks go to Penelope Middelboe, Edith Olivier's great-great-niece, who has been entirely supportive of this project from the outset and who knows more about Edith than anyone. Her generosity and hospitality have been supreme. She has lent me books, letters, photographs and her own research as well as allowing me to while away magical hours in her kitchen poring over Rex's letters to Edith and plundering boxes filled with Edith's papers, photographs and scrapbooks. Her own published book of extracts from Edith's diaries has been my constant companion and she has let me quote liberally from Edith's books, diaries and letters and to reproduce family photos. Her kindness, friendship and unfailing support have been paramount to me.

Similarly, my greatest thanks go to Rex Whistler's nieces Frances Whistler and Robin Ravilious. Robin welcomed me into her home and showed me many fascinating things from Rex's archive. Frances and Robin kindly read my text, offering me both encouragement and insightful comments and suggestions. Their kindness and extraordinarily generous support of this project have enabled me to quote freely from Rex's letters, from Laurence's letters and books and also to reproduce Rex's letters and paintings. I also owe an enormous debt to Laurence Whistler and to his wonderful biography, *The Laughter and the Urn*. It has been vital to my understanding of Rex.

This project had an earlier incarnation as an MPhil thesis and I would like to thank Peter Warburton and Margaret de Fonblanque, my comrades on the Biography MA programme at the University of Buckingham. Thank you too to later Buckingham friends, especially Wynn Wheldon, Victoria Fishburn and Judith Paisner. I would also like to thank Frances Wilson and Frances Spalding who examined my thesis and encouraged me to publish this work. I am eternally grateful to my inspirational tutor at Buckingham, Jane Ridley, for her intelligence, good humour and encouragement.

Very special thanks to Hugo Vickers for his help, hospitality and enthusiasm. Thanks too, for fascinating conversations, for showing me the letters sent to him by Stephen Tennant and for a memorable visit to Wilsford Church to see Stephen's grave. In his capacity as executor of Cecil Beaton's literary estate he has also been incredibly helpful and generous. Warmest thanks to Charles Duff for his generosity, for great conversations and lovely lunches, for helping me to see his mother, Caroline Duff, in a new light and for letting me use his memoirs and other unpublished material. Many thanks to Joanna Ling of the Cecil Beaton Studio archive at Sotheby's for her patience, enthusiasm and generosity. Thank you also to Katherine Marshall for digging out negatives from drawers and responding to my every Beaton whim.

I should like to thank the archivists at (what was then) the Wiltshire and Swindon Record Office who were so helpful during the time I spent working on Edith Olivier's diaries. I have very happy memories of my time there. Thank you to the staff at Plas Newydd and to the library of St John's College, Cambridge. The Salisbury and South Wiltshire Museum now houses the Rex Whistler Archive and I would like to acknowledge the help of its Director, Adrian Green, and the museum staff.

In Wilton, I owe enormous thanks to David and Maureen von Zeffman for inviting in the loitering stranger at their gates, for letting me snoop around every nook and cranny of Edith's childhood home and for their friendship. The tenants of the Daye House kindly let me wander around and take endless photographs. At Wilton House, many thanks to Lord Pembroke and I am indebted to Ros Liddington who told me countless stories about Wilton, showed me Rex's Long Room panels, which she has lovingly preserved, tramped through woodland with me and revealed every hidden corner of the estate.

Thank you to Andrew Ginger and Roger Barnard for discovering

Acknowledgements

Stephen Tennant's marvellous drawing of Edith, to Nikki Frater for lending me her excellent MA dissertation and to the late Lord Anglesey for answering my questions. Thank you also to John Byrne for showing me his beautiful first editions of Rex's books, to Nancy Morland for a fascinating tour of Wilton, to John Kennett of the Eltham Society for his talk on Rex Whistler's early years at Eltham and to Wendy Reed and Sue Robertson for sharing their memories of Pickering during the Second World War. I would also like to thank the following for their help and support: David Ellender; Maureen Emerson; Edward Franklin; Sarah Gibson; Hayley Gilman; Amanda Gregor; Laura Jordan; Balazs Korchmaros; Emily Korchmaros; Patricia Low; Charlotte Malcolm; Simon Mawbey; Jeremy McMinn; Karen McMinn; Richard McMinn; Sherman McMinn; Erik Munro; Pascale Pinxt; Damien Taylor; Elise Taylor; Julia Thomasson; Kevin Thomasson; Leo Walsh.

Thank you to Dusty Miller, Nicholas Blake, Zennor Compton and Jennifer Kerslake at Macmillan. Thank you too to my copyeditor Mary Chamberlain and proofreader Nicole Foster for their hard work. I am deeply grateful to Tania Wilde for her help and extraordinary patience and care. It has been a pleasure to work with my editor Georgina Morley. Immense thanks go to her. She is wise, great fun, passionate, always right and simply brilliant. Ed Wilson of Johnson & Alcock, has gone far beyond the call of duty, being at once confessor, therapist, sage and midwife. I feel incredibly lucky to have him as my agent.

Thank you to Milona von Habsburg de Rambures for her hospitality and friendship and to Damon McMinn for his computer wizardry. My thanks and love, as always, to my dearest friend Anne Marsham, to my ever-inspiring brother Edward Thomasson and to Mark Barker. My grandfather Eric Stubbs died just as I was beginning to work on this project but his unfailing belief that I was doing the right thing has kept me going long after he has gone. I would not have been able to write this book without the support and encouragement of my parents, Peter and Annette Thomasson. My mother has been a dedicated and enthusiastic research assistant and travelling companion. She has patiently endured countless readings of the text and knows it almost as well as I do. My love and eternal thanks go to her. My beloved husband, Trent McMinn, quickly realized he was marrying three people and he has cheerfully learnt to live with us all. He has trekked around Wiltshire with me and taken photographs of everything I pointed at. For those things and for his patience, his continuous faith in me, for his love and for everything really, I thank him from the bottom of my heart.

In addition to Penelope Middelboe, Frances Whistler, Robin Ravilious and Charles Duff, I would also like to thank the following for their generous permission to quote from published and unpublished works: Queen Elizabeth The Queen Mother's letter to Rex Whistler is quoted with the permission of Her Majesty Queen Elizabeth II; extract from *Albion: The Origins of the English Imagination* by Peter Ackroyd © Peter Ackroyd 1981, reproduced by permission of Sheil Land Associates Ltd on behalf of Peter Ackroyd and with the permission of Random House; Barry Hugill's *Observer* interview with Peter Ackroyd is reproduced with the consent of *The Guardian*; extract from Mark Amory's *Lord Berners: The Last Eccentric* is reproduced with permission of Curtis Brown Group Ltd, London, on behalf of Mark Amory, copyright © Mark Amory 1999; Brook Ashley and Brockman Seawell, as representatives of the Estate of Tallulah Bankhead, for kind permission to quote from her autobiography; Hugo Vickers for permission to quote from the books and other unpublished material © The Literary Executors of the late Sir Cecil Beaton, 2015; Ana Vicente for kind permission to quote from *Diaries and Letters of Marie Belloc Lowndes;* Mark Bostridge and T. J. Brittain-Catlin, Literary Executors for the Vera Brittain Estate for kind permission to quote from Vera Brittain's article in the *Manchester Guardian*; Stephen Calloway for permission to quote from *Baroque, Baroque;* the extract from Lewis Carroll's diary is quoted with the permission of A. P. Watt at United Agents on behalf of the Executors of the C. L. Dodgson Estate and Scirard Lancelyn Green; extracts from *Autobiography* by Diana Cooper, reproduced by permission of the Estate of Diana Cooper and the Felicity Bryan Literary

Acknowledgements

Agency; extracts from *The Duff Cooper Diaries, 1915–1951*, edited by John Julius Norwich, reproduced by permission of the Estate of Duff Cooper and the Felicity Bryan Literary Agency; excerpt from *Henry Brocken* by Walter de la Mare is reproduced by permission of The Literary Trustees of Walter de la Mare and The Society of Authors as their representative; Anne Somerset for kind permission to quote from Daphne Fielding's autobiography; Victoria Glendinning and David Higham for the extract from *Edith Sitwell: A Unicorn Among Lions*; David Herbert's autobiography is quoted courtesy of the Earl of Pembroke; extract from his article in *Apollo* by kind permission of John Jolliffe; *Serious Pleasures* © Philip Hoare, 1990, by courtesy of Philip Hoare; Yale University Press for permission to quote from *The Fall and Rise of the Stately Home* by Peter Mandler; extracts from *Stylistic Cold Wars: Betjeman Versus Pevsner* by kind permission of Timothy Mowl; the extract from *The Sacred Flame* by Somerset Maugham is quoted with the permission of A. P. Watt at United Agents on behalf of the Royal Literary Fund; extract from *Enigma of Arrival*, copyright © V. S. Naipaul, 1987 used by permission of The Wylie Agency (UK) Ltd; extract from 'Design For (Queer) Living' by kind permission of Christopher Reed; Jane Ridley for permission to quote from Ursula Ridley's unpublished letters to her mother; extracts from *Siegfried Sassoon (1886–1967)* by John Stuart Roberts, new edition, Metro Publishing, 2014, copyright © John Stuart Roberts 1999, 2005, 2014; extracts from Siegfried Sassoon's poetry, diaries and letters, copyright Siegfried Sassoon by kind permission of the Estate of George Sassoon; the Estate of Osbert Sitwell and David Higham for permission to quote from an article and *Noble Essences or Courteous Revelations* by Osbert Sitwell; Penguin Books and Farrar, Straus and Giroux for permission to quote from *Against Interpretation and Other Essays* by Susan Sontag and Copyright © Susan Sontag 1961, 1962, 1963, 1964, 1965, 1966; Yale University Press for permission to quote from *Sassoon: The Worlds of Sybil and Philip* by Peter Stansky; extract from a letter from Lytton Strachey, courtesy of The Society of Authors as agents of the Strachey Trust; quotation from an article in *Tatler*, courtesy of *Tatler*; Stephen

Acknowledgements

Tennant's letters and his unpublished essay on Rex Whistler by kind permission of The Hon. Tobias Tennant; extracts from *Lolly Willowes* by Sylvia Townsend Warner, copyright the Estate of Sylvia Townsend Warner and by permission of Little, Brown Book Group; extracts from *The Times* copyright © *The Times*; extracts from *Vogue*, courtesy of *Vogue* © The Condé Nast Publications Ltd; Audrey Stanley of Alderley / *Vogue* © The Condé Nast Publications Ltd; Edith Olivier/ *Vogue* © The Condé Nast Publications Ltd; *Brideshead Revisited: The Sacred and Profane Memories of Captain Charles Ryder* by Evelyn Waugh (first published by Chapman & Hall 1945, Penguin Classics, 1999) copyright © 1945 Evelyn Waugh; *Decline and Fall* by Evelyn Waugh (Penguin Books, 1937) copyright © Evelyn Waugh, 1928 and by permission of Little, Brown and Company; extracts from Rex Whistler's letters © the Estate of Rex Whistler reproduced by courtesy of the Rex Whistler archive housed at The Salisbury Museum.

Notes

❖

ABBREVIATIONS

CP   Caroline Paget
EO   Edith Olivier
HS   Hester Sassoon
HU   Henry Paget, Earl of Uxbridge,
       later 7th Marquess of Anglesey
HV   Hugo Vickers
LW   Laurence Whistler
RW   Rex Whistler
SS   Siegfried Sassoon
ST   Stephen Tennant

SOURCES

BA   Cecil Beaton Archive at St John's College, Cambridge.
BBC 'Rex Whistler', BBC TV, 1980, BBC Research Central.
EOA Edith Olivier's archive in the possession of Penelope Middelboe.
EOC Edith Olivier's correspondence, Wiltshire and Swindon
       Archives, Chippenham.
EO Diary   Edith Olivier's diaries, Wiltshire and Swindon Archives,
       Chippenham.
National Trust   Rex Whistler's papers owned by the National Trust
       and held at Plas Newydd, on Anglesey.
RWA Rex Whistler's archive at the Salisbury and South Wiltshire
       Museum.
STE   Stephen Tennant, essay on Rex Whistler, 1948, private
       collection.

Notes

MAIN WORKS AND EDITIONS USED

Works by Edith Olivier

Country Moods	Country Moods and Tenses: A Non-Grammarian's Chapbook (Batsford, 1941)
Four Victorian Ladies	Four Victorian Ladies of Wiltshire (Faber & Faber, 1945)
Jane	As Far as Jane's Grandmother's (Secker, 1928)
Love Child	The Love Child (Virago, 1981)
Mildred	Mildred (The High House Press, 1926)
Moonrakings	Moonrakings: a little book of Wiltshire stories told by members of the Women's Institutes (Coates and Parker, 1930)
Mary Magdalen	Mary Magdalen (Peter Davies, 1934)
Night Thoughts	Night Thoughts of a Country Landlady (Batsford, 1943)
Secrets	Secrets of Some Wiltshire Housewives: a book of recipes collected from the members of the Women's Institutes (Coates and Parker, 1927)
Seraphim	The Seraphim Room (Faber & Faber, 1932)
Walkley	Without Knowing Mr Walkley (Faber & Faber, 1938)

Works by other authors

Ashcombe	Cecil Beaton, Ashcombe: The Story of a Fifteen-Year Lease (Batsford, 1949)
Book of Beauty	Cecil Beaton, The Book of Beauty (Duckworth, 1930)
Brideshead	Evelyn Waugh, Brideshead Revisited (Penguin, 1962)
Initials	Laurence Whistler, The Initials in the Heart (Michael Russell, 2000)
L&U	Laurence Whistler, The Laughter and the Urn (Weidenfeld & Nicholson, 1985)

Life and Drawings	Laurence Whistler, *Rex Whistler: His Life and Drawings* (Art and Technics, 1948)
Noble Essences	Osbert Sitwell, *Noble Essences or Courteous Revelations* (Macmillan, 1950)
PM	Penelope Middelboe, *Edith Olivier: From Her Journals, 1924–1948* (Weidenfeld & Nicolson, 1989)
Self-Portrait	Cecil Beaton, Richard Buckle, ed., *Self-Portrait with Friends: Selected Diaries, 1926–74* (Penguin, 1982)
Wandering Years	Cecil Beaton, *The Wandering Years: Diaries, 1922–39* (Weidenfeld & Nicolson, 1961)

BEFORE

Edith

1 Edith Olivier, *Without Knowing Mr Walkley* (London: Faber & Faber, 1938), p.144.
2 *Walkley*, p.148.
3 *Walkley*, p.145.
4 Edith Olivier, ed., *Mildred* (Shaftesbury: The High House Press, 1926), p.7.
5 *Walkley*, p.148.
6 *Walkley*, p.24.
7 *Walkley*, p.25.
8 *Walkley*, p.74.
9 *Walkley*, pp.70–1.
10 *Walkley*, p.176.
11 *Walkley*, p.178.
12 Morton N. Cohen, *Lewis Carroll: A Biography* (London: Macmillan, 1995), p.188.
13 *Walkley*, p.165.
14 *Mildred*, pp.11–12.
15 *Mildred*, p.79.
16 *Mildred*, p.28.
17 *Walkley*, p.185.
18 *Walkley*, p.203.

19 *Walkley*, p.199.

20 *Walkley*, p.213.

21 *Walkley*, p.23.

22 *Walkley*, p.23.

23 *Mildred*, p.7.

24 *Walkley*, p.23.

25 *Walkley*, p.152; p.153.

26 *Mildred*, p.8.

27 *Mildred*, p.28.

28 Terry Castle, 'Contagious Folly: *An Adventure* and Its Skeptics', *Critical Inquiry*, Vol. 17, No. 4 (Summer 1991), pp.741–72.

29 *Walkley*, p.233.

30 *Walkley*, p.225.

31 *Walkley*, p.226.

32 *Walkley*, p.231.

33 *Walkley*, p.224.

34 *Walkley*, p.226.

35 *Walkley*, p.188.

36 *Mildred*, p.23.

37 *Walkley*, p.183; *Mildred*, p.15.

Rex

1 LW to Haileybury School (undated, 1980s), Haileybury School Archive.

2 Laurence Whistler, *The Laughter and the Urn: The Life of Rex Whistler* (London: Weidenfeld & Nicolson, 1985), p.28.

3 *L&U*, p.87.

4 Cynthia Asquith, *Haply I May Remember* (London: Barrie, 1950), p.91.

5 BBC TV, 'Rex Whistler', 1980, BBC Research Central.

6 Charles Castle, *Oliver Messel* (London: Thames & Hudson, 1955), p.8.

7 Stephen Tennant, essay on Rex Whistler, summer 1948, private collection.

8 *L&U*, p.62.

9 STE, p.2.

10 *L&U*, p.66.

11 Walter de la Mare, *Henry Brocken* (London: Collins, 1904), p.1.

12 *L&U*, p.64.

13 V. S. Naipaul, *The Enigma of Arrival* (New York: Vintage, 1998), p.190.

14 Philip Hoare, *Serious Pleasures: The Life of Stephen Tennant* (London: Hamish Hamilton, 1990), p.10.

15 Hoare, p.11.

16 *L&U*, p.37.

17 Edgar Allan Poe, *Collected Tales and Poems of Edgar Allan Poe* (London: Wordsworth, 2004), p.730.

18 *L&U*, p.65.

19 Hoare, p.19.

20 *L&U*, p.60.

21 Hoare, p.30.

22 Hoare, p.30.

23 Evelyn Waugh, *Brideshead Revisited* (London: Penguin, 1962), p.206.

24 *Brideshead,* p.33.

25 *L&U*, p.72.

26 Hoare, p.34.

Spring

1 EO Diary, 25 November 1924.

2 *Walkley*, p.136.

3 *Walkley*, p.38.

4 EO Diary, 26 December 1924.

5 Penelope Middelboe, *Edith Olivier: From Her Journals, 1924–1948* (London: Weidenfeld & Nicolson, 1989), p.14.

PART ONE: THE LOVE-CHILD

1: San Remo

1 EO Diary, 29 March 1925.

2 Cecil Beaton, Richard Buckle ed., *Self-Portrait with Friends: Selected Diaries, 1926–74* (London: Penguin, 1982), p.5.

3 *Walkley*, pp.255–6.

4 EO Diary, 29 March 1925.

5 EO Diary, 30 March 1925.
6 Hoare, p.38.
7 EO Diary, 31 March 1925.
8 EO Diary, 1 April 1925.
9 EO Diary, 15 April 1925.
10 *L&U*, p.78.
11 EO Diary, 7 April 1925.
12 EO Diary, 7 April 1925.
13 EO Diary, 2 April 1925.
14 EO Diary, 2 April 1925.
15 EO Diary, 7 April 1925.
16 EO Diary, 4 April 1925.
17 EO Diary, 12 April 1925.
18 EO Diary, 12 April 1925.

2: *The Daye House*

1 RW to EO, 14 May 1925, EOA.
2 RW to EO, 14 May 1925, EOA.
3 EO Diary, 18 May 1925.
4 EO Diary, 30 May 1925.
5 RW to EO, 28 May 1925, EOA.
6 *Walkley*, p.244.
7 *Walkley*, p.247.
8 Adam Nicolson, *Earls of Paradise: England & the Dream of Perfection* (London: HarperCollins, 2008), p.10 and p.12.
9 *Self-Portrait*, p.6.
10 EO Diary, 30 May 1925.
11 EO Diary, 31 May 1925.
12 EO Diary, 24 June 1925.
13 EO Diary, 23 September 1925.
14 EO Diary, 31 May 1925.
15 EO Diary, 1 June 1925.
16 EO Diary, 1 June 1925.

3: 'At the Shrine of Beauty'

1 'Wilton House, 1544–1944, and the Earls of Pembroke – II', *Country Life* (28 January 1944), p.157.

2 EO Diary, 2 June 1925.

3 RW to EO, 4 June 1925, EOA.

4 Edith Olivier, 'Wilton House and the Earls of Pembroke 1544–1944 – I', *Country Life* (21 January 1944), p.115.

5 Arthur F. Kinney, ed., *Cambridge Companion to English Literature 1500–1600* (Cambridge: Cambridge University Press, 2007), p.100.

6 EO Diary, 23 September 1925.

7 EO Diary, 26 September 1925.

8 EO Diary, 26 September 1925.

9 EO Diary, 20 September 1929.

10 RW to EO, 28 September 1925, EOA.

11 *L&U*, p.19.

12 *L&U*, p.80.

4: *The Darling*

1 Joseph Hone, *The Life of Henry Tonks* (London: Heinemann, 1939), p.201.

2 Charles Castle, *Oliver Messel* (London: Thames & Hudson, 1955), p.11.

3 Asquith, p.92.

4 Hone, p.182.

5 EO Diary, 25 September 1925.

6 EO Diary, 27 May 1927.

7 Asquith, p.111.

8 *L&U*, p.61.

9 Laurence Whistler, *Rex Whistler: His Life and Drawings* (London: Art and Technics, 1948), p.1.

10 *L&U*, p.88.

11 EO Diary, 10 January 1926.

12 EO Diary, 10 January 1926.

13 Aitken to Duveen, December 1926, Tate Archive, Tate History file, TG 3/4/3.

14 *L&U*, p.92.

15 *L&U*, p.93.

16 EO Diary, 25 March 1926.

17 RW to EO, 21 June 1926, EOA.

18 EO Diary, 28 August 1926.

19 EO Diary, 29 August 1926.

20 Martin Green, *Children of the Sun: A Narrative of Decadence in England After 1918* (London: Pimlico, 2001), p.157.
21 *Brideshead*, p.34.
22 EO Diary, 10 December 1926.
23 EO Diary, 29 November 1926.
24 EO Diary, 29 August 1926.
25 EO Diary, 28 August 1926.
26 PM, p.41.
27 EO Diary, 7 November 1926.
28 EO Diary, 6 November 1926.
29 PM, p.41.
30 EO Diary, 16 September 1928.
31 EO Diary, 11 August 1927.
32 EO Diary, 31 May 1925.
33 EO Diary, 2 June 1925.
34 EO Diary, 20 December 1926.
35 EO Diary, 8 November 1926.
36 EO Diary, 24 November 1926.
37 RW to EO, 27 November 1926, EOA.
38 EO Diary, 10 November 1925.
39 EO Diary, 8 November 1926.

5: 'A Dream Change'

1 Edith Olivier, *Night Thoughts of a Country Landlady* (London: Batsford, 1943), p.v.
2 *Walkley*, p.291.
3 *Walkley*, p.290.
4 Edith Olivier, *The Love Child* (London: Virago, 1981), p.10.
5 *Love Child*, p.12.
6 *Love Child*, p.15.
7 *Love Child*, p.14.
8 *Love Child*, p.16.
9 *Love Child*, p.29.
10 *Love Child*, p.80.
11 *Love Child*, p.80.
12 *Love Child*, p.30.
13 *Love Child*, p.117.
14 *Love Child*, p.119.

15 *Love Child*, p.116.
16 *Love Child*, p.195.
17 *Love Child*, p.149.
18 *Love Child*, p.179.
19 *Love Child*, p.208.
20 Hermione Lee, ed., Introduction to *The Love Child*.
21 Sylvia Townsend Warner, *Lolly Willowes or The Loving Huntsman* (Chicago: Academy Chicago Publishers, 1999), p.78.
22 Townsend Warner, p.238.
23 Townsend Warner, p.243.
24 *Love Child*, p.26.
25 *Love Child*, p.64.
26 *Love Child*, p.65.
27 *Love Child*, pp.65–6.
28 *Love Child*, p.32.
29 *Love Child*, p.24.
30 *Love Child*, p.56.
31 *Love Child*, p.34.
32 *Saturday Review,* 2 June 1928.
33 *Love Child*, p.9.
34 *Love Child*, p.14.
35 *Love Child*, p.24.
36 *L&U*, p.87.

PART TWO: TABLEAUX VIVANTS

6: *Bright Young People*

1 EO Diary, 21 February 1927.
2 EO Diary, 23 February 1927.
3 EO Diary, 10 March 1927.
4 EO Diary, 2 March 1927; 3 March 1927.
5 EO Diary, 1 March 1927.
6 EO Diary, 11 March 1927.
7 EO Diary, 10 March 1927.
8 EO Diary, 17 January 1927.
9 EO Diary, 12 January 1927.

10 EO Diary, 15 January 1927.

11 *Love Child*, flyleaf.

12 *Love Child*, flyleaf.

13 *Saturday Review*, 20 August 1927.

14 EO Diary, 6 March 1927.

15 EO Diary, 26 February 1927.

16 EO Diary, 12 March 1927.

17 EO Diary, 28 February 1927.

18 Hugo Vickers, *Cecil Beaton* (London: Phoenix Press, 2003), p.97.

19 Vickers, p.96.

20 Cecil Beaton, *The Wandering Years: Diaries, 1922–39* (London: Weidenfeld & Nicolson, 1961), p.164.

21 *Wandering Years*, p.164.

22 EO Diary, 3 March 1927.

23 EO Diary, 10 March 1927.

24 EO Diary, 1 March 1927.

25 *Vogue*, 14 December 1927.

26 *Wandering Years*, p.150.

27 *Self-Portrait*, p.1.

28 Stephen Calloway, *Baroque, Baroque: The Culture of Excess* (London: Phaidon, 1994), p.35.

29 Calloway, p.47.

30 Vickers, p.99.

31 Susan Sontag, 'Notes on Camp' in *Against Interpretation* (London: Vintage, 1994).

32 'William Hickey', *Daily Express*, 1927.

33 Christopher Reed, 'Design For (Queer) Living: Sexual Identity, Performance, and Décor in British Vogue, 1922–1926', in *GLQ: A Journal of Lesbian and Gay Studies*, Volume 12, Number 3, 2006 (Durham: Duke University Press), p.379.

34 EO Diary, 16 June 1927.

35 EO Diary, 14 June 1927.

36 *Wandering Years*, p.171.

37 EO Diary, 1 September 1927.

38 EO Diary, 5 September 1927.

39 7th Marquess of Anglesey to author, July 2005.

40 *L&U*, p.55.

41 RW to EO, 15 December 1926, EOA.

42 EO Diary, 31 May 1927.

43 BBC.
44 *Wandering Years,* p.167.
45 *Wandering Years,* p.165.
46 RWA.
47 *L&U,* p.214.
48 *Graphic,* 1 October 1927.
49 Evelyn Waugh, *Decline and Fall* (London: Penguin, 2003), p.81.
50 *Wandering Years,* p.162.
51 *Wandering Years,* p.165.

7: *Town and Country*

 1 EO to CB, 21 March 1927, BA.
 2 PM, p.50.
 3 EO to CB, 21 March 1927, BA.
 4 *Vogue,* late July 1927.
 5 EO to CB, 27 July 1927, BA.
 6 EO to CB, 5 July 1927, BA.
 7 EO to CB, 10 July 1927, BA.
 8 EO to CB, 15 August 1927, BA.
 9 *Wandering Years,* p.164.
10 *Secrets of Some Wiltshire Housewives: a book of recipes collected from the members of the Women's Institutes* (Warminster: Coates and Parker, 1927), p.45.
11 *Secrets,* p.ii.
12 EO Diary, 12 July 1927.
13 EO Diary, 27 February 1933.
14 EO Diary, 29 December 1927; 21 December 1927.
15 EO Diary, 14 January 1928.
16 EO Diary, 22 December 1927.
17 EO Diary, 20 February 1929.
18 Edith Olivier, *As Far as Jane's Grandmother's* (London: Secker, 1928), p.29.
19 *Walkley,* pp.293–4.
20 *Walkley,* p.293.
21 *Jane,* p.217.
22 EO Diary, 29 October 1927.
23 RW to EO, 4 November 1927, EOA.
24 RW to EO, 14 September 1927, EOA.

25 RW to CB, Autumn 1927, BA.

26 EO Diary, 12 September 1927.

27 *The Times,* 21 November 1927.

28 Edith Olivier, *In Pursuit of Rare Meats – A Guide to the Duchy of Epicurania with some Account of the Famous Expedition* (London: Tate, 1954).

29 EO Diary, 15 December 1927.

30 EO Diary, 29 October 1927.

31 EO Diary, 19 December 1927.

32 RW to EO, 12 July 1927, EOC.

33 EO Diary, 2 September 1927.

34 EO Diary, 14 May 1927.

35 *Walkley,* pp. 272–3

36 *Vogue,* October 1928.

37 EO Diary, 1 November 1927.

8: *Revels*

1 Jean Moorcroft Wilson, *Siegfried Sassoon: The Journey from the Trenches 1918–1967* (London: Duckworth, 2003), p.197.

2 Moorcroft Wilson, p.197.

3 Michael Holroyd, *Lytton Strachey* (London: Vintage, 1995), p.590.

4 EO Diary, 16 October 1927.

5 Max Egremont, *Siegfried Sassoon* (London: Picador, 2005), p.310.

6 Egremont, p.214.

7 Moorcroft Wilson, p.195.

8 John Stuart Roberts, *Siegfried Sassoon* (London: Metro, 2005), p.218.

9 Moorcroft Wilson, p.197.

10 Roberts, p.217.

9: *'Adored Sons'*

1 *Sketch,* 30 November 1927.

2 *Sunday Times,* 27 November 1927.

3 EO Diary, 23 November 1927.

4 *Tatler,* 30 November 1927; *Sunday Herald,* 27 November 1927.

5 EO to CB, 24 November 1927, BA.

6 *Daily Express,* 28 December 1927.

7 *Sunday Herald,* 27 November 1927.

8 EO Diary, 30 November 1927.
9 *The Times,* 1 December 1927.
10 EO Diary, 30 November 1927.
11 EO Diary, 2 June 1927.
12 EO Diary, 1 May 1929.
13 EO Diary, 3 May 1929.
14 EO Diary, 23 October 1929.
15 *L&U*, p.127.
16 *L&U*, pp.125–7.
17 EO Diary, 27 August 1927.
18 EO Diary, 31 August 1927.
19 EO Diary, 3 September 1927.
20 EO Diary, 15 November 1930.
21 *L&U*, p.102.
22 *L&U*, p.102.
23 EO Diary, 10 October 1927.

10: Bird Songs

1 EO Diary, 31 December 1927.
2 EO Diary, 8 January 1928.
3 EO Diary, 19 January 1928.
4 RW to EO, 8 December 1927, EOA.
5 *Manchester Guardian,* 13 November 1928.
6 *Walkley*, p.237.
7 *Walkley*, p.238.
8 Alfred Lord Tennyson, *Idylls of the King* (London: Penguin, 1983), p.290.
9 PM, p.72.
10 EO Diary, 6 March 1928.
11 RW to EO, 8 March 1928, EOA.
12 EO Diary, 20 April 1928.
13 *Self-Portrait*, p.5.
14 EO Diary, 20 April 1928.
15 EO to CB, 27 April 1928, BA.
16 EO to CB, 21 March 1928, BA.
17 EO to CB, 1 February 1928, BA.
18 EO to CB, 9 May 1928, BA.
19 EO Diary, 7 May 1928.

20 *Vogue*, 30 May 1928.

21 EO to CB, 31 May 1928, BA.

22 EO to CB, 11 August 1928, BA.

23 RW to EO, 22 July 1928, EOA.

24 EO to CB, 9 May 1928, EOA.

25 EO Diary, 7 July 1927.

26 Jane D. Wise, transcribed, *Last Poems of Elinor Wylie* (New York: Knopf, 1943), p.ix.

27 EO Diary, 30 August 1926.

28 Wise, p.ix.

29 EO Diary, 23 July 1927.

30 EO to CB, 27 July 1927, BA.

31 EO Diary, 8 May 1928.

32 Nancy Hoyt, *Elinor Wylie: The Portrait of an Unknown Lady* (New York: Bobbs-Merrill, 1935), p.172.

33 Hoyt, p.173.

34 Hoyt, p.185.

35 Wise, pp.vii–viii.

36 Wise, p.viii.

11: Król Dudziarz

1 *Daily Mail*, 1 December 1927.

2 EO Diary, 3 October 1927.

3 *Daily Chronicle*, 22 November 1927.

4 Osbert Sitwell, 'This Strange Country', *Architectural Review* 64 (July 1928), p.403.

5 EO Diary, 18 March 1928.

6 *L&U*, p.166.

7 EO Diary, 30 June 1932.

8 *L&U*, p.175.

9 Anne Massey, *Interior Design of the Twentieth Century* (London: Thames & Hudson, 1996), p.124.

10 RW to EO, 2 January 1928, EOA.

11 *L&U*, p.109.

12 EO Diary, 30 October 1927.

13 EO Diary, 22 January 1928.

14 EO Diary, 22 November 1928.

15 STE, p.4.

16 EO Diary, 3 March 1928.

17 *L&U*, p.109.

18 RW to EO, 20 May 1928, EOA.

19 EO Diary, 10 July 1927.

20 EO Diary, 12 August 1927.

21 EO Diary, 31 August 1927.

22 EO Diary, 9 September 1928.

23 *L&U*, p.124.

24 EO Diary, 2 September 1927.

25 EO Diary, 17 October 1932.

26 PM, p.66.

27 EO Diary, 23 January 1928.

28 EO Diary, 4 March 1928.

29 EO Diary, 22 January 1928.

30 *L&U*, p.121.

31 RW to EO, 17 June 1928, EOA.

32 RW to EO, 17 June 1928, EOA.

33 RW to EO, 29 April 1928, EOA.

34 *L&U*, p.118.

35 RW to EO, 10 May 1928, EOA.

36 RW to EO, 3 July 1928, EOA.

37 RW to CB, 9 July 1928, BA.

38 RW to EO, 3 July 1928, EOA.

39 RW to EO, 17 June 1928, EOA.

40 EO to CB, 27 August 1928, BA.

41 EO Diary, 25 August 1928.

42 EO Diary, 27 August 1928.

43 EO Diary, 28 August 1928.

44 EO to CB, 27 August 1928, BA.

45 EO Diary, 25 November 1932.

46 *Walkley*, p.257.

47 EO Diary, 27 August 1928.

48 Victoria Glendinning, *Edith Sitwell: A Unicorn Among Lions* (London: Phoenix, 1999), p.154.

49 Glendinning, p.157.

12: 'The Trail of the Serpent'

1 EO Diary, 16 September 1928.
2 EO Diary, 15 January 1928.
3 *Daily Express*, 14 July 1928.
4 *Daily Express*, 11 July 1928.
5 EO Diary, 16 July 1928.
6 EO Diary, 18 July 1928.
7 EO Diary, 26 November 1928.
8 *The Times*, 30 November 1928.
9 EO to CB, 2 October 1928, BA.
10 EO Diary, 6 November 1928.
11 EO Diary, 4 November 1928.
12 EO Diary, 20 November 1928.
13 RW to EO, 19 October 1928, EOA.
14 EO to CB, 23 November 1928, BA.
15 EO Diary, 24 November 1928.
16 EO Diary, 2 December 1928.
17 EO Diary, 5 December 1928.
18 EO Diary, 6 December 1928.
19 EO Diary, 7 December 1928.
20 EO Diary, 7 December 1928.
21 EO Diary, 1 January 1929.
22 EO to CB, 15 January 1929, BA.
23 *Walkley*, p.258.
24 EO Diary, 7 January 1929.
25 Roberts, p.221.
26 EO Diary, 29 November 1930.
27 EO Diary, 24 February 1929.
28 EO to CB, 10 March 1929, BA.
29 EO Diary, 23 February 1929.
30 EO Diary, 24 February 1929.
31 Hoare, p.131.
32 Moorcroft Wilson, p.197.
33 *L&U*, p.65.
34 *L&U*, p.132.
35 *L&U*, p.112; EO Diary, 25 March 1929.
36 EO Diary, 25 March 1929.

37 *L&U*, pp.131–132.
38 *L&U*, p.134.
39 *L&U*, p.134.
40 PM, p.55.
41 EO Diary, 28 March 1929.
42 EO Diary, 28 March 1929.
43 EO Diary, 9 April 1929.
44 EO Diary, 5 April 1929.
45 EO Diary, 8 April 1929.
46 EO Diary, 2 April 1929.
47 EO Diary, 10 April 1929.
48 EO Diary, 20 April 1929.
49 EO Diary, 21 April 1929.
50 PM, p.93.

13: 'Bells at Midnight'

1 EO Diary, 30 May 1929.
2 EO Diary, 31 May 1929.
3 Johanna Hirth to EO, 6 May 1929, EOC.
4 RW to CB, 27 September 1928, BA.
5 EO to CB, 10 March 1929, BA.
6 EO Diary, 22 May 1929.
7 RW to EO, 2 July 1929, EOA.
8 Mark Amory, *Lord Berners: The Last Eccentric* (London: Pimlico, 1999), p.113.
9 Amory, p.113.
10 RW to EO, 2 July 1929, EOA.
11 Amory, p.113.
12 EO Diary, 26 September 1928.
13 EO Diary, 8 June 1929.
14 EO Diary, 16 June 1929.
15 EO Diary, 17 June 1929.
16 EO Diary, 17 June 1929.
17 EO Diary, 28 June 1929.
18 RW to EO, 12 April 1929, EOA.
19 Donald Albrecht, *Cecil Beaton: The New York Years* (New York: Rizzoli, 2011), p.11.
20 Vickers, p.119.

21 EO to CB, 15 January 1929, BA.
22 EO to CB, 10 March 1929, BA.
23 Hoare, p.138.
24 EO Diary, 15 July 1929.
25 EO Diary, 10 August 1929.
26 EO Diary, 10 August 1929.
27 EO Diary, 14 August 1929.
28 EO Diary, 14 August 1929.
29 Hoare, p.145.
30 EO Diary, 23 October 1929.
31 EO Diary, 10 November 1929.
32 EO Diary, 23 July 1929.
33 EO Diary, 7 December 1929.
34 EO Diary, 7 December 1929.
35 EO Diary, 9 December 1929.
36 EO Diary, 22 September 1929.
37 *Walkley*, p.295.
38 Edith Olivier, *The Triumphant Footman* (London: Secker, 1930), p.35.
39 *Harper's Magazine*, June 1930.
40 EO Diary, 1 January 1930.
41 EO Diary, 12 December 1929.
42 EO Diary, 12 December 1929.
43 EO Diary, 31 December 1929.

PART THREE: REVERSIBLE FACES

14: Moonraking

1 PM, p.107.
2 EO Diary, 19 February 1930.
3 EO to CB, 3 November 1930, BA.
4 EO Diary, 9 November 1931.
5 Stephen Lloyd, *William Walton: Muse of Fire* (London: Boydell & Brewer, 2001), p.80.
6 EO Diary, 3 December 1930.
7 Cecil Beaton, *Ashcombe: The Story of a Fifteen-Year Lease* (London: Batsford, 1949), p.14.

8 Julia Strachey and Frances Partridge, *Julia: A Portrait of Julia Strachey* (London: Phoenix, 2000), p.111.

9 *L&U*, p.203.

10 Edith Olivier and Margaret K. S. Edwards, eds., *Moonrakings: a little book of Wiltshire stories told by members of the Women's Institutes* (Warminster: Coates and Parker, 1930), p.4.

11 A. G. Street, 'Memories of Edith Olivier', *Mercury: A Review of the Arts* (Bournemouth: Autumn 1948), p.15.

12 ST to HV, September 1980, private collection.

13 Vickers, p.96.

14 Cecil Beaton's diary, undated, private collection.

15 EO to CB, 1 August 1929, BA.

16 EO to CB, 7 October 1930, BA.

17 EO to CB, 3 October 1930, BA.

18 PM, p.113.

19 EO to CB, 12 November 1930, BA.

20 Cecil Beaton, *The Book of Beauty* (Duckworth, 1930), p.33.

21 Vickers, p.101.

22 *Book of Beauty*, p.37.

23 EO to CB, undated, BA.

24 EO Diary, 6 April 1930.

25 EO Diary, 6 April 1930.

26 EO to CB, 2 September 1929, BA.

27 *Ashcombe*, p.3.

28 EO Diary, 6 April 1930.

29 *Ashcombe*, p.5.

30 EO Diary, 6 April 1930.

31 *Ashcombe*, pp.5–6.

32 EO to CB, 11 April 1930, BA.

15: Ashcombe

1 EO Diary, 8 August 1932.

2 EO Diary, 19 February 1930.

3 *L&U*, p.150.

4 *L&U*, p.154.

5 EO Diary, 29 May 1930; 5 June 1930.

6 EO Diary, 7 June 1930.

7 STE, p.4.

8 EO to CB, 18 April 1930, BA.

9 PM, p.109.

10 EO to CB, 30 April 1930, BA.

11 EO Diary, 3 May 1930.

12 *Ashcombe,* p.8.

13 EO to CB, 4 May 1930, BA.

14 EO to CB, 30 June 1930, BA.

15 EO Diary, 9 June 1930.

16 EO Diary, 16 October 1930.

17 EO Diary, 13 August 1930.

18 EO Diary, 24 August 1930.

19 EO Diary, 24 August 1930.

20 *Walkley*, pp.294–5.

21 EO Diary, 21 October 1930.

22 *Wandering Years*, p.223.

23 *Wandering Years*, p.222.

24 EO Diary, 17 May 1931.

25 EO Diary, 9 November 1930.

26 Charlotte A. E. Moberly, *An Adventure* (Faber & Faber, 1931), p.24.

27 Moberly, p.28.

28 EO Diary, 7 December 1930.

29 EO to CB, December 1930, BA.

30 EO Diary, 28 December 1930.

31 EO Diary, 29 December 1930.

32 EO Diary, 17 January 1931.

33 EO Diary, 10 April 1931.

34 EO Diary, 18 April 1931.

35 EO to CB 30 April 1931, BA.

36 *Wandering Years*, p.246.

37 *L&U*, p.153.

38 EO Diary, 29 May 1932.

39 RW to EO, 7 June 1932, EOC.

40 *Ashcombe*, p.42.

41 EO Diary, 3 December 1930.

42 EO Diary, 11 February 1931.

43 EO Diary, 24 October 1933.

44 EO Diary, 2 January 1937.

45 EO Diary, 11 February 1931.

16: 'Peintre de Luxe'

1 Ronald Fuller and Laurence Whistler, *The Work of Rex Whistler* (London: Batsford, 1960), p.4.
2 *L&U*, p.157.
3 EO Diary, 1 August 1933.
4 Peter Mandler, *The Fall and Rise of the Stately Home* (London: Yale University Press, 1997), p.265.
5 Mandler, p.279.
6 Joseph Mordaunt Crook, *The Rise of the Nouveaux Riches* (London: John Murray, 2000), pp.185–6.
7 Henry Channon, ed. Robert Rhodes James, *Chips: The Diaries of Sir Henry Channon* (London: Phoenix, 1996), p.202.
8 Channon, p.63.
9 *L&U*, p.159.
10 EO Diary, 9 November 1930.
11 EO Diary, 1 May 1931.
12 EO Diary, 2 May 1931.
13 RW to EO, 4 May 1931, EOA.
14 RW to EO, 12 August 1932, EOC.
15 Susan Lowndes, ed., *Diaries and Letters of Marie Belloc Lowndes 1911–1947* (London: Chatto & Windus, 1971), p.129.
16 Peter Stansky, *Sassoon: The Worlds of Sybil and Philip* (London: Yale University Press, 2003), p.171.
17 EO Diary, 10 August 1931.
18 *L&U*, p.162.
19 Channon, p.323.
20 *L&U*, p.163.
21 RW to EO, 8 October 1931, EOA.
22 EO Diary, 25 November 1931.
23 RW to EO, 2 January 1932, EOA.
24 EO Diary, 16 January 1932.
25 STE, p.4.
26 EO Diary, 16 February 1932.
27 EO Diary, 3 March 1932.
28 EO Diary, 3 December 1930.
29 RW to EO, 12 October 1933, EOA.
30 *L&U*, p.134.

31 *L&U*, p.134.

32 Bryan Connon, *Beverley Nichols: A Life* (Portland: Timber Press, 2000), p.161.

33 Beverley Nichols, *The Unforgiving Minute* (London: WH Allen, 1978), p.225.

34 *L&U*, pp.184–5.

35 RW to EO, 1 April 1932, EOA.

36 EO Diary, 18 January 1932.

37 EO Diary, 20 March 1932.

38 EO Diary, 27 March 1932.

39 EO Diary, 28 March 1932.

40 Edith Olivier, *The Seraphim Room* (London: Faber & Faber, 1932), p.198.

41 *Seraphim*, p.37.

42 *Seraphim*, p.25.

43 *Walkley*, p.294.

44 *Seraphim*, p.175.

45 *Seraphim*, p.176.

46 EO Diary, 24 April 1932.

47 EO Diary, 23 June 1932.

48 RW to EO, 24 June 1932, EOC.

49 EO Diary, 19 July 1932.

50 EO Diary, 21 July 1932.

51 EO Diary, 7 August 1932.

52 EO Diary, 9 August 1932.

53 RW to EO, 6 September 1932, EOC.

54 EO Diary, 6 November 1932.

55 EO Diary, 5 November 1932.

56 EO Diary, 10 December 1932.

57 EO Diary, 5 November 1932.

17: The 'Storm Touched Soul'

1 RW to EO, 11 February 1930, EOA.

2 EO Diary, 8 July 1930.

3 EO Diary, 17 July 1930.

4 EO Diary, 1 September 1930.

5 EO Diary, 3 May 1930.

6 EO Diary, 19 September 1930.

7 EO Diary, 1 January 1931.

8 Hoare, p.163.

9 EO Diary, 7 February 1931.

10 EO Diary, 8 February 1931.

11 EO Diary, 7 July 1931.

12 EO Diary, 11 May 1931.

13 EO Diary, 27 February 1931.

14 EO Diary, 14 March 1931.

15 EO Diary, 16 January 1931.

16 Roberts, p.249.

17 EO Diary, 28 March 1932.

18 EO Diary, 10 June 1932.

19 EO Diary, 28 May 1931.

20 RW to EO, 12 August 1932, EOC.

21 ST to EO, 28 December 1932, EOC.

22 Hoare, p.180.

23 Roberts, p.245.

24 EO Diary, 31 May 1933.

25 EO Diary, 4 June 1933.

26 Roberts, p.251.

27 *Ashcombe*, p.44.

28 EO Diary, 17 September 1933.

29 EO Diary, 29 October 1933.

30 EO Diary, 29 October 1933.

31 Moorcroft Wilson, p.283.

18: 'The Happy Heartbreak'

1 RW to EO, 11 February 1933, EOC.

2 EO Diary, 30 March 1933.

3 *Queen*, 20 April 1932.

4 EO Diary, 16 June 1933.

5 EO Diary, 22 June 1933.

6 EO Diary, 1 July 1933.

7 PM, p.144.

8 EO Diary, 12 July 1933.

9 *L&U*, p.173.

10 *L&U*, p.176.

11 EO Diary, 3 July 1933.

12 EO Diary, 14 August 1933.

13 RW to EO, 12 October 1933, EOA.

14 Miranda Seymour, *Ottoline Morrell: Life on a Grand Scale* (London: Sceptre, 1998), p.535.

15 EO Diary, 20 July 1933.

16 EO Diary, 21 July 1933.

17 *Walkley*, p.259.

18 EO Diary, 26 July 1933.

19 EO Diary, 22 September 1933.

20 EO Diary, 2 December 1933.

21 EO Diary, 3 July 1933.

22 EO Diary, 28 February 1934.

23 EO Diary, 4 February 1934.

24 EO Diary, 14 March 1934.

25 RW to EO, 12 April 1934, EOA.

26 RW to EO, 14 April 1934, EOA.

27 EO Diary, 22 March 1934.

28 EO Diary, 22 March 1934.

29 *L&U*, p.175.

30 EO Diary, 3 July 1933.

31 Poe, p.730.

32 *L&U*, p.177.

33 BBC.

34 Arthur Ware Locke, trans., 'Beethoven's Instrumental Music', translated from E. T. A. Hoffmann's *Kreisleriana, Music Quarterly,* 1 January 1917, p.128.

35 C. S. Lewis, *The Pilgrim's Regress: An Allegorical Apology for Christianity, Reason and Romanticism* (Grand Rapids: Wm. B. Eerdmans, 1992), Afterword.

36 RW to EO, 20 May 1928, EOA.

37 STE, p.3.

38 RW to EO, 2 July 1929, EOA.

39 *Life and Drawings*, p.19.

40 EO Diary, 3 December 1933.

41 EO Diary, 19 March 1931.

42 EO Diary, 4 October 1927.

43 RW to EO, 2 July 1929, EOA.

44 RW to Helen Whistler, 4 July 1929, RWA.

45 *L&U*, p.163.

Notes

13: Sex

1 ST to EO, 22 April 1934, EOC.
2 EO Diary, 16 April 1934.
3 Rex Whistler, 'Instructions for Roses', 1937, National Trust, Plas Newydd.
4 BBC.
5 EO Diary, 28 September 1928.
6 *Book of Beauty*, p.34.
7 *L&U*, p.185.
8 Hoare, p.211.
9 Joel Lobenthal, *Tallulah: The Life and Times of a Leading Lady* (London: Aurum Press, 2005), p.125.
10 Tallulah Bankhead, *My Autobiography* (Jackson: University Press of Mississippi, 2004), p.324.
11 *L&U*, p.184.
12 *L&U*, p.185.
13 EO Diary, 24 June 1934.
14 EO Diary, 30 June 1934.
15 EO Diary, 26 June 1934.
16 EO Diary, 8 July 1934.
17 Edith Olivier, *Alexander the Corrector: The Eccentric Life of Alexander Cruden* (London: Faber & Faber, 1934), p.57.
18 *Walkley*, pp.295–6.
19 PM, p.154.
20 EO Diary, 8 July 1934.
21 EO Diary, 29 June 1934.
22 *Walkley*, p.296.
23 *Walkley*, p.297.
24 EO Diary, 4 July 1934.
25 EO Diary, 3 December 1934.
26 EO Diary, 7 July 1934.
27 Edith Olivier, *Mary Magdalen* (London: Peter Davies, 1934), p.47.
28 *Mary Magdalen*, dedication.
29 EO Diary, 8 October 1934.
30 EO Diary, 28 October 1934.
31 EO Diary, 25 November 1934.
32 EO Diary, 31 December 1934.

495

PART FOUR: LANDSCAPES

20: *Distance*

1 EO Diary, 29 March 1935.
2 EO Diary, 7 January 1935.
3 EO Diary, 6 January 1935.
4 EO Diary, 8 November 1934.
5 EO Diary, 7 January 1935.
6 EO Diary, 6 January 1935.
7 EO Diary, 7 January 1935.
8 EO Diary, 20 March 1935.
9 *The Times*, 6 December 1935.
10 EO Diary, 16 April 1935.
11 EO Diary, 18 April 1935.
12 EO Diary, 21 May 1935.
13 EO Diary, 24 May 1935.
14 EO Diary, 27 January 1936.
15 EO Diary, 29 April 1935.
16 EO Diary, 23 April 1935.
17 EO Diary, 24 August 1926.
18 EO Diary, 15 May 1935.
19 EO Diary, 7 January 1935.
20 EO Diary, 15 May 1935.
21 EO Diary, 15 May 1935.
22 EO Diary, 26 March 1938.
23 *Book Window*, Vol. IV, no. 7, Spring 1937.
24 EO Diary, 30 June 1935.
25 EO Diary, 27 June 1935.
26 EO Diary, 14 July 1935.
27 EO Diary, 16 July 1932.
28 EO Diary, 17 July 1932.
29 EO Diary, 17 July 1932.
30 EO Diary, 17 July 1932.
31 Timothy Mowl, *Stylistic Cold Wars: Betjeman versus Pevsner* (London: John Murray, 2000), p.72.
32 Edith Olivier, *Country Moods and Tenses: A Non-Grammarian's Chapbook* (London: Batsford, 1941), p.34.

33 *Mary Magdalen*, p.165.
34 Mowl, p.72.
35 Mowl, p.120.
36 Mowl, p.64.
37 Mowl, pp.57–8.
38 Mowl, p.73.
39 Edith Olivier, *Four Victorian Ladies of Wiltshire* (London: Faber & Faber, 1945), p.71.
40 EO Diary, 27 September 1935.
41 EO Diary, 29 August 1935.
42 EO Diary, 12 October 1935.
43 EO Diary, 6 November 1935.
44 EO Diary, 5 November 1935.

21: An 'Eventful Year'

 1 EO Diary, 28 October 1934.
 2 ST to EO, 7 December 1935, EOC.
 3 ST to EO, 10 December 1935, EOC.
 4 EO Diary, 18 March 1936.
 5 EO Diary, 5 December 1935.
 6 EO Diary, 6 December 1935.
 7 EO Diary, 14 December 1935.
 8 EO Diary, 25 December 1935.
 9 EO Diary, 31 December 1935.
10 EO Diary, 9 January 1936.
11 EO Diary, 19 January 1936.
12 EO Diary, 20 January 1936.
13 *Walkley*, p.284.
14 EO Diary, 21 January 1936.
15 EO Diary, 28 January 1936.
16 EO Diary, 28 January 1936.
17 EO Diary, 9 February 1936.
18 EO Diary, 10 February 1936.
19 EOA.
20 EO Diary, 7 March 1936.
21 EO Diary, 5 June 1936.
22 EO Diary, 24 June 1936.
23 PM, p.183.

24 EO Diary, 12 October 1936.

25 EO Diary, 3 December 1936.

26 EO Diary, 31 December 1936.

27 EO Diary, 9 December 1936.

28 EO Diary, 5 December 1936.

29 EO Diary, 10 December 1936.

30 EO Diary, 11 December 1936.

31 EO Diary, 29 November 1936.

22: *La Belle Dame*

1 *L&U*, p.203.

2 *L&U*, p.206.

3 Diana Cooper, *Autobiography* (Salisbury: Michael Russell, 1979), p.91.

4 Charles Duff, 'Sex, Slate and Snowdon', p.15.

5 Caroline Duff, 'Facts about "Journal to Caroline" and letters to me from Duff Cooper', manuscript fragment, private collection.

6 EO Diary, 2 December 1935.

7 EO Diary, 13 October 1935.

8 EO Diary, 23 June 1938.

9 David Herbert, *Second Son: An Autobiography* (London: Owen, 1972), p.22.

10 John Julius Norwich, ed., *The Duff Cooper Diaries* (London: Weidenfeld & Nicolson, 2005), p.239.

11 Duff Cooper, p.240.

12 Caroline Duff.

13 Duff, p.14.

14 *L&U*, p.221.

15 7th Marquess of Anglesey, letter to author, July 2005.

16 *L&U*, p.193.

17 EO Diary, 6 January 1937.

18 EO Diary, 6 January 1937.

19 EO Diary, 29 January 1937.

20 EO Diary, 5 February 1937.

21 EO Diary, 13 February 1937.

22 EO Diary, 10 April 1937.

23 EO Diary, 12 May 1937.

24 EO Diary, 23 May 1937.

25 EO Diary, 7 June 1937.

26 EO Diary, 21 June 1937.

27 EO Diary, 23 June 1937.

28 EO Diary, 27 June 1937.

29 EO Diary, 15 July 1937.

30 EO Diary, 19 July 1937.

31 EO Diary, 10 July 1937.

32 EO Diary, 12 July 1937.

33 EO Diary, 14 June 1937.

34 EO Diary, 12 July 1937.

35 *L&U*, p.213.

36 EO Diary, 15 September 1937.

37 RW to 6th Marquess of Anglesey, 11 December 1938, National Trust, Plas Newydd.

38 National Trust, Plas Newydd.

39 RW to EO, 27 January 1939, EOA.

40 Laurence Whistler, *The Initials in the Heart* (London: Michael Russell, 2000), p.19.

41 RW to CP, Tuesday 20th, no year, National Trust, Plas Newydd.

42 RW to EO, 8 March 1937, EOA.

23: 'Out of the Ordinary'

1 EOA.

2 EO Diary, 21 April 1938.

3 PM, p.199.

4 EO Diary, 19 June 1936.

5 *Moonrakings*, p.5.

6 Barry Hugill, '"Cultists" Go Round in Circles', *Observer,* 28 August 1994.

7 Peter Ackroyd, *Albion: The Origins of the English Imagination* (London: Vintage, 2004), p.449.

8 EO Diary, 19 June 1936.

9 *Walkley*, pp.267–8.

10 *Walkley*, p.17.

11 *Walkley*, p.226.

12 *Walkley*, p.256.

13 *Walkley*, P.249.

14 *Walkley*, p.247.

15 *Walkley*, p.8.

16 EO Diary, 8 July 1934.

17 *Walkley*, p.25.

18 *The Times*, 6 May 1938.

19 EO Diary, 29 May 1938.

20 EO Diary, 29 August 1938.

21 EO Diary, 31 August 1938.

22 EO Diary, 10 September 1938.

23 EO Diary, 11 September 1938.

24 EO Diary, 14 September 1938.

25 EO Diary, 23 September 1938.

26 EO Diary, 21 September 1938.

27 EO Diary, 26 September 1938.

28 EO Diary, 30 September 1938.

29 EO Diary, 1 October 1938.

30 EO Diary, 27 June 1938.

31 *Western Gazette*, 5 October 1938.

32 *Evening Standard*, 10 November 1938.

33 *Evening News*, 12 January 1939.

34 EO to Wilton residents, 23 December 1938, EOA.

24: 'Another Season'

1 EO Diary, 5 May 1938.

2 Queen Elizabeth to RW, 1 May 1938, RWA.

3 EO Diary, 15 September 1937.

4 EO Diary, 10 May 1938.

5 EO Diary, 21 May 1938.

6 EO Diary, 22 July 1938.

7 Duff Cooper, p.250.

8 RW to CP, 17 February 1938, National Trust, Plas Newydd.

9 RW to CP, undated, National Trust, Plas Newydd.

10 *L&U*, p.219.

11 EO Diary, 11 August 1938.

12 EO Diary, 22 August 1938.

13 *L&U*, p.221.

14 RW to EO, 27 January 1939, EOA.

15 EO Diary, 16 March 1939.

16 EO Diary, 20 March 1939.

17 EO Diary, 28 April 1939.

18 Terence Pepper, *Howard Coster's Celebrity Portraits* (London: National Portrait Gallery, 1985), p.vii.

19 Osbert Sitwell, *Noble Essences or Courteous Revelations* (London: Macmillan, 1950), p.265.

20 EO Diary, 7 January 1935.

21 *Self-Portrait,* p.59.

22 RW to EO, 16 June 1939, EOC.

23 EO Diary, 17 October 1938.

24 Henry Tonks to Mary Adshead, 26 September 1925, Mary Adshead Papers, private collection.

25 Asquith, p.98.

26 *L&U,* p.92.

27 *Brideshead,* p.260.

28 *Brideshead,* pp.215–16.

29 *Brideshead,* p.216.

30 EO Diary, 17 October 1939.

31 EO Diary, 15 May 1939.

32 Roberts, p.275.

33 Roberts, pp.277–8.

34 EO Diary, 5 June 1939.

35 EO Diary, 12 September 1939.

36 RW to HU, 21 October 1939, National Trust, Plas Newydd.

37 RW to HU, February 1939, National Trust, Plas Newydd.

38 *L&U,* p.223.

39 *Night Thoughts,* p.1.

PART FIVE: PAINTING FROM LIFE

25: *Commission*

1 *Night Thoughts,* p.6.

2 *Night Thoughts,* p.9.

3 EO Diary, 10 May 1940.

4 EO Diary, 13 May 1941.

5 EO Diary, 9 October 1941.

6 EO Diary, 21 October 1940.

7 *Night Thoughts,* p.13.

8 EO Diary, 27 September 1939.

9 EO Diary, 2 October 1939.

10 EO Diary, 3 October 1939.

11 *L&U*, p.231.

12 EO Diary, 12 November 1939.

13 Jenny Spencer-Smith, *Rex Whistler's War* (London: National Army Museum, 1994), p.26.

14 *Self-Portrait*, p.146.

15 Channon, p.323.

16 *Night Thoughts*, p.45.

17 *L&U*, pp.238–9.

18 *L&U*, p.235.

19 *L&U*, p.236.

20 RW to EO, 18 April 1940, EOA.

21 RW to HU, undated but received 12 March 1940, National Trust, Plas Newydd.

22 EO Diary, 10 June 1941.

23 EO Diary, 19 May 1940.

24 EO Diary, 21 May 1940.

25 *Life and Drawings*, p.45.

26 *L&U*, p.236.

27 Spencer-Smith, p.52.

28 Duff, p.15.

29 Ursula Ridley to Emily Lutyens, June 1940, Ursula Ridley Papers, private collection.

30 RW to HU, 27 May 1940, National Trust, Plas Newydd.

26: 'The Conditional'

1 EO Diary, 25 December 1939.

2 *Queen*, December 1939.

3 *Night Thoughts*, p.14.

4 *Vogue,* January 1940.

5 EO Diary, 26 March 1938.

6 *Daily Express*, 6 January 1940.

7 *The Times*, 23 December 1939.

8 *L&U*, p.242.

9 EO Diary, 11 April 1940.

10 EO Diary, 25 April 1940.

11 EO Diary, 10 May 1940.

12 EO Diary, 17 May 1940.

13 EO Diary, 23 May 1940.

14 EO Diary, 4 June 1940.

15 EO Diary, 13 June 1940.

16 EO Diary, 14 June 1940.

17 EO Diary, 11 October 1940.

18 EO Diary, 23 June 1940.

19 RW to EO, 26 June 1940, EOA.

20 Frances Spalding, *British Art Since 1900* (London: Thames and Hudson, 1989), p.137.

21 Spalding, p.138.

22 EO Diary, 1 July 1940.

23 Cooper, pp.55–6.

24 EO Diary, 30 June 1940.

25 EO to Wilton residents, 6 July 1940, EOA.

26 *Ashcombe*, p.76.

27 EO Diary, 6 December 1940.

28 *Night Thoughts*, p.28.

29 *Country Moods*, p.1.

30 *Country Moods*, p.4.

31 *Country Moods*, p.5.

32 *Country Moods*, p.7.

33 *Country Moods*, p.18.

34 *Country Moods*, p.115.

35 *Country Moods*, p.10.

36 Katharine Allison Gurley to EO, 13 April 1944, EOC.

37 Malcolm Fry to EO, 4 May 1943, EOC.

27: Home

1 EO Diary, 9 October 1940.

2 RW to CP, 17 October 1940, National Trust, Plas Newydd.

3 Daphne Fielding, *Mercury Presides* (London: Eyre & Spottiswoode, 1954), p.201.

4 John Jolliffe, 'Rex Whistler', *Apollo*, August 2005.

5 EO Diary, 20 March 1941.

6 EO Diary, 20 March 1941.

7 *Night Thoughts*, p.13.

8 *Night Thoughts*, p.29.
9 EO Diary, 18 April 1941.
10 EO Diary, 12 June 1941.
11 RW to EO, 19 May 1941, EOA.
12 EO Diary, 13 June 1941.
13 EO Diary, 15 June 1941.
14 *L&U*, p.249.
15 EO Diary, 20 June 1941.
16 EO Diary, 22 June 1941.
17 EO to CB 17 September 1941, BA.
18 EO Diary, 22 September 1941.
19 EO Diary, 7 October 1941.
20 EO Diary, 9 October 1941.
21 EO Diary, 1 January 1942.
22 EO Diary, 28 October 1941.
23 *Night Thoughts*, p.31
24 EO Diary, 29 April 1942.
25 EO Diary, 5 October 1941.
26 *L&U*, p.252.
27 EO Diary, 4 October 1941.
28 *Ashcombe*, p.79.
29 RW to HU, undated, National Trust, Plas Newydd.
30 *Self-Portrait*, p.103.
31 RW to CB, undated, BA.
32 EO Diary, 27 December 1941.
33 EO Diary, 12 February 1942.
34 EO Diary, 26 April 1942.
35 EO Diary, 27 April 1942.
36 *Ashcombe*, p.80.
37 RW to CB, 1942, BA.
38 EO Diary, 6 June 1942.
39 EO Diary, 7 June 1942.
40 EO Diary, 21 June 1942.
41 RW to EO, 27 June 1942, EOC.
42 EO Diary, 19 July 1942.
43 EO Diary, 18 August 1942.
44 EO Diary, 31 August 1942.
45 EO Diary, 12 September 1942.
46 EO Diary, 3 September 1942.

47 *Night Thoughts*, p.7.
48 *Night Thoughts*, p.viii.
49 *Night Thoughts*, p.vi.
50 *Night Thoughts*, p.47.
51 *Night Thoughts*, p.40.
52 *Night Thoughts*, p.86.
53 As repeated by Henry Uxbridge in a letter to Edith, HU to EO, 16 June 1944, EOC.
54 *Ashcombe*, p.109.
55 EO Diary, 12 September 1942.
56 EO Diary, 6 March 1942.
57 EO Diary, 7 March 1942.

28: 'In the Long Ago'

1   EO Diary, 15 June 1942.
2   EO Diary, 18 August 1942.
3   EO Diary, 13 September 1942.
4   Roberts, p.285.
5   *Initials*, p.133.
6   RW to EO, 13 January 1943, EOA.
7   EO Diary, 26 February 1943.
8   EO Diary 26 February 1943.
9   RW to EO, 2 May 1943, EOA.
10 *L&U*, p.260.
11 *L&U*, p.230.
12 *Vogue*, March 1943.
13 EO Diary, 14 April 1943.
14 EO Diary, 30 April 1943.
15 EO Diary, 5 June 1943.
16 EO Diary, 6 June 1943.
17 EO Diary, 7 June 1943.
18 RW to EO, 21 February 1944, EOA.
19 ST to EO, 14 January 1943, EOC.
20 EO Diary, 18 January 1943.
21 EO Diary, 18 January 1943.
22 EO Diary, 18 January 1943.
23 EO Diary, 27 January 1944.
24 RW to EO, 25 January 1944, EOA.

25 Fielding, p.201.
26 EO Diary, 28 December 1941.
27 *Brideshead*, p.330.
28 *Brideshead*, p.288.
29 *Brideshead*, p.288.
30 RW to EO, 1 August 1943, EOA.
31 RW to EO, undated, EOA.
32 *Four Victorian Ladies*, p.9.
33 EO Diary, 8 December 1943.
34 EO Diary, 9 December 1943.
35 EO Diary, 10 December 1943.
36 EO Diary, 29 December 1943.
37 EO Diary, 26 January 1944.
38 EO Diary, 4 February 1944.
39 EO Diary, 6 February 1944.
40 EO Diary, 29 February 1944.
41 PM, p.282.
42 EO Diary, 11 March 1944.

29: Action

 1 Spencer-Smith, p.134.
 2 Helen Turner to EO, 25 April 1944, EOA.
 3 Spencer-Smith, p.151.
 4 Spencer-Smith, pp.135–6.
 5 Asquith, pp.112–13.
 6 EO Diary, 6 June 1944.
 7 EO Diary, 6 June 1944.
 8 EO to CB, 20 June 1944, BA.
 9 EO Diary, 7 June 1944.
10 PM, p.287.
11 EO Diary, 16 June 1944.
12 RW to EO, 18 June 1944, EOA.
13 EO Diary, 20 June 1944.
14 EO Diary, 21 June 1944.
15 RW to EO, 9 July 1944, EOA.
16 EO Diary, 18 July 1944.
17 *The Times*, 19 July 1944.
18 EO Diary, 25 July 1944.

19 EO Diary, 25 July 1944.
20 Spencer-Smith, p.164.
21 *L&U*, p.284.
22 RW to EO, 16 July 1944, EOA.
23 *Life and Drawings*, p.44.

AFTER

'The Loving Spirit'

1   EO Diary, 26 July 1944.
2   *L&U*, p.295.
3   EO to LW, 28 July 1944, RWA.
4   Hoare, p.266.
5   Moorcroft Wilson, p.339.
6   EO Diary, 27 July 1944.
7   *Self-Portrait*, p.146.
8   EO to CB, 28 July 1944, BA.
9   EO Diary, 29 July 1944.
10 Helen Turner to EO, 28 July 1944, EOC.
11 EO Diary, 1 August 1944.
12 EO Diary, 31 July 1944.
13 EO Diary, 28 July 1944.
14 *Initials*, p.208.
15 EO Diary, 9 August 1944.
16 EO Diary, 13 October 1944.
17 EO Diary, 19 April 1945.
18 Francis Portal to HS, 'Eyewitness Account of the Death of Rex Whistler', August 1944, EOC.
19 Portal, August 1944, EOC.
20 EO Diary, 28 July 1944.
21 EO Diary, 4 August 1944.
22 EO Diary, 12 September 1944.
23 EO Diary, 19 September 1944.
24 EO Diary, 12 October 1944.
25 EO Diary, 13 September 1944.
26 EO Diary, 23 August 1944.

27 EO Diary, 23 August 1944.
28 EO Diary, 29 November 1944.
29 LW to EO, 1 May 1946, EOC.
30 EO Diary, 29 April 1946.
31 LW to EO, 14 July 1946, EOC.
32 LW to EO, 24 January 1947, EOC.
33 Helen Turner to EO, 12 March 1946, EOC.
34 *L&U*, p.297.
35 EO Diary, 4 October 1944.
36 EO Diary, 6 October 1944.
37 EO Diary, 23 December 1944.
38 Helen Turner to EO, EOA.
39 EO Diary, 24 December 1944.
40 EO Diary, 31 December 1944.
41 EO Diary, 23 March 1945.
42 ST to EO, 6 April 1945, EOC.
43 EO Diary, 8 May 1945.
44 EO Diary, 9 May 1945.
45 EO Diary, 30 October 1944.
46 EO Diary, 24 June 1945.
47 EO Diary, 26 July 1945.
48 EO Diary, 14 July 1945.
49 *Ashcombe*, pp.120–1.
50 EO to CB, 1 September 1945, BA.
51 EO Diary, 14 October 1945.
52 EO Diary, 19 November 1945.
53 EO Diary, 14 August 1946.
54 EO to CB, 8 December 1946, BA.
55 *Self-Portrait*, p.196.
56 EO to CB, 6 October 1947, BA.
57 EO Diary, 28 January 1948.
58 EO to CB, 5 December 1947, BA.
59 EO to LW, 20 April 1947, RWA.
60 SS to EO, 20 January 1945, EOC.
61 EO Diary, 11 January 1948.
62 EO Diary, 27 January 1948.
63 EO Diary, 27 January 1948.
64 EO Diary, 27 February 1948.
65 EO Diary, 3 April 1948.

66 EO Diary, 3 March 1948.

67 EO Diary, 8 March 1948.

68 *The Times*, 12 May 1948.

69 Cecil Beaton, *Salisbury Journal*, May 1948.

70 Herbert, p.157.

71 *Ashcombe*, dedication.

72 ST to CB, undated, Cecil Beaton Archive, Sotheby's.

73 *Mercury*, 1948, p.16.

Legacies

1 *Noble Essences*, p.264.

2 *The Times*, 23 September 1944.

3 Christabel McLaren to CP, 1 August 1944, National Trust, Plas Newydd.

4 Diana Cooper, p.962.

5 *Self-Portrait*, p.145.

6 Cooper, p.686.

7 Roberts, p.286.

8 *L&U*, p.297.

9 Edith Olivier, 'Memories of Rex Whistler', *Country Life*, 1 September 1944.

10 *Initials*, p.208.

11 *L&U*, p.297.

12 Charles Duff, in conversation with author, 2014.

13 The *Spectator*, 24 November 2012.

14 Stanley Olson, *Elinor Wylie: A Life Apart* (New York: The Dial Press/ James Wade, 1979), p.269.

15 Naipaul, p.17.

16 *Walkley*, p.247.

Select Bibliography

❖

MANUSCRIPT SOURCES

When I began researching this book Edith Olivier's diaries and correspondence were held at the Wiltshire County Record Office in Trowbridge. They are now housed in the archive at the Wiltshire and Swindon History Centre in Chippenham. Almost all of Rex Whistler's letters to Edith Olivier are in the possession of her great-great niece Penelope Middelboe, along with the rest of Edith's archive. A selection of Rex's letters to the Paget family is on display as part of the museum that is dedicated to him at Plas Newydd (National Trust). Until recently Rex Whistler's archive was in the possession of his family, it is now at the Salisbury and South Wiltshire Museum. Cecil Beaton's papers, including Rex and Edith's letters to him, are at St John's College, Cambridge University.

BOOKS BY EDITH OLIVIER

The Love-Child (London: Secker, 1927)
The Underground River (London: Thomas Nelson, 1928)
As Far as Jane's Grandmother's (London: Secker, 1928)
The Triumphant Footman (London: Secker, 1930)
Dwarf's Blood (London: Faber & Faber, 1931)
The Seraphim Room (London: Faber & Faber, 1932)
Alexander The Corrector: The Eccentric Life of Alexander Cruden (London: Faber & Faber, 1934)
Mary Magdalen (London: Peter Davies, 1934)
Without Knowing Mr Walkley (London: Faber & Faber, 1938)
Country Moods and Tenses: A Non-Grammarian's Chapbook (London: Batsford, 1941)
Night Thoughts of a Country Landlady (London: Batsford, 1943)

Select Bibliography

Four Victorian Ladies of Wiltshire (London: Faber & Faber, 1945)

Wiltshire (London: Robert Hale, 1951)

In Pursuit of Rare Meats – A Guide to the Duchy of Epicurania with some Account of the Famous Expedition: Being the Story of the Mural Paintings by Rex Whistler in the Restaurant of the Tate Gallery (London: Tate, 1954)

The Love Child (London: Virago, 1981)

With Others

Mildred (Shaftesbury: The High House Press, 1926)

Secrets of Some Wiltshire Housewives: a book of recipes collected from the members of the Women's Institutes (Warminster: Coates and Parker, 1927)

with Margaret K. S. Edwards: *Moonrakings: a little book of Wiltshire stories told by members of the Women's Institutes* (Warminster: Coates and Parker, 1930)

with Charlotte A. E. Moberly: Olivier, Edith, preface, *An Adventure* (London: Faber & Faber, 1931), 4th Edition

with Robert Byron: *Shell Guide to Wiltshire* (London: The Architectural Press, 1935)

with Mabel Morrison: 'The Quest of Joy: Fragments from the manuscript of Mabel Morrison' (Privately printed, 1937)

with others, *Tribute to Walter de la Mare on his seventy-fifth birthday* (London: Faber & Faber, 1948)

OTHER WORKS

Ackroyd, Peter, *Albion: The Origins of the English Imagination* (London: Vintage, 2004)

Albrecht, Donald, *Cecil Beaton: The New York Years* (New York: Rizzoli, 2011)

Amory, Mark, *Lord Berners: The Last Eccentric* (London: Pimlico, 1999)

Anon, *Mottisfont Abbey: Garden, House and Estate* (London: The National Trust, 2004)

Anon, *Rex Whistler 1905–1944: A Memorial Exhibition* (London: The Arts Council, 1960)

Select Bibliography

Anon, *Wilton House* (London: Pitkin Pictorials, 1974)

Asquith, Cynthia, Lady, *Haply I May Remember* (London: Barrie, 1950)

Banham, Joanna, ed., *Encyclopaedia of Interior Design* Vol.I, (London: Fitzroy Dearborn, 1997)

Barrett Browning, Elizabeth, *Aurora Leigh and Other Poems* (London: Penguin, 1995)

Bankhead, Tallulah, *My Autobiography* (Jackson: University Press of Mississippi, 2004)

Beaton, Cecil, *The Book of Beauty* (London: Duckworth, 1930)

———, *Ashcombe: The Story of a Fifteen-Year Lease* (London: Batsford, 1949)

———, *The Wandering Years: Diaries, 1922–39* (London: Weidenfeld & Nicolson, 1961)

———, *The Years Between* (London: Weidenfeld & Nicolson, 1965)

Beaton, Cecil, Buckle, Richard, ed., *Self-Portrait with Friends: Selected Diaries, 1926–74* (London: Penguin, 1982)

Birchall, Heather, *In Pursuit of Rare Meats: The Rex Whistler Mural Tate Britain Restaurant* (London: Tate Publishing, 2003)

Birns, Nicholas, *Understanding Anthony Powell* (Columbia: University of South Carolina Press, 2004)

Blow, Simon, *Broken Blood* (London: Faber & Faber, 1987)

Buckton, Henry, *Artists & Authors At War* (Barnsley: Leo Cooper, 1999)

Calloway, Stephen, *Baroque, Baroque: The Culture of Excess* (London: Phaidon, 1994)

———, *Rex Whistler: The Triumph of Fancy* (Brighton: Royal Pavilion, 2006)

Carpenter, Humphrey, *The Brideshead Generation* (London: Weidenfeld & Nicolson, 1990)

Castle, Charles, *Oliver Messel* (London: Thames & Hudson, 1955)

Castle, Terry, 'Contagious Folly: *An Adventure* and Its Skeptics', *Critical Inquiry*, Vol. 17, No. 4, Summer 1991 (Chicago: University of Chicago Press)

Channon, Henry, James, Robert Rhodes, ed., *Chips: The Diaries of Sir Henry Channon* (London: Phoenix, 1996)

Cohen, Morton N., *Lewis Carroll: A Biography* (London: Macmillan, 1995)

Connon, Bryan, *Beverley Nichols: A Life* (Portland: Timber Press, 2000)

Cooper, Diana, *Autobiography* (Salisbury: Michael Russell, 1979)

Cooper, Emmanuel, *The Sexual Perspective: Homosexuality and Art in the Last 100 Years in the West* (London: Routledge, 1994)

Select Bibliography

Core, Philip, *Camp: The Lie That Tells the Truth* (London: Plexus, 2008)

de la Mare, Walter, *Henry Brocken* (London: Collins, 1904)

Duff, Charles, 'Sex, Slate and Snowdon' (unpublished manuscript)

Ellis, Lionel, *Welsh Guards at War* (Aldershot: Gale & Polden, 1946)

Egremont, Max, *Siegfried Sassoon* (London: Picador, 2005)

Emerson, Maureen, *Escape to Provence* (Cuckfield: Chapter and Verse, 2008)

Felmingham, Michael, *Rex Whistler: An Exhibition of his Graphic Work* (Leicester: Leicester College of Art and Design, 1967)

Fest, Joachim, *Plotting Hitler's Death: The German Resistance to Hitler 1933–1945* (London: Weidenfeld & Nicolson, 1996)

Fielding, Daphne, Marchioness of Bath, *Mercury Presides* (London: Eyre & Spottiswoode, 1954)

Flaubert, Gustave, Steegmuller, Francis, trans., *Intimate Notebook 1840–1841* (London: WH Allen, 1967)

Foss, Arthur, *Country House Treasures* (London: The National Trust / Weidenfeld & Nicolson, 1980)

Fraser, David, *Wars and Shadows: Memoirs of General Sir David Fraser* (London: Allen Lane, 2002)

Freud, Sigmund; McClintock, David, and Phillips, Adam, *The Uncanny* (London: Penguin, 2003)

Fuller, Ronald, and Whistler, Laurence, *The Work of Rex Whistler* (London: Batsford, 1960)

Gannett, Cinthia, *Gender and the Journal* (New York: State University of New York Press, 1992)

Gardiner, Juliet, *Wartime Britain 1939–1945* (London: Review, 2005)

Glendinning, Victoria, *Edith Sitwell: A Unicorn Among Lions* (London: Phoenix, 1999)

Green, Martin, *Children of the Sun: A Narrative of Decadence in England After 1918* (London: Pimlico, 2001)

Hastings, Selina, *Evelyn Waugh: A Biography* (London: Vintage, 1995)

———, *Rosamond Lehmann: A Life* (London: Vintage, 2003)

Herbert, David, *Second Son: An Autobiography* (London: Owen, 1972)

Higdon, David Leon, 'Gay Sebastian and Cheerful Charles: Homoeroticism in Waugh's *Brideshead Revisited*', *ARIEL: A Review of International English Literature*, 25.4, 1994 (Calgary: University of Calgary)

Hill, Oliver, 'Mr Rex Whistler at Port Lympne', *Country Life* (4 February 1933)

Hoare, Philip, *Serious Pleasures: The Life of Stephen Tennant* (London: Hamish Hamilton, 1990)

———, 'I Love a Man in a Uniform: The Dandy Esprit de Corps', *Fashion Theory: The Journal of Dress, Body & Culture*, Volume 9, Number 3, September 2005 (Oxford: Berg Publishers)

Holroyd, Michael, *Lytton Strachey* (London: Vintage, 1995)

Hone, Joseph, *The Life of Henry Tonks* (London: Heinemann, 1939)

Hoyt, Nancy, *Elinor Wylie: The Portrait of an Unknown Lady* (New York: Bobbs-Merrill, 1935)

Hussey, Christopher, 'Paintings at 36 Hill Street', *Country Life* (25 March 1939)

———, 'The Rex Whistler Room at Plas Newydd', *Country Life* (22 February 1939)

———, 'Mottisfont Abbey', *Country Life* (6 May 1954)

Jackson, Stanley, *The Sassoons: Portrait of a Dynasty* (London: Heinemann, 1989)

Jackson-Stops, Gervase, 'Rex Whistler at Plas Newydd', *Country Life* (4 August 1977)

Jameson, Anna, *Legends of the Monastic Orders* (London: Longmans, Green and Co., 1867)

Jolliffe, John, 'Rex Whistler', *Apollo* (August 2005)

Keegan, John, *Six Armies in Normandy: From D-Day to the Liberation of Paris* (London: Pimlico, 2004)

Kennett, John, *Rex Whistler in Eltham* (The Eltham Society Publications Committee, 2005)

Kinney, Arthur F., ed., *Cambridge Companion to English Literature 1500–1600* (Cambridge: Cambridge University Press, 2007)

Kite, Edward, 'Wilton House, and its Literary Associations', *Wiltshire Notes and Queries* 5, June 1907, p.433 (Devizes: George Simpson)

Lees-Milne, James, *Ancestral Voices & Prophesying Peace: Diaries 1942–1945* (London: John Murray, 1995)

Lewis, C. S., *The Pilgrim's Regress: An Allegorical Apology for Christianity, Reason and Romanticism* (Grand Rapids: Wm. B. Eerdmans, 1992)

Light, Alison, *Forever England: Femininity, Literature and Conservatism between the Wars* (London: Routledge, 1991)

Lloyd, Stephen, *William Walton: Muse of Fire* (London: Boydell & Brewer, 2001)

Lobenthal, Joel, *Tallulah: The Life and Times of a Leading Lady* (London: Aurum Press, 2005)

Select Bibliography

Lowe, Norman, *Mastering Modern British History* (London: Macmillan, 1991)

Lowndes, Susan, ed., *Diaries and Letters of Marie Belloc Lowndes 1911–1947* (London: Chatto & Windus, 1971)

McBain, Audrey and Nelson, Lynette, *The Bounding Spring: A History of Teffont in Wiltshire* (Teffont: Black Horse Books, 2003)

McLaren, Christabel, Lady Aberconway, *A Wiser Woman?* (London: Hutchinson, 1966)

Mandler, Peter, *The Fall and Rise of the Stately Home* (London: Yale University Press, 1997)

Massey, Anne, *Interior Design of the Twentieth Century* (London: Thames & Hudson, 1996)

Maugham, W. Somerset, *The Sacred Flame,* (London: Heinemann, 1928)

Middelboe, Penelope, ed., *Edith Olivier: From Her Journals, 1924–1948* (London: Weidenfeld & Nicolson, 1989)

Mitford, Nancy, *Love in a Cold Climate* (London: Penguin, 1976)

———, *The Pursuit of Love* (London: Penguin, 1970)

Moorcroft Wilson, Jean, *Siegfried Sassoon: The Journey from the Trenches 1918–1967* (London: Duckworth, 2003)

Mordaunt Crook, Joseph, *The Rise of the Nouveaux Riches* (London: John Murray, 2000)

Mowl, Timothy, *Stylistic Cold Wars: Betjeman versus Pevsner* (London: John Murray, 2000)

Naipaul, V. S., *The Enigma of Arrival* (New York: Vintage, 1988)

Nichols, Beverley, *The Unforgiving Minute* (London: WH Allen, 1978)

Nicolson, Adam, *Earls of Paradise: England & the Dream of Perfection* (London: HarperCollins, 2008)

Norwich, John Julius, ed., *The Duff Cooper Diaries* (London: Weidenfeld & Nicolson, 2005)

Olson, Stanley, *Elinor Wylie: A Life Apart. A Biography* (New York: The Dial Press/James Wade, 1979)

Owens, Susan, *Watercolours and Drawings from the Collection of Queen Elizabeth The Queen Mother* (London: Royal Collections Publications, 2005)

Pepper, Terence, *Howard Coster's Celebrity Portraits* (London: National Portrait Gallery, 1985)

Poe, Edgar Allan, *Collected Tales and Poems of Edgar Allan Poe* (London: Wordsworth, 2004)

Pugh, Tison, 'Romantic Friendship, Homosexuality, and Evelyn Waugh's *Brideshead Revisited*', *English Language Notes*, 38.4, 2001 (Boulder, University of Colorado)

Reed, Christopher, 'Design For (Queer) Living: Sexual Identity, Performance, and Décor in British Vogue, 1922–1926', in *GLQ: A Journal of Lesbian and Gay Studies*, Volume 12, Number 3, 2006 (Durham: Duke University Press)

Ridley, Jane, *Edwin Lutyens* (London: Pimlico, 2003)

Roberts, John Stuart, *Siegfried Sassoon* (London: Metro, 2005)

Sassoon, Siegfried, *The Complete Memoirs of George Sherston* (London: Faber, 1972)

Schenkar, Joan, *Truly Wilde: The Story of Dolly Wilde, Oscar's Unusual Niece* (London: Virago, 2001)

Seymour, Miranda, *Ottoline Morrell: Life on a Grand Scale* (London: Sceptre, 1998)

Shakespeare, Nicholas, 'A light that shines brightly still', *The Times* (31 October 1985)

Sitwell, Osbert, 'This Strange Country', *Architectural Review* (July 1928)
——, *Noble Essences or Courteous Revelations* (London: Macmillan, 1950)

Skipwith, Joanna, *The Sitwells and the Arts of the 1920s and 1930s* (London: National Portrait Gallery, 1994)

Sontag, Susan, *Against Interpretation* (London: Vintage, 1994)

Spalding, Frances, *British Art Since 1900* (London: Thames and Hudson, 1989)
——, *The Tate: A History* (London: Tate Gallery, 1998)

Spencer-Smith, Jenny, *Rex Whistler's War* (London: National Army Museum, 1994)

Steegman, John, 'The Artist and the Country House', *Country Life* (1949)

Stansky, Peter, *Sassoon: The Worlds of Sybil and Philip* (London: Yale University Press, 2003)

Strachey, Julia Frances and Partridge, Frances, *Julia: A Portrait of Julia Strachey* (London: Phoenix, 2000)

Street, A. G., 'Memories of Edith Olivier', *Mercury: A Review of the Arts* (Bournemouth: Autumn 1948)

Swift, Jonathan, *Gulliver's Travels* (London: Cresset Press, 1930), 2 vols.

Taylor, A. J. P., *English History, 1914–1945* (Oxford: Oxford University Press, 1965)

Taylor, D. J., *Bright Young People* (London: Chatto & Windus, 2007)

Taylor, John, *A Dream of England: Landscape, Photography and the Tourist's*

Select Bibliography

Imagination (Manchester: Manchester University Press, 1994)

Townsend Warner, Sylvia, *Lolly Willowes or The Loving Huntsman* (Chicago: Academy Chicago Publishers, 1999)

Tennyson, Alfred, *Idylls of the King* (London: Penguin, 1983)

Vickers, Hugo, *Cecil Beaton* (London: Phoenix Press, 2003)

Waugh, Evelyn, *Brideshead Revisited* (London: Penguin, 1962)

———, *Vile Bodies* (London: Penguin, 2000)

———, *Decline and Fall* (London: Penguin, 2003)

Whistler, Laurence, *Rex Whistler: His Life and Drawings* (London: Art and Technics, 1948)

———, 'Rex Whistler', *Everybody's* (October 1948)

———, *The Königsmark Drawings* (London: Richards Press, 1952)

———, *An Anthology of Mine* (London: Hamish Hamilton, 1981)

———, *The Laughter and the Urn* (London: Weidenfeld & Nicolson, 1985)

———, *The Initials in the Heart* (London: Michael Russell, 2000)

Wilcock, Roland, 'A Casualty of "Goodwood"', *Guards Magazine* (Autumn 1984)

———, 'Rex Whistler at Pickering', *Welsh Guards Regimental Magazine* (1989)

———, 'Whistler calls the tune in Pickering', *The Dalesman* (December 1993)

Willsdon, Claire, *Mural Painting in Britain 1840–1940* (Oxford: Clarendon Press, 2000)

Wise, Jane D., transcribed, *Last Poems of Elinor Wylie,* (New York: Knopf, 1943)

Wyndham, Ursula, *Astride The Wall: A Memoir, 1913–1945* (London: Century, 1988)

Ziegler, Philip, *Diana Cooper: The Biography of Diana Cooper* (London: Hamish Hamilton, 1981)

———, *Osbert Sitwell* (London: Random House, 1998)

Index

Index

Beaton, Cecil xviii, 25, 40, 49, 84–7, 94,
      177, 179, 185, 270, 273, 275, 317,
      459–60
   affair with Doris Castlerosse 264–5
   in America 164, 181–2, 186, 199, 221,
      239–40, 305, 376–7, 434–5, 460
   anti-Semitism 376–7
   arriviste 94–6
   and Ashcombe 205–9, 212–14,
      216–20, 222–4, 231, 236, 247, 258,
      264–5, 297, 325, 327, 376, 395,
      401, 441–3, 446–7
   Ashcombe publication 447, 451
   backlash against the youthful exploits
      of 90–2, 105
   and Edith 84–5, 97–100, 104–5,
      121–2, 129–30, 133–8, 145, 155–6,
      162–4, 167, 182–3, 186, 193–4,
      196, 199–208, 212–14, 216–26,
      239–40, 245–8, 253, 264–5, 284,
      292, 312, 322, 325–7, 345–7,
      375–7, 387–8, 395, 399–400,
      405–6, 411–13, 420, 424, 434–5,
      439–48, 451, 457
   exhibitions 121–3, 182
   films *The Sailor's Return* at
      Ashcombe 297, 318
   financial success 209, 221, 305
   and the Great Mayfair War 160
   Heil Cinderella production 377–8
   Official War Photographer 377, 395, 400
   and Peter Watson 217–18, 223
   photography 85–6, 90, 96, 97–8, 116,
      134, 201–2, 209, 325–6, 376–7,
      395, 400, 460, 462
   portraits of Edith 346, 347, 375,
      411–12
   posthumous tribute to Rex 354–5
   prose 201–2
   at Reddish House 446, 460
   and Rex's death 434–5, 443, 455–6
   on Rex's love for Penelope Dudley
      Ward 263
   and Rex's Port Lympne commission 232
   Scrapbook 322
   and the Second World War 366, 377,
      386, 395, 399, 400, 417, 434–5

   set design 460
   and the Sitwells 86–7, 95–6
   and Stephen's house parties 115–17, 130
   and Tallulah Bankhead 277–8, 279
   The Book of Beauty 201–3, 225, 277–8
   in Venice 351–2
   and *Vogue* 134–5, 181, 182, 221, 460
   Windsor Wedding photographer 325–6
Beaton, Lady Mary 95
Beaton, Nancy 122, 125, 135, 160, 186,
      202
Beauchamp, William Lygon, 7th Earl
      159–60
Beaumont, Hugh 'Binkie' 422
Beckford, William 111, 140, 409
Beddington, Jack 211, 298
Beerbohm, Max 186, 313
Beeton, Mrs 50
Behrman, S. N. 133
Bell, Clive 50
Bell, Vanessa 145
Benét, William Rose 137, 139, 140–1
Bérard, Christian 219–20
Berners, Gerald Tyrwhitt-Wilson, Baron
      153–4, 156, 178–9, 219, 221, 223,
      228–9, 233, 235, 264–5, 299,
      327
Betjeman, John 25, 64, 297–8, 300
Biddesden 224, 241, 247
Bismarck, Jacky 224
Blagdon 367, 391
Blanche, Anthony 64, 348
Bledisloe, Charles Bathurst, Viscount 20
Blitz 370, 386
Bloomsbury Group 196
Blow, Detmar 19
Blunden, Edmund 177, 183, 313, 448
Board of Agriculture 10
Bodnant 391
Bonham Carter, Lady Violet xvii, 14, 345,
      399
Book Window magazine 295–6, 311, 326
Borenius, Tancred 194, 310
Borley, Mr 206, 212–13, 442
Boucher, François 55
Bradley, General Omar 402
Breccles Hall 411

Index

Index

Index

Index

Index

Index

Index

Index

in Rome 259–60
as *salonnière* 263, 265, 340
and Sassoon 166–9, 171–4, 182–3,
    185–7, 199–200, 249–57, 294–5,
    296, 305, 326, 339, 407–9, 425,
    441, 444, 449, 450, 457
scholarship to Oxford University 7–8
and the Second World War 341–4, 347,
    353, 358–60, 363–6, 373–82,
    384–9, 392–406, 409–15, 417–28,
    433–8, 440–4
snob 65
spinsterhood 8–9, 157–8
and Stephen's house parties 117–18, 130
and the suffragettes 15
supernatural experiences of xvi–xvii,
    16–18, 184, 274, 339
and Tallulah Bankhead 277, 279–80,
    291–2, 306, 308, 313
and *Vogue* xvii, 98–100, 134–5, 375–6,
    411–12
and William Walton 194–5, 220–1, 237,
    241, 247, 253, 283–4, 302–3, 339,
    457
work
    BBC radio broadcasts 335, 400, 418,
        443
    becomes a writer 68–9
    begins book about Wiltshire 419, 438,
        443, 445, 450
    begins memorial to Rex 437–8,
        448–50, 456, 458
    biographies 280–3, 285, 299
    book censorship projects 295
    book reviews 137, 295–6, 311, 326
    chairperson of the Rural Cottage
        Improvement Society for
        Wiltshire 346
    contributes essay to *A Tribute to Walter
        de la Mare on His Seventy-Fifth
        Birthday* 448
    contributes to *Mildred* 68, 458
    *Country Moods and Tenses – A
        Non-Grammarian's Chapbook*
        387–9, 405
    Director of the County ARP
        Executive 343, 363, 389

edits *Moonrakings: A Little Book of
    Wiltshire Stories* 197–8
film scripts 294
Four Victorian Ladies of Wiltshire 418,
    425
Girls' Diocesan Association lectures
    61
governor of Southampton University
    College 322
on the Invasion Committee 397
invents story to Rex's Tate mural
    ('Guide to the Duchy of
    Epicurania') 108–10, 132,
    145, 162
journalistic ambitions 294–6, 298,
    311, 326, 346–7, 437
magistrate 381, 397
Mayor of Wilton 344–7, 373–6, 385,
    396–7
member of the Conservative
    Association 131
memoirs, *Without Knowing Mr
    Walkley* 301, 311, 326, 336–41
on the National Council of Women
    130–1
*Night Thoughts of a Country
    Landlady* 68 403–5, 413
novels 273–4, 335–6
    As Far As Jane's Grandmother's 3,
        102–6, 130, 162, 166–7, 182
    Dwarf's Blood 189, 196–7, 215–16,
        218, 221–2, 230, 242, 293
    The Love-Child xiii, 68–77, 82–3,
        99, 103, 104, 132, 136–7, 149,
        242, 268, 274, 443, 457,
        458
    The Seraphim Room 227, 230,
        241–3, 246, 418
    The Triumphant Footman 163, 179,
        187–8
    Without Knowing Mr Walkley
        129
and the Order of St John
    Ambulance 397
private tutor 61
secretary of the Salisbury Women's
    Diocesan Council 130

Index

Index

Index

Index

Index

extracts reading groups

competitions books new

discounts extracts

competitions extracts

books new events

reading groups extracts discounts

events books reading groups

extracts new interviews books

new titles reading groups

events extracts extracts events

discounts books

new books events events

events new interviews books extracts

discounts extracts discounts

www.panmacmillan.com

extracts events reading groups

competitions books extracts new books